NAPOLEON'S PROCONSUL in EGYPT

Bernardino Drovetti, engraving by Franz Gau, c. 1818

NAPOLEON'S PROCONSUL in EGYPT

EGYPT

The life and times of Bernardino Drovetti

Ronald T. Ridley

THE RUBICON PRESS

The Rubicon Press
57 Cornwall Gardens
London SW7 4BE

British Library Cataloguing-in-Publication Data

A catalogue record for this book is available from the British Library.

ISBN 0-948695-59-5

Printed and bound in Great Britain by
Biddles Limited of Guildford and King's Lynn

Contents

List of Illustrations

Acknowledgements

My sincerest thanks are due to all the institutions holding documents relative to Drovetti which gave me access to them, notably the Ministry of Foreign Affairs in Paris, the Public Record Office in London, the archives of the University in Torino and the State Archive there.

Of people, so many have contributed so much but some deserve very special mention: first and foremost Don Giuseppe Buzzo, priest at Barbania and indefatigable researcher in local history; Prof. Jean Leclant, Permanent Secretary of the Académie des Inscriptions et Belles-Lettres in Paris, Egyptologist of renown; Dr Maurizio Cassetti, Archivist at Vercelli; Dr Mario Capitolo of the General Cemetery at Torino; Prof. Antonio Pizziola, Istituto Agnelli, Torino; to Thames and Hudson for their gracious permission to reprint illustrations 5 and 10; Bruce Allardice, who recommended me to The Rubicon Press; Ingrid Barker, who transcribed the text; and Thérèse, who has accompanied me on every expedition and edited every page.

Finally, as almost one and a half centuries of history comes to an end, I wish to record my thanks to the Reading Room in the greatest library in the world, the British Library. Without its resources, this book could not have been written.

Dedicated
to the memory of
I.E.S. (Eiddon) Edwards
and for
Elizabeth Edwards
who contributed so much

Introduction

By any account, Bernardino Drovetti is an important and fascinating figure of his time, both Revolutionary and Napoleonic Europe and newly emerging Egypt. I cannot remember how long ago he attracted my attention, and slowly I began to gather the enormous bibliography relating to him. I was delighted to discover the first volume of his *Epistolario*, which I took with me on microfilm to read in Tokyo in 1982 (but that is another story). Perhaps it was in the same year that my wife and I first visited Torino and the wonderful Egyptian Museum. We found it one of the most beautiful and unjustly neglected cities of Italy, and it never fails to charm us. When I mentioned to the then Director of the Museum my Drovetti project, he waved his hand uncomprehendingly: 'But Marro has done it all', he said.

My first thoughts must have been simply the project of putting together all the scattered materials. As I delved more deeply, I became more disconcerted. The standard reference works could not get a thing right about the man, not even his place of birth, or the fact that he did *not* take part in the Egyptian expedition of 1798; they made the grossest blunders in attempting - or even failing to see the need to do so - to evaluate him in the indispensable political and archaeological contexts of his time. There was also the manifest sloth in failing to consult the most obvious categories of evidence: to take just two examples, the published volumes of his consular correspondence, and the multitude of references by contemporary travellers in Egypt.[1]

Worse still, if that were possible, childish prejudices underlay many references: rivalry between Italian and French writers, given Drovetti's dual connections, and between these and English writers, the last of whom see him as a public enemy thwarting English control of Egypt, before the days of Lord (Overbaring) Cromer. There is also the Champollionic question: the adherents of that towering figure also see Drovetti as a bête-noire; while the English for their part have adopted as their own an Italian, Belzoni, whose brilliant account of his achievements, written in English, convinced many that Drovetti was almost a murderer.

All the above prejudices may be viewed by me as an outsider. I do not mean that I have no sides to take, but these attitudes are not inborn in me as with the writers just mentioned. As a 'colonial', these Old World feuds are not mine, and I can judge them from a (considerable) distance. I am an historian, with long-standing interest in the history of Egyptology, and the history of archaeology in general, as well as the history of biography and travel.

There are three people above all others who have laid the foundations on which any biographer of Drovetti must build. The first, taking them in alphabetical order, Georges Douin (1884- ?) is unknown to any standard biographical dictionary, including the *Dictionnaire de biographie française*. Yet from the 1920s he began an indefatigable labour of publishing thousands of documents relating to Egypt from the time of the French expedition of 1798. Most indispensable to Drovetti's biographer are those presenting the correspondence of the French Consuls in Egypt: *L'Egypte de 1802 à 1804*; *Mohamed Aly, Pacha du Caire, 1805-1807*; *L'Egypte de 1828 à 1830*. In addition, Douin edited many volumes of documents on special episodes: *Une mission militaire française auprès de Mohamed Aly* (the Boyer mission of 1824-1826); *Mohammed Ali et l'expédition d'Alger, 1829-1830*; *Navarin, 6 juillet-20 octobre 1827*; *Les premiers frigates de Mohamed Aly, 1824-1827*.

The second is Edouard Driault (1864-1947), a high school teacher until 1920, and close collaborator with Douin in the publication of archival documents. He filled in the other three volumes of Drovetti's official correspondence: *Mohamed Aly et Napoléon, 1807-1824*; *La formation de l'empire de Mohamed Aly de l'Arabie au Soudan, 1814-1823*; and *L'expédition de Crète et de Morée, 1823-1828*. They were but a small part of his prodigious activity, centering mainly on Napoleon, of whom he was a more than devoted adherent. This was to lead to his undoing. His anxiety to recover the ashes of Napoleon's son from Hitler induced him to express his gratitude in the unfortunate year 1940. He was disowned even by the Bonapartists, and his remorse is said to have hastened his death.

The work of these two French scholars means that, allowing for any editing which they may have judged prudent, the major part of the French diplomatic archives relating to Drovetti's period as French representative in Egypt is easily accessible in six volumes of correspondence, as well as the other supplementary volumes cited. If only the archives of the English consuls Missett and Salt were so readily at hand! For those one must consult the many volumes in manuscript in the Public Record Office.

The third foundation figure is the Italian scientist Giovanni Marro (1875-1952), professor of anthropology and clinical psychiatry in the University of Torino. He had been involved with Egyptology since 1912, collaborating with Schiaparelli, Director of the Egyptological Museum, and in 1922 he was sent to represent his city at the centenary celebrations for the decipherment of hieroglyphs. Preparing for this congress, Marro came across Drovetti's papers in Barbania. His life was never the same thereafter. He wrote dozens of papers on every aspect of Drovetti's life, but most importantly began the publication of his personal letters, his *Epistolario*. The first volume was published in 1940 with a shortly-to-appear sequel which had not materialised by the time Marro died in 1952. In 1986, the contents of the original volume were republished, along with what purported to be the remainder of the letters, in an amazingly lacunose and careless volume.

Marro was a complex man, as anyone who has read all his Drovettiana can attest. Pretentious (he never got over his audience with King Fuad in 1930, and also boasts of his meeting Vittorio Emanuele in 1942), his contributions were repetitious and uncritical (he was chided even by Italian colleagues, and his anxiety to tell only one side of the story neglected even such perfectly accessible and famous sources as Champollion's letters). Worst of all, he was infected with the disease of Fascism: there is much chatter about the 'razza italiana' and justification for contemporary Italian presence in Africa because of Italians who had served Mehemet Ali or even visited the continent in his time.[2] Woe betide the intellectual who prostitutes himself to the ideology of a regime, especially a dictatorship!

Where do I stand in regard to Drovetti? The adulators are surely wrong. Drovetti was not a saint. On the other hand, he has often not received his due, especially from the English. He was politically too astute and established for the English Consuls to counter him, and Belzoni, his rival in antiquities, knew the advantage of leaving his side of the story in print. The most fascinating body of evidence is, in fact, the voluminous correspondence, notably in the *Epistolario*, for all the frustrations of the edition on which we are forced to rely. This collection demonstrates the ties of gratitude and affection which bound him to so many people, whether those he had known since his youth, colleagues, political figures, travellers, scientists or intellectuals across Europe. Drovetti was a man of great bravery, political skill and personal attraction. He began as a revolutionary, but in some ways seems to have become more conservative as he grew older. He could be generous to a fault, but at the same time jealously guarded the resources over which he held a monopoly.

The real picture is much more complex and more true to life than the stereotypes produced by either adulators or enemies, and not in the slightest surprising to historians and biographers, those best acquainted with the mélange of virtues and vices which make up the character of most human beings. To keep the balance according to the evidence is where the historian's professional training is indispensable.

What this book assuredly is not is a history of Egypt during the reign of Mehemet Aly, under whom Drovetti spent the central part of his life, between the ages of twenty-seven and fifty-three, and to the development of whose country he made a substantial contribution. A choice has been made of those episodes considered by this biographer to be most illustrative of Drovetti in all his facets. A modern biography is also needed, for example, of Henry Salt; and for the years 1816-1827 it would be entirely different.

The organisation of the biography requires a little explanation. The first five chapters tell the story of a very complex life. Drovetti's various activities could have been divided into neat chapters or little sections: for example, political and diplomatic career, archaeological interests, personal life. This is not, however, how he lived his life, and would be a grave distortion. As Consul and Consul-General in Egypt he had literally every day to deal with French, Egyptian and even European and Oriental politics at the highest level, while looking after any visitor from any European country who chanced to land on his doorstep, and protecting anyone who called on his help, and seeing to his own extensive interests in antiquities, to mention only the most obvious categories. The difficulty of making a connected narrative out of all this is exactly, I suggest, what it must have been like to Drovetti, who lived it all.

Thousands of letters of Drovetti's official and personal correspondence have been perused, along with some twenty volumes of the records of the English Consuls-General, as well as the accounts of dozens of contemporary travellers to Egypt and the memoirs of any contemporary who may have known him. The resulting thickly woven tapestry takes the reader through Revolutionary and Napoleonic France and Piedmont; the Egypt of Mehemet Ali, against a backdrop of the faltering Ottoman Empire and the Greek war of independence; European policies in the eastern Mediterranean in the first thirty years of the nineteenth century; Restoration Europe and Piedmont, and the Italian prelude to the Risorgimento; and not least, the age of the heroes in the history of Egyptology, when in the brief half century following the opening of Egypt to Europe Champollion made the hieroglyphs speak once again, and the major collections which are the pride of European museums were gathered in Egypt.

One small note: throughout this book the famous city of Torino appears in the only form possible for those who know it well, and to whom the anglicised form is unbearably ugly.

I   The making of a lawyer, soldier and diplomat

Thirty kilometers from Torino in the Canavese lies the small village of Barbania. The road from the capital runs north-west across the Piedmontese plain to Caselle, then to S. Francesco, called significantly al Campo. The setting and vegetation become more sub-alpine. The trees are dominated by acacia, but there are many birch and oak. The main crop seems to be corn, but vineyards are scattered about.[1] The road winds and climbs sharply over a small ridge to reach Front and then more gently up to Barbania, at an altitude of 362 metres.

The main piazza of the town is dominated by the seventeenth century facade of S. Giuliano (ill. 2). On the streets that run parallel to the hill above the piazza the dwellings are often grand town-houses, but there are also northern Italian farmhouses built on the centuries-old model, with an open upper storey consisting of great barns full of hay; bunches of vegetables such as corn and peppers hang drying from the upper balconies. The circle of the Alps is very close. In summer the land is lushly green; in winter Barbania lies under a thick blanket of snow. The population in the early nineteenth century was 1,600.

Here on 4 January, 1776 Bernardino Drovetti, a subject of king Vittorio Amedeo III, was born (ill. 3). This same year the Americans won their independence, and in London a literary sensation was created when Edward Gibbon published the first volume of his *Decline and Fall of the Roman Empire*. The parish registers of 1776 have the following entry:

> ('Druett' in the margin): 'die quarta januarii natus et baptizatus fuit a Rd. Michaele (surname indecipherable) priore Bernardinus Michael Maria filius D. notarii Georgii et Annae Victoriae iugalium de Druetto. Susceptores fuere d. notarius Dominicus Maccario et dominica uxor Georgii 'Taramino.'[2] (ill. 4)

Drovetti's father Giorgio Francesco was a lawyer, and his mother, Anna Vittoria Vacca, came from another famous family in the district: her father was the senator Francesco Vacca. Bernardino was the second son: an elder brother Giuseppe was to follow his father's profession in the law,

1

2. Main square of Barbania with the church of S. Giuliano, in winter

and a younger brother Luigi became a priest. There was also a sister, whose name is unknown.

The name Drovetti was one of the most prominent in the district, although it changed its form over the centuries. It can be seen earlier as Dro, Droy, Droenghi. Drovetti himself was registered in the above register as Druetto and sometimes used the slight variant Druetti. Perhaps Druent was named after the family – or the other way round. In a list of the mayors of Barbania from 1668 to 1904, the name Drovetti occurs twice.[3] As befits the parochial church, that of Barbania commemorates the local notables. Various chapels and altars belong to such families. The first on the right in S. Giuliano belongs to the Drovetti.

The Canovese[4] is one of the many components of the modern region of Piedmont.[5] At the time of Drovetti's birth, this was the kingdom of Sardinia, ruled by the house of Savoy, which dates back to the end of the first millennium. It had become a duchy in 1416, and a monarchy in 1720 by the acquisition of the island of Sardinia. The history of the dynasty is proverbially turbulent. Amedeo VIII (1391-1434) later served for nine years as Pope Felix V. Vittorio Amedeo II (1675-1730) abdicated, but then decided to resume the throne, was arrested by his son, and died in prison in 1732. Carlo Emanuele IV (1796-1802) abdicated twice and hardly ruled, dying as a Jesuit in Rome in 1819. Vittorio Emanuele (1802-1820) ruled only in Sardinia until the fall of Napoleon in 1815.

3. The house in Barbania in which Drovetti was born

The eighteenth century saw the emergence of Savoy as a strong military state. It had long been under the influence of its most powerful neighbour, France. There were occasional attempts at a different policy, as in the War of the Spanish Succession (1701-1713), which resulted in a French invasion, but also the acquisition of Sicily in 1713, which was exchanged for Sardinia in 1720. The new kingdom was then caught up in another of the endless wars of succession, this time the Austrian (1740-1748). One of the many theatres of this war was the struggle between Spain and Austria for the control of Italy, and Piedmont was again invaded. The settlement of this war by the Treaty of Aix-la-Chapelle brought about a balance of power between the Spanish Bourbons and the

4. Handwritten document recording Drovetti's baptism on 4 January, 1776

Hapsburgs, and marginalised Sardinia. This was sealed by the Treaty of Aranjuez (1752) between Spain and Austria, and the Treaty of Paris (1756) between France and Austria. Carlo Emanuele III (1730-1773) refused to take up the offer of alliance with the new major power, Prussia. The centre of European politics had shifted away from the Mediterranean.

As the century progressed, much the same crisis afflicted Piedmont as developed in France, although on a more restricted scale. There was an economic collapse as new technologies brought unemployment, food shortages and inflation. The desire for political reform of the absolute monarchy affected notably the more educated and professional classes. The inevitable repression only exacerbated the revolutionary passions. There were executions and imprisonments, while many went into exile in the face of police and military intervention. Vittorio Amedeo III (1773-1796), ruling when Drovetti was born, was reactionary and bigoted.

By the later eighteenth century, however, Piedmont had the largest army in Italy and the makings of a modern state in its diplomatic service and bureaucracy. The capital, Torino, had a population of only 75,000:

> The population amounts to 75,000, of whom 22,000 are idle: 4,000 soldiers, 2,000 monks and priests, 8,000 so-called nobles, 7,000 servants of luxury and about 1,000 beggars.[6]

When Drovetti was merely a youth of thirteen, the States-General summoned by the French king met at Versailles (May, 1789). The French Revolution had begun, which was to ensure, among many other things, that Italy 'reentered the mainstream of European civilisation'.[7] On 14 July, the Bastille was stormed. The Declaration of the rights of man and citizen was issued on 27 August. As Paris fell prey increasingly to warring clubs and factions of the Revolutionaries, Louis decided that his position was untenable and attempted to flee (20 June, 1791).

The arrest of the king finally induced the other European powers to intervene as if the spreading of French revolutionary doctrine throughout the continent and the crowds of noble emigrés were not enough. The First Coalition against France (1792) comprised Austria, Prussia and Sardinia. The first engagement, at Valmy (20 September), was a victory for the French over the Prussians; Speier, Mainz and Frankfurt were occupied, then Nice and Savoy, which were annexed on 27 November.

On the execution of the king (21 January, 1793), England, the Netherlands and Spain joined the coalition. Soon the whole of France was gripped by the Terror and French armies suffered defeat, until the tide turned at the end of the year and new armies pushed the allies back across the Rhine. They overran the Netherlands and set up the Batavian

Republic. By the Treaty of Basel (April, 1795) an exhausted Prussia withdrew from the war, followed by Spain.

On the dissolution of the Convention in October 1795, the Directory took over and planned a three-pronged attack on Austria, directed at Vienna via the lower and upper Rhine, and at Italy. The first two offensives failed, but Bonaparte defeated the Sardinians, then the Austrians at Lodi (10 May 1796) and Rivoli (14 January, 1797). Peace was made by the Treaty of Campoformio, mainly to the detriment of Prussia. The left bank of the Rhine was surrendered to France, Venice ended its thousand years as an independent republic, and Modena, Ferrara, Bologna and the Romagna were added to the Cisalpine Republic.

Sardinia was a member of the First Coalition, as already mentioned, and the maelstrom of European events did not fail to leave their mark. On the outbreak of the Revolution, Piedmont became one of the refuges of the dispossessed aristocrats, and Vittorio Amedeo was ready to offer armed support, a policy disapproved by even the Emperor Leopold, Marie Antoinette's brother. The French army invaded Piedmont in September 1792. The king called for Austrian reinforcements, but that help was so half-hearted that the French took Savoy and Nice. Further military advances by the French in 1794 were followed by diplomatic initiatives in 1795, trying to win over Piedmont by the offer of Milan, but Vittorio Amedeo still honoured the Austrian alliance. The war continued, and the French under Kellerman and Scherer pushed back both the Austrians and Piedmontese. The French command fell to Bonaparte in 1796, and within a month he forced Torino to sign an unconditional surrender (27 April). This separate peace was viewed with hostility by Austria. The Peace of Paris (15 May) ratified the loss of Savoy and Nice, and Vittorio Amedeo died of apoplexy in October.

University Years

It was precisely during these momentous events that Drovetti was gaining his secondary education and studying law at Torino University.

Of his earliest education, as one might suspect, the records are sparse. His secondary studies were under D. Uccelli, a famous grammarian, and D. Castagneri, rector at Vauda Inferiore di Front, south of Barbania.[8] Much more important, of course, were his university studies.

Drovetti obtained his baccalaureat on 13 August, 1791, at the age of fifteen. On the same day also matriculated Count Carlo Botta. One of the examiners was the president of the college of law, Avvocato Bruno. The young student carried on his studies at one of the most interesting educational institutions in Italy, the Collegio delle Provincie.[9] This had been founded in 1729 for clever and willing students who lacked means ('giovani di esser, ingegnosi e vogliosi di studiare, ma privi di corrispondenti facoltà'). It was a royal college, designed to produce leading servants of the crown, and therefore unlike other colleges, which were set up to commemorate their founders and meant for the ecclesiastical and noble classes. Every city and district chose candidates, and scholarships were awarded proportionately across the state. The aims of the college were secular, although the governor was always an ecclesiastic, with the exception of the very first.

The College produced many of the leading Piedmontese intellectuals. It was located in Piazza Carlina. The staff consisted of eight tutors, who received their lodging and food, along with a meagre salary. They were young graduates, gaining experience and awaiting appointments. From the 1750s there were between 120 and 230 students with scholarships. They were paid 25 lire a month, and provided their own black uniform, bed, books and paper. They were well fed, although conditions in general were spartan.

The students attended lectures at the University, and also had tutorials at the College. Their curriculum was more demanding than that of ordinary students, especially regarding preparation for examinations: they could not, in fact, sit without college permission.

Candidates for a place in the Collegio delle Provincie had to provide proof of poverty (from the local council), morality (from the priest) and good studies (from their teachers). How did a youth like Drovetti, from one of the leading local families in Barbania, and professional at that, gain entrance? The explanation lies in the process of selection which constituted a contravention of Vittorio Amedeo's intentions in establishing the College. The selection board in each community was composed of the local élite, people such as doctors, lawyers and merchants. Among the second the most numerous were the notaries, 'the key to local life', because they monopolised the administrative and judicial offices and witnessed all property transactions. A large proportion of the scholars thus came from this class. Many also came from that of the landowners. In short, those who had means simply claimed that they could not support children at University because of debt, taxation or natural disasters. On the other hand, one third of candidates' fathers had died, and their families were obviously genuinely at a disadvantage. When 1,000 lire was a good salary, a degree in law or medicine cost 1,500-2,000 lire. The case of Drovetti illustrates perfectly the customary process of selection for a scholarship at the College.

The completion of his legal studies was marked by the granting of his Licentia on 26 April, 1794 before Avvocato Gastaldi, the then president of the law faculty, and his Laurea (degree) on 1 April, 1795 before Avvocato the Rev. Spanzotti. The University records show the subjects on which he was examined for the Licentia, one of each of ecclesiastical and civil law, chosen by lot: the former 'de criminibus qui gaudeant privilegio fori' (the clergy's exemption from civil jurisdiction) and the latter, 'de legatis et fideicommissis. De legato pure in diem, vel sub conditione relicto' (on legacies and trusts). The professors who examined him were Viotti, Marchetti, Piceo and Cecidani. The examination was indeed gruelling, since out of the whole corpus of church and secular law, two subjects were chosen at random, and the candidate was examined orally – and therefore most searchingly – by a panel of professors. The next candidate was brought in an hour later, so each had been under scrutiny for that length of time. There were five emeritus doctors and fifteen 'ordinary' doctors on the examining panel. It seems that four examined each student. Drovetti was presented by Doctor Emeritus Carena.[10]

If one casts one's eye down the list of students in April 1795, the year of Drovetti's graduation, on the 14th of the same month there matriculated Giulio Cordero di S. Quintino, the man who was to be the first curator of the Museum in Torino where Drovetti gave his first collection of antiquities nearly thirty years later.

Drovetti thus graduated in law at the age of little more than eighteen. This was, in fact, the normal age.[11] Within a year, however, he had enrolled in the army.

First military service

There are a number of sources for Drovetti's earliest military service. The two major documents are the nomination for the criminal court in Torino in 1801 by General Colli[12] and Drovetti's own statement preserved in his dossier in the archives of Foreign Affairs in Paris.[13]

By his own statement he enlisted in June 1796 as a soldier in the 27th Légère.[14] In this regiment he was promoted to Caporal Fourrier (Quartermaster Corporal) and Maréchal de Logis (Sergeant) and served as secretary to the General Staff of the Cavalry.[15] He is said to have fought at the siege of Mantova (July 1796-February 1797).[16] By September 1797, he was at Gorizia, near Trieste.

In that same month he made the crucial passage from non-commissioned to commissioned rank, and was promoted from Second to First Lieutenant two months later. He was attached to the General Staff of the Cisalpine Army, under General La Hoz.[17]

To understand these earliest military years in Drovetti's career, we must follow the French campaigns in Italy in 1796 (ill. 5). Bonaparte was appointed commander of the Army of Italy on 2 March. He inherited an army that was without clothing or arms, and starving. The Austrian commander was Beaulieu, allied to the Piedmontese under Colli.[18] After reorganising and equipping his men, Bonaparte split the allies, driving the Piedmontese back to Torino and the Austrians to Milan, before defeating them at Montenotte, Dego and Mondovi (12-21 April). Italian Republicans were delighted, but the Directory was not in favour of collaboration with them, nor was Bonaparte, who preferred to treat with the king.

There followed the rapid advance to Piacenza, where the French crossed the Po. The first major and hard-fought victory over the Austrians was the storming of the bridge at Lodi (10 May), which left the way open to Milan. It was now that there began that odious policy of including artistic plunder among the conditions of surrender, the most famous example of which was the Treaty of Tolentino. Bonaparte was ordered south by the Directory, to ravage Lombardy, but he protested, and the order was rescinded. He promised independence to Lombardy, and gave its National Guard a red, white and green flag. The liberal middle class did not, however, have the support of the conservative lower classes, which rose in revolt. Pavia was sacked and many protesters were shot or exiled.

The campaign now centred on Mantova, which held out against the French. There were moves for redrawing the whole frontier between Brussels and Munich, whereby the Austrians might be granted Northern Italy in return for giving up the Rhine. On the advance of Beaulieu's successor, Wurmser, Bonaparte was driven back, but then defeated the Austrians in three engagements, including that against Wurmser at Castiglione (5 August); the latter however managed to circle back and enter Mantova. Austrian reinforcements under Alvintzi defeated the French at Caldiero near Verona (12 November), but were then beaten in a bitter three days' battle at Arcola. A further attempt at relief by Alvintzi resulted in his utter defeat at Rivoli on 14 January, 1797, and the surrender of Mantova on 2 February.

The First Coalition crumbled with the following victories over Archduke Charles as the French moved on Vienna. The danger was averted only by the Treaty of Leoben (18 April), which was the prelude to the Treaty of Campoformio (17 October).

The 27th Légère in which Drovetti served[19] set out from Calizzano, near the Alps, in April 1796, and crossed the Po at Piacenza on 20 April. It took part in the capture of Lodi and then operated mostly in the vital campaigns around Lake Garda. The fortress of Salò was captured on 30 July, but on the advance of the Austrians, the 27th retreated to Brescia. It then tried to relieve the beleaguered 29th at Gavardo, but could not get through. It defeated the Austrians at Termini, then captured the seemingly impregnable stronghold of Rocca d'Anfo on Lago d'Idra before returning to Lake Garda where it took the fort of Mori in September. In the new

States under
direct French rule

States under
indirect French rule

Allies of France

mls   0   300
kms   0   500

5. Map showing Napoleon's Empire at its greatest extent

year, the 27th took part in the push to the east, crossing the Piave under heavy fire, and capturing three hundred Austrians at Sacile. The Tagliamento was similarly crossed against considerable odds. The operations of the 27th were halted by the signing of the preliminaries of Leoben.

The light infantry made a crucial contribution to the Italian campaign of 1796. This was a war of 'columns and movements rather than lines and positions'. In the lightning campaigns, the light infantry was perfectly suited to plains and mountains of northern Italy.[20]

The major results were the setting up of the Lombard Republic on 16 May 1796 and the dismemberment of the Cispadane Republic in June. 'The failure of the Cispadane Republic marked the end of any official pretence of allowing the Italians freedom of choice.'[21] With the north under French control, the way lay open to Rome. Pius VI was forced to conclude the Peace of Tolentino (19 February, 1797), by which he ceded the Romagna, Bologna and Ferrara. This did not save him. In February 1798, Rome was occupied by the French under Berthier. A Republic was established and the Pope was deported to France. Within another two months, the French armies occupied Switzerland and proclaimed the Helvetian Republic in April.

With Europe under control, Bonaparte now tried to strike a mortal blow at England by blocking her access to India. On 18 May, 1798, he sailed from Toulon with 35,000 men and a vast array of scientists, and landed in Egypt on the first day of July. Following the famous Battle of the Pyramids (21 July), Cairo fell. It was, however, only a week later that Nelson destroyed the French fleet in harbour at Aboukir, leaving the whole expeditionary force isolated in Egypt. The interest of the Egyptian campaign for Drovetti was probably minimal. He was not to know that he would soon spend nearly thirty years of his life there. He was fully occupied with the arduous beginnings of his military career and his swift promotion through the ranks, although that was quite normal for the gifted in these times, as well as his important part in the Piedmontese Provisional Government. It has, however, many times been asserted that Drovetti took part in this famous expedition. The temptation to explain his later position in Egypt by his accompanying Bonaparte in 1798 has been irresistible to too many works of reference and even specialist writers, and has led simply to invention and fantasy.[22]

Vittorio Amedeo's successor as king was Carlo Emanuele IV (1796-1802). 'Not an unintelligent man, he was weak physically and had a weak and bigoted personality.'[23] He was instantly the target of plots to kidnap or assassinate him, which resulted in many executions. There were Republican risings throughout Piedmont. Military action against these disturbances, which were all suppressed, involved crossing Ligurian territory. Genova refused an accord, and invaded Piedmont. France then intervened to impose peace, exacting the surrender of the Torino citadel (July 1798). This was bound to excite further unrest and justify further intervention. After armed clashes, General Joubert, commander of the army in Italy, denounced the king and took over. Carlo Emanuele abdicated on 8 December and a government of fifteen members assumed power.

The Provisional Government, 1798-1799[24]

The new government issued a hymn to freedom and the French liberators, and freed the political prisoners of the old regime. Given the notorious Catholicism of the state, it was most welcome to the government to have the strongest support from Carlo Buronzi, archbishop of Torino. Committees of government were established, and the members, divided according to these ministries, were:

Public Safety: Sartoris, Bertolotti, Colla;

Legislation, Justice and Education: Faurat, Galli, Bon, Baudisson, Braida;

Finance, Trade and Agriculture: Bottone, Favella, S.Martino, Fava, Bossi;

Public Works: Cavalli, Rocci, Fava;

Foreign Relations and War: Bottone, Bossi, Rocci.

To these fifteen were added another ten on 19 December: Balbis, Botta, Chiabrera, Capriata, Simian, Avogadro, Bunico, Bellini, Cerize and Guymet.[25] A National Guard was set up. The University and the Collegio delle Provincie, closed earlier during the troubles, were reopened.

The nightmare which haunted the government was the financial crisis. The economy was flooded with letters of credit and debased coinage. Drastic devaluation was introduced. At the same time the French army demanded two million lire. With the treasury bare, the money was raised by a tax on the rich. And when the army needed horses, these were found by requisitioning all 'luxury' animals. The rich thereupon dismissed their coachmen, but were ordered to pay them four months' wages.

Opposition to the government was shown by the need to set up seven local courts to try political crimes. That opposition took on a very serious character at the end of December with the uprising at Alba and Asti, put down very rigorously by the army.

To meet the financial crisis, religious property was expropriated in January. In a similar vein, the Superga cult of the deceased sovereigns was abolished, and the basilica reserved for the tombs of patriots. Political opposition continued unabated. It was ascribed to 'aristocratic fanatics', who cleverly undermined confidence on all fronts by claiming that letters of credit would be completely dishonoured, that the National Guard was really to provide recruits for the army, and that attacks would be made on religion. Patriots in reply offered their letters of credit for public burning, and illuminations were held for the anniversary of the execution of Louis XVI. National property worth 14 million lire was offered for sale.

The University was freed from all religious interference: the governing Magistrato della Riforma was abolished, as was the students' oath. New chairs of obstetrics and chemistry were established, and lectures could be given in Italian as well as Latin. The Collegio dei Nobili was abolished and its building given to the Collegio delle Provincie. The Inquisition in Piedmont was abolished.

By February, 1799, however, the dominant question was the most fundamental of all: whether Piedmont should become part of France. Many reasons were advanced for annexation, and they are highly interesting: Piedmont was closer in language and customs to France than to neighbouring Italians; it had borne the brunt of defending Italy, so that the other Italians benefited without cost to themselves; annexation would be a protection against Austria; and it would put an end to aristocrats' plots. The dream of an independent Italy, it was admitted, was too costly. This report was signed by the leading supporters of annexation, Botta, Bossi and Colla.

Attempts at social reform, despite the economic crisis, continued; for example, 10% of the price of tickets for entertainments was to go to the poor; and betrothal, which led to endless disputes, was to be replaced by a written agreement to marry within three months, otherwise compensation might be paid. By 19 February, overwhelming acceptance of the proposed annexation was reported. Piedmont became a department of France (the 27th.). All Piedmontese, subjects previously of the Sardinian monarchy, became French citizens. Drovetti thus underwent the vital change which made possible the most important post in his whole career.

The initiatives continued. A commission of arts and sciences was established, which was to draw up a plan for education. All feudal rights were abolished, with a public surrender and burning of all documents granting such rights (1 March).

There had, however, been further revolts, at Acqui and Alessandria, which required the intervention of Generals Grouchy, Flavigny and Seras. Strevi, the centre of the uprising, had been burned to the ground, and four hundred people had lost their lives. Six tribunals were set up to try criminal cases. At the same time there were reforms in penalties: prison was replaced by public work, as was the death penalty for many crimes, and torture was abolished. The government was hostage to its bankruptcy, however, and rather than harm the poor by a general tax, a loan was exacted from traders and merchants of nearly half a million lire.

As a consequence of the plebiscite, the provisional government was ended by decree of the Directory in Paris on 15 March and replaced by a commissioner, Joseph Musset. Piedmont was divided into four departments. Torino was the capital of the Eridano which had five administrators: Bertolotti, Avogadro, Botta, Guymet and Favrat. The end was not, however, far off.

The first sign came on 30 April, when General Grouchy called on his 'intrepid companions in arms', warning them that the enemy threatened their liberty and property, and that the scourge of war might devastate Piedmont at any moment. Rumour-mongering closed shops and houses on 2 May, and soon reports came in of Frenchmen being murdered and troops fired upon by bands of robbers. The National Guard was called upon to organise pickets, and citizens were asked to illuminate their windows to make this easier at night. On 10 May the enemy was identified: non-Catholic Russians and Germans! The administration moved to Pinerolo, 36 kms south-west of Torino. It was admitted that there was danger of civil war and the archbishop called for calm and obedience. Food became scarce, and the government had to step in to ensure supplies of bread and polenta. Although the death penalty was imposed for anti-Republican and anti-French activity, a unanimous vote of the judges was still required, a remarkable testimony to Republican ideals.

On 16 May it was reported that the Austrians had crossed the Po at Ponte Stura but had been driven back, as had the Russians at Bassignone where 700-800 were killed and 2,000 drowned. General Moreau, commander of the Army in Italy, warned the Piedmontese to stop the murder and devastation, or he would bring iron and fire and leave no stone unturned. Enemies of the French told the inhabitants of Torino that the French would abandon them to a sack. The National Guard failed to report to their post. On 26 May a final proclamation announced that the enemy and a mass of brigands were drawing near. The city was under siege. The civil authorities were ordered to remain at their posts.

The policies of the Provisional Government had been bold and radical. It had attempted many reforms affecting every aspect of Piedmontese life. It was fiercely anti-monarchist and noticeably anti-ecclesiastical. It had, however, been gravely divided over relations with France, but the vote for annexation had been overwhelming. In these daring and bitter events the recently promoted young Captain Drovetti had taken part. He was a member of the Provisional Government. When it fell he fled to France.

In the Torino archives exists a complete list of the officials of the government. These names, complete with profession, show that the overwhelming support came from the educated: lawyers (such as Drovetti) above all others, doctors and teachers, but also the religious and the aristocracy, and even the peasants.[26]

On 1 March, 1799, the president of the government, Bertolotti, wrote to Druetti (sic), *uomo di legge* (lawyer):

> The proofs given by you of your firm patriotism induced the government, which recognises your talents, to summon you to participate in its labours, nominating you as Secretary General in the Committee for Public Safety, with a monthly salary of 250 lire.
>
> In entrusting to you such an important post, the government intends to give you an attestation of the consideration in which it holds you. It is your duty to confirm that, and to render yourself ever more worthy of national gratitude.
> Greetings and fraternity[27]

There could not, as Bertolotti implied, be a more striking testimony to the trust placed by the government in the twenty-three years old

Captain than this appointment in the last most difficult days as Secretary in the Committee of General Safety.

There were also twenty-one 'commissioners' of the government, one for each of the same number of centres. On 3 March, 1799, Botta nominated Drovetti as Commissario for Torino.[28] He was, in short, the chief Commissioner, since he represented the capital.

In his capacity as Secretary in the Committee of General Safety, Drovetti wrote on various occasions in March and April to the Committee of Foreign Affairs and War.[29] He passed on petitions of notables to be named municipal councillors; notified changes in the command of the National Guard, and the mutiny at Rivara over the election of a Captain; and sent out a proclamation to encourage enlistment.

The most important letter of all, however, is addressed to him, from the Committee of War, and dated 26 March, complimenting him on his reestablishment of order at Favria. He had dismissed the commander of the National Guard there. His measures were declared 'secure and just'. On 2 March there had been a very grave anti-French uprising, led by Dr Porta at the head of some eight thousand men, which attempted to take Alessandria. General Colli sent the First Half Brigade (Drovetti's unit) to suppress it, which it did ruthlessly.[30]

Other traditions of the time were preserved by Drovetti's family, such as that on the fall of the government, the various members would have been captured by the enemy had Drovetti not loaded all the documents on mules and led his colleagues to safety, ultimately in France, even carrying the aged Capriata on his shoulders 'as Aeneas did with his father Anchises'.[31] Drovetti's biographers refer to decrees issued by him, in which he alluded to his youth, 'which some thought was perhaps an obstacle to the proper execution of the functions entrusted to (him)', but which, he asserted, was no reason to refuse him confidence; it was rather a guarantee of his deference to citizens' advice, which because of his age they could offer in all frankness. He called upon his fellow citizens to assist him in redressing the 'calamitous situation to which the past despotic government had reduced the country'.[32] If these documents are reliably reported, much of Drovetti's remarkable character is instantly apparent in his frankness and sincerity, and the combination of the awareness of his extraordinarily young age for the post he held with an equally remarkable self-confidence in publishing the fact and turning it to his advantage.

The family of the Drovetti were very numerous, and seem to have been unanimously pro-French. Under the restoration in 1800, a list was compiled of all the officers of the Provisional Government.[33] At Barbania the president of the local administration was none other than a Bernardino Druetti, but if his profession is given correctly as 'flebotomo' (doctor or surgeon), he cannot be the lawyer. Also named is Giovanni Antonio Druetti. Our Bernardino is named, but at the end of the list, as 'Commissario della Direzione Centrale', now absent. His brother Giuseppe, the notary, had also been absent but was now noted as returned.

The memoirs of Felice Bongioanni give a very vivid picture of Piedmont on the collapse of the Provisional Government in April 1799.[34] His own wanderings were very arduous, including the crossing of the flooded Po on the back of a porter. He crossed the Alps under unbelievable conditions with Bessone, Giacca, Bertoni and Bernardi. A central episode in the memoirs is the reactionary revolt of Bongioanni's own city, Montovi. The conditions were those of anarchy, terrorism and civil war: 'It is under cover of the shadows of night that we abandoned districts populated only by anarchy, rage and the spirit of vengeance'.[35]

The Republican government of Piedmont withdrew to Fenestella in May, then Briançon by the next month, and to Grenoble by July. Drovetti was one of the many who fled to France.

He was at Pinerolo on 26 May, 1799, as proven by letters he wrote from there. One concerns the sale of national property – one of the major hopes, as we have seen for the solution to the economic crisis. Another complains to the Secretary of the Commissariate about the failure to impose payment of duties, 'a measure which, in the present circumstances, is of the greatest importance'. The third, to Bonardelli, an additional commissioner, complains of the dissensions of the time and urges him to put an end to them. These letters, as difficult as they may now be to place in context, show Drovetti clearly as a member of the government in exile in the most difficult circumstances and, indeed, continuing retreat who fully merited the trust put in his bravery and patriotism by his appointment, and conscientiously continued to do his duty and implement the government's policies.

In Briançon, Drovetti received a letter from Carlo Botta,[37] who confided in his old friend that Italy had been betrayed by those who governed France (the Directory), but at the same time expressed his belief that things might improve (they could hardly get worse!). The French were still arguing over the future of Italy, whether it might be one republic or two, or whether Piedmont and Liguria might be annexed to France and the rest be made a republic! Botta hoped that Generals Moreau and Macdonald might be victorious, and informed Drovetti that he had been dining in Paris with Joubert, Jourdan, Angerau, Marbot, Bernadotte, Garat, Lucien and Joseph Bonaparte, Salicetti and Desaix (one might well envy Botta such brilliant company!). He ended, however, on a human note which all too vividly reminds us of the problems of most exiles. He might dine with the leading political and military figures, but his own movement around Paris was very difficult. Carriages were too costly, and he had callouses on his feet.

Drovetti is next mentioned in Grenoble by Bongioanni, who calls him Avvocato Druetti.[38] Grenoble, as one of the most Republican cities in France, was the great centre for Italian emigrés and the headquarters of the French army being assembled for the reconquest of Italy.

In August, Carlo Botta again wrote to his friend, telling him of the damaging dissensions among the patriots. He hoped to see Drovetti soon, given Joubert's victories. (He did not know of his death a week before at Novi.) Botta also spoke of the 'cruel destiny' of Avogadro.[39]

Meanwhile a second great coalition had been formed against France, comprising Russia, England, Austria, Naples, Portugal and Turkey. It began badly for the allies with the French overthrow of the Kingdom of Naples and the proclamation on 23 January 1799 of the Parthenopean Republic. In March the Grand Duchy of Tuscany was overrun. Then the French lost ground. Scherer was defeated at Magnano (5 April) by the Austrian Kray; Moreau was defeated at Cassano (27 April) by Melas and Suvorov and the Cisalpine Republic was overthrown. Torino's pro-French days were thus numbered, and the capital was occupied by Suvorov on 27 May. At the battle of Trebia in June, Suvorov defeated MacDonald, and the Parthenopean and Roman Republics fell. A new French army under Joubert was crushed at Novi (15 August) and its general killed.

The whole European situation was transformed, however, by the return of Bonaparte from Egypt to France in August. On 9 November occurred the infamous Coup d'Etat, in which he overthrew the Directory and had himself appointed first Consul of the Republic for ten years.

The campaign of the Reserve Army in Italy, 1800

Just before his appointment to the Provisional Government in March 1799, in February of that same year Drovetti had been promoted to Captain in the First Piedmontese Half Brigade, at the hands of the famous General Championnet.[40] The half brigades were formed by the Provisional Government, to compensate for the weakness of the Piedmontese army. Three regiments were each made into half brigades. The First Half Brigade was composed of the Savoia, Aosta and Lombard regiments, which became the new battalions. The Savoia was destined for the Tuscan expedition, cut short by Suvorov's arrival, and was disbanded after the French defeat. The Aosta followed General Scherer and fought at Verona, Bassignana and S. Germano. The Lombard was at Alessandria. It and the Aosta surrendered to the Austrian-Russian army.[41]

A striking series of further promotions for Drovetti followed. In March 1800 he was attached to the General Staff of the Reserve Army, of the cavalry to be precise.[42] He fought at Marengo on 14 June.

Many sources claim that he was, in fact, aide-de-camp to General Murat, who led the cavalry on his famous campaign.[43] The family tradition calls him captain of the light cavalry in the Italian expedition.[44] His relations with Murat were certainly close.[45] There is, however, no sign of Drovetti in the two volumes of Cugnac's documents, including the many appendices with lists of officers of the various corps. Most importantly, he is not mentioned in Murat's own account of Marengo, in which he names three of his aides-de-camp (Colbert, Beaumont, Didier) and also a Piedmontese officer (Didetes).[46] Nor is Drovetti listed in the wounded and killed in the battle 'par suite de quelque action d'éclat'.[47] One source, however, mentions something passed over by all others. When Chateaubriand met Drovetti in Egypt in 1806, he noted that he had suffered damage to one hand, and it has been assumed that this happened at Marengo.[48]

This is all we know of Drovetti's participation in one of the most remarkable French military undertakings of the Napoleonic wars, the reconquest of Italy by the Reserve Army. Drovetti's recent colleague in the Provisional Government, Carlo Botta, scathingly summarised Bonaparte's motives:

> To a supreme degree master of the art of seduction, the First Consul gave out that he returned to Italy, in order to found a well-regulated liberty in Lombardy, to give peace to Naples and Tuscany, to restore religion, to protect the clergy, and, finally, to reinstate the Roman Pontiff to his rightful seat. To all he spoke of peace, of humanity, of the termination of existing evils, of an age of prosperity about to commence for the general happiness of the human race.[49]

The Reserve Army was created on 8 March, 1800 and existed for little more than three months.[50] It comprised six divisions of infantry, the Italian legion under Lechi, and eleven regiments of cavalry under Murat (in which Drovetti served), a total of 50,000 men. It assembled at Dijon, and on 2 April, Berthier became in fact lieutenant-commander. Whatever had been the original strategy of cooperation with the Rhine Army, all was changed in April by the victory of the Austrians under Melas, who besieged the Italian Army under Massena in Genova. The crossing into Italy of the Reserve Army was mostly via the Great Saint Bernard (14-23 May), which took ten days instead of the two which Bonaparte had calculated. The magnificent painting by David of Bonaparte on horseback on the peaks is one of the greatest travesties of history: he came in a carriage, then crossed on a mule, and nearly plunged to his death. His most serious mistake, however, was the complete underestimation of the resistance of the fort at Bard, which did not capitulate until 12 June. This meant that the army campaigned in Lombardy for three weeks with only six canon and had only twenty at Marengo. The capture of Ivree, key to the Val d'Aosta, was the initiative of the ever-daring Lannes. This allowed Murat with the vanguard to set off for Milan; Drovetti presumably accompanied him. This was the pressure intended by Bonaparte to force the Austrians to leave Genova. Murat's forces entered Vercelli on 27 May, forced their way over the Sesia river on 29 May, fought a bitter battle to cross the Tessino two days later, and finally entered Milan on 2 June. The Austrians were defeated at Malignano and then Lodi (4 June) and retreated to Mantova. The French could thus cross the Po, and Murat occupied Piacenza (7 June). The last key was Stradella, to cut Melas off from his bases. Massena had not, however, been able to hold out for so long: Genova capitulated[51] and the Austrians massed at Alessandria. The final battle was fought at Marengo on 14 June, and 'changed the lot of Europe for fourteen years'.[52]

It is one of the great ironies of history that this vital struggle was first lost by the French. They retreated from Frontinone by 2 pm and fell back some seven kilometres. Melas incredibly failed to press his advantage. The second engagement was won by the bravery of Desaix's men, at the cost of their general's life, and by the charge of Kellerman's cavalry on the enemy left.[53]

The Reserve Army had thus in one month fought more than twenty battles and conquered the entire Po valley. It was 'suppressed' on 23 June, 1800 and incorporated in the Italian Army.

The next month, Drovetti was appointed first officer in the Ministry of War in Piedmont,[54] and one month later Squadron Leader (i.e. Cavalry Major) of the First Piedmontese Hussars.[55] These hussars were formed in July 1800, on the instructions of General Massena. There were to be two squadrons. Drovetti was therefore commander of half the entire body. In August General Brune reorganised them into one regiment composed of four squadrons. A year later they were incorporated into the French army and were disbanded in 1814.[56] The letter of appointment as Squadron Leader both tells of Drovetti's qualities and gives some flavour of the times:

> The commission of government having noted the valour which you displayed under the Republican flags in defense of the common cause and your constant resolution in following the path of honour, and now wishing to appoint as leaders of the new Piedmontese troops persons who unite integrity of behaviour and a true love of country

with civil and military skills, has by the accompanying decree named you Squadron Leader in the Regiment of the Piedmontese Hussars. Greetings and Brotherhood.[57]

One can also imagine him in his uniform: the green dolman (the hussar's jacket with the sleeves hanging loose) and breeches, white braid and buttons, collar and cuffs both edged with red, and the shako (a word derived from Hungarian to denote the cylindrical hat with peak and plume), and finally the regimental plate in white metal in the form of a lozenge worn on the chest.

Following Bonaparte's victories, Torino had again fallen to the French, and a governing commission was established under Count Cavalli d'Olivola. This Piedmontese government was, however, too independent for the liking of the French, especially given the parlous state of the economy, and was replaced in October 1800 by an Executive Commission of three. Piedmont was occupied in April 1801, and Jourdan was appointed administrator, to be succeeded by Joachim Menou (1802-1808) and Camillo Borghese (1808-1814). By the Peace of Luneville (9 February, 1801), Austria recognised French dominion of northern Italy.

It was on 19 March 1801 that Drovetti, aged barely twenty-five, reached the pinnacle of his distinguished military career. He was appointed by Lorenzo Corte, Minister of War in Piedmont, as Chief of Staff under General Colli of the Piedmontese Division of the French army in Italy.[58] In the *Epistolario* is the letter of Colli to Drovetti telling him to bring his troops to Cremona to form a division with the French troops. He went on to explain that the most important job in an active division was the Chief of the General Staff. Such a man must be conversant with all arms, have a detailed knowledge of administration, have a military eye for what was needed, be able to give leadership, be active and work easily. Colli assured the young major that he had all these qualities and more: he had the confidence of everyone, especially his commanding general. Colli summed up by saying that it was dear to his heart, useful and pleasant to have a friend such as Drovetti for this post, and that he thought with pleasure of the cooperation which would exist between them.[59]

Drovetti was not to exercise his new and eminent military post for very long. The new government required able administrators, notably lawyers.

Criminal judge in Torino
In October 1801, Drovetti was appointed one of the judges of the new criminal tribunal in Torino, a post he held until March 1803.[60] In the month of his appointment the French government, with the usual decree signed by the First Consul, completely reorganised the courts in Piedmont.

Eleven tribunals of first instance were established throughout the state (the judges in Torino received 2,400 frs salary), as well as one tribunal of appeal consisting of thirty judges in three sessions (each receiving 4,200 frs), and three special tribunals of criminal justice. The judges in Torino received 4,200 frs, and numbered eight. The president was Bertolotti, who was one of the special appeal judges as well. There were two civilian judges, and the other five were military. Drovetti was one of these last, along with two other Piedmontese (David, a brigade commander, and Rubini, a captain of dragoons) and two Frenchmen (Pont-Carre and Heymard, both squadron commanders in the gendarmes).[61]

This post also was owed to Colli, whose recommendation of his friend survives.[62] He gave a brief outline of Drovetti's career, then summed him up as 'a lawyer, very well educated with great abilities, of an honesty and incorruptability beyond any description' ('homme de loi, Beaucoup d'instruction et de moyens, d'une Probité et d'une incorruptibilité au-dessus de tout ce que l'on peut en dire'). The contrast with the other three officers whom Colli recommended is striking: they are 'probe et integre', 'laborieux', 'incorruptible'. Equal to this assessment was the memory still retained by the famous political exile, Ferdinando dal Pozzo, a quarter of a century later. He recalled when they were in public service after Marengo. They had not seen each other since, and dal Pozzo was now in exile in London, but he told his friend that he preserved a profound impression of his qualities 'which made you dear and esteemed by all who knew you'.[63]

The Torino archives preserve the decisions of the criminal court from 1802. The standard formula tells of the interrogation of suspects, their defence, and the support of the local mayor. By virtue of article 15 of the law of 27 January, 1801, the accused is then set free. The President (Bertolotti) usually signs the decision, occasionally others, but never Drovetti, because he was so soon transferred to his most famous post.[64] The difficulties of these courts are revealed by letters to Jourdan, stating that the tribunal is 'paralysed' by the fact that it does not possess copies of the necessary laws, regulations and decrees which it is supposed to be administering. Not easily forgotten is the Prefect of Marengo informing Jourdan that no-one knows how to build a guillotine, and asking him to send a model. The judges also suffered considerable delays in the payment of their salaries.[65]

A summary of the operations of the court until May 1802, just six months before Drovetti's departure, shows fifteen death penalties, thirteen prison terms of ten to twenty years, but most of one to six months, in all eighty-four condemnations and no fewer than eighty-three persons freed, in just four months from January to April. Four hundred and sixty-four, however, were still awaiting judgement, and an appeal for help was made to reduce this backlog.[66] Drovetti's early biographers record his tireless efforts precisely in bringing forward cases which had been neglected for years, and his visits to prisons which resulted in his contracting typhus, which nearly cost his life.[67] It is significant, then, that in his history Carlo Botta singled out the Piedmontese legal system at this time as the best part of the administration and some compensation for lost liberties:

> The amelioration of the judicial laws, both civil and criminal, was great, and so immense a benefit was derived from their prompt decisions, that it afforded some consolation for the loss of independence.[68]

Drovetti's term as judge was served under very difficult circumstances, but the Torino court was responsible for exonerating as many people as it condemned.

Meanwhile, peace finally came to Europe by the Treaty of Amiens (March, 1802), although it lasted only until May 1803. Vittorio Emanuele succeeded his brother Carlo Emanuele in Sardinia in June 1802 by the latter's abdication, and thought to win his restoration from Bonaparte by a more pro-French policy. In September, however, Piedmont was again annexed to France. For the second time in his life Drovetti became a French citizen, which he was to remain until 1815. New possibilities opened up for the career of the brilliant young officer and judge.

The post which was to immortalise him was offered to him immediately following the annexation. By decree of the First Consul, on 20 October, 1802, he was appointed Deputy-Commissioner of Commercial Relations (Sous Commissaire des Relations Commerciales) at Alexandria in Egypt.[69] The office was, of course, what would be known more ordinarily as Vice-Consul – but the title of Consul now had a very special application in the French Republic. The story behind his appointment, at the age of twenty-six, to such an important post is revealed by a letter to him dated 13 August, from none other than General Colli.[70]

> My wishes have been fulfilled. The First Consul has decided to name you commissioner of foreign relations (sic) as we call a consul. This post will bring you 18,000 livres (i.e. francs) a year, clear nett and legal, not counting the rest. Murat wants you to accept.

Colli went on to urge Drovetti to reply poste haste, gratefully accepting the appointment, wherever the First Consul might want to post him: he was to make the letter convincing! At this stage, then, Colli seems not to have known that the post had been fixed, but the two people behind the nomination are clear: Colli and Murat. Even as late as October, Colli was hoping that the young man whom he had come to appreciate so highly would not be sent too far away from France.

Drovetti belonged precisely to the first class to enter what was shortly to become the imperial Napoleonic service, the educated middle class; the aristocracy soon followed.

> Obedience was the prerequisite of service in the Napoleonic state....
> Moderate republicans and conservative royalists, former Jacobins and nobles of ancient lineage merged in the *amalgame* which Napoleon transferred from the mass armies of the Revolution (where the term was first used in 1793) to civil society.[71]

And so Drovetti left behind for nearly thirty years the great political arena in which he had spent his formative years, that of Revolutionary Europe, to travel across the sea to represent the new Empire in one of its most strategic posts where Napoleon himself had made one of his extravagant gambles just five years before and to which he never ceased dreaming of returning. Drovetti's own nation, Piedmont, had been one of the most radically affected parts of Europe in upheaval. Now Drovetti was a French citizen. We may join him in casting a look back at the continent he was now leaving and which the régime he represented was to attempt to mould even closer to one man's will:

> In all his relations with Europe, Napoleon probably had little coherent policy, beyond a desire to make conquered countries satellites of France and adjuncts to his own dynastic ambitions. He certainly followed no consistent policy of arousing nationalities against their governments, doing so only as expediency dictated. He worked out no principles for organising his empire, beyond the general introduction of the French legal codes and administrative system. How he organised it in fact varied according to the military needs of the moment and the requirements of his Continental System, and as he was never at peace for long, the pressure of these necessities was constant and decisive. Likewise the results of his conquests varied according to the conditions of each country, and to the existing diversities of European states he added not uniformity, but merely further complexity.[72]

At the urging of Murat and Colli, however, Bonaparte did send Drovetti to Egypt.

II Drovetti's first consulate, 1803-1815: the rise to power of Mehmet Ali

At the beginning of the nineteenth century Egypt was sliding into ever deeper chaos. The Ottoman Empire was in danger of collapse, and the viceroyal Mameluke dynasty which had formally ruled the country from 1250 until 1517 and had regained effective control in the eighteenth century from the normal Turkish rulers had been overthrown by the French in 1798. The major European powers, notably France and England, but also Russia, were ready to intervene in most decisive ways, to protect their own interests or to aid their supposed allies. England, for example, had long been pro-Turkish as a mainstay of her control of the route to India.

Into this seething confusion entered almost simultaneously the two figures who were to dominate Egyptian politics for the first third or more of the new century: Mehemet Ali and Bernardino Drovetti. It was the French Consul who in fact was to be decisive in bringing the Albanian condottiere to power and in keeping him there.

From the French evacuation to the arrival of Drovetti

The French army evacuated Egypt by the end of 1801. An English force under Sir Ralph Abercromby had landed at Aboukir on 8 March. Despite some reverses, Rosetta was taken, Belliard surrendered Cairo on 22 June, and Alexandria was taken from Menou on 26 August. The French were all delighted to be repatriated.[1]

> The French occupation of Egypt came to an inglorious end. But it had been far from fruitless. It had shaken Mameluke power; it had fully awakened English minds to the strategic importance of a country placed midway between East and West; it had illustrated Turkish incompetence; and incidentally it had brought to Egypt an Albanian adventurer, Muhammed "Ali".'[2]

What is missing here is paradoxically the most lasting of all the effects of the French expedition: the first full-scale scientific recording of the remains of the ancient civilisations and the awakening of all Europe to Egypt's cultural importance, so that henceforth both savants and ordinary visitors flocked to visit it.

Egypt in 1801 instantly became the subject of contention between the Ottoman government in Constantinople and the Mameluke beys in the country, who now with the support of the English, since they had suffered so much at the hands of the French, attempted to regain the control they had lost in 1798. Not to be outdone, and despite the failure of their military occupation, the French maintained a lively intelligence service. On 16 October, 1802, a roving ambassador, Horace Sebastiani, arrived. He had been sent by the First Consul to go everywhere, to speak to everyone. The situation was complicated, and his major instruction, significantly, was not to compromise Bonaparte: say 'that I love the Egyptian people, that I desire Egypt's happiness and that I speak often of her', the First Consul pompously and ineffectually told him.[3] This kind of non-policy gained the French nothing. Bonaparte's master stroke, although he undoubtedly did not realise it, was the appointment on 20 October, 1802, of Drovetti as 'Deputy-Commissioner of Commercial Relations' in Egypt. That he did not understand the young diplomat's abilities and crucial importance can easily be proved: he appointed someone quite ineffectual as his superior.

Sebastiani was intensely interested in the evacuation of the English force under General Stuart. There were still 4,500 English in Alexandria. In Middle Egypt were 3,000-4,000 Mamelukes, swelled by 700-800 French and English deserters. Sebastiani informed the French Foreign Minister, Talleyrand,[4] that so great was the enthusiasm for the French in Egypt that he was welcomed as taking possession of Alexandria in the name of the First Consul.[5] With intelligence of this naiveté one may understand the complacency of French policy. Drovetti would soon set the record straight.

The nominal Viceroy was Khosrev, who seems to have been leaning towards French support, because of the notorious English preference for the Mamelukes.[6] General Stuart certainly offered his mediation in an attempt to reach agreement between the Viceroy and the beys.[7] Sebastiani, who went to see Khosrew, however, heard him speak of exterminating the Mamelukes, despite being beaten in battle by them five times. He asked for Bonaparte's intervention with the Porte. The French envoy reported that all the sheiks in Cairo were desperately pro-French; he satisfied their yearnings by handing out innumerable portraits of the First Consul. General Stuart replied by cunningly giving the Viceroy an old letter of

Bonaparte from 1799 on Egyptian independence, but Sebastiani won him over. Such were the intrigues into which Drovetti was soon to be plunged. Sebastiani described the ruler as a Georgian slave who knew only how to cut off heads. His main message was clear: the Turks with an army of 16,000 were detested, and the Mamelukes were not loved and numbered only 3,000. The French could easily conquer Egypt![8]

Moves in Egypt were forestalled early in 1803, however, by the success of the British ambassador to the Porte, Lord Elgin, who negotiated a treaty with the Sultan on behalf of the Mamelukes, by which they could stay at Aswan but had to be subjects of the Sultan without English protection.[9] General Stuart in Egypt was a little embarrassed: he regretted that the arrangement was not more favourable to the beys, given their attachment to the English. Since the Turks were facing total ruin, it was only through his intervention, he claimed, that the Mamelukes were induced to withdraw south.[10]The old rulers of the country were in notorious and total disarray. It is essential to understand the factions. The Mamelukes

> moved in Upper Egypt under four chiefs: Ibrahim, the "doyen" of the Corps, but now so enfeebled in body and mind that the "most inferior" Mameluke could disobey him with impunity, Bardissy, the basis of whose character was formed by vanity and arrogant ignorance, Elfi, the "bête noire" of his colleagues – an energetic barbarian, not entirely unattractive – and Osman Hassan, the keeper of the best of the traditions of the race. It was Bardissy and Elfi who counted for all practical purposes.[11]

It was only on 7 March 1803 that Bonaparte finally decided to appoint another diplomatic representative in Egypt, a superior to Drovetti. The form of the decree shows his indecision. Matthieu de Lesseps was also appointed 'Deputy-Commissioner of Commercial Relations' at Damietta, but in the interim was to be Commissioner-General in Cairo![12] His instructions stated that he was to leave for Egypt together with Drovetti, and that when he arrived he was to observe the utmost prudence and circumspection, and not to become involved in the struggle between the Turks and Mamelukes. In other words, Bonaparte was not taking sides, unlike the English and unlike Drovetti, as we shall soon see.[13] Basil Fakre, an appointment of Sebastiani, was to continue as Deputy-Commissioner at Damietta; de Lesseps was left to make his own nomination for Rosetta. As for the Mamelukes, they made clear what they thought of the First Consul: one of their leaders, Elfi, went to London to try to gain the King's support.[14]

It was also in March 1803 that the English army which had driven out the remains of Bonaparte's expedition evacuated Egypt. General Stuart left behind as England's representatives, and therefore the rivals of de Lesseps and Drovetti, Samuel Briggs in Alexandria and Ernest Missett as Resident in Cairo. As Consul, the government appointed Charles Locke, but he died in Malta in September before he could reach Egypt. Missett thus became the leading English diplomat in Egypt and was to remain Consul until 1816.[15] He was of Irish ancestry and a soldier. He first appears in the army lists in 1794 as a captain and was in the Irish Brigade in 1798 and Stuart's Minorcans (later the 97th Queen's Germans) the next year. In this regiment he took part in the English expedition in 1801. The most extraordinary thing about him is that by c.1805 he was paralysed in his lower limbs and confined to a wheelchair.[16] His instructions in 1803 were that he was to act as a conciliator between the Mamelukes and the Sultan, but his own clear preference was for the former, and was to lead to national disaster.[17]

Events in Egypt moved, as always, very suddenly. In April, the Albanian troops, yet another ingredient in the turmoil and jockeying for power, bombarded Khosrew's house in Cairo, forcing him to flee. The Albanian commander, Taher, was now master of the city and hoped to be the same of the country.

The arrival of Drovetti

By a curious irony, the man who was to play such a dominating role among Europeans in Egypt for the next twenty-six years made an almost unnoticed entrance into the country. On 29 May, 1803, after a crossing of fifteen days from Toulon, a brig carrying Drovetti and de Lesseps with nine staff arrived in Alexandria. The dragomans and the firmans which should have come from Constantinople had not yet arrived, and so they disembarked privately and without any publicity. They were noticed only by an Italian merchant, Antonio Goddard.[18]

It was in Alexandria that Drovetti was to spend most of his time as consul. It is therefore essential to have some impression of it in the early nineteenth century. One of the most informative descriptions comes from the eminent English traveller and Orientalist William Lane, in his *Notes and views in Egypt and Nubia made during the years 1825-1828*, in c.1825.[19]

> The quarter occupied by the Europeans is the south-eastern part of the town, by the shore of the New Harbour. This situation appears to have been chosen for their residence because it was convenient to the loading and shipping of their merchandise: but now that the Old Harbour is open to their vessels the situation is not so advantageous to them...

The houses are generally built of white calcareous stone, with a profusion of mortar and plaster. Some have the foundation walls only of stone and the superstructure of brick. They have plain or projecting windows, of wooden lattice work. The windows of the houses belonging to the Europeans and those of the palaces of the Ba'sha and the governor of Alexandria and a few others are of glass. The roofs are flat and covered with cement. There is little to admire in the interior architecture of the houses, and the town altogether has a mean appearance. Many ancient columns of granite and marble have been used in the construction of the mosques and private dwellings. The inhabitants are supplied with water from the cisterns under the site of the ancient city, which are filled by subterranean aqueducts from the canal during the time of the greatest height of the Nile; but in consequence of the saline nature of the soil through which it passes from the river, the water is not good. Almost every house has its own cistern, which is filled by means of skins borne by camels or asses, and there are many wells of brackish water in the town. The number of the inhabitants is about 15, or 16,000.

As the emporium and key of Egypt, Alexandria is a place of considerable importance, but otherwise it is in no respect a desirable residence. It is a poor, wretched town; its climate is unhealthy; and nothing but the sea and desert meets the eye around it. Ancient writers have extolled the *salubrity* of the air of Alexandria. This quality of air was attributed, according to Strabo, to the almost insular situation of the city: the sea being on one side, and the lake Mareotis on the other. The *insalubrity* of the climate in later years has been regarded as the result of the conversion of the lake into a salt marsh.... The damp and the rain during the winter at Alexandria, and the heavy dew at night throughout the year, have a particularly baneful influence. I may add that this town is one of the few places where the plague generally makes its appearance many days earlier than in the interior of Egypt. (ill. 6)

There was, then, little which was attractive in the location where Drovetti was to spend most of the next three decades of his life, and much that was dangerous. As it transpired, one of the major reasons for his return to Europe in 1829 was the severe damage done to his health. His life was to be in quite direct danger on numerous occasions for political reasons. When the two French diplomats landed, de Lesseps could not go to Cairo, given the state of civil war, and he instantly requested instructions from his direct superior, the ambassador in Constantinople.[20] Greater

6. View of the city and new harbour of Alexandria from the powder tower to the Meidan

difficulties arose for him in June when Bardissi, who controlled Cairo, invited him to reside there, so that he was fearful of compromising himself.

A mere twenty-three days after taking power, Taher had been assassinated and the Mamelukes controlled the capital. The Sultan nominated a new Viceroy, Ali Pasha, who hastily levied 1,500 men and arrived on 8 July. The Mamelukes, however, captured Damietta and Rosetta, so that they controlled all Egypt except Alexandria, on which they were marching. De Lesseps informed Talleyrand of this, and that he knew a little Arabic![21] He met the new Viceroy and found him pro-English, but finally screwed up courage and made his way to Cairo in August, fearing reprisals from the beys. (ill. 7) The two leaders, Bardissi and Ibrahim, were well disposed to the French (in contrast to Elfi); Ibrahim spoke of conquering Egypt and handing it over to the French in exchange for Syria. By the end of August, however, de Lesseps had still not received any instructions from France.

Harmony was reported reigning between the Mamelukes and the Albanians that month, but was soon shattered. The apple of discord was military pay: the Albanians demanded 10,000 purses (5 million piastres). The beys oppressed the population to pay this and also extorted 'loans' from the Europeans. The Albanians were threatening to pillage Cairo, the Mamelukes were planning to starve it. De Lesseps described the situation as 'frightful' and awaited orders. The strain was beginning to tell: an unspecified illness which had afflicted him in France flared up, and he began to talk of returning to Europe.[22]

The first mention of Drovetti in the official correspondence is in September 1803: the French ambassador to the Porte, Brune, informed Talleyrand that he had had news from him, but not from de Lesseps.[23] We must admit that the Deputy Commissioner had a much easier time than his superior. Alexandria had so far been untouched by the civil war raging in the rest of the country. It was also much easier for him to get news out of Egypt, being at the main port. Alexandria was now, however, in danger. Although Bardissi had retreated to Cairo, the Europeans asked for seals to be put on their houses to protect them. Ali Pasha had refused, but they intended to ask the same of the beys, through the Spanish consulate. The consuls were embarking their valuables and were ready to do the same with their families. And here for the first time the Drovetti we have known so well in Italy and who will soon prove his character in Egypt makes a telling entry onto the stage: he alone of all the diplomatic corps took no such measures. 'His calm attitude produces a favourable reaction.' A man who had survived the Napoleonic wars in Europe and reached the rank of major would not be troubled by such provincial disturbances – or at least would not deign to show it.

The first example of Drovetti's correspondence in the official edition is dated 6 October, and addressed to the Viceroy.[24] It also is characteristic. He protested against the sequestration of the goods of the French agent Fakre and threatened that if this protest were disregarded, there would be an 'interruption to official relations' between himself and Ali Pasha. The

7. The Sphinx in Drovetti's time

difference in character between him and de Lesseps could not be clearer. And when communications between Alexandria and Cairo were cut, Drovetti simply threatened to go straight to Constantinople. The Viceroy was forced to grant him the right to a courier. De Lesseps praised him to Talleyrand for having combined wisdom with firmness.[25]

Drovetti's courtesy and diplomatic skills were demonstrated in the same month. An English ship arrived with an English officer who bore the strange name of Taberna. He was, like Drovetti, a Piedmontese, and better known in Egypt as Captain Vincenzo. He had helped the beys against the French and then joined the English. Relying on their shared nationality, Drovetti skilfully entertained him and discovered his mission. The same letter revealed the Consul's keen interest in matters commercial: he noted the arrival of Spanish ships carrying lead. This expanding trade with Egypt could endanger French interests.[26]

De Lesseps in Cairo was not faring so well. He reported that Europeans were being massacred in their houses, that there was famine, and that forced loans were being extorted. He had been well received by Bardissi in his camp, but now that the bey was in Cairo he seemed less friendly. De Lesseps complained of the lack of instructions (presumably from Brune or Talleyrand) and of replies from Bonaparte; for he was being utterly outwitted by agents of countries with more decided policies: Rosetti, the Austrian agent, was bribing shamelessly to gain trade controls, and the English were promising the beys protection, even from India.[27]

The diplomatic crisis in Alexandria

The first note of what was to develop into a dangerous crisis, in which Drovetti was to play a leading role, came in mid November 1803 when he reported to de Lesseps that the European quarter was no longer safe. Troops passed through it daily, firing indiscriminately, especially on Sundays and holidays just at the time for church services. Three days previously Drovetti himself had been shot at from thirty paces. Ali Pasha, always at the head of these troops, was never to be found when protests were made.[28] The next day the houses of the French, English and Imperial (Austrian and Russian) consuls were fired at; the windows especially were targeted when someone was thought to be looking out. The consuls wrote in concert to Ali Pasha, demanding respect for their persons and property.

On 20 November, the Alexandrian consuls met at the house of Fantozzi, the Swedish representative. That morning Turkish troops had fired at his coat of arms, and Goddard, the Russian Consul, and Soler, the Spanish, both complained of firing at their windows. Amidst great emotion, the Russian flag was shown with four bullet holes in it. The very radical decision was taken that all should seek asylum for their families with the Turkish admiral, and commit the care of their nationals to that officer as well as Kurchid Pasha (governor of Alexandria) and Ianib Effendi, the Customs chief. An official complaint was to be sent to Constantinople, and the report of the consuls was signed by all six.[29]

This threat to leave their posts was carried out on 22 November at 3 pm and the consuls embarked on ships in the harbour. The only French company in Alexandria, the Maison Batthalon (sic), also left and went on board a Russian ship. If Drovetti went to the same ship, this may have been the beginning of an intimacy which was to change his life.

The consuls kept their promise to appeal to Constantinople on 27 November. Apart from the matters already raised, they complained of the turning of a promenade near the European quarter into a place of public execution and its being used for military exercises. One of Drovetti's staff had been arrested and given two hundred strokes. The Pasha was overturning court decisions in favour of Europeans by hearing appeals in his own house. Diplomatic correspondence between Alexandria and Cairo was blocked, and the helpful director of the post at the former was imprisoned and perhaps strangled. Ali refused to give written answers to anything which he did not like, as beneath his dignity. When the consuls embarked, reports favourable to Ali were extorted from leading figures in Alexandria under threat of death.[30]

At precisely this juncture, Bonaparte told Talleyrand to send an express message to de Lesseps saying that he wished the Mamelukes well and would help them, but not to the point of upsetting the Porte, and asking them exactly what they needed. One is left astounded at this piece of clumsiness. He also asked de Lesseps to send messages in code and by express.[31] Through Briggs, the British agent at Alexandria, however, a treaty was made between the Porte and the beys in November. Unaware of this, a courier was sent via Trieste to Egypt to assess the two contending parties and judge the likely outcome. Perhaps also unaware of this, on 1 December Drovetti made his first political recommendations.[32] He told Brune that Ali Pasha had failed in his attempt to crush the revolt of the Mamelukes, but was backed by the Ottoman Vizier, who was anti-French. The French should therefore work against him. This did not mean that they should support the Mamelukes; for they had been bought by the English. The only pro-French actor was the Turkish admiral, the Captain Pasha, who frequented Drovetti's house. Drovetti obviously considered both the present Viceroy and the Mamelukes as unworthy of French support but realised that the successful contender would have to have the Porte's approval – a remarkable presage of his triumphant policy. De Lesseps, on the other hand, thought that the French could win the Mamelukes over from the

8. Mehemet Ali, Viceroy of Egypt

English.[33] This view did not, of course, even begin to consider their fitness to rule.

While international negotiations were thus underway which were, in fact, to have little effect on the situation in Egypt, the crisis in Alexandria was settled. After two weeks of asylum on the ships in harbour, the consuls disembarked on 6 December to a seventeen-gun salute from the Turkish admiral. The agreement with the Viceroy included provisions that a guard be provided at night in the European quarter, that the esplanade not be used for executions or exercises, that the man responsible for the maltreatment of Drovetti's agent and the troops who had thrown stones and fired shots at the consuls' houses be punished. De Lesseps implies that it was Drovetti's plan to embark and seek the Sultan's protection, but also claims some credit for himself.[34] It was indeed a brilliant move which gained the desired result and bears all the hallmarks of Drovetti's legal mind and decisiveness. And de Lesseps kindly reminded Talleyrand of his colleague's enormous expenses: hiring a ship, sending despatches to Constantinople, and offering hospitality (to the members of the Maison Balthalon?).

The fall of Ali Pasha

The Viceroy left Alexandria on 25 December to move to Cairo. De Lesseps predicted that he would ally with the Albanians against the Mamelukes. Drovetti stated simply that he would have difficulty getting into the city.[35] It is interesting to compare the reliability of the two predictions. In January 1804 the two armies faced each other at Cairo. The beys refused to let Ali enter with more than one hundred men. The Albanians were mostly loyal to the Viceroy and numbered 8,000; the latter himself had 4,000 men, whereas the Mamelukes were only 1,000, although they had many Arab allies.[36] The denouement was sudden and shocking. The Viceroy realised that he could not in fact pacify the whole country, and 'fearing his troops', in January he surrendered to the Mamelukes. The main part of his army was to be sent to Syria, but within days news came that these soldiers had been cut to pieces in the desert, and there were rumours that Ali himself had been killed.[37] By early February it was known that he was dead.[38] The Mamelukes were thus again rebels against the Porte.

The name of Mehemet Ali appears for the first time in the official correspondence at this time. (ill. 8) De Lesseps strangely thought that the Mamelukes had acted with the Porte's approval. They asked Kurchid, Pasha of Alexandria, to come to Cairo, but intended to control the whole country themselves. With a rare flash of insight, de Lesseps suggested that the Albanians 'seem to me a great obstacle to their plan'. He also began to talk endlessly of fears for his life. He believed that the English would engineer a union of the Mamelukes and Kurchid Pasha. To counter this, he secretly informed the beys that the French ambassador Brune was willing to negotiate for them with the Porte. De Lesseps continued to be hopeful of winning them over, and undermining the English.[39]

For this plan Drovetti in Alexandria was crucial to sound out Kurchid. He was in touch with both him and the moderate Ianib Effendi, trying to ensure that the beys should wait for the Porte's reaction to their attempt to install Kurchid as the next Viceroy.[40] One must stress that the French diplomats were at a tremendous disadvantage, being left, as de Lesseps often complained, without instructions.[41] In strong contrast, just at this moment an English frigate put in at Aboukir, and the English Consul was able to consult with the captain. By his considerable contacts, Drovetti was able to find out that the English were supporting Kurchid's move to Cairo and a Mameluke takeover of Alexandria! He also found out that the English captain had had a three hour interview with the Consul after seeing Kurchid. On a pretext, Drovetti visited him and was able to confirm by deduction from indirect replies that the English were supporting the above policy.[42] One can only be amazed at the skills as an intelligence agent demonstrated by the young Consul. Within a few more days he had won over Kurchid's secretary and then uncovered more details of the English contacts with the Pasha. The English were claiming that the French still had designs on Egypt and that the Old Port of Alexandria had to be blocked to prevent their fleet anchoring there. Drovetti realised that this meant that a Turkish fleet coming to put down the Mamelukes would also be unable to anchor; he suspected that the whole plan did not originate with the English government, but only with the captain and the English diplomats.[43]

In mid February Elfi returned from England on an English ship.[44] Drovetti instantly foresaw that this would change the whole political outlook of the Mamelukes and produce a struggle for power. His predictions were borne out within days. Bardissi allied with Mehemet Ali, the Albanian leader, and on the night of 19-20 February, Elfi's supporters were massacred in their tents by Osman's men. Elfi's base had been at Gizeh; after the pillage 'only the walls of this unhappy town remained'.[45] Elfi had escaped the massacre at Rosetta and was heading for Cairo. Mehemet Ali attacked him, and he managed to escape only on a commandeered camel; his life was spared only because his enemies stopped to plunder. The struggle among the Mameluke beys which was to ensure their ultimate annihilation had begun.

This only heartened the Albanians who now demanded their eight months' arrears of pay and threatened Bardissi that they would deal with him as with Elfi and pillage Cairo as well. At this point Mehemet Ali turned to de Lesseps for French protection. The Consul saw that he sought only power for himself, and offered the remarkable judgement: 'I do not believe that he has the ability to conceive a grand plan or the means to carry it out'.[46] The feeble political judgement of de Lesseps was once again demonstrated; his deputy would not make the same mistake. He did, however, give evidence of his personal bravery. When the beys demanded 'loans' of the Europeans in Cairo and sent troops to extort the money, de Lesseps stood in his doorway with drawn sabre and told them they would have to kill him first. Such were the trials of European diplomats in Egypt at this time. Shots were also fired at de Lesseps in his own garden, and his attempts to escape to Alexandria on the pretext of consulting Drovetti were refused.[47]

The latter was meanwhile trying to discover what response Kurchid had given to the English pressure upon him. It seemed that he had refused to block the harbour. Drovetti alerted the Captain Pasha that this was simply a device to assist the Mamelukes and he was furious.[48]

It was only early in March 1804 that de Lesseps finally arrived in Alexandria to join Drovetti. The Albanian mutiny in Cairo and the pillage made his remaining there impossible. On his way, escaping Arabs who were massacring travellers on the Nile, he called at Rosetta to give the Albanian commander a letter from Mehemet Ali. De Lesseps now urged Kurchid to resist the Albanians with the help of the Mamelukes, although he clearly saw the possibility of the beys being defeated by the Albanians. Such were the inconsistencies in his policies. And precisely now Talleyrand wrote saying that he had just received letters written up to the end of October (four months ago!), and telling de Lesseps to remain in Cairo and use the crisis to show his energy, zeal and devotion.[49] To Drovetti four days later he wrote approving the convention with Ali Pasha made on 6 December,[50] but that Viceroy had been dead for a month. What hope was there of a coherent French foreign policy in Egypt directed from Paris?

The short reign of Kurchid Pasha

On 11 March 1804 the Albanians in Cairo marched on the houses of the beys Bardissi and Ibrahim. It was claimed that they wounded them, but this was later found to be untrue; they had, however, forced them to flee. Kurchid was declared Viceroy. Within two days there was talk of a bloody conflict between the two discomforted leaders, and they were said to have killed each other – again totally unfounded.[51] On 26 March, Kurchid entered Cairo, and de Lesseps achieved a major victory in installing his choice as the Viceroy's dragoman instead of the person favoured by the English.

The beys now massed their armies outside Cairo: they numbered 12,000 with their Arab allies. The Albanians made a sally against them but were worsted. Kurchid had, in fact, no firman and no resources. To complicate matters, Djezzar Pasha had been named by the Sultan as the new Viceroy. In April, however, the beys retreated to the Fayum. Mehemet Ali told de Lesseps that he was pro-French.[52] In the face of these developments, at the urging of Brune in Constantinople, the Turkish government offered to send four ships and 3,000 men. By the end of the month it was reported that Kurchid had been granted a firman as Viceroy. The Mamelukes inflicted a heavy defeat on the Albanians near Sakkarah in May.[53] It was then discovered that Djezzar Pasha had been dead for months. His body had been embalmed and shown at his window! Cairo was blockaded by the Mamelukes, who by now had 20,000 Arab allies.

This simply strengthened de Lesseps' old intention of backing them: if the English favoured Elfi, the French could support Bardissi and Ibrahim.[54] And this despite his realisation that the Mamelukes 'respect the French but hate them mortally'. The Albanians were again defeated on 17 May, and the Mamelukes were at the gates of Cairo, but constantly jockeying for position among themselves. After apparently receiving approval from Talleyrand to negotiate with them, de Lesseps contacted Bardissi, who handed him his 'shopping list': from Napoleon he demanded 3,000 men, 5,000 rifles, 10 canon, 5 mortars, 1,000 sabres and a loan of 2 millions. Confronted with this, de Lesseps reported that he was, as instructed, using all prudence.[55]

At this vital juncture, as the fate of Cairo hung in the balance, Talleyrand in Paris granted de Lesseps the leave which he had so long sought: the Minister had no idea what was happening in Egypt. A third French diplomat arrived, however: Saint-Marcel, Deputy-Commissioner at Rosetta. Kurchid tried to win over the Albanians with honours, and de Lesseps was so deluded as to believe that Mehemet Ali was devoted to him, while his rival Hassan was more in favour of the Mamelukes. Although Mehemet Ali had 6-7,000 troops, only some 2,000 were ready for action.[56]

Despite the almost total lack of communication between Paris and Alexandria, on 21 August 1804, Bonaparte promoted de Lesseps to Commissaire-Général, but he was not to hold the post for very long. A major upset in Cairo nearly resulted in the massacre of all the French. In a feud between a Greek doctor and a Frenchman, an Albanian was killed. De Lesseps' prompt intervention saved his countrymen's lives, but Cairo was in anarchy, and they mostly took refuge in Alexandria. Kurchid resorted to the usual extortion to pay the Albanians.

The Mamelukes were in their customary disarray, with Bardissi at Asyut, Elfi in the Fayum, and Hassan at Aswan. They thus failed to strike while the Albanians were disaffected. Finally in October, a force of 3,000 Turks and Egyptians left Cairo to confront the Mamelukes in the south. The joint commanders were the Seliktar (general) of Kurchid and Mehemet Ali. They lacked discipline and tactics and were defeated in the Fayum; the Albanians were terrified.[57] At this most inauspicious moment, de Lesseps left Egypt for leave in Europe. He was not to return. The crossing to Livorno took twenty-two days, with the English fleet looking for him. His last report emphasised the stupidity of Kurchid, who, anxious to win the Sultan's favour, had claimed that Egypt was pacified. Now that Kurchid needed help, he could not ask for it! He was a hostage to the Albanians, his only weapon against the Mamelukes.[58] While this political instability dominated Drovetti's world, a momentous political development took place in Europe, as another political parvenu attempted to establish himself on a loftier and undoubtedly permanent plane. In May Bonaparte, the First Consul, transformed himself into the Emperor of the French. The French Revolution had come to a sudden end. Drovetti was now the representative of the French Empire.

The year 1804 also saw a momentous change in Drovetti's personal life. In June, Rose Balthalon demanded a separation from her husband, Joseph, a leading merchant in Alexandria. The grounds were that she had been brutally attacked by him when she revealed that she was pregnant again, although it was ten years since the birth of her previous child. He accused her of expecting the child of another than himself. Rose was the daughter of Rey, a wealthy baker, now dead. She and her mother were owners of the building in which the French consulate was housed. The man with whom she had formed a liaison was Drovetti. The matter was public knowledge: two dragomans of the consulate in November stated that Drovetti had seduced Mme Balthalon eleven months earlier, so at the end of 1803 or the very beginning of 1804. However that may be, their first child Giorgio was born in 1812, and the first mention of Mme Drovetti is during the English invasion in 1807.[59]

Drovetti as acting Consul-General

It was early in the new year, 1805, that Francesco Benzi, chaplain to Caroline Murat, soon to be queen of Naples, replied to a letter from Drovetti which sought help and reassurance.[60] Benzi assured him that Murat was pleased with him and that he would have de Lesseps' post, since he was sure that he would not return to Egypt. Benzi also passed on to Murat Drovetti's request for an increase in salary: Murat had promised another 4,000 frs. The expenses of the French representative were onerous. There were, however, returns to be made for connections in such high places: Caroline wanted a pair of gazelles! As usual, Drovetti saw clearly the keys to the character of the main actors. Of Kurchid he stated bluntly that having good advisers and listening to them compensated for his own lack of ideas.[61]

In a battle in January 1805 between the Albanians and the Mamelukes, several beys were killed, but Mehemet Ali was defeated in an attack on Minieh, the key to Upper Egypt. When it fell to the Turks in March, supplies again reached Cairo and the price of wheat halved.

Drovetti was, of course, totally aware of the ultimate cause of the Mamelukes' defeat: their disunity and their falling numbers (their best men, Drovetti notes, had been killed) and diminishing supplies. Their headquarters were at Asyut and their army at Manfalut in Middle Egypt.[62] On 23 April Mehemet Ali entered Cairo at the head of 4,000 men and demanded money for his troops. Drovetti realised that Kurchid's Kurdish allies, the so-called delis, were unlikely to resist such a demand, and he stated instantly that the Albanians had always wanted the pashalik of Cairo. Events were soon to confirm his analysis. Within a week the demand had risen from 2,000 purses to 12,000 (six million piastres).[63] With Cairo in chaos, the Mamelukes there withdrew to Gizeh. It was at this point, on 6 May, that Drovetti wrote to Paris asking for instructions in case Mehemet Ali should gain power![64]

Kurchid's response to Mehemet Ali's move demonstrated his own weakness: he declared him Pasha of Djedda. In a riot orchestrated by his rival, Kurchid was arrested, but escaped and took refuge in the Citadel, where he was to remain. Drovetti provided a masterly analysis of the situation as always, describing Mehemet as machiavellian, increasing discontent in the capital and seeking popular support for himself, while pretending to be a loyal servant of the Sultan. There was no evidence that he was in league at this time with the Mamelukes, the Consul stated, unless with Elfi against Bardissi. Drovetti's main concern, however, was his own delicate position: how could he help Mehemet Ali without upsetting French relations with the Sultan. This was, in short, his fundamental task, and its justification was always the same: to prevent at all costs English influence in Egypt.[65]

Mehemet Ali, Pasha of Cairo

Drovetti's estimate of the Albanian's ambitions was almost instantly fulfilled. On 12 May 1805, he had himself declared Pasha of Cairo. It is time to introduce more formally the man who was to rule Egypt for the next forty-four years. He was born in 1769, the same year as Wellington and Bonaparte. Nothing is known of his first thirty years. He was born at Kavala in Macedonia, and came to Egypt in 1799 as a volunteer with other Albanians, to drive out the French. He landed with the Turkish fleet at Alexandria and was nearly drowned. The English like to take credit for saving him: he was pulled into the gig of Sir Sydney Smith. He returned to the Dardanelles and did not come back to Egypt until 1801, from which time he was one of the leaders of the unruly Albanian militia. He was now to found the dynasty which ruled Egypt until the revolution in 1952.

Drovetti instantly employed agents to influence the new ruler in a number of directions: to retain the Sultan's favour, to gain the support of the French, and not to make any agreement with the Mamelukes. It is interesting that at this time Drovetti regarded the Russian consul, Rosetti, not Missett, as the greatest enemy of France in Egypt.[66] He informed the Foreign Minister bluntly that French interests would be better served by Mehemet Ali than by Kurchid: he was strong enough to rule the country and could be used by an outside government which wished to have influence.[67] Drovetti was most anxious to prevent Mehemet Ali bringing the Mamelukes into the government, given their endemic dissensions and the violently anti-French sentiments of beys such as Bardissi and Elfi. And in the middle of 1805, rumours of an English invasion were still strong.

With Kurchid still holding out in the Citadel, there was an uprising of the population against the soldiery in June, but Mehemet Ali managed to restore order, whereupon Kurchid began bombing the city; the Pasha replied with bombardment of the Citadel.

Drovetti's despatches went not only to Paris but also to Constantinople, where they were of the greatest use to the French ambassador there. The Sultan in this way was finally convinced that the English might invade, and so he determined to send out the Turkish admiral, the Captain Pasha, to restore order in the country. The Equerry arrived first, however, by 10 July, and in the Sultan's name appointed Mehemet Ali as governor (Kaimakam) of Cairo; Kurchid was ordered to Alexandria.[68] This arrangement was confirmed by the Captain Pasha who arrived in the same month, but with only a few ships and three hundred men. He was not in any position to enforce the Sultan's wishes.

At this dramatic juncture, the instructions which Drovetti had sought back in May finally arrived.[69] The message was incredible: on no account to become involved in politics. Commercial agents were *not* diplomats, he was told – which meant that France in effect had no diplomats in Egypt. He was to recognise as legitimate whatever authority was in power, await the outcome of events, and on no account abandon his post! One can only be astounded at the complete lack of understanding of the importance of Egypt by Napoleon, who had himself invaded the country only a few years before, but whose attention was now directed elsewhere as the Third Coalition of England, Austria, Russia and Sweden formed against him. Drovetti's obviously intelligent reports might, however, have drawn forth more support and encouragement. The triumph of French influence was to be due, then, to the Consul's efforts alone. The irony of the injunction not to become involved in politics was not lost on Drovetti, who often referred to it in the sequel.

While Kurdish troops ravaged Lower Egypt, the Mamelukes fought each other, but by August Drovetti thought that the latter would support Kurchid, which delighted the English. He went himself to see the Captain

Pasha's dragoman, to reinforce Mameluke disunity, on which the Turks were relying. When the English Consul Missett and the Mamelukes went to see the Captain, claiming that they alone could restore order, he replied that Mehemet Ali was Viceroy of Cairo and that the English had enough troubles of their own without mixing in the Sultan's provinces. In his letter to Talleyrand, Drovetti revealed that this last damaging point had been provided by him: he had given the Captain copies of European newspapers![70]

A major development came with Kurchid's withdrawal from the Citadel on 7 August and retirement to Alexandria. The Mamelukes then made one of their most foolish moves. At dawn on 18 August, four hundred of them under six beys entered Cairo in a triumphant procession. When they reached the Bab Zouwaila gate, they were set upon by the population and two were killed. They thereupon tried to retreat but their way was blocked. All were killed or taken prisoner.[71] It transpired, as Drovetti was later to discover, that they had been summoned by letters to support the Cairenes, who were being harassed by the soldiers. The remaining beys and Kurchid, whom Drovetti visited, were relying on the English. They had suffered a severe loss, but the beys were still utterly suspicious of one another. Drovetti now sent a trusted agent to them to sound them out. They were supporting Ali Pasha on condition that Mehemet Ali was handed over 'dead or alive'. Elfi and Bardissi both claimed to be their leaders, but the English clearly supported the former. Drovetti thus thought it his duty to counter the English influence. In setting this out to Talleyrand, he again stressed his difficulties without instructions, and claimed to be following the policy of his recent superior, de Lesseps.[72]

Negotiations between Mehemet Ali and the beys began in September, but did not last long. The Pasha proposed that they should live at Gizeh, and that their widows and daughters should marry Turks and Albanians! He was attempting to get money from the European consuls to pay his troops, which placed Drovetti in a delicate situation: he could not risk his favoured position by supporting these protests. He noted to Talleyrand that the Sultan's appointment of Kurchid to Salonika indicated that he was not totally sure of Mehemet Ali.

By mid October the negotiations had failed, as expected. Drovetti gave a clear verdict on the state of the Mamelukes, prescient as ever: they were 'no longer those brave warriors devoted to their masters to the death; there was no longer any order or obedience among them'.[73] The Sultan's pathetic attempt to settle the power struggle in Egypt by diplomacy ended on 13 October when the Captain Pasha set sail for Constantinople. Drovetti realised that he was not taken in by Mehemet Ali's pretence at submission to Ottoman authority.

Power struggles even more far-reaching were taking place at precisely the same time in Europe. In the war of the Third Coalition, Napoleon won a major victory over the Austrians at Ulm on 17 October 1805, but just four days later, Nelson at Trafalgar ensured British domination of the seas. It little troubled Napoleon, who entered Vienna, while General Massena forced the Austrians out of Italy. The greatest French success was, however, over the combined Austrian-Russian army at Austerlitz on 2 December.

Drovetti saw that the main rival of Mehemet Ali was Hassan; Bardissi and Ibrahim were blocking communications with the south. The long awaited combat came in December, when the Pasha defeated the beys at Gizeh, but he was forced almost immediately to return to Cairo because his troops were unreliable.[74]

By January 1806, however, most of the beys were again ready for negotiations.[75] Drovetti was instrumental in inducing Mehemet Ali to break off contacts with Elfi because he was supported by the English. He admitted, however, that the Pasha was quite unable to stand against the bey, because his troops were insubordinate. Elfi defeated Hassan at Reka, then ravaged the Fayum. The situation was so bad that by March all Europeans were leaving Cairo and taking refuge in Rosetta and Damietta. In April Elfi ravaged the Delta with 6,000 men. Since the Mamelukes controlled all the provinces, Mehemet Ali's desperate need for money for his troops had to be satisfied by Cairo alone. When Elfi tried to besiege Damanhur, he was forced to retire, but he was clever enough to send an envoy to Constantinople, backed by the English, hoping for recognition.

Drovetti suffered greatly in the middle of the year from the English confidence that their protégé would be recognised. There were great celebrations for the birthday of King George, and a magnificent reception for the visiting Lord Valentia. The French Consul's response was some diplomacy of his own. He obtained a declaration of loyalty to France from Bardissi, by convincing him of Napoleon's power.[76] The French ambassador in Constantinople, Sebastiani, however, on 21 June was given clearer instructions on French foreign policy than Drovetti, who was on the spot. Napoleon declared finally that France's whole policy was tied to that of Turkey and that he would not support any rebel against the Sultan, not even old friends.[77] That message was delivered in the midst of Drovetti's cooperation with Mehemet Ali to outwit the English, which he saw as the duty of any Frenchman. He admitted in his report to Talleyrand the need to claim indulgence for this. The Pasha had declared that he had gained Egypt by the sword and would lose it only by the same means. He was frightened of English intervention and foresaw the need to ask for French help. This was the first time, we may note, that Drovetti was able to report such explicitly pro-French statements by Mehemet Ali. If need be, he promised to retire to the Citadel and hold out.[78]

The Porte, meanwhile, had decided to try once again to solve the Egyptian problem. The Captain Pasha returned on 27 June with seven ships, offering Mehemet Ali the choice of the pashalik of Salonika or Crete, and urging the Cairenes to rise against him. The English had obviously won over the Sultan. Far from disheartened, Drovetti told Talleyrand that he was sending an agent to win over the French in the service of Elfi to the pro-French Bardissi. His propaganda weapon was an Arab translation of the account of the battle of Austerlitz! Elfi replied bluntly that Napoleon might defeat the Russians and Austrians, but not the English. (His political perspicacity must be rated highly; Drovetti was obviously well matched.) The Consul claimed that Elfi had paid the English 700,000 piastres and promised them control of the senna and nitron trade. In the face of this, Mehemet Ali tried to negotiate with the Mamelukes in Upper Egypt, and some indication of his personality may be gained from his inducing his officers and troops in Cairo to forego five of the six months' pay owing to them by revealing a plot to overthrow him. Among Drovetti's sources at this time was Mme Murad Bey, widow of the great leader killed in 1801, who stressed the power of Bardissi as a counter to Elfi.[79] It is incredible to discover in July that Talleyrand had shown all Drovetti's despatches to Napoleon, and that the Emperor simply had no instructions.[80]

The Captain Pasha could make no headway against Mehemet Ali, mainly because of the vast popular support he had in Cairo. The latter felt the need, however, of more tangible backing and asked Drovetti to obtain five hundred good French soldiers, a request the Consul supported. In early August there was an engagement between Mehemet Ali and Elfi at Naguile, in which neither side prevailed, and Elfi returned to trying to reduce Damanhur. The garrison of four hundred Albanians and Turks resisted strongly and Drovetti reported that even the women chanted insults from the ramparts against their assailants' cowardice and effeminacy. Elfi's tactics included the diversion of the town's water-supply, which in fact cut off the Alexandrian cisterns. Drovetti was instrumental at this time in unnerving the Captain Pasha by telling him that a change in the Sultan's policy was imminent under French pressure and Mehemet Ali's bribery.[81] He was amazed, however, that the Admiral did not do more to assist Damanhur. He was, in fact, sufficiently alienated from Drovetti to forbid his captains to return the courtesy visits made to them by the consul. He did, however, begin negotiations with Mehemet Ali, and Elfi tried the same without success, until left in a very difficult situation by the Captain's departure again for Constantinople on 18 October.[82]

Drovetti's spirits must have been much raised by the visit at this juncture of a most eminent Frenchman, none other than le Vicomte de Chateaubriand, who stepped ashore at Alexandria on 20 October, 1806, on his famous tour from Paris to Jerusalem and return. He was lodged at the consulate on the very seashore, and Drovetti cared for his servant Julien, who had a fever, while the author went sight-seeing. He returned to Alexandria on 13 November, and spent the last week with Drovetti, seeing the city, the necropolis and the desert.

Chateaubriand is the first of the many European visitors who are to tell us so much about Drovetti in Egypt. He mentions the aviary on the roof of his house where he raised quail and partridge. The two men talked long of France and agreed, among other philosophical musings, that they required 'some little retreat in our homeland'. One notes that Drovetti seems to have been talking as if he were a real Frenchman.

It is from the famous travel account of Chateaubriand that there comes the following tribute to Drovetti:

> Le 20, à huit heures du matin, la chaloupe de la saïque me porta à terre, et je me fis conduire chez M. Drovetti, consul de France à Alexandrie. Jusqu'à présent j'ai parlé de nos consuls dans le Levant avec la reconnaissance que je leur dois; ici j'irai plus loin, et je dirai que j'ai contracté avec M. Drovetti une liaison qui est devenue une véritable amitié. M. Drovetti, militaire distingué et né dans la belle Italie, me reçut avec cette simplicité que caractérise le soldat, et cette chaleur qui tient à l'influence d'un heureux soleil. Je ne sais si, dans le désert où il habite, cet écrit lui tombera entre les mains; je le désire, afin qu'il apprenne que le temps n'affaiblit point chez moi les sentiments; que je n'ai point oublié l'attendrissement qu'il me montra lorsq'il me dit adieu au rivage: attendrissement bien noble, quand on en essuie comme lui les marques avec une main mutilée au service de sons pays! Je n'ai ni crédit, ni protecteurs, ni fortune; mais si j'en avais, je ne les emploierais pour personne avec plus de plaisir que pour M. Drovetti.[83]

This must, by any standards, be accounted a remarkable tribute, singling out Drovetti from all the other Levantine consuls. It will, however, be seen to be quite characteristic of the gratitude expressed to the Consul by all European travellers to Egypt. Chateaubriand's description includes something very important not mentioned by anyone else: Drovetti's 'mutilated hand', the legacy of his war-service. As for the writer's desire to return the Consul's kindness, he was to obtain his wish in 1822, when he became Foreign Minister, just at the beginning of Drovetti's term as Consul-General.

The anomalous French diplomatic situation in Egypt was finally made clear by the news in November that de Lesseps would not be returning from leave; he had been posted to Livorno. Drovetti straight away applied for the post of senior representative. He was not successful. He remained, incredibly, until the end of his first term in 1815 only Vice-Consul, although carrying out the duties of Consul-General. One is reminded of Napoleon's similar behaviour over the government of Rome, supposedly the 'second city' of the empire.

Then Mehemet Ali's position suddenly deteriorated. He was in desperate need of money and men, and his troops at Minieh mutinied, whereupon the Mamelukes offered them four months' pay. Elfi was, on the other hand, offered Russian help, and had the great fortune to be rid of his major rival, Bardissi, whose death was, of course, attributed to poison. Elfi failed, however, in one last attempt on Damanhur and retired to the south, after greatly weakening his own side by exiling Bardissi's friends. Through all this, Drovetti remained in favour of Mehemet Ali, telling Talleyrand at the end of 1806 that 'this man has gigantic ideas',[84] in short that he was the man to watch.

Major events had meanwhile been reshaping the map of Europe. One result of the battle of Austerlitz at the end of 1805 was the establishment of Napoleon's brother Joseph as king of Naples in March, 1806. In August of the same year, the Holy Roman Empire was dissolved, to be succeeded by the Confederation of the Rhine. It was at this incredible moment that Prussia, so far neutral, declared war on France. The Prussians were totally defeated at Jena in October, 1806, and Berlin was occupied. Russia was now to bear the brunt of the fighting in hard-fought battles at Nylau in February and Friedland in May 1807. The result was the Treaty of Tilsit on 25 June between Alexander I and Napoleon, which divided Europe into French and Russian spheres of influence.

1807: the year of decision

In January 1807, Mehemet Ali decided to attempt an encounter with Elfi, who was near Cairo. A minor battle took place in that month, but neither side was very damaged. The Pasha could do little more while he was unable to pay his troops, and his rival was isolated from the perennially disunited other beys.

Mehemet Ali's first great stroke of luck came on 27 January: Elfi died, either of apoplexy or poison.[85] His most daunting rival was now out of the way. This event may have led to the rumours reported by Drovetti of an English invasion as the only way to secure Mameluke influence. The Pasha, however, marched south against the other beys. Drovetti warned him of the need to defend the coast at the same time, so he sent all his northern troops to secure it. Drovetti also saw with absolute clarity the fact that the governor of Alexandria, Emin Bey, was pro-English. For at least a year, in fact, the English Consul, Missett, had been suggesting to his government that if it were judged 'expedient to interfere by force of arms in the affairs of Egypt, a very small armament would be sufficient'.[86]

On 13 March an English ship arrived at Alexandria and the English Consul there, Briggs, went on board; immediately after couriers were sent to Cairo and Rosetta. 'By means of some sacrifice', Drovetti reported to Sebastiani, he was able to find out what news was conveyed: that an English invasion was imminent and that the beys were called north to join it. Drovetti replied by sending express couriers to warn Mehemet Ali to cut off communications with the beys. One thousand Albanians were thereupon despatched to Alexandria to garrison it and the English consuls did everything possible to incite the Alexandrians not to admit them.[87]

On 15 March an English 74-gun ship arrived to announce the fact that England and Turkey were at war and to offer terms of capitulation to Egypt. It is well known that the English invaded because of the insistence of the English Consul Missett, who assured his government that the garrison was inadequate, that the fortifications were very poor, and that the population and more importantly the beys were very pro-English. An expedition of 6,600 men under Major-General Mackenzie Fraser sailed from Sicily on 6 March and landed on the 17th.[88]

Drovetti announced to Sebastiani that his presence at Alexandria was no longer 'useful' and that he had requested a passport for Rosetta. The governor, Emin Bey, refused this unless he went by sea, the route controlled by the English fleet. Drovetti, in one of the most daring exploits of his long career, managed to gather two dozen French and Italian sailors to accompany him in a dash by land. When he came to the city gate, he found it closed against him. Gun in hand, he threatened to sell himself dearly. He finally extorted a passport, and the same night as the English landed (17 March) he reached Rosetta, thanks to the help of two Arab chiefs who acted as his guides. It transpires that Mme Drovetti remained in Alexandria.[89]

Immediately on reaching relative safety, Drovetti asked the governor of Rosetta to send reinforcements to Alexandria. They were delayed for two days, and only then did Drovetti go on to Cairo (where he was to remain until 1812). From there he sent more express couriers to tell Mehemet Ali everything and to urge him to extract some capitulation from the Mamelukes, while Drovetti worked on the beys belonging to Bardissi's faction.[90] By this time he was able to assess the English invasion more calmly. He demonstrated to Sebastiani their indecision, having been seen off the port as early as 15 March and then being so occupied with only one thousand Albanians and now the beys. While Mehemet Ali was dealing with the south, Drovetti kept an eye on Cairo, interviewing the leading sheiks, whom he considered not very reliable, and at the same time sending envoys to the Bardissi faction to keep them neutral at least. To prevent the beys' conjunction with the English was his central care – and this was decisive in the outcome.[91]Alexandria capitulated quickly enough, on 20 March. Just three days later Missett told General Fraser that the city contained enough food only for two weeks. It was therefore necessary to occupy in addition Rosetta and Ramanieh.[92] The English accordingly attacked Rosetta on 31 March, entered the unexplored town, and were ambushed with heavy losses (200 dead, 150 wounded). From prisoners it was now known that the invading force was made up of the 31st and 35th infantry regiments, the 78th Scottish regiment, the Roll regiment and foreign 'Chasseurs', commanded by General Alexander Mackenzie Fraser (it had earlier been thought that the invasion was led by the same General John Stuart who had been one of the commanders of the expedition of 1801).

Mehemet Ali returned to Cairo on 13 April, after winning victories in the south over the beys. Drovetti immediately had a two hours' interview with him. The Pasha had left the remaining Mamelukes in the south on condition that they made no alliance with the English. (This was obviously a more trusting Mehemet Ali than he showed himself four years later, but there was no opportunity to do more.) Drovetti was justifiably sceptical that they would maintain the agreement. He stated bluntly to Sebastiani that they lived only from day to day and could not contemplate the future. The late Bardissi was the only one of them who 'could put two political ideas together'.[93]

Further English attacks on Rosetta brought only more reverses, and disastrous losses in the attack on el Hamed on 21 April.[94] The English invasion was one of the major debacles of the Napoleonic wars. Those who knew the truth, like the famous Sir John Moore, blamed first Missett for his deceit, then General Fraser for dividing his forces.[95] Not to be overlooked, however, was the totally incompetent political direction in England: 'The Cabinet sent six thousand men to Alexandria for a vague object which it could not define.'[96]

The irony was that Drovetti, who was to have been killed in the invasion, was now asked by Fraser to help protect the English prisoners. In the first attack on Rosetta all English prisoners were massacred. After the second attack, Drovetti convinced Mehemet Ali to give his men twice as much for a live prisoner as he had previously offered for a head.[97] Major Vogelsang wrote to Fraser from the Citadel on 1 May to inform him that he was a captive, along with 466 others, and that Drovetti was doing everything to help the condition of the captured and wounded.[98] General Fraser's letter of thanks for all this may be quoted:

Alexandria 7th May 1807

Major-General Fraser to Consul Drovetti
The kindness and attention you have shown to the unfortunate British prisoners call for my most sincere and unfeigned thanks. Not only this Army but the British Nation will ever feel indebted to you, and I shall send to H.M.B. Government my public testimony of the honourable and generous conduct shown by you to the Nation at large in the persons of those distressed individuals. Whatever expense you have been or may be at for them will be most thankfully acknowledged and repaid in such manner as you may wish; and it would give me the truest satisfaction to have an opportunity of returning to you or any of your nation, the obligations I feel to you for your generous and honourable humanity.

Madame Drovetti, who remained here at her own request, now wishes to go to Cairo. She has my free permission to stay here or to go wherever she pleases, and I only wait your commands respecting her and any other matter in which you may be interested.'[99]

The personal dossier of Drovetti in the Paris archives preserves an even more remarkable document.[100] This is a copy of the letter of the English ambassador at Constantinople, Robert Adair, dated 27 June, 1810. He records that two of the English prisoners were sent there, namely Major Vogelsang and Lieutenant John Love. It was Drovetti who induced Mehemet Ali to send the major at least to Turkey.[101] They and other prisoners were lodged in the palace of the ambassador at Pera, where they would, Adair asserts, have been in great need had Love not brought a letter from Drovetti to John Berzolese, stating that he would be personally responsible for everything furnished to the two prisoners. On this assurance Berzolese, obviously a banker, paid Love large sums which were guaranteed by bills drawn on the lieutenant's father. These bills were, astoundingly, dishonoured and returned to Love. By March 1809 with interest they amounted to £690 sterling. Love also owed the banker 3,700 Turkish piastres. Three years after the English invasion, the money had still not been repaid. Adair urged the British government to give the most serious attention to settling these accounts with the French government, on the grounds that every encouragement should be given to cooperation between English and French diplomats 'in distant latitudes' regarding prisoners of war on either side.

The whole episode is extraordinary. English prisoners were sent to Constantinople, apparently for negotiations, relying on the financial guarantees of the French Consul in Egypt. What was the British ambassador in Constantinople supposed to be doing? What were the prisoners' relatives doing? It is inconceivable that Love would have drawn such a sum against his father if he knew he were unable to pay, yet the bills were returned, dishonoured.[102]

Despite the parlous English situation, Mehemet Ali realised that he was hardly in a position to force the invaders out of Alexandria. Negotiations therefore commenced in May. Fraser asked for the protection of English trade and a guarantee that no 'European army' would be allowed into Egypt. When the Pasha showed Drovetti these conditions, the latter thought it wiser not to emphasise the uselessness of the negotiations, because a military operation would only cost Mehemet Ali his best soldiers. He instead described the terms as 'insignificant', and so gave his support.[103]

Mehemet Ali asked Drovetti to negotiate with the Mamelukes. The Consul described his situation at the time in vivid terms as 'sailing at the whim of the whirlpools of a stormy sea, without rudder, oars or sail', with only a 'general political compass' for a guide. He spoke unrestrainedly about his great rivals, Rosetti, the Russian Consul-General, who also acted for the Austrians, and Petrucci, the English Vice-Consul, who also represented the Swedes, as 'political hermaphrodites', who continued to manoeuvre for the enemy and who could not be touched because of their double roles.[104] His agents went to see the Bardissi faction, to ensure their inactivity until the next inundation, by which time they would be useless to the English. He gained reassurances that they would not support them, but they also feared a trap by Mehemet Ali if they came to Cairo (their fears were to be dramatically fulfilled four years later). By July the English had received reinforcements and were again 5-6,000 strong, but decisions were being made in England, albeit on totally outdated information. The Minister of War, Castlereagh wrote to General Henry Fox, English commander in Sicily, on 14 June that he was convinced that the occupation of Alexandria would require that also of Rosetta, Ramanieh and perhaps Damietta, which would mean 15,000 men. The choice was, then, either Egypt or Sicily, which meant that there was no choice. The main problem was France in Italy. The English were therefore to withdraw from Egypt.[105] With Mehemet Ali owing his troops nine months' pay, and his revenues much restricted by granting the Mamelukes the southern provinces, 'loans' were exacted from the Europeans in Cairo. 10,000 Turkish piastres and 40 quintals of both iron and lead were required from those under Drovetti's protection – which was much less than what was exacted from the others.

Drovetti discomforted

One would have thought that with the services rendered to Mehemet Ali by the French Consul, nothing less than the saving of his entire regime, the latter's position would have been as high and favoured as it was to be during most of his period of office in Egypt. Almost immediately, however, Drovetti found himself under the strongest attack from his rivals. The first signs were hopeful: he was entrusted with the censorship of the mail of the English prisoners. In July, however, he lost this right, to a Greek protégé of the Austrian-British agent, Petrucci.[106] Some of Drovetti's own letters also were lost. He complained to Sebastiani that he could not compete with the bribes paid out by his rivals, and that money was the 'surest means' in Egypt.

To distract his payless troops, Mehemet Ali marched on Alexandria and began negotiations with the English. He showed Drovetti the terms they offered and claimed that he would demand their evacuation as a precondition of negotiations. The Consul described the Pasha as 'very prolific in machiavellian tricks' and acknowledged that he could not combat the daily insinuations of his enemies. To crown everything, he had to decline an invitation to accompany the Pasha to Alexandria. His influence was on the decline, at least momentarily.[107]

Mehemet Ali in fact went to Damanhur and there on 15 August Rosetti and Petrucci spent the day with him. Drovetti was prevented from being present by solemn celebrations: it was Napoleon's birthday. The result was a notable cooling in relations between the Pasha and the Consul. Drovetti began to fear that he would agree to privileges for English commerce and policies, and was convinced that his two rivals had persuaded Mehemet Ali that an accommodation with the English was the key to his independence. The English, on the other hand, had much to gain for their control of the Mediterranean and the route to India. To add to his cool relations with the Pasha, Drovetti had not received one letter from Sebastiani since he had come to Cairo, and this fact was well enough known to be used to discredit him.[108]

The treaty of evacuation with the English was signed on 14 September. With the English went the man most responsible for the invasion, the English consul Ernest Missett, who retired to Sicily, and was not to return to Egypt for four years. English interests were henceforth served by Petrucci.[109] The English expedition had been an entire fiasco. In the view of an English historian, the main result was that Mehemet Ali acquired 'the one quality alone he lacked', that of national hero: 'this was bestowed on him by the folly of our government.'[110]

Further exactions were made of Europeans in Cairo, but this time Drovetti paid 1,500 piastres, instead of the 4,000 demanded, from his own purse. He begged Sebastiani to put an end to this abuse – by obtaining an order from the Sultan.

Mehemet Ali returned to Cairo on 3 October, and two days later granted Drovetti a long audience. The Consul protested vigorously at the disregard of French diplomats, and the Pasha in some embarrassment hoped that their old close relations would continue. His troops were now behaving with greater arrogance than ever. Drovetti was insulted by one in the street, and thought of complaining, but Mehemet Ali himself was fired at and nearly killed on 14 October. Houses were being plundered, and women and children assaulted. A grave mutiny broke out on the 26th, when five hundred Turks and Albanians marched on the Pasha's house, which they then bombarded. Mehemet Ali retired to the Citadel, and his house was plundered. In the midst of these upheavals, brave as ever, Drovetti visited the French quarter and gained assurances from the sheiks for its protection.[111]

With the English gone, Mehemet Ali was able to turn his attention again to the Mamelukes. Chain, leader of the Elfi faction, was to be given the Fayum and Gizeh. It was presumed that this was another clause in the treaty with the English, since he was the leading pro-English bey.

Much of the new year, 1808, was taken up with continued negotiations between Mehemet Ali and the English over the exchange of prisoners, notably those remaining in private hands. The Pasha had a striking success against yet another bey, an Albanian named Yassin, who threatened to become very powerful because he was supported by the Arabs. He was induced to come to Cairo by the offer of the pashalik of Jedda, was promptly arrested and deported to Syria. Communications reopened between Upper and Lower Egypt. Drovetti was, however, again outwitted by Petrucci. Both Mehemet Ali and the Mamelukes wanted the French Consul to mediate between them, but Drovetti could not do so, for he had no instructions. The parties thus turned to Petrucci, who seized the chance. Drovetti's report to Talleyrand in April was very pessimistic.[112] Mehemet Ali claimed to be the servant of the Sultan, but acted in total independence. His main maxim was to humour indiscriminately all powers; for he was quite erratic in his dealings with European diplomats. He was entirely dependent on his army since the mutiny, and Egypt was faction-ridden and unstable, with the wretched peasants worst off. Drovetti's great influence seemed to have evaporated completely, and the English had the upper hand.

A further blow to French prestige came in July, when a ship entered Rosetta from Malta under a Jerusalem flag. The French Consul there, Saint-Marcel, attempted to sequester its cargo as being in reality English. It was well known that the Jerusalem flag could easily be bought, and thus the English could bring goods from Egypt for their garrison in Malta, notably linen for the navy. Drovetti intervened with Mehemet Ali in support of his colleague, but to no avail. An appeal was then made to the French Chargé d'Affaires at Constantinople to gain a firman from the Sultan. When it did arrive, it was based on the misunderstanding that the ship was English, and the vessel was confiscated.[113] This long wrangle did much to sour relations further between the Pasha and the Consul. In August, however, he again asked Drovetti to accompany him on a visit to Damietta, Rosetta and Alexandria, in order to win local support against an attempt by the Sultan to impose a Turkish commander of Egyptian ports. Again Drovetti had to decline, because he still had no instructions![114]

Just how seriously Petrucci had outwitted Drovetti is made abundantly clear by the English Foreign Office records. In September 1808 Mehemet Ali offered through the English agent a secret pact to unite his interests with those of Great Britain for the duration of any war between the European powers and the Porte. This was just when the Pasha was about to take up the Sultan's offer to conquer Yambo and Jedda. The motive seems to have been mainly commercial; for Mehemet Ali wanted a commercial treaty with the East India Company.[115] The treaty came about, in fact, in 1810.

Drovetti may not have known of a sad event which occurred in March 1809 at Alessandria in Piedmont. His most devoted patron, General Luigi Colli, died. After their service together in Piedmont, Colli had been appointed commander of the 23rd military division of the Empire (Corsica), but his administration was damaged by scandals, and he had retired in 1806. His name is on the Arc de Triomphe.

In the same month Petrucci scored another coup, when he brought the Superior of the Order of the Holy Land in Alexandria under his protection instead of that of France.[116] At the same time came news of Mehemet Ali's peace with the Mamelukes in the south, except that they objected to the tribute (*miri*) which they had to pay: 300,000 piastres and 100,000 ardebs of grain each year. Drovetti himself thought the amounts insignificant, but predicted that they would attempt to regain their independence at the first opportunity.

Mehemet Ali received a sabre and kaftan from the Sultan in confirmation of his position as Viceroy. The Sultan's motive was clear: the new Viceroy was ordered to march against the Wahabites, the religious rebels in Arabia. The Pasha was, however, unwilling to endanger his control over Egypt by such a venture. All troops were now commanded by his relatives or allies. The army numbered ten thousand, but was paid as if it was three times more numerous, requiring endless extraordinary exactions. One of the results, Drovetti reported to the Foreign Minister

Champagny, was that wheat was six times dearer than under the French ten years earlier. And for Drovetti himself, this was a very depressing period. He spoke of 'this barbarous country where I have vegetated(!) for five years in the midst of every kind of danger, disturbance and privation, and where my health has been considerably weakened.'[117]

Finally in April, after rebuking Drovetti for consulting the Ambassador in Constantinople rather than the minister, Champagny stated that he approved of the consul's refusal to become involved in negotiations with the Mamelukes, because they were too unstable and would compromise him, and also of his not accompanying Mehemet Ali in the tour of the northern ports.[118] A rare coup for Drovetti in these frustrating times was his obtaining possession of the letter of August 1809 from Chain to the English commander in the Mediterranean, offering to be completely submissive to the English in return for help in gaining control of Egypt and 15,000 purses.[119] By September, as Champagny had foreseen, negotiations had broken down and the Mamelukes retreated to Asyut. Three months later Mehemet Ali made another expedition to the south and convinced them to settle near Gizeh and pay him tribute.

Events in Europe could not have been without interest to, and influence on, Drovetti. Joseph Bonaparte was transferred in 1808 from Naples to Spain. The new king of Naples was none other than Drovetti's patron, Joachim Murat, husband of Caroline. In February of the same year, a French army under General Miollis had occupied Rome, leading to the disastrous kidnapping of Pope Pius VII in July 1809, and a French government of occupation (1809-1814).

Austria re-entered the war in 1809 by invading Bavaria, but three months later was overwhelmingly defeated at Wagram in July. The resulting Treaty of Schönbrunn ceded enormous territory and population to France. This year may be seen as the high point of Napoleon's empire which Drovetti represented in Egypt.

Early the next year Drovetti was convinced that another English invasion was imminent, and was naturally desperate concerning his course of action in that event; for he was still in the most 'cruel incertitude' over the Minister's reaction to his actions in 1807.[120]

In May the commercial treaty between England and Egypt was announced, to safeguard trade with India, which might have been blocked by a war of Russia or France on Turkey. English ships were guaranteed entry to all ports under Egyptian control, including the Red Sea, without duty, cargoes when landed were to be protected, and deserting sailors were to be restored. English goods going to India were to pay only 3% duty.[121]

Mehemet Ali, meanwhile, was busy building a fleet at Boulaq for use in the Red Sea. The Peace of Schönbrunn between France and Austria meant that Austrian ships, moreover, were not being used to take Egyptian cargoes to the British in Malta. It was in March also that Champagny finally wrote to Drovetti on what action to take in the event of another English invasion – although how much later he actually received the letter we can only guess. The advice was that the Consul was to wait until the invasion occurred![122] Nothing could more clearly reveal the total incompetence of central French foreign policy; there obviously was no policy at all.

Drovetti continued to complain that the English were buying the right to load their ships in Alexandria. He then suddenly found himself in a very dangerous situation. His enemies told the Pasha that he was dealing with the Mamelukes. The Consul rushed to the Citadel to find Mehemet Ali. He arrived at one of the least auspicious moments, just as the Pasha was about to enter his harem. Drovetti fortunately still had enough credit with him to explain himself and to effect a reconciliation before the suspicions led to more serious consequences. It was a narrow escape in such a volatile moment. He obtained from Mehemet Ali as well a promise that he would not place himself under English protection at all, and that, although he was in fact powerless to stop English warships entering Alexandria or to stop supplies going to Malta, he would tax them as highly as possible. This was a convenient solution for the Pasha, who would thus ameliorate his endemic impecuniousness.[123]

Meanwhile, in May the Mamelukes had advanced to Gizeh and the factions were more united: Chain had been appointed head of the Murad faction, equal in influence to Ibrahim. For some reason they withdrew again to the Fayum, but the decisive encounter was approaching. Drovetti in June described Mehemet Ali's position: as critical as at any time since he became Pasha. The campaign was marked, however, by a speedy success. Within weeks his troops had captured el-Minya, Manfalut and Asyut, four beys deserted to him, and reinforcements were arriving from Syria. In the middle of July and in August, the beys were defeated three times.[124] Mehemet Ali wrote to Drovetti informing him of these successes, and claiming 600 dead or prisoner: 'the tyranny of the Mamelukes has been destroyed.'[125] Chain submitted, and Ibrahim with the remainder of the beys retired to Aswan.

By the end of the year, Drovetti's close relations with the Pasha seem to have been reestablished. He had a long interview with the ruler, in which the latter told him that he wished to be a commercial power in the Mediterranean and the Red Sea with the support of France. He desperately wanted Drovetti's agreement to this plan, which of course he could not grant without consulting his Foreign Minister. Mehemet Ali was again put out, and Drovetti told Champagny that once more the English agents had outmanoeuvred him, for they were able to make promises of support.[126]

The expedition against the Wahabites was finally to be undertaken, and Tusun, the Pasha's son still in his teens, was chosen to lead it.

The Cairene Vespers (ill. 9)

On 1 March, 1811, occurred in Cairo an event which Drovetti instantly described accurately and succinctly as 'the catastrophe which has astonished everyone, dismayed the Pasha's enemies, and removed the few supporters the English had in Egypt.'[127] The Cairene Mamelukes had been summoned to the Citadel to witness the investiture of Tusun with the command against the Wahabites. Mehemet Ali claimed to have evidence that these beys had been conspiring with those in the south and that they had corresponded with Soliman Pasha, governor of Syria. When they assembled in the Citadel, suddenly the Albanians loyal to the Pasha opened fire and the entire body was massacred: 500 Mamelukes, 25 beys and 60 cachefs. The party of Elfi was annihilated with one blow. Their houses in the city, some 120 of them, were then pillaged; the booty was estimated at ten million piastres. The only remaining factions were those of Ibrahim, Osman Hassan, Selim and Murandgy, and in the same month Ibrahim died.[128]

Despite this appalling event, Drovetti had to carry on with his day to day representation of French interests. He remonstrated yet again with

9. Cairo, the Citadel and tombs of the Mamelukes, photo by Tancredi Dumas, 1860s

Mehemet Ali over the trade with the English, contrary to the directions of the Sultan and Napoleon's wishes. The Pasha replied bluntly that he needed the money, that this export removed the excess of grain in Egypt created by the payment of taxes in kind, and that the English were threatening him with the idea that forces which had to withdraw from elsewhere (such as Portugal) might come to Egypt. Besides, they were sending him arms. The man who had just dealt so decisively with his enemies joked to Drovetti that the bullets which the Engish gave him might be used against themselves! The Consul was amazed at the disregard for the Sultan by both the Pasha and the English. He wondered whether the last were trying to embroil Mehemet Ali with the Porte, and warned him of the possibility.[129] He noticed a change in the Pasha. In Drovetti's view he was no longer the man of uncommon abilities, and he put this down to his advisers being won over by the English. It was rumoured that they had offered him refuge in India if it came to the worst and his bid for independence failed. They brilliantly undermined Drovetti by claiming that he had no influence with the French government – and the Foreign Ministry's total apathy regarding Egypt as revealed in the official correspondence certainly supports this assessment. Mehemet Ali, on the other hand, felt very confident. His income for 1811 was estimated at 45-50 million piastres, and he would soon have an army of 20,000 men. He confided bluntly to Drovetti that he mistrusted the English and the French equally![130]

In June 1811 Colonel Vincent Boutin arrived in Egypt. He was said to be seeking commercial information. His purpose was, of course, political. As early as September 1810, Napoleon was asking his Minister of the Navy about sending 40,000 men, 500 artillery carriages and 200 horse to Egypt.[131] A captain in the Imperial army, Boutin had been sent to Constantinople and attached to the army of the Grand Vizier in Silistria in 1808, then sent to reconnoitre in Algiers before coming to Egypt. He made two tours, the first to Aswan and Cosseir, then across the Red Sea to Yambo and Sinai; the second to the oasis of Siwah, where he was nearly killed by the natives. Missett warned Mehemet Ali that the first journey could only be to sound out the Mamelukes in the south and the Wahabites in Arabia against the Pasha. He replied that he had nothing to fear from the former and that the English navy could defend Egypt from a French invasion.[132] Boutin left Egypt in March 1814 to explore Syria, and in July or August 1815 was murdered by bandits near Hamah. In connection with this visit of Boutin, Drovetti wrote a long report on the present state of Egypt, and the picture was not reassuring.[133] The Mamelukes in the south, as he had predicted, were waging a most damaging 'partisan war', and the peasants, he thought, would rise at the first success to join them. The massacre in

March had made Mehemet Ali 'an object of public execration', and his troops (understandably) did not trust him as before. 3,000 of his 15,000 men were tied down in the south, and not all of the rest could be relied upon. In the event of an invasion, the Pasha had prepared a retreat with cavalry to Syria or Arabia. The coincidence of this great detail about Mehemet Ali's intentions in the event of an invasion and the arrival of the French military investigator is striking. Drovetti's colleague at Alexandria, Saint-Marcel, was similarly reporting on the defences there and had to admit that the city would fall easily to an artillery attack. And English arms continued to flow to the Pasha in return for grain: 8,000 bombs in August alone.[134]

In the midst of such vital political calculations, however, it is extraordinary to find Drovetti occupied as always with friends. He had asked Leinon, the Consul in Tunis, to obtain more presents for Caroline Murat: gazelles, ostriches, dates and exotic women's clothing.[135] Perhaps they illustrate the major interests of the Bonaparte women.

And finally in July 1811, the architect of the English invasion of 1807 returned to his post: Consul-General Ernest Missett. His difficulties continued to be many. He had to explain to the English government why he had not returned sooner, long after the restoration of peace: he had not received permission to do so, despite his repeated requests! In order to make amends for his actions in 1807 he had to spend no less than 900 pounds on presents for the Pasha and all his leading officials. Mehemet Ali was highly offended with him over the English government's refusal to approve his plan to send an Egyptian frigate into the Red Sea via the Cape of Good Hope. And finally, in his absence, Drovetti had made excellent use of his influence 'to form successful intrigues' and to win over to his side 'persons about the Pasha formerly in the British interests'.[136]

The Wahabite war

In late July or early August, 1811, Tusun left Cairo for Suez with 6,000 men. Pressure had long been brought to bear on Mehemet Ali by the Sultan to act against the sect which had taken over so many of the holy places of the Islamic religion. Its ideas were based on the fundamentalist teachings of Ibn al-Wahhab (c.1700-c.1790), who called for a return to original Islam based on the Koran and who taught that all opponents deserved death. Armed with an assurance that those of them who fell would immediately enter Paradise, his soldiers flung themselves against all odds.

Tusun crossed the Red Sea and landed in Arabia. After fierce resistance, Yambo was captured. Thirty thousand Wahabites, however, were reported ready to defend Mecca and Medina. At this very interesting juncture in both internal and external politics, on 17 November, Drovetti left Cairo with Colonel Boutin for a visit to Upper Egypt, apparently the first time he had done so during his eight years in the country.[137] He was not to return until the end of January in the next year.

Meanwhile, disaster struck in Arabia. In December Tusun was at Bedr, preparing to pass the very narrow gorges of Soffra. The Wahabites attacked and captured the Egyptian camp, forcing Tusun back to Yambo. The situation was critical, and he called desperately on his father for reinforcements. In Upper Egypt, however, another son of the Pasha, Ibrahim, pushed the Mamelukes back, and they retired to Dongola. Mehemet Ali's interest in the navy also began to show results. He had tried to send a ship around Africa to the Red Sea, but the English blocked his plan. They recompensed him handsomely, however, by fitting out the ship with a copper bottom, thirty canon and three hundred rifles, at a cost of 5,000 pounds. To this corvette were soon added eight merchant ships, and a frigate was under construction.[138]

Shortly after Drovetti's return from Upper Egypt, one of the most remarkable visitors ever to come to Egypt, Hester Stanhope, arrived from Rhodes in February 1812. She met the Consul in Cairo and was invited by him, along with two other English visitors, Milner and Calthorpe, to witness the opening of a mummy:

> A French surgeon performed the dissecting part, which consisted in dividing a vast number of folds of fine linen or cotton, which bandaged the body tight around from head to foot. When these were removed, the right hand was found to hold a papyrus. The features were not in good preservation. But M. Drovetti had in his possession the head of one so little changed that the spectator could with little difficulty persuade himself of its great antiquity, as the features, hair and teeth still existed in good preservation. The surgeon drew a tooth from the mummy before us, which broke in the extraction, as a recent one would do.[139]

This is significantly the earliest evidence for Drovetti's interest in antiquities, and coincides precisely with his visit to Upper Egypt in late 1811. It is also a fascinating description of the operations performed at this time in semi-scientific conditions on the physical remains of the ancient Egyptians.

Hester Stanhope stayed only a few months in Egypt, and when she left for the East where she was to make herself eternally famous, she was accompanied by two French Mamelukes, thanks to Drovetti and Mehemet Ali.

From conversations with the Pasha, Drovetti was amazed to learn that he was not at all alarmed about the reverses in Arabia (which perhaps explained the tardiness in sending reinforcements), because had success been easy, some of the army commanders might have been difficult to control! One wonders how far the plight of his teenage son concerned him. By April, however, the Pasha was talking of raising 4-5,000 reinforcements, and even of leading them himself. A month later the planned reinforcements were said to number 12,000.[140]

In the south Ibrahim had been appointed governor of Upper Egypt and two hundred Mamelukes had surrendered to him, leaving the others wondering where to take refuge.[141] In May Drovetti reported another massacre, this time of all those who had sought refuge with Ibrahim. He described it as an 'inexcusable, atrocious' action. At the same time Mohammed Ali married the widow of the Pasha of Derna, who had been the brother of the Pasha of Tripoli. This was seen as an obvious attempt to lay claim to Cyrenaica.[142]

In June sales of food to the English and Spanish totalled more than three million piastres. Drovetti was furious at the discrimination against any ships but English in the matter of trade and the right to sell prizes. Alexandria, he claimed, was run by the English consuls. At the same time he estimated that ten thousand French and Italian sailors were serving under the English flag because they had no means of repatriation.[143]

The situation at Yambo, meanwhile, had deteriorated seriously. Dysentery was carrying off fifteen to twenty men a day. All the stories of massive reinforcements were undercut by others about negotiations to bribe the Wahabites to leave Medina and Mecca. Not unexpectedly, unrest began to surface at home: in August four Albanian army leaders were accused of plotting against Mehemet Ali and were deported, while there were revolts of the peasants in the south against taxes, revolts which required military intervention. Drovetti at this time was unwell, and so went to Alexandria 'for a few months' to recuperate.[144] He was to remain there until the end of his first period of service in 1815. By September, Mehemet Ali had lured to Cairo and decapitated the man Drovetti described as his only military rival in Egypt, Hamged Aga. Any remaining enemies were all in fear of murder or deportation.Following the disaster of December 1811 in Arabia, Tusun regained the Soffra gorges, won over 20,000 Wahabites by bribery, and awaited the reinforcements which left Cairo in October.[145] His father seemed about to accompany these troops, but on the news of the reported occupation of Medina by Tusun, he returned to Cairo. The real reason was that there had been a revolt of the Arabs in the Fayum.

Drovetti reported constantly on the growing English control of the Egyptian economy and was bitter at Mehemet Ali's supposed impartiality towards Europeans. He in fact favoured the English above all others, 'because he fears them less and they flatter his ambition and satisfy his avarice'. They were, besides, considered the best guarantors of his independence.[146]

Seventy Arab chiefs joined Tusun, and those in Medina, which he reached by November, were ready to hand over to him. The city fell by the end of the year.

In June of this year more than half a million men had crossed the Niemen river and invaded Russia. They occupied the capital, but the Russians burned it and refused to treat for peace. In October the army of invasion was forced to begin its retreat. Only some 100,000 men were to survive. The 29th Bulletin of 26 December revealed the truth. One wonders how long it took for people like Drovetti in Egypt to hear the news.

For Drovetti personally, 1812 had been a year of great disturbance, but also some joy. His health was causing great concern. He was told by a colleague in Chios not to take too much notice of the doctors and to ask Murat to intercede with Napoleon for a change of climate. His colleague in Cairo, Asselin de Cherville,[147] told him that a sickness of the spirit was as damaging to the health as one of the body, and that he should think of a happier future and tear himself away from upsets and chagrins; being with Saint-Marcel in Alexandria would diminish his distress. Even Hester Stanhope heard of his troubles, and sent him a coin of the Ptolemies in remembrance of their meeting. Boutin wrote, mentioning a skin disease (*dartre*) and advising him to trust more in medicine than confession (!) and to take walks.[148] The joyful event was the birth of his son Giorgio in October.[149]

The new year, 1813, found him ill to the point of requesting leave.[150] Every day it became worse: 'transports d'humeurs à la tête'.[151] Alexandria was, in fact, ravaged by plague which carried off between sixty and eighty persons each day. By March it had killed one third of the population. It could have been avoided had Mehemet Ali followed French advice on quarantine, but these measures were not enforced until too late. The Pasha himself went to Upper Egypt to escape the disease, but returned by April. It reached Cairo in May, but was not so serious or lasting. The most famous victim was Mehemet Ali's own doctor, Mandrici.[152]

News of the crucial victories in Arabia at the end of 1812 arrived: the capture of Jedda and Mecca. Mehemet Ali's youngest son, Ishmael, aged about fifteen was to take the keys to Constantinople to present them to the Sultan.[153] By the middle of the year, the Pasha talked of touring his Arabian conquests. This was partly out of fear that they were not stable, but also because he wanted to make a triumphant pilgrimage to Mecca.

Others were less fortunate on the field. In the middle of the year a subscription was taken up in Alexandria for the remounting of the cavalry of the Grand Army. Eight contributors offered 2,000 francs, of which

Drovetti paid 625.[154] The fantastic and disastrous adventure of the Napoleonic regime was, however, almost over. The old allies saw their chance. Prussia and Austria took up arms again, and the decisive battle was fought at Leipzig on 16-19 October, 1813. Within six months Napoleon was forced to abdicate.

At the same time Mehemet Ali was taking vital steps in the consolidation of his own power and preparations for him to play a larger part on the eastern stage. The 'new army' was being formed, to allow him to break free from his dependence on the Turks and the Albanians. It was to be formed of negroes and fellahs.[155]

There were, however, as always, blots on the list of successes. Laty Pasha had accompanied Ishmael to Constantinople, and was highly honoured by Mehemet Ali. His head was then turned by fortune-tellers, and he revolted and was executed on 15 December. That at least was the first version. Drovetti later reported that there was a more sinister possibility: that Mehemet Ali was angry at his reception by the Sultan and his demand of the Pasha's daughter in marriage. The new sherifs of Mecca and Jedda also had to be deposed.[156] Mehemet Ali's worst fears soon began to be realised. The Wahabites regrouped in Arabia, and the Mamelukes took over Sennar and began returning to Egypt.

Drovetti is replaced

The abdication of Napoleon on 11 April, 1814 and the return of the Bourbons produced the appropriate reaction in the French diplomatic service. Saint-Marcel spoke of the joy at the restoration after the tyranny of a usurper, of the hoisting of white flags, and of Te Deums. Drovetti's words at this time are not preserved, but we know how he responded to the One Hundred Days the next year. These momentous changes, the collapse of the world in which he had come to maturity and office, affected him very deeply, although his official and personal correspondence unfortunately reveals little. The most telling is a letter from his old friend Boutin, in Aleppo in July 1814, also a fervent Bonapartist, bemoaning the collapse of the Empire. Drovetti had clearly expressed concern over his anomalous position as a Piedmontese. Boutin replied that he was in exactly the same position as other French officials and had no reason to fear worse treatment. Despite the reestablishment of Piedmont, Boutin advised him to remain firm, that is, to remain French. Boutin was a close friend who was anxious that Drovetti's services were retained by France. He even promised to write to the Ambassador at Constantinople, since Drovetti thought that it might help, but assured his friend that Murat would see that justice was done.[157] Little did either realise that this other luminary of the regime was so soon destined to fall.

On 25 September, the Foreign Minister, again Talleyrand,[158] wrote to Joseph Roussel, Consul-General at Patras in Greece, appointing him to Alexandria.[159] The same month Drovetti was informed of this and directed not only to hand over all his papers to his successor, but also to give him 'all the information that your experience has enabled you to acquire in Egyptian affairs'. He was furthermore instructed to come immediately to Paris, in order to be introduced to the King. That was not to be. Drovetti was not to leave office for another year, and he was to stay in Egypt.

In January 1815 Drovetti wrote to Talleyrand assuring him that the restoration of the Bourbons would contribute much to the reestablishment of peace and order in Europe, and that he had participated 'actively and sincerely' in the celebrations. This is one of the few cases where he may be convicted of hypocrisy. Both Drovetti and the Minister were old Bonapartists, and the Consul reminded him of their service together at an earlier time.[160]

This last year of his first tour of duty was a momentous one for Drovetti. In February his father died.[161] Then the apparent end of the Napoleonic era was rudely shattered by the One Hundred Days (20 March-29 June), which reawakened the Consul's loyalties, doubtless not requiring much encouragement. There is one version of what happened from an English visitor, William Turner:

> I gave Mr Drovetti credit for more prudence than he possesses. Letters from Cairo that arrived this morning inform us that he has written to the government there, of his intention to hoist the tri-coloured flag; and required them to order that it be saluted in every port of Egypt with a hundred and one canons, as a royal standard; this, however, they have refused to do.

This under 13 June; in September the details have changed:

> On Sunday Mr Drovetti hoisted the white flag again, which, til now he had refused to do, under pretence of not having orders; yet he hoisted Bonaparte's flag before without any orders, or rather took down the king's, for the French merchants here could not formally consent to his hoisting Bonaparte's and he dared not do it of his own authority alone.[162]

Whatever the contradictions of Turner's account, it is certain that the Hundred Days met a warm response in Drovetti, contrary to his suggestion of joy at the Bourbon restoration which was required for official consumption. That dream ended with Waterloo on 18 June. (ill. 10)

10. Map of Europe according to the settlement of the Congress of Vienna

Although English, William Turner was not hostile to the French Consul. He arrived in Egypt in the middle of the Hundred Days and is an interesting example of the cordial relations Drovetti maintained with all nations, even at such a critical juncture, and of his generosity and hospitality.

> In the morning I received a visit from Mr Drovetti, French consul, a man whom I could not help respecting, for his kind protection of the English prisoners taken in our second invasion of Egypt. He is Piedmontese and devoted to Bonaparte ... he was once captain of a regiment of Murat's cavalry, and is still devoted to that royal adventurer. For a year or two after our second invasion of Egypt, he enjoyed a yearly pension of 50,000 Turkish piastres, as a recompense for the advice and assistance he had given the Turks against our army.[163]

Turner was to see Drovetti's growing collection of antiquities.[164] In June he noted that 'all the Franks, except the colonel (i.e. Missett) and Mr

62

Lee' (English consul at Alexandria) had shut up their houses because of the plague. Turner also gives us details of one of the endless cases of protection Drovetti must have been involved in, this time a domestic case of some interest.[165] The wife of an Italian doctor Duzap who was living with the Spanish Consul turned out to be the wife of a wealthy Armenian banker in Constantinople. She had eloped with the doctor, bringing 25,000 piastres worth of jewels with her. Her lover demanded them, but she refused to hand them over, whereupon he claimed that she had the plague, poisoned her and beat her. The woman ran to Drovetti, who gave her refuge. Duzap attempted to escape with the jewels, but Drovetti 'extorted them from him by threatening messages sent by his janissary'. Duzap apparently went to Cairo and set up practice there. What happened to the woman Turner does not, unfortunately, say. These then were the problems with which Drovetti had to deal while the fate of Europe hung in the balance.

Meanwhile, on 15 May during the Hundred Days a much more momentous visitor arrived: Giovanni Battista Belzoni. (ill. 11) He was to become one of Drovetti's most notorious rivals, and to win a very considerable space in the history of Egyptology. Born in Padua in 1778 (two years younger than Drovetti), he went to Rome in his teens and toyed with hydraulics and the idea of a career in the priesthood. He won great celebrity in London in 1803 as a strong man at Sadler's Wells. In 1813 he was recruited for Mehemet Ali in Malta to make improvements to Egypt's irrigation system. When that failed he was to perform more sensational archaeological feats than anyone of his generation: removing the head of

11. Giambattista Belzoni from the
frontispiece to his *Narrative*

Ramesses II (Memnon) from Thebes for the British Museum, opening the temple of Abu Simbel, discovering the tomb of Seti in the Valley of the Kings and the entrance to the Pyramid of Chephren at Gizeh. He died in Africa in 1823.[166]

Drovetti's *Epistolario* contains no fewer than eight letters from Belzoni during his stay in Egypt, and they are of vital importance, for they throw an entirely different light on their relations from the way in which they are depicted in Belzoni's famous *Narrative of operations in Egypt and Nubia*. The first is dated 2 August, 1815, when Belzoni was trying to interest Mehemet Ali in his hydraulic machine. The Consul's advice, he declared, would be most valuable. Belzoni was nervous on many counts: he was not sure of the Egyptians' sincerity, found them ungenerous, and feared he might be duped ('when the bird is in the cage, one thinks no more of the birdlime'). He thus planned to build a small machine worked by one ox, and after agreement had been reached then to build others which required no animals. Drovetti at this stage had made him a loan. When he wrote again in twelve days, he had been granted a living allowance by the government. It seems, however, that the main burden of this letter was to ask Drovetti to send him a barrel of wine from Alexandria, for which he sent 80 piastres. Before the end of the month, however, he told Drovetti that his advice to confide in Bokhty, Swedish Consul and a kind of Minister of Industry, was useless: he was not a man to trust, he would not help foreigners, he was jealous to excess, malicious to the point of madness, and hypocritical. (One can say that, almost from this point, the chances of Belzoni's success with his machine were non-existent.) Belzoni assured Drovetti that Bokhty was *his* enemy also, although the Consul thought that he was a friend. Belzoni accordingly had his own plans afoot, which he confided to Drovetti. He had noticed land near the Nile at present quite useless, because it was never flooded; this he proposed to lease on cheap terms and then irrigate it, but all this had to be done before the Pasha saw the machine. Drovetti was obviously to be a beneficiary in the scheme.[167]

In November Belzoni informed Drovetti of his public falling out with Bokhty over his friend the chemist Giovanni Baffi.[168] Bokhty had made hypocritical charges against Baffi, saying that he had betrayed their friendship and offended him, the purest man in the world. Belzoni claimed that he had stopped him short by asking who had instigated another Italian to set up a rival nitrate factory, and by accusing him of unnatural control over the Pasha. Drovetti had to intervene immediately, and we have Bokhty's reply, defending himself from any form of favouritism or corruption: he had to help *all* 'professors and artists'. Concerning Baffi, however, he stated that there had been some confusion: the minister did not interfere in such matters, and he advised Drovetti to apply to Mehemet

Ali or the Kiaya Bey. At the same time he offered to be as helpful as ever, not as director of factories (which came under the Kiaya and the Defterdar), but as assistant in the preparation of machines. It seems, then, that Drovetti had intervened on Baffi's behalf, but Bokhty's response is very ironic. He asks the Consul and others not to try and invest him with a pelisse as director of factories, and to help protect him against such an increase in his responsibilities. Yet he writes in the second person, and signs himself 'your affectionate friend'. This letter was written three days after the arrival of Drovetti's temporary replacement as consul. Relations between Drovetti and Belzoni will be resumed by means of the latter's *Narrative* in 1816, when the former is mentioned for the first time.

Belzoni was, in fact, witness soon after his arrival in Egypt to very serious troubles. In August 1815 the troops rose in revolt against the attempt to introduce European training into the army. Belzoni describes the siege of the Citadel, the street fighting, the terror of the Europeans shut up in their quarters, and the sack of the city.[169] Drovetti in Alexandria was not directly involved but must have been concerned for the survival of the Pasha. The troubles were apparently calmed by the latter's promise that the new policies would be abandoned. As always with him, however, they were simply postponed.

On 13 October, at Pizzo in southern Italy, a firing-squad brought an untimely end to the sensational career of the one time king of Naples, Joachim Murat. After fighting alongside Napoleon at Leipzig, he had negotiated with the Allies in a desperate attempt to keep his throne, which was obviously impossible. Realising that they had no more use for him after Napoleon's fall, he turned to championing Italian independence against Austria. Advancing north, he occupied Rome and Bologna, but was crushed at Tolentino on 2 May, 1815. The Bourbons were restored. Murat escaped to France, but then made a desperate last attempt to regain his kingdom. He was easily captured and court-martialled. Drovetti thus lost one of his greatest patrons and one of his closest associates from his early military days.

The man who was to relieve Drovetti of the burdens of office, Pierre Thédénat-Duvent, the new Vice-Consul, arrived in Alexandria on 14 November.[170]

In a letter in 1819 Drovetti summed up his first period in office as 'a laborious and arduous post, encompassed by every kind of privation and danger, in a country which during this time was the theatre of six different revolutions.'[171] A stable regime under Mehemet Ali had, however, now been established and had survived many tests. Apart form his own qualities as a politician, Mehemet Ali had no-one to thank for that more than Drovetti.

Yet despite his overwhelming role in Mehemet Ali's survival in 1807, for much of the following period Drovetti fought a losing battle against the British and their agents. The reasons for this are crystal clear. French 'policy' in Egypt was non-existent. Bonaparte himself had not the faintest idea of the political events unfolding there and how to deal with them, but dreamed only of another invasion. The Ministry of Foreign Affairs was no better. When Drovetti asked what he should do in the revolutions or in the case of the English invasion, he was told to do nothing. His initiatives in crucial diplomacy were thwarted and his position made to look ridiculous. As if all that were not enough, on the rare occasions that communications were sent, they inexplicably took months, and there were conflicts and jealousies between Paris and the Ambassador in Constantinople.

The English, on the other hand, despite the invasion of 1807, saw exactly what the Viceroy wanted, and provided it: money, commercial treaties, arms and ships.

Drovetti's first period of office had, however, demonstrated his fundamental qualities once again. His bravery was manifested in 1803 and 1807. His enormous talent for diplomacy was illustrated in his dealings with Captain Taberna, his winning over of Kurchid's secretary, his use of newspapers to disconcert the Turkish admiral, and his contacts with Mme Murad. Most notable was his political insight, in striking contrast to his superior de Lesseps. He very early saw Mehemet Ali as the man most likely to win power.

III   The interregnum, 1815-1821: politics, archaeology and exploration

Drovetti came out to meet Thédénat-Duvent, and arranged a great reception for him, which the new Vice-Consul protested was more fitting for a Consul-General. Drovetti told him that all of this was necessary to make a show of French dignity. Thus the next day, 15 November 1815, Thédénat came ashore in all his finery, to salvoes of twenty-one canon and to find representatives of all the other diplomats, as well as French merchants and Egyptian troops awaiting him. The next day, accompanied by Drovetti, he had an audience with Mehemet Ali.[1]

With someone installed to take over the consulate, Drovetti was thus free to do as he liked. He in fact remained in Egypt during the five and a half years between his two periods as Consul, more active than ever, and not least in politics. He was also free to devote himself to archaeology, an interest he had recently discovered. As if that were not enough, the ex-consul took part in a number of very interesting and important exploring expeditions. It is, indeed, rather extraordinary that he remained in Egypt, given the impression which he conveyed of his situation to his friend Rignon in Torino, of 'disastrous circumstances', and given the way the latter went on to talk of 'living always menaced by the plague or a massacre, or of being the victim of the inclemency of the climate'.[2] A major consideration may, however, have been arrangements for the sale of his first collection, already being discussed in 1816.[3]

The English diplomatic service also underwent a shake-up. Missett's successor had been appointed in 1815, but did not arrive until March 1816: Henry Salt.[4] (ill. 12) He was four years younger than Drovetti, and had begun life as an artist. On meeting Lord Valentia, he had accompanied him to the East as secretary and draftsman (1799-1806). Their tour included India, the Red Sea, Abyssinia and Egypt. This experience induced Canning's government in 1809 to send him again to Abyssinia to investigate trading possibilities. On Missett's resignation, he obtained the consulship in Egypt through the influence of friends such as Sir Joseph Banks. He was to devote himself to antiquities (his two

12. Portrait of Henry Salt, by John Halls

collections went to the British Museum and the Louvre) and so create considerable rivalry with Drovetti. He was a scholar (knowing Greek, Latin, French, Italian and Arabic) and interested in the decipherment of hieroglyphs: Champollion praised his work. A most charming man, he was six feet tall, but his health was never sound after a fall from a horse in 1812.

Egypt was at this time seething not only with the plague,[5] but also with rumours of invasion. In the event of a war by Russia and Austria on Turkey, a landing by a 'third power' was feared. The French agent in Cairo, Asselin de Cherville, had the sense to offer various arguments against the possibility of the English returning in force. Mehemet Ali was seen, however, as fearing to offend them, because of their influence with the Mamelukes (what remained of them) and with the Pasha's secretary, Boghos, who made sure that his master saw no-one without his own presence. Salt's previous activity on his mission to Abyssinia made the French regard him with suspicion, and look with energy to the establishment of a French agent at Moka.

This incident introduces us to Youssef Boghos (1768-1844), an Armenian, and probably the most influential figure under Mehemet Ali after the Pasha himself. He was his secretary, and so all foreigners interested in travel or antiquities needed his support for firmans and introductions to Mehemet Ali. They all mention him, but tell very little about him. He was also Minister of Commerce from 1826.[6]

The first letter to Drovetti dated after the handing over to Thédénat and preserved for us is from the Piedmontese nobleman, his friend Giovanni Rignon, thanking him for his many presents (perfumes, dates, etc), and begging him to return to his friends, although he was only too well aware that Chateaubriand's predictions of further employment were bound to be difficult.[7] The letter is characteristic of the intense bonds of friendship which Drovetti inspired.

The journey to the Second Cataract

In the spring of 1816, meanwhile, Drovetti set off on one of his most impressive journeys, to the Second Cataract and Abu Simbel. He was accompanied by Jean Jacques Rifaud[8] and Frédéric Cailliaud.[9] An important contemporary reference is a letter to Drovetti from Boghos, replying to Drovetti's account of the journey.[10] The only interest signified by the Pasha's secretary, however, is in the existence of iron and silver mines near Aswan. Here may be a major part of the inspiration for the whole undertaking, which perhaps had government support.

The visit to Abu Simbel remains the most memorable part of the journey. An uncritical source, always anxious to give Drovetti more credit than he deserves, claims that he was the first European of this period to see the great temples.[11] It is certain, however, that he was preceded by both John Lewis Burckhardt in 1813 and William Bankes in 1815.[12] Further information on Drovetti at Abu Simbel comes from the account of the Belzoni expedition, accompanied by the two English naval captains Irby and Mangles in 1817, when in one of the most incredible exploits in the history of Egyptology, at the risk of their very lives and by superhuman effort, for the first time in the modern era the great temple was entered (ill. 13). Irby and Mangles noted with satisfaction in their account that Drovetti had tried to persuade the local chief to open the temple for 300 piastres (seven pounds ten shillings at the then exchange rate!) but that he had refused.[13]

The main source is the narrative of Frédéric Cailliaud, a mineralogist who arrived in Egypt in 1815.[14] It was on 5 March, 1816 that the travellers first caught sight of Abu Simbel. The major problem, of course, was to obtain entry, which could be achieved only with the help of the natives. Drovetti used every means of persuasion, and after three days they agreed, promising to accomplish the clearing of the entrance while the party visited the Cataract. Drovetti paid them 300 piastres. Imagine our surprise, says the naive Cailliaud, on the return eight days later to find nothing done! The reason was characteristic: an old sheik, regarded as an oracle, had

13. Abu Simbel at the time when Belzoni first opened the temple

declared that opening the temple would bring disaster on the tribe and that the Europeans were only interested in carrying off the 'treasures' within. The chiefs had the delicacy, Cailliaud notes, to return the 300 piastres. The names of Rifaud and Drovetti are incised on the pilasters of the first room of the small temple.[15]

The most primary source for the whole expedition comes, so to speak, from the hand of Drovetti himself: a series of graffiti marking the main stages of the journey. Drovetti's name appears at Amada,[16] in the small temple at Abu Simbel as we have already noted, at Wadi es Sebua,[17] at Dendur,[18] and Kalabscha.[19] It has been suggested that because of the mis-spelling at Dendur (Droveti) it was engraved by someone else and that Drovetti was in such a hurry that he did not even stop to check it. Rifaud is, then, the obvious candidate.

Belzoni steals the limelight

Drovetti was certainly on his way back from the south in July, for on the 15th of that month he met Belzoni at Manfalut.[20] Drovetti was in the company of Mehemet Ali's son Ibrahim, who was going to Cairo, and he already knew that Belzoni was going to try to remove the colossal head of

'Memnon' (Ramesses II) from Thebes. He told Belzoni that the Arabs there would not work, but he also gave him a granite sarcophagus lid in one of the tombs, since he had been unable to get it out himself. Drovetti had obviously been at Thebes, engaged in further antiquities work.

In August, Belzoni was at Thebes, where most famously he managed to move the Memnon head, despite every conceivable obstruction placed in his way (ill. 14). These were the usual calculations and apathy of the Arabs, about which Drovetti had warned him, but Belzoni also believed that 'antiquities collectors' at Alexandria were implicated in it.[21] As for the granite sarcophagus lid (that of Petau, 12th century BC, and now in the BM) which Drovetti said he could have, when he came to remove it the Cachef told him that it had been sold to Drovetti, some of whose agents had just arrived.[22] These are unnamed, but in October there appeared two agents whom Belzoni calls 'Messrs Jacque and Caliad', obviously Rifaud and Cailliaud. They attempted to dissuade Belzoni from trying to move the head of Memnon, and when he returned at the end of the year to embark it, he found it impossible to get a boat and claimed that this was due to these two men.[23]

The new French Consul, Roussel, finally arrived in Egypt on 25 August, 1816. Since his appointment to Egypt, he had spent ten months in Smyrna. With more than thirty years' service, he was the doyen of the consuls in the Levant.[24] He complained bitterly about the state of the consular house in Alexandria which required repairs. Affected by ophthalmia, by the end of the year he was asking to be returned to Smyrna, should a vacancy occur! One sees the trials, great and small, which the health of a European suffered in such posts, and also the perseverance of a man like Drovetti who had already held it for twelve years.

14. Belzoni moves the Head of Memnon

A heavy blow had meanwhile struck the house of Mehemet Ali. His son Tusun, hero of the Wahabite war, died in November at the age of twenty, 'des oeuvres d'une belle Georgienne qu'il avait trop aimée'.[25] He was to be succeeded as commander in Arabia by his brother Ibrahim.

Frédéric Cailliaud returned from his first mineral expedition in January 1817. Following his participation in Drovetti's expedition to Abu Simbel, he was introduced to Mehemet Ali by the ex-consul and was commissioned in August 1816 to search for mines in the eastern desert between the Nile and the Red. Sea.[26] Yet another European thus owed his honours in Egypt to Drovetti. It was therefore to him that Cailliaud announced his discovery of a hitherto unknown temple, fifty kms east of Redesieh.[27] He described it as having ten square pillars covered with hieroglyphs, with three divinities in the sanctuary, and with two colossal statues in low relief. We now know that the temple was built by Seti I of the nineteenth dynasty. Cailliaud's description seems a little confused. The portico is supported by four columns and the inner room by four square pillars.[28]

More importantly, Cailliaud had reports of Belzoni, and they were bad. When he had gone, on Drovetti's instructions, to give gifts at Kurneh, he was confronted by an enraged Belzoni, who told the natives to despise such presents and that he would give them twice as many. He had to be driven away after he became abusive.

Drovetti's Italian rival had, however, become a celebrity. In January, Alexandria was electrified by the arrival of the head of Memnon. This amazing feat caused some gloating. The English boasted that one man had been able to do more than the entire French army. Roussel had to uphold his country's honour by retorting that the French had had enemies on all sides, and that the English had not been able to remove even Cleopatra's Needle. He undoubtedly called on Drovetti's help in his report to Richelieu, the Minister of Foreign Affairs: it was really a head of Isis, he claimed, and the measurements of it did not accord with those of the foot in the Memnonium made by Drovetti in 1816. According to Roussel, Salt now had a firman to excavate in the Great Pyramid and was forming a committee to carry out this work, which would contribute to his reputation and profit. Salt and Briggs were, in fact, financing Caviglia's researches.[29]

There are several striking testimonies to the very high prestige that Drovetti continued to enjoy in Egypt, even as a private citizen. In February, Richelieu wrote to Roussel, expressing the French government's anxiety to profit from the ex-consul's influence with Mehemet Ali and his willingness to continue to serve French interests. Roussel was urged to conciliate Drovetti and to show the government's gratitude for his 'praiseworthy and disinterested conduct'.[30] Drovetti was, in fact, constantly consulted by the

Egyptian government at this period, on matters such as the establishment of a salt fish industry, and the construction of the Mahmudieh canal.[31] In a lighter vein, he was asked to recommend and find some books on the history of ancient Egypt, to be translated for the Viceroy, and religious houses were begging him to obtain wine for them from Cyprus.[32] And he received a report on the Arabian war from one of the French officers participating in it, Vaissière. The campaign in early 1817 centred on Canakie, and Vaissière told of a night attack on a large and rich tribe of Arabs, which was ruined because Ibrahim's men lit a fire and alerted the enemy.[33] We may assume that this French officer in Egyptian service owed much to Drovetti's patronage.

In the same month of February, Belzoni set off on his second expedition to the south. At Minieh in March his party saw two of Drovetti's agents, unnamed Copts, but dressed like Franks. They were supposedly hastening up the Nile to Thebes to forestall Belzoni's acquisition of antiquities by taking possession of territory likely to yield them.[34] When Belzoni arrived at Thebes, by his own forced march, it was not, however, Drovetti whom he blamed for what happened. It was Salt, who failed to reply to a letter from the Defterdar (Treasurer), and then proceeded to excavate for himself where Belzoni had dug in the previous year, near the sacred lake, using the services of a Piedmontese doctor, Moroki. He had uncovered a number of 'lion-headed sphinxes', apparently statues of the goddess Sekhmet, which later fell into Drovetti's hands.[35] When the latter's agents did arrive, they took up every worker, so that Belzoni was obliged to move over to the west bank, and finally the Defterdar forbade anyone to work for him or to sell anything except to Drovetti, so that he had to leave Thebes altogether.[36]

Lascaris, chevalier di Ventimiglia, who was tutor in French to another of Mehemet Ali's sons, Ishmail, died in April.[37] He had been given this post thanks to Drovetti, noted Roussel, who recorded in the same vein that the all-powerful Youssef Boghos owed his fortune to the same person. The death of Lascaris was fraught with danger for the ex-consul. He had carried on a lively and satirical correspondence with the tutor, with comments on the court knaves and ignoramuses. Salt had put seals on all the dead man's effects, including his papers. Were these to fall into the wrong hands, Drovetti's position would be utterly compromised. It is a great shame that none of these letters have come down to us. Someone – why not ultimately Drovetti himself? – saw to their destruction, but they hint at least at a very interesting side to Drovetti's character and would have been fascinating insights on the court of Mehemet Ali. It is undoubtedly connected with these events that Drovetti expressed a sudden desire to go home and to ship his antiquities to Livorno, but he also talked of going to Upper Egypt or Syria. He feared that he would be poisoned and believed that Lascaris had died in this way. Roussel's advice was sound and his judgement generous: he told Drovetti to go to France and take citizenship, and he advised the Foreign Minister that he should have been given the Légion d'Honneur in 1807. No-one knew Egypt better than he: Drovetti was a 'walking dictionary'.[38]

He did not leave Egypt, and instead took up another of the above-mentioned options. In July he was at Asyut; for he met there his old friend Cailliaud. Drovetti was on his way to Thebes 'to oversee the excavations which he had sponsored for some time with the greatest success.'[39] Irby and Mangles claim that in 1817 he was searching 'for a temple and an Egyptian road, which are said to have been seen by the jelabs [slave-traders], at one day's journey, in the desert, from Madfuni, the ancient Abydos.'[40]

Perhaps Drovetti's choice of Upper Egypt was fired by two further amazing coups of Belzoni. On 1 August, 1817, in company with Irby and Mangles he succeeded in doing what Drovetti had failed to manage, despite his enormous influence with the natives, to open Abu Simbel, and on 18/19 October he discovered the incredibly rich tomb of Seti I at Thebes in the Valley of the Kings.[41] The tomb of this king of the Nineteenth Dynasty is most famous for the exquisite alabaster sarcophagus (now in the Soane Museum in London), but also for the brilliant painted decoration. It is one of the most beautiful tombs in the whole valley and stretches some 350 feet down from its entrance, through long descending corridors and five pillared halls. The walls are decorated with the finest reliefs and hieroglyphs, with texts of the *Book of what is in the Underworld* and the *Book of Gates*, not to mention the astronomical ceiling of the burial chamber. There are two places where the continuation of the tomb is concealed by steps beneath the floor, the first approximately half way, the second behind the burial chamber and this corridor has never been fully cleared.[42]

Drovetti's nervousness about the situation following the death of Lascaris was solved, then, by removing himself to Upper Egypt, where Roussel claimed that he was speculating in ostrich feathers from Dongola![43] The plague was again raging in the north, another good reason for absenting oneself. The Spanish Consul's wife had been a victim. From the pen of an English traveller, Robert Richardson, we know what Drovetti was doing on 20 November, 1817. Richardson travelled to Upper Egypt with Salt and they were welcomed at Thebes by Belzoni; Richardson claimed to be the first European to be shown the newly discovered tomb of Seti.

On the 20th we visited the newly discovered tomb in company with the ci-devant French consul, whom we found an agreeable and intelligent man and one of the most zealous and successful collectors of antiquities in Egypt. He is the only Frenchman that I saw in all my life completely run out of the small change of compliment and admiration. He was so lavish of his civilities on entering the tomb, and everything was so superb, magnifique, superlative and outstanding, that when he came to something which really called for epithets of applause and admiration, his magazine of stuff was expended, and he stared in speechless astonishment, to the great entertainment of the beholders.[44]

There is much here that is suspect. Richardson at least admits that Drovetti was 'agreeable and intelligent', but then concentrates on his supposed failures in civilities, which is undercut completely by his own failure to realise that Drovetti was, in fact, not a Frenchman! It is all too much a piece of English Schadenfreude. Far more significant is the evidence which it offers for Drovetti's relations with Salt and Belzoni, not the bitter and unforgiving rivalry one might imagine. A most interesting sidelight on the whole episode is thrown by the claim made by Salt's biographer that Drovetti offered to buy the alabaster sarcophagus for 10,000 Spanish dollars (2,000 sterling).[45] If, moreover, this were told to illustrate Drovetti's shrewdness outwitted, when the sarcophagus had been transported all the way to England it was sold to Sir John Soane for precisely that amount. A final irony made Belzoni's name. When he returned to Thebes in August, he had found two of Drovetti's agents working at Gurneh. They were Rosignani and Lebolo.[46] It was thus because Drovetti was crowding him out of that area famous for its tombs that he turned his attention to the Valley of the Kings.[47] Had he remained at Gurneh he may never have discovered the tomb of Seti.

Yet another vignette from the same circumstances is provided by the famous Athanasi. He was with Lord Belmore (travelling with Richardson), Salt and Drovetti at Thebes in 1817. Three old Arabs came to offer their services to the English in their excavations, but were rejected. They worked by themselves, but found only two 'idols', black and ordinary, and so gave up. One of them, however, took the two idols to the river, where he found the three Europeans.

The Arab no sooner saw them than he addressed himself to the last mentioned (Drovetti), who offered him fifty paras for them both; the Arab demanded twenty more, making in all a piastre and a half of the country, a sum sufficient, as he said, to buy food for himself and his two companions; but as M. Drovetti would give no more than he at first offered, the man furiously threw one of the idols on the ground, when, to the astonishment of all present, a large papyrus rolled out of it. M. Drovetti, who never imagined that this sort of idol could contain such things, was wonder-struck, and the Arab, being delighted at this discovery, again addressed himself to M. Drovetti, and asked him, with a contemptuous air, whether he would now add anything to the price he had offered before the two idols. M. Drovetti, who had made so many difficulties about the disputed twenty paras, now found himself obliged to pay a much larger price for the papyrus and the other idol than was at first demanded for them. From that moment this mystery of the ancient Egyptians, or more properly of their priests, was no longer a secret to the inhabitants of Gourna.[48]

The story is again interesting on various counts. If it is meant to show Drovetti as ungenerous to the Arab excavators, it conflicts with everything else told about him in this respect; the 'idols' are, however, admitted to be both ordinary and unattractive. Egyptologists will be interested in this account of the first discovery that such funerary figures could contain secrets. It is unlikely that this was not known before 1817, but the knowledge has led to the destruction of untold antiquities, in the search for treasures hidden within them.

On 1 November, meanwhile, there had arrived in Alexandria a man who was to play a leading role in Egyptian architecture and engineering for the next ten years, Xavier Pascale Coste. In his lengthy *Mémoires d'un artiste*, he tells of the various projects with which he was associated, such as the saltpetre factory near Memphis, the Mahmudieh canal, the telegraph line between Alexandria and Cairo, the palace on the Citadel, and many other canals. He was, in fact, Minister of Works in Lower Egypt from 1823. It is extraordinary that in his book he does not mention Drovetti once, but only his nephew at Thebes in May 1821.[49]

By December 1817, Drovetti returned to Alexandria, complete with antiquities and feathers. Roussel wondered whether his speculations in the latter would finance the 'ruinous struggle' with Salt over the former. The English Consul, he noted, had carte blanche from Mehemet Ali.

Somehow Drovetti missed the arrival of one of the most prestigious European visitors during his whole twenty-six years in Egypt, none other than the comte de Forbin, member of the Institut de France and Director-General of French museums. He mentioned the 'intensity' with which all who knew Drovetti spoke of him, and stated that it would be impossible to have 'an exact idea' of Egypt if he did not consult him. He had a mere forty days in the country on a mission to acquire antiquities for the Louvre. He wanted Drovetti, in fact, to carry out excavations for him, and suggested that it was time to obtain a share of the success gained by the English, whom he at the same time accused of exploiting others' weakness and ignorance! He also wanted to see Drovetti's collection.

On 12 January 1818 Forbin went off to Thebes. What is extraordinary is that Drovetti did not accompany such an eminent royal emissary. No reason is hinted at, and no blame attached to him; for Forbin became a most warm supporter. The excavations at Thebes were a success, aided by Drovetti's agent Rifaud. Drovetti was left to get everything safely to Alexandria, not forgetting the 'colossal arm'. As well there were two sphinxes and two mummies in triple cases acquired from Joseph the Mameluke. To Forbin's fury, Belzoni carried off an arm in pink granite from Karnak: 'Do not let us walk on our bellies', thundered Forbin; 'be sure that a lawful and firm act of resistance will always be approved in Paris.' Drovetti's agents did not need encouragement, as events were shortly to show. Forbin returned to Alexandria at the end of February, where he did meet Drovetti and see his collection. The ex-consul also arranged a highly successful meeting with Mehemet Ali.[50]

In the account of his travels, the Director of Museums paid high compliments to the man who had helped him so much:

> M. Drovetti has given many proofs of the disinterested benevolence that tempers his character, and of the noble use he makes of that entire confidence (of Mehemet Ali) which he possesses. In his solicitude for the welfare of others, it may be conceived that his excellent bias has often contrived to forget himself. He presumes no otherwise on his favour than to avail himself of the privilege (whereof he is not a little proud) of pursuing his researches and attempts, without molestation, to explore the sandy excavations of Thebes and Memphis.[51]

The Wahabite war

The war in Arabia dragged on. By November 1817 Ibrahim was claiming to have captured Raz, Cabra and Inize; in January 1818, Shakra, three days from Dhariya. In proof of his victories, he sent 1,200 pairs of ears to Cairo! Early reports of the capture of the capital, Dhariya, however, soon proved false. Roussel gave vivid accounts (what was his source?) of the way four Wahabites could mount the same camel, and survive for a week with one bag of water and one of flour, whereas the Egyptian army of 7,000 men needed 40,000 camels. It was not until September that Dhariya fell. The Egyptian victory was a miracle, for the Arabs had blown up Ibrahim's munition stores, leaving him without ammunition for twenty-five days, but had then failed to follow up this overwhelming advantage. The muftis of the Wahabites had their beards and teeth pulled out as a punishment for heresy. The 'Lernean Hydra', as Roussel so aptly termed this war, seemed to have been crushed.

A major reason for the victory probably lay in the French military adviser Joseph Vaissière, who had earlier written to Drovetti.[52] After Ibrahim lost one third of his army at Rass, he listened to the Frenchman's advice, and the latter captured Enesa, despite its ramparts sixteen feet thick, whereupon his reputation was made. He gives a marvellous description of Dhariya, defended by no fewer than eighty canon.

Another vital source are the letters to Drovetti from the Italian doctor Andrea Gentili, who also took part in the campaign.[53] He gives a memorable description of the explosion of the munitions store at lunch time, one of the greatest explosions he had ever heard, even though he was a kilometre away. All the tents collapsed, and sixty or seventy caught fire, seventeen men were killed and several were blown off their feet. Gentili lost a leg in the war and was operated on by doctors Tedeschini and Scotti, evidence of the significant Italian presence in the Egyptian army. We need have little doubt as to why such a person wrote to Drovetti, even though he was a private citizen now, given the Consul's vital contribution to the later medical history of Egypt. Scotti also wrote to Drovetti, telling of the surrender of Abdullah to Ibrahim, and of the civilised reception granted to him.[54]

The celebrations for the victory in Egypt were spectacular and included a reenactment of the siege of Dhariya. Drovetti was meanwhile in Thebes, and relations with Belzoni reached an all-time low.

In the same year a momentous and life-long friendship and collaboration for Drovetti began, and one which did him great honour. He was introduced to Edme Jomard, the geographer and antiquarian who had been a member of the Napoleonic expedition of 1798 and who had since 1807 been editing the *Description de l'Egypte*. He had now been elected to the Académie des Inscriptions, but sought the help of the man who knew Egypt perfectly and had a famous collection of antiquities. He needed precise information on the excavations and discoveries made since 1798. Any illustration or inscription which Drovetti cared to offer would be published under his name.[55] It is opportune here also to mention another call for help with the same project the next year, from Jean Dubois Aymé, another member in 1798 as an engineer and naturalist, and who had from 1811 been Director of Customs. He resorted to Drovetti for help to complete the *Description* since no-one more than he had the means to do so. Aymé was urging the government to give the ex-consul a copy of the enormously expensive work, normally reserved for royal donations. Aymé was particularly interested in what Drovetti could provide on the costume and domestic life of the ancient Egyptians. The latter was known, therefore, for his interest in the less spectacular aspects of Egyptian antiquities, which was a feature of his collecting. The correspondent then took the opportunity to mention his own interests: he collected mummies, and sought Drovetti's help in sending him a 'stone' which he had seen at Menouf in the Delta.[56] We know that Drovetti sent him a mummified cow! The result was one he must have been very used to: Aymé then asked for one or two ibises, a crocodile, a snake, not to mention ancient bread and various modern weapons from Upper Egypt. Drovetti as usual sent off many of these.[57]

The battle lines are drawn in Thebes

The liveliest descriptions of antiquarian rivalry in Upper Egypt around Thebes come from 1818. Frédéric Cailliaud does not mention Drovetti, who was a close friend, but the following picture must include him:

> Je trouvai à Thebes beaucoup d'Européens réunis, qui travaillaient à des fouilles intéressantes, à Qourneh, sur les ruines de Medynet Abu et de Memnonium; tout l'espace occupé par les ruines de Karnak était couvert par les lignes de démarcation qui séparaient le terrain des Français, celui des Anglais, celui des Irlandais, celui des Italiens ecc. Des dames Européennes parcouraient les ruines et pénétraient dans les catacombes, ainsi que les autres voyageurs. Tous cherchaient à recueillir ou acheter des antiques; nul n'était sensible à la chaleur ni aux fatigues. A toute heure de nuit et de jour, les voyageurs parcouraient les tombeaux ou la plaine. A milieu de cette ardeur générale pour satisfaire une juste curiosité ou pour découvrir des antiquités ignorées, il est survenu quelquefois des différens sérieux entre les agens de plusieurs des voyageurs de nations diverses; on est en même venu jusqu'à se menacer des armes: heureusement les querelles n'ont pas été plus loin. J'ai remarqué que les Arabes aiment assez ces disputes, qui tournent presque toujours à leur avantage. Aujourd'hui les hommes ne suffisent plus pour les fouilles: ils emploient leurs femmes à fouiller aussi les catacombes: elles parcourent sans cesse les plus grands et les moindres tombeaux: et, jusqu'à leurs enfans depuis l'âge de neuf ans, tous travaillent incessament à porter le terre au dehors. Cette manie est poussée à un tel point, que si les *kachef* ou les *qaymaqam* n'obligeaient avec rigueur les Arabes à travailler à la culture, ceux-ci abandonneraient entièrement leurs terres pour se livrer uniquement à la recherche des antiquités.

Dans la vallée des tombeaux des rois, je trouvai M. Henry Salt, consul général d'Angleterre, connu par son talent et par son savoir autant que par son voyage en Abyssinie; il avait une longue suite: les uns étaient campés sous les tentes; les autres, dans les tombeaux mêmes. C'est alors que je vis le magnifique tombeau que M. Belzoni a découvert à force de persévérance, et qu'il a trouvé enseveli sous trente ou quarante pieds de sable et de décombres....[58]

Various contemporary visitors tell us of Drovetti's agents at Thebes at this time (ill. 15). The comte de Forbin was there in January 1818, and mentioned a French Mameluke, Yousef working for Drovetti on the west bank, and Riffo (sic), a Marseillais, at Karnak.[59] Cailliaud says that Joseph was an Italian from Torino, who had come to Egypt with Napoleon. When the French withdrew, he was ill, and so remained, and married into a good family connected with the Mameluke beys. He took service with Ibrahim bey.[60]

'Riffo' was Jean-Jacques Rifaud, of whom we now know much thanks to the labours of Jean-Jacques Fiechter, who has discovered his papers at Geneva.[61] He was born at Marseille in 1786, and trained as a sculptor. He was conscripted in 1806 and sent to Spain, but was captured or deserted. In 1810 he went to the East, and finally arrived in Egypt in January 1814, where he attached himself to Drovetti, who took him to Cairo in 1816. Here he was briefly architect to Mehemet Ali! When Salt sought his services, Drovetti indignantly announced that he would serve the French. He accompanied Drovetti to Abu Simbel in 1816, and worked at Thebes 1817-1823, then in the Fayum 1823-1824, and later in the Delta, notably at Tanis, until 1826. Although the impression is given that he was merely Drovetti's agent, he was a member of the Société royale des Antiquaires, and corresponding member of many French academies; he was also awarded the Légion d'Honneur. He published notably *Voyage en Egypte, en Nubie* (6 vols), 1830, containing hundreds of plates. In an assessment of his work and collections by the Société de Géographie, Jomard and others gave him credit for discovering many temples at Karnak, by which they meant his topographical drawings. He was often criticised by others for inaccuracy in architectural detail and the hieroglyphs: Champollion was among his detractors.[62] Cailliaud also describes him at this time:

un homme ardent pour les recherches d'antiquités, M. Riffaut, habitait Louqsor, où il faisait des fouilles pour M. Drovetti avec autant de bonheur que d'intelligence; il avait déjà trouvé, quand je le vis, une grande quantité de statues de la plus belle conservation, et découvert plusieurs petits temples jusqu'alors inconnus.[63]

15. Drovetti and his team at Thebes 1818-1819. From the left: a Nubian guide, Linant de Bellefonts. the Count de Forbin (in Turkish dress, giving alms to a woman), a servant at his feet, Drovetti with arm extended, Rifaud, Rosignani, Lebolo and another servant

It would be appropriate at this point to mention another of Drovetti's agents, Antonio Lebolo, of whom the liveliest picture is provided by his fellow Piedmontese, Carlo Vidua.[64] He was, like Drovetti, from the Canovese, had served in the carabinieri in Piedmont and in the French army. Praising Piedmontese ingenuity, Vidua exclaimed that 'it was quite a jump from the gendarmes to antiquities'. Lebolo found so much for Drovetti that he was allowed to make excavations on his own account, and he had a small collection. His house in the middle of the ruins was full of mummies, papyri and statuettes, and his fire was fed, as seems de rigueur at the time, with pieces of sarcophagi.

The question of a territorial division around Thebes is of some interest, for it may provide vital evidence for the provenance of important items found at this time by both Drovetti and Salt. As early as 1816, Ambrose Firman Didot talks of a division between the two men, but he refers to the whole of Egypt.[65] Irby and Mangles describe Thebes in August 1817 as suffering a vast inflation in the value of antiquities, owing

16. Karnak in Drovetti's time, seen from the east, showing the Hypostyle Hall and the obelisks of Tuthmosis and Hatshepsut

to the opposition between the two men. Papyri which previously sold for 8-10 piastres now cost 30-50. A dozen of the leading characters of Gourneh had formed their fellows into two digging parties, one French, one English: 'these are constantly occupied in searching for new tombs, stripping the mummies, and collecting antiquities.' One can imagine the devastation being wrought on the pitiful and defenceless dead of old Egypt. The various notables were bribed to support one party or the other, from the local Defterdar down. According to the two English captains, Drovetti obtained an order from him that the natives should neither sell anything to, nor work for, the English (this was also Belzoni's version) and a cashief was severely bastinadoed by order of a bey in Drovetti's presence for disobeying.[66] When Belzoni returned to Thebes in May 1818, he found 'that all the grounds on each side of the Nile were taken, partly by Mr Drouetti's agent, and partly by Mr Salt himself, who marked the grounds before his return to Cairo the last time.' He thus turned to the Valley of the Kings. As for the territorial division, he shows that it was unstable; for both Drovetti and Salt excavated near the Colossi of Memnon, where the latter found, after the former had abandoned it as unfruitful, a temple.[67] This was none other than the mortuary temple of Amenhotep III. And the educated German traveller, Gustav Parthey, spoke in 1822 of a riverine agreement: the right bank with Karnak and Luxor was in the hands of the French, the west bank belonged to the English (ill. 16). He went on to explain the differences in the various collections which derived from this: Drovetti's was rich in statuary, while Salt's had many mummies and sarcophagi, funerary and domestic objects, and papyri.[68] It is striking what an impression was made on all travellers at this time by the way in which Thebes was being worked, and by the rivalry between the French and the English. Some kind of territorial division did exist. It was the only way to keep peace! In his first extant letter, in 1822, Rifaud referred back to a division of territory in 1816.[69]

The Belzoni incident

Another batch of letters from Belzoni in the last months of 1818 allows us a glimpse of the state of relations between himself and Drovetti.[70] The latter was in Thebes in October, when Belzoni wrote to ask if he had heard the rumour that a native had offered to show the 'tomb of Apis' (i.e. Seti) to one of Drovetti's agents for 100 piastres and that when this price was refused, he had sold it to Belzoni. His enemies would obviously stop at nothing to discredit his discoveries. Belzoni protested that it would be the easiest thing to check if anyone had been paid 100 piastres by him, since both he and Drovetti were in Thebes. Belzoni regarded Drovetti's reply as stalling: the latter said that he had to wait for his agent Giuseppe Rosignani. Belzoni instead insisted that Drovetti assemble all the villagers, and if anyone admitted receiving 100 piastres, Belzoni would give Drovetti 500! Within another three days, he was tormenting Drovetti again about the source of this story, and claiming that the other did not understand his repeated letters. It transpired that Rosignani had told him the story, which shocked Belzoni's estimate of this 'young man of character'. Drovetti had congratulated Belzoni on finding the entrance to the second pyramid at Gizeh, but perhaps with some irony; for the latter replied that he did not expect 'honours or immortality', but only to stay in peace far from malice and calumny. The reader of Belzoni's letters in all of this exchange wishes that Drovetti's side of the correspondence had survived.

A very different picture emerges from Belzoni's *Narrative*. Salt was also at Thebes, along with William Bankes and Baron Sack. 'One evening when the whole party was assembled, Mr Drovetti happened to be there'; this indicates a close enough relationship between the two consuls. Drovetti raised the matter of a servant of his who had drowned while travelling down the Nile on a boat belonging to the English.[71] Belzoni said nothing of the language used during these social gatherings: Salt spoke both French and Italian.

On 14 November, Drovetti allotted Belzoni places to dig in Luxor. He furthermore told Belzoni that someone who looked very much like him had been seen lurking in the ruins of the temple, and that he believed that this person wanted to harm him, Drovetti. Belzoni was naturally alarmed at this, realising that it could be a pretext for harming *him*. Drovetti, he says, 'laughed at the story, and observed that I could not be so easily imitated'.[72] Although the story has its sinister possibilities, it might just as easily have been intended only as a joke. If Drovetti had a sense of humour, Belzoni did not.

Following this, Drovetti invited Salt and Belzoni to his house in the ruins of Karnak, where they took sherbets and Belzoni told of his recent journey to Berenice. The obelisk at Philae was then mentioned, of which Belzoni had taken possession for Salt. Drovetti claimed that he had paid the natives to ship it down to him, but then graciously ceded any rights he had to Salt. On 16 November, Salt, Bankes, Sack, Beechey, Linant and Ricci all set off to recover the obelisk. Drovetti's agents were at this time occupied at Edfu, and here the English passed Lebolo. When they arrived at Philae, they found that he had claimed the obelisk for Drovetti. Drovetti had also written, claims Belzoni, to the Aga, forbidding anyone to take it away. These ploys were disregarded, as was the appearance of an (unnamed) agent of Drovetti. By brilliant manoeuvres, the obelisk was loaded on a boat and passed through the rapids, arriving at Thebes on 24 December.[73] It is difficult to know what to make of all these rival claims. On the one hand, such underhand behaviour by Drovetti, especially in dealing with a man of Salt's character and standing, is rather incredible; on the other, the rivalry over antiquities was at fever-pitch, but Belzoni's status as a witness is not to be rated very highly.

As his correspondence shows, Drovetti was at the end of 1818 at Thebes. A French traveller, Edouard Montulé, gives us a remarkable picture at this time:

> In the midst of the ruins of Karnak, the finest in Thebes, the most splendid of Egypt and the world, rises a lofty portal sixty feet high, where Mr Drovetti, the ancient French consul in Egypt, has caused an earthen house to be constructed, from which he appears to command the precious relics of antiquity that surround him and which, truly speaking, he frequently rescues as from the tomb.[74]

Another traveller arrived in Egypt at this time, in the company, indeed, of the already mentioned Baron Sack: Franz Christian Gau. He fell out with his patron and was thus penniless, and was taken in by a doctor and then a Greek family, and made a living by sketching. At the end of November he reached Thebes. After confirming Montulé's description of Drovetti's house on the top of the pylon, he continues:

> I owe to the zeal and perseverance which this distinguished man has employed to help me the success of my enterprises in Egypt and Nubia.[75]

Gau went on to make a long journey into Nubia, to the Second Cataract (1818-1819), then spent three months in Thebes (April-July) on his return, before going on to Syria and Palestine. Seven of his letters are preserved in the *Epistolario*, and they reveal exactly what he meant by the above words in the preface to his book. Being penniless, he was given money by Drovetti.[76] The close friendship thus established unfortunately ended in 1824; for Gau was a phil-hellene.

It was the mooring of the obelisk from Philae at Luxor which almost cost Belzoni his life. On Boxing Day, 1818, he set out on a donkey, with a Greek servant and two Arabs, to continue his digging. Three hundred yards from the great pylon of the temple of Karnak, he was accosted by thirty Arabs led by Lebolo and Rosignani. Lebolo held both the donkey and Belzoni's coat and abused him for taking away the obelisk and depriving him of profits. Rosignani levelled a double-barrelled gun at his chest. At this point another band of Arabs ran up, headed by Drovetti himself (whose house, as we have seen, was just by). The latter accused Belzoni of stopping his men from working and told him to dismount (which he had not yet done, considering it safer to remain on the donkey). When, however, a pistol was fired somewhere behind him, he did get down, whereupon Drovetti assured him that he was not in danger.

The whole fracas had been instigated on the pretext that Belzoni was obstructing Drovetti's men in their work. The real cause, however, was clearly the taking away of the obelisk, and Belzoni stated that Drovetti lamented that act. The result was that Belzoni determined to leave Egypt immediately.[77]

There was, in a sense, a witness. Edouard Montulé was drawing the Memnonium that very morning when Belzoni rode by on his way to the tombs. He was then on the west bank, but heard the whole story from many people later that day when he crossed back to the east. His account agrees in all essentials with that of Belzoni. He adds, however, that he had seen the evening before the Arab chiefs with Drovetti speaking very strongly against Belzoni, whom they called the colossus. He stresses at the same time that Drovetti did 'all in his power to calm this vindictive spirit on either side'.

> It may now be asked of me who was in the wrong? I firmly believe that Messrs Drovetti, Salt and Belzoni are not to blame, but their Agents, who are frequently rewarded in proportion to the value of the discoveries which they make, and consequently nourish mutual animosities against one another.

The conflict was between Italians, Belzoni and Drovetti's agents. The French and English (Drovetti and Salt) were not, he says, present.[78]

The sequel to the assault involved many important people, notably Belzoni's old employer, Henry Salt. In a letter to none other than the famous antiquarian William Hamilton, dated 4 May, 1819, Salt reported:

> There has lately been a grand fracas between him and Drovetti's agents, the former having been attacked by them at Karnak, with an intent, as he declared in an affidavit, to take away his life. He wrote to me officially in the matter, and I ordered affidavits to be taken and laid before the French Consul-General (Roussel). This has put Drovetti in a raging passion, he being in some degree implicated in the cause.[79]

When Belzoni laid the case in Alexandria, Salt paid all the expenses. After a fruitless attempt to visit Siwah oasis, Belzoni returned to Cairo in June, and attempted to settle the matter. He states that Drovetti tried to make the case one between himself and Salt, instead of between Belzoni and the two agents. On Roussel's retirement, Pillavoine took over. Lebolo and Rosignani were finally induced to come to Alexandria, only to have the new Consul end the case by saying that since the accused were Piedmontese, the case could be settled only in Torino. Belzoni left Egypt in September, 1819.[80]

At almost the same time as the attack on Belzoni, in the last days of December 1818, occurred another event very damaging and upsetting to Drovetti. While he and Rifaud were at Luxor, an excavation was under way at Karnak using children to carry away the debris. A native supervisor allowed the excavation to reach a depth of some ten metres without shoring up the sides. The inevitable happened: they collapsed, entombing the children. Half of them were saved, but apparently six were killed. The story would not be known to us but for Rifaud's papers. The local population reacted with great emotion, and Drovetti is shown by Rifaud as expecting his finds to be pillaged.[81] This tragedy throws an additional light on the very tense situation at Thebes.

In January 1819 Roussel was granted leave on the grounds of health. He complained of damp autumns and winters in Alexandria. He was to be replaced provisionally by Alexandre Pillavoine from Jean d'Acre.

Drovetti's *Epistolario* contains a letter by him dated 11 January, 1819, unfortunately without address.[82] It is to someone going up to Nubia, between the first and second cataracts. It is mostly taken up with complaints about the loss of the obelisk – so Drovetti had not really given it to the English. He confesses that his last visit to the Thebaid was sad and unfortunate: probably the accident with the children. He had left with the village chief two fine mummy cases, two dozen bottles of wine, four of rum, six of vinegar and four of Lucca oil, obviously the remains of his last stay, to be shared between the recipient of this letter and M. Lachaise. The provisions are interesting as an indication of what a European had to take with him, and as an index of Drovetti's lavishness and continuing Italian tastes. The mention of Lachaise, however, is the vital clue to the identity of his correspondent. Lachaise was a French engineer later associated with Jean Huyot in the perfecting of the Mahmudieh canal. On his arrival in Egypt, Huyot was sent by Drovetti to draw all the monuments in Nubia, and ascended the Nile to the Second Cataract.

An English visitor to Egypt between November 1818 and August 1819, who met and was very impressed with Drovetti, was John Hyde.[83] At Karnak in January he met the Belzonis, who were setting off with the sarcophagus of Seti. The next month he met Salt with Buchy (i.e. Beechey), Bankes and Ricci at Abu Simbel, and continued south with the last three. They were only five or six days from Dongola when forced to turn back by hostile sheiks. Despite his English connections, who were most hostile to Drovetti, Hyde was well-disposed, for he had been given letters of introduction by Father Raffaelli to 'the learned Mr Drovetti' who was at this time in 'higher Egypt'. He must also have been influenced by Father Ladislaus of the Propaganda of the Faith at Girgeh, 'a very friendly, kind-hearted man with great politeness of manner'. So it was that on 21 January, 1819, above Girgeh he met Drovetti's boat on the Nile, went on board and breakfasted with him, spending an hour together. 'Mr Drovetti is considered one of the most learned men of the French Institute and is highly accomplished in oriental literature'. Here are two matters about Drovetti which no-one else records, and the former is certainly wrong. For all his honours, including academic, membership of the Institut de France was not one. One wonders what transpired over the breakfast table on the Nile that January morning to give Hyde the impression that Drovetti knew much of oriental literature. Perhaps he showed him some papyri. It was characteristic, however, that Drovetti gave Hyde a collection of classical coins.[84]

At Thebes Hyde met Rifaud, busy making drawings of the temples and collecting flora and fauna. Again he offers singular information, not vouchsafed by other sources: Rifaud was 'about 24-28 years of age and of most agreeably prepossessing manners.' At the same place on the return journey, he met Lobelau (i.e. Lebolo). He mentions finally several of Drovetti's excavations: at the temple of Shanhour, two hours from the Nile on the east bank, about three hours from Koptos, and tombs near Abydos, which contained wonderful 'sculptured tablets'.[85]

Back in Cairo, survival was of close concern to Thédénat-Duvent, who wrote to the new Foreign Minister, Dessolle:

Ah Monsieur, there is some merit for diplomats, especially for those who, like me, are fathers of a large family, in serving the King and the country in countries like these, where death is unceasingly before our eyes, apart from being ruined by the enormous expenses which one is obliged to undertake to live decently here.[86]

It is rare to have such personal and emotional observations in the official correspondence, and they may be equally well applied to Drovetti, soon to resume duties, even if his own family was not 'numerous'.

The same letter announced the beginning of the Yemen campaign under Mehemet Ali's nephew Kalil Pasha, supposedly to gain control of the Moka coffee trade, according to Thédénat. At the news of the first victories, all the consuls went to the Viceroy to congratulate him. He assured them that he did not want territory, only to free Yemen from the rebel Hamud. His following remarks about coffee, however, gave the contrary impression.

The journey to Dakhla Oasis

In 1821 Jomard published a book entitled *Voyage à l'oasis de Thèbes et dans les déserts situés à l'orient et à l'occident de la Thébaide*. The main narrative is, in fact, travels by Frédéric Cailliaud, notably in the eastern deserts, to rediscover the lost emerald mines in late 1816 and between November 1817 and January 1818. Following the latter journey, Cailliaud also visited Kharga oasis in June-July 1818.[87] Appended, so to speak, to his narrative is a short chapter with the strange title, *Journal d'un voyage à la vallée de Dakel par M. le chevalier Drovetti, Consul-Général de France en Egypte, vers la fin de 1818*. The imprecision of the date is striking in comparison with Cailliaud's exact calendar.

There is an account of Kharga oasis, devoted to a listing of the main settlements and the distances between them, and with no description of any matters of interest, whether anthropological, topographical or archaeological. The prelude, the journey from the Nile to the oasis, a distance of 200 kms, is dismissed in one sentence, which tells us that it takes three or four days.

The way thence to Dakhla adds up, in Drovetti's stage by stage account, to about thirty hours. The description of this outer oasis is only a little more detailed: occasional notes on temples, tombs, agriculture (they grew dates, apricots, oranges, pomegranates and figs), architecture (double-storey houses), funerary customs (funerals with singing and dancing) and bathing in sulphur springs with resultant blindness. The most extended note describes the temple at Deir el Hagar, which Drovetti rightly thought later than Ptolemaic (it is Roman). The journey back from Dakhla to the Nile is again dismissed in a sentence as requiring five days. The Nile was regained at Manfalut.

It is thus clear that Drovetti travelled to Kharga from Asyut, which took four days, traversed that oasis from north to south and back again, then continued north-west to Dakhla, and returned from the outer oasis to Manfalut in five days (ill. 17).

Even today, the word 'oasis' conjures up visions of lushness in the midst of the desert. What was the great Kharga oasis like in the early nineteenth century? A description of what Drovetti passes over with such lack of interest is offered by Cailliaud, who had been there only some months earlier. He had come across from Esneh due west to reach the southern part of the oasis, and returned due east from the northern end to Abydos. The inhabitants of Beyreys, the second town of the oasis, welcomed him, but thought that he might have come to survey them for taxes. Cailliaud tried to reassure them by asking about the existence of mines, whereupon the villagers were sure that he was looking for treasure – and never let him out of their sight! The six hundred inhabitants of the town he described as miserable, living on poor crops of rice, grain and dates. The farmers had strict turns in getting water for their fields, which were separated from each other by earthen walls. The poor farms were

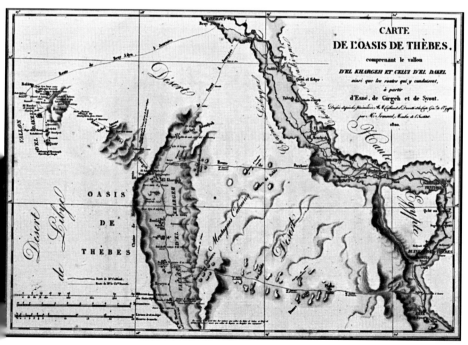

17. Map of Drovetti's journey to the southern oases

sometimes only 24 feet square with five or six date palms. Beyreys was constantly invaded by sand, and instead of clearing it away, some inhabitants preferred to raise the walls of their houses. Polluted water made it anything but healthy.

A little south was the temple of Osiris. An hour's march north of Boulaq was another Egyptian temple, with a subterranean chamber under the sanctuary. Kharga, the chief town, had a population of two thousand, and an abundance of rice and fruit. The town had covered streets to protect them from the sun and sand. The ruler of the whole oasis lived here, and the inhabitants seemed to be 'perfectly independent' of Mehemet Ali; all of them were armed, noted Cailliaud. A league to the north-west was the greatest temple of the area, with three pylons and the walls covered with fine hieroglyphs, and all surrounded by groves and fruit trees (ill. 18). Cailliaud spent days here, at some peril to himself, copying many Greek inscriptions. Even here the water was so unhealthy that it produced pimples all over not only the Europeans, but also the camels.

It is obviously a very great shame that Drovetti's journal does not provide us with information on the outer oasis, Dakhla; for Cailliaud did not visit it and so cannot fill the gap. This is even more the pity in the light of Jomard's claim that this oasis was unknown before Drovetti, that is, that he was the first to visit it.[88]

In this connection, our interest is aroused by the account of the travels of a Scot, Archibald Edmonstone. He was encouraged to visit the

18. General view of the main temple at Kharga

oases near Thebes by none other than Belzoni, whom he met on the Nile. The result has a particular piquancy, in the light of recent clashes in Thebes. On reaching Asyut on 7 February, 1819, Edmonstone found that Drovetti had set out three days earlier. Scottish canniness triumphed. Edmonstone went straight to Dakhla, and can thus claim to be the first European to have visited the outer oasis. He then returned east to Kharga:

> Nor far from here we met M. Drovetti, who having visited the nearer Oasis was now on his way to the further which we were leaving. His intention was to penetrate if possible from that into the more northern, the Oasis Parva, but I have not heard whether he succeeded in his undertaking.

The irony of the last note is especially wicked. The meeting referred to is later specified as having taken place on 21 February, about three or four in the afternoon, half a day's journey from Ballata (Dakhla).[89]

Edmonstone went on to note some bizarre features of the map provided by Jomard, the result of Drovetti's failure to give distances and sites. Dakhla was shown oriented north-south instead of east-west.[90]

The date of Drovetti's visit is thus crucial for giving credit to the first European in modern times to reach the outer oasis. Drovetti's journal gives no precision whatsoever. We have noted, indeed, the very strange title given to the published account: 'towards the end of 1818'. Was it rather early 1819? The answer is given in the French consular correspondence. Roussel wrote to Dessolle on 15 February, 1819, that Salt was going to the Second Cataract and that Drovetti was going to the Little Oasis.[91] To this we can add even more direct evidence. When Herbert Winlock surveyed Dakhla for the Metropolitan Museum in the 1930s, one of his colleagues found a graffito of Drovetti dated 26 February, 1819.[92] The date of Drovetti's visit was thus, indeed, February 1819, and Edmonstone preceded him.[93]

The French visitor Edouard Montulé, who was in Egypt 1818-1819, has already been mentioned as being at Thebes on Boxing Day, 1818. Early in the new year he came to Abydos, the temple famous for its vaults and arcades. 'By means of some researches made under the auspices of M. Drovetti (the French consul) you penetrate beneath the ceiling of the temple'.[94] We know that Drovetti was active at this site, but Montulé's note is invaluable in specifying the great temple still at this time buried under the sand.

A very important offer was made to Drovetti shortly after his return from the oases. In March 1819, Luigi Spagnolini, one of many friends who had looked forward to seeing him back in Italy after he had lost the consulate, asked him if he would be interested in representing the King of Sardinia in Egypt if Carlo Felice decided to set up a consulate there. He would have the freedom to live in either Cairo or Alexandria, as he chose. It was a confidential question, but authorised by the Minister of Foreign Affairs.[95] As it happened, a Sardinian consulate was established in 1824, but by that time Drovetti had, of course, been reappointed as French Consul-General. The man who was then appointed was none other than his son-in-law. How different Drovetti's life might have been, however, had he accepted the offer. His influence would have been so much smaller had he represented his own modest country. Fascinating would have been Drovetti's reply to this offer, had it survived among his papers. As Dubois Aymé put it, 'You have adopted France by shedding your blood for her. You must not abandon us.'[96]

In May, Roussel at last obtained his wish and sailed for France, leaving Thédénat-Duvent as acting Consul-General.[97] We do know what Drovetti wrote to Baron de Barbania in April about his future plans. He had long sighed after a life in peace in the bosom of his family and with his friends, but 'vicissitudes which he had never been able to overcome' had always prevented this; he hoped, however, that the time was not too far distant when he might spend some years with those who had most claim on his attention.[98]

In the middle of the year, Frédéric Cailliaud returned to Egypt, this time with the support of the French government, to visit Siwah oasis and Nubia.[99] Jomard recommended him to Drovetti – as if that were necessary – and told him how Cailliaud never ceased telling everyone how kind Drovetti had been to him before. Drovetti provided Cailliaud with information to help him on his further travels.[100]

Jomard also wrote very intimately to Drovetti, whom he had never met, we must constantly remember, about his life's greatest work, the *Description de l'Egypte*. It was now approaching completion, and Jomard referred with pride to the enormous work required for the whole undertaking, notably the engraving of the nine hundred plates. It was, he declared, a 'unique opportunity to erect a kind of monument to the glory of France'. We know the great hopes that Jomard had that Drovetti would contribute to this monumental work, and it must have been highly gratifying to the ex-consul to see such confidence placed in his scientific assistance.

At long last the honour so long denied to Drovetti was granted him. On 27 July, the *Moniteur universel* announced that he had been awarded the Légion d'Honneur for his services to the sciences and arts and his help to the French in Egypt. The decoration was to be taken to him by Cailliaud.[101]

The consulate of Alexandre Pillavoine

The situation for Drovetti in Egypt was not, however, very comfortable. He had been on the best terms with Roussel, who happily followed the government's instructions in this regard, but Pillavoine was another matter. He arrived in July, 1819, admittedly to find a very difficult situation. The European consuls were being asked to control their nationals, who were pouring into Alexandria and who were at best rowdy, at worst criminal. According to Pillavoine, the worst offenders were Genovese sailors who stormed around the streets at night shouting political slogans, assaulting people, and even threatening the consuls' lives. It was necessary to demand a police force from the governor to protect the Frankish quarter. One hundred and fifty arrests were made, and many were deported.[102]

Then arose the problem of what presents were to be given to the Pasha. The English had hit upon a brilliant solution which showed up French slackness: they gave him Bordeaux wine! Mehemet Ali was known not to think highly of crystal or porcelain (obviously favourite French gifts). Pillavoine suggested a French carpet – but with flowers, not figures, of course – and pistols for his son-in-law.

It was, however, the state of the consulate which most aroused the new Consul's ire. He claimed that he found no archive of instructions, inventories or despatches, no list of people who were under French protection, and that the flag was so small and battered (presumably the one Drovetti had been so unanxious to fly, in 1815). These problems should obviously be considered more the fault of Roussel than of Drovetti, who had not held office now for five years. He was soon, however, brought to Pillavoine's attention. Charges had been laid against his agents, a Piedmontese and a Turk, by Salt's 'Roman assistant'. This refers, of course, to the Belzoni case; he was from Padova, and his two assailants were Italian! It was Pillavoine who sent the case on to Torino. These turmoils caused him to remark that coming from Jean d'Acre to Egypt was like passing from calm into a storm. Drovetti's name caused him fury in another connection, one which we can only regard as astounding. The French Consul's house in Alexandria belonged to Mme Drovetti, whose father had bought it from the French army – obviously between 1798 and 1801 – and repairs were at the expense of the renter. Pillavoine claimed that the house was uninhabitable; Roussel had also complained about such matters, as we know. And that was not all that was not in order. Tourneau, supposedly French agent at Rosetta, in fact lived in Alexandria, leaving Rosetta to a dragoman who represented Russia as well, and sometimes mixed up the correspondence! The new Consul, on the other hand, had no dragoman, which created enormous difficulties, since Mehemet Ali spoke only Turkish.

One must admit that Pillavoine had run into a whole nest of problems, but there is more than a suspicion that his own character was not easy. That fact was fully confirmed, little did he realise, by the last matter that he raised with the Minister for Foreign Affairs: was the Vice-Consul to have a chair next to him in church and to receive the same honours?[103] Here was a stickler for the rules, with an over-keen sensitivity to his own importance.

The anniversary of Louis XVIII was celebrated with the éclat we might expect from Pillavoine. Mehemet Ali provided an orchestra, and there was a banquet for twenty-four people, and a ball for one hundred and thirty, attended by all the other consuls. Nothing is recorded of such celebrations, and on such a scale, in the days of Drovetti or Roussel. Pillavoine was obviously a devoted monarchist, and the old guard in the diplomatic service caused him much anguish. He reacted with a heavy hand, relying on the regulations.

The economic situation also caused him great difficulties. All but one of the French merchants owed money to Mehemet Ali. How could the Consul protect people who had ruined themselves by their own excesses or even fraud? No European was, in fact, allowed to leave Egypt without permission, following the flight of one debtor. In sum, only the Consuls of France, England and Russia were not the Pasha's 'slaves'. Pillavoine's evidence does not seem to be very coherent. Most of the nations established their consuls in Alexandria; those of England, Austria and Sweden lived, by contrast, in Cairo; this meant, according to Pillavoine, that they had to follow Mehemet Ali around everywhere, even on his travels. This was then stated to be a disadvantage for the French, because they had only an agent there, Gaspery. It is obvious that Pillavoine was far from possessing the diplomatic skills of a Drovetti, and was facing dilemma after dilemma.[104]

Drovetti was at this time in Alexandria, living in fact in a part of the consulate previously used by the janissaries. He stated that he would leave Egypt in October, but soon put off his departure until spring. He was partly retained by the continuing dispute over the Philae obelisk with Bankes. Drovetti called for arbitration, while Bankes asked that the English Consul should decide! It was at least realised that if Mehemet Ali were called in, he would not only take the object for himself but also forbid excavations in the future. Bankes therefore was allowed to have it. For once Pillavoine was on Drovetti's side: he was sorry that it was not obtained for France.[105]

In the same month, Henry Salt married. The story behind this is so extraordinary that it cannot be passed over.[106] An Austrian merchant had received a 'mail-order bride' from Italy, a very beautiful girl of seventeen. Before he could marry her, however, Salt saw her, proposed and was accepted. Given what we know of Salt's charm, the story so far is quite credible. A furious feud resulted, however, between the Austrian and English consulates, and an arbitrator was called in, who wickedly decided the case on commercial principles. 'Goods' had been taken after being landed, but before they reached the warehouse, but Salt was acquitted of 'pilfering' on the grounds that they were not properly 'packaged'. He was, at the same time, ordered to reimburse all transport costs. This, then, was a most celebrated event in 1819. Pillavoine was asked to be a witness at the wedding, and it is highly likely that Drovetti also attended. If so, his gift may not have been lavish. With the collapse of the Portalis-Praximandi company, he is said to have lost 130,000 piastres. As for Salt, the romantic courtship ended in grief. The beautiful young girl died three years later, on 16 March, 1823, from puerperal fever.[107]

At the beginning of the new year, Pillavoine informed the new Foreign Minister, duc Pasquier, that Drovetti was enormously in debt, owing Mehemet Ali 200,000 piastres and his son Ibrahim 30,000. The collapse of the Portalis company was therefore a heavy blow to him, and he may have been relieved when Portalis was unanimously condemned to repay his creditors.

Pillavoine then proceeded to indulge in endless recriminations against the ex-consul, revelations of a most indiscreet nature for official correspondence with his minister, and which only revealed the totally untenable position into which Pillavoine had manoeuvred himself. He admitted that he was not liked at all by the French in Egypt, especially the old diplomatic staff. The general community blamed him for consorting with the 'foreign' consuls, but Pillavoine asserted that they were more civilised than his fellow-Frenchmen. He then went on to assert that Drovetti and Thédénat-Duvent headed a cabal to undermine his authority.

There seemed some substance to this claim when he described how Drovetti was head of the trading house Tourneau-Balthalon. Tourneau was the French agent at Rosetta, while Balthalon was Drovetti's step-son by his wife's first marriage. Now Thédénat, the Vice-Consul, had also set up a trading company. 'God deliver me from Thédénat, Drovetti and Company, both of them turbulent lawyers, both of them Vice-Consuls (sic), both of them businessmen, both of them supporters of anarchy and wanting to be in charge', cried Pillavoine in anguish. He complained bitterly that his authority was not respected, but he hesitated to use it for fear of failure and the resulting shame. Drovetti, on the other hand, he claimed, gained everything he wanted by using his old title of consul, and everyone thought that it was Pillavoine who was making the request!

Despite economic problems, Drovetti knew where his duties lay. On the triumphal return of Ibrahim from the Wahabite war in December

1819, everyone gave him presents. The ex-consul, according to Pillavoine, contributed forty cases of wine. Mehemet Ali, on the other hand, was ruthless in calling in his debts, and even Tourneau-Balthalon were being dunned for a quarter of what they owed.[108] In the midst of all these troubles, Drovetti made one of his most spectacular journeys of exploration.

The journey to Siwah Oasis

Perhaps the most intrepid of all his travels in retirement was that to Siwah early in 1820, a trek of almost two weeks through the desert to an independent and isolated state inhabited and guarded by fierce desert Arabs. It must be admitted, however, that the ex-consul did have a large military escort; for he was in fact accompanying the expedition sent by Mehemet Ali to bring the oasis under his control.

Drovetti was by no means the first European to go there. William Edward Browne had been there as long ago as 1792, and Friedrich Hornemann in 1798,[109] not to mention Frédéric Cailliaud, only months before.[110] Perhaps a special stimulus to Drovetti's anticipation, however, was the fact that Belzoni in 1819 claimed to have reached Siwah.[111] He was mistaken; he was the first European to visit Baharia.

Cailliaud had marched from the Fayum to Siwah in eighteen days, arriving on 10 December, 1819. He was accompanied by Pierre Letorzec, a French naval midshipman, an Arab sheik called Gouroum, and a Siwan called Yousef, who acted as the guide and interpreter. They had, of course, a firman from Mehemet Ali, but the chiefs of the oasis could not understand it and suggested sending it to Cairo for explanation! At first everything went well, with permission granted to the visitors to see everything except the island, and all inhabitants were warned of penalties if they harmed the travellers. Under increasing difficulties, however, Cailliaud visited the catacombs of Geleb Mouta to the north-east and the antiquities to the west. There remained the major monument of the oasis, Omm-Beydah, the temple of Amon. This required another long consultation with the local council; for the natives suffered from the superstition that the Europeans could make the water sources dry up. Cailliaud was being followed wherever he went and had to bribe heavily to be able to draw anything, and the area he was allowed to visit was continually shrinking. He could write only at night. An attempt to send Yousef to get wax impressions of the temple inscriptions failed, and then everyone was forbidden to speak to the visitors. Permission to visit the temple was finally granted. It was just then that a trading caravan from Benghazy visited the oasis on its way to Alexandria, and Cailliaud was warned that this was his only way of returning safely. The editor of his

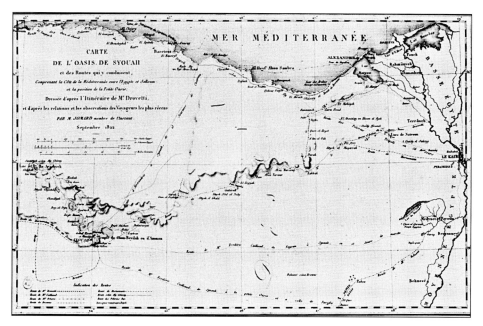

19. Map illustrating Drovetti's journey to Siwah

account, Jomard, rightly stresses the dangers that such travellers underwent for the sake of geographical and antiquarian studies and the incredible difficulties they had to surmount in order to obtain the simplest results. This then was the condition of the oasis just before Drovetti arrived. The major antiquarian question still to be solved was the most important: where was the seat of the famous temple of Jupiter Amon?

By February 1820, Mehemet Ali decided to send a military expedition to Siwah. Hassan, governor of Bahyreh province, offered to conquer it, and in March he set out with 1,500 or 2,000 men, as well as artillery. Drovetti obtained permission to accompany them, and with him came the artist Linant de Bellefonds, Alessandro Ricci, and Enegildo Frediani.[112] Setting out from Terraneh on the Nile a little below Cairo, the route curved north along the bottom of lake Mariut, the south-west to Hammameh, south to Lebbak, and then south-west again to Siwah. The distance was about 650 km (ill. 19).

The interest of the expedition is manifold. The oasis still today has great romantic attraction and still involves a dangerous journey. 'After the fatigue of the road and the monotony of the rocky desert, the reddish hills and the palm plantations, the blue patches of the surfaces of water, the evening colours make a profound impression on the traveller.'[113] As well, the remains of antiquity are now much fewer, so the records of the Drovetti expedition are all the more precious.

20. The town of Siwah from the south, painting by Linant de Bellefonds

The conquest of the oasis required a three hours' battle. Drovetti's map indicates that only about one tenth of the area of the oasis was fertile, producing dates and fruit. The soil was sandy and salty, but that did not harm the fertility or affect the sources of fresh water. There was a salt lake to the west (Arachyeh), with two small islands. The main trees grown were palm, olive, pomegranate, apricot, fig, plum and apple, as well as grapes. Some of the fruits were dried and exported. The olives produced excellent oil; the dates were of five qualities, the best of them superior to anything in Egypt. The animals kept were sheep, cattle, asses, goats, camels, buffaloes. The population at the time was estimated at five thousand, all devoted Muslims.

The oasis was governed by a divan of twenty-two sheiks, according to Cailliaud; Drovetti says twelve. Their deliberations were carried on in public; a judge (cadi) came from Cairo. Wrongs less than criminal were punished by a fine, but a murderer was handed over to the family of his victim to do with as they liked. The character of the Siwans was notoriously difficult: sombre, savage, intractable, opinionated and zealous, says Jomard.

The town of Siwah was divided in two: one part for married people, the other for widows and young unmarried men. The streets, flanked by multi-storeyed houses (extra storeys were added to houses for newly married members), were so tortuous that even at midday a lamp was useful. The whole town was a fortress. The basic building material was salt, cut in blocks in the neighbouring mountains and covered with gypsum (ill. 20).

Of the remains of the temple of Amon, placed also by Drovetti at Omm Beydah, two sections were still discernible in the location proposed by Drovetti. One was a room or corridor (37.5 m. long), with part of a door still standing, the other remains of a peristyle with columns three metres in circumference; there were also traces of an outer surrounding wall, 110 m x 90 m. The temple was, in short, almost destroyed, and Jomard regretted this especially because of the fine decoration that it once had boasted. Still recognisable were lines of deities and priests, with the ram-headed god naturally dominant (ills. 21-22). Jomard quoted at length Drovetti's views on the topography of the ruins: he believed that the standing sections could not be the main room of the temple, but were simply a corridor, because they were too close to the entrance door on the north, and because of the great mass of fallen stone to the south. Drovetti suggested the remains were of a typhonium, as at Edfu. The nearby village of Gharmy, to the east of Siwah on a steep height, was taken by Drovetti to be the citadel.

To the north-west of Siwah, one hour across the salt plain, then two hours through the sand, beyond the salt lake and a mountain on a sandy plain, were the ruins of the temple of A'moudeyn. Only the facade was standing, but the dimensions of the building were 29 m x 8 m. A little further north was the Greek or Roman temple of Kasr-Roum, in the Doric order. Much further to the north ($2^1/_2$ days from Siwah) lay the lake of Arachyeh, which Drovetti was the first of modern travellers to penetrate. To everyone's amazement, no antiquities of any kind were to be seen.

This was the standard account of the 1820 expedition, published by Jomard, along with Cailliaud's earlier notes, in 1823. In the interval, another of the participants published his own version, much to the displeasure of both Cailliaud and Drovetti. This was Enegildo Frediani, who wrote a letter to the famous sculptor, Antonio Canova.[114] It is much more detailed than the later 'official' version on dates and the itinerary. The party

21. View of the ruins of the temple of Umm Abayada, painting by Linant de Bellefonds

22. Decorations on the door of the temple of Umm Abayada. Erroneously identified by Drovetti as the temple of Amon, it was blown up in 1897. Drawing by Alessandro Ricci

left the Nile on 2 March and arrived at Siwah on the 17th. After the first battle, some three days were occupied in negotiations for a capitulation. Frediani mentions that the Siwans offered gifts of 'women, sheep, rather fine figs, and dates'. The terms, to Frediani's satisfaction, were that the 'republic' should remain on the old basis, paying an annual tribute to Cairo.

The invaders were allowed to enter the town on the 29th. Frediani also stressed the narrowness and darkness of both the streets and the interior of the houses. At the summit of the town was an open space where the council held its deliberations. Frediani had the sense of theatre to date his letter 30 March, 'from the ruins of the temple of Jupiter Amon'. The letter finishes with a brief note on the Europeans as they collected, drew and recorded. Drovetti was collecting flora (undoubtedly, as usual, for some botanical friend), using his influence for preservation of the Siwans' independence, and encouraging the others. Here are precious and characteristic insights into Drovetti's character, illustrating his customary traits in an unusual and arduous, even dangerous, situation.

There is yet another account, probably from Drovetti himself, preserved by Cailliaud in his *Voyage à Meroe*.[115] This records the return of Drovetti, Linant and Ricci to Cairo in April. He adds interesting details.

The Siwans flooded the ground to block the army; only the artillery broke their resistance. The Siwans lost forty men, the Egyptians fifteen. The Siwans had enlisted to fight for them a hundred Arabs from the caravan from Benghazy. Hassan imposed on them a fine of 10,000 talaris as a war indemnity, and a tribute of 2,000 loads of dates per annum, but Drovetti intervened to have this much reduced, and offered himself as a personal guarantor to the Pasha.

It was on his return to Cairo that Drovetti introduced Cailliaud to Ishmael, who was just about to set out on his Nubian expedition. When he was rejected by the cabal around this son of Mehemet Ali and had to return to Cairo, Drovetti along with Boghos was again instrumental in getting him new firmans.

Perhaps the most interesting relic of Drovetti's visit to the oasis was not known until 1934. Jomard knew that he had made some notes on the language of the Siwans, but it was not until that year that they were published, having been found among his papers.[116] The lexicon contains 35 words for food and drink, seven for clothing, seventeen for parts of the body, and ten verbs. The list may have been used by Drovetti during his visit to the oasis for simple communications, or compiled merely out of curiosity, and was presumably provided by one of the interpreters. This modest list should not, however, be overrated; compare the 470 word vocabulary in alphabetical order published by Cailliaud.[117]

Later visitors to Siwah included Baron von Minutoli in 1821, Bayle St. Jean in 1847 and James Hamilton in 1852. The last claimed that not Um Ebeida but Ahgurmi, visited by the 1820 expedition, was the site of the oracle. This was verified by Georg Steindorff in 1900.[118] In this important respect, then, the 1820 expedition had not solved all the problems.

On his return to Cairo from the expedition, Drovetti was again subjected to intensified vilification by Pillavoine. He belittled the Siwan trip by saying that Drovetti had tried 'to make himself useful' simply to make some money, but that he had risked his life for nothing.[119] He gave a damning summary of his career: having turned to trading after 1815, he had become enslaved by debt; he then (sic) turned to antiquities, and having failed to be appointed as Consul-General for France or Sardinia (to the contrary he must have rejected the offer by the latter)[120] he was now depleting the collection offered to France for 400,000 francs by making gifts to the Prince of Carignano. This campaign by Pillavoine was soon to have quite the opposite of the desired effect.

There were personal grievances to keep the feud alive. In the previous December there had been floods in Alexandria which had damaged the consular dwelling. Now in July the rent was due to Mme Drovetti, and Pillavoine refused to pay any increase. He handed the case over to the

Foreign Minister in Paris to decide. There were also the political antipathies we have already noted: Pillavoine attacked Drovetti, Thédénat and Asselin de Cherville as a 'revolutionary club opposed to authority', and he looked forward to getting rid of the second and sending the last to Constantinople. Thédénat he described again as a crooked lawyer who would destroy anyone opposed to him and stop at nothing to protect his friends.[121]

Pillavoine's failing competence was demonstrated by the end of 1820, when he suggested that European ambassadors at Constantinople should obtain an order for free trade in Egypt and that the only solution was for the pashalik of Egypt to rotate on an annual basis! He was most disturbed by the embarrassment of the visiting French commander in the Levant, Admiral des Retours, who was lavishly welcomed by Mehemet Ali with gifts valued at 25,000 piastres, but could give only two boxes of wine in return. After informing the Naval Ministry about the requirements of Eastern etiquette, Pillavoine went on to claim that such benefits should be offered to the permanent consul, not to a passing officer! After showing such alertness to his own advantage, he then refused to help French workers who had not prospered and wished to return their families to France. A ministerial note asks: can one not help people really in need? And finally, in the belief that the French in Cairo were absolutely debauched, Pillavoine tried to close down the inns where they sought entertainment. The Foreign Minister did not hesitate to criticise his actions in the deportation of Noyane, the so-called Robespierre of Smyrna, who was tutor to Thédénat's children (once again Pillavoine was taking out his personal and political prejudices):[122] his actions were not always legal and he was far too ready to resort to extremes. The last trace of this unpleasant man in the diplomatic correspondence is a falling out even with his favoured European colleagues, this time the Neapolitan Consul, over equal rights in the churches of the Holy Land.

And still the visitors seek him

As a counterbalance to Pillavoine's enmity, many other impressions of Drovetti come from this period, from Italian, French and German visitors.

In December 1819, the Piedmontese Carlo Vidua had arrived in Egypt; he was to stay until August 1820. Perhaps because he was a fellow Piedmontese, he tells us much about Drovetti at the end of his period as a 'private citizen' between his consulates; he provides, indeed, the liveliest impressions we have of him in these years:

> He filled this post during the whole of Bonaparte's time with the greatest distinction, and acquired such great personal esteem that now, even if he is no longer consul, he makes more impression and

has more influence than all the other consuls. Mehemed Ali the Viceroy of Egypt likes him enormously, and would have made him a very rich man, but he has nothing except what is his own and always helps with great generosity the poor foreigners who arrive in Egypt. He is still young, with a very lively intelligence, exquisite manners, and most ready to oblige.[123]

Vidua saw clearly that Drovetti's position had not suffered from his loss of the consulship (thus confirming Pillavoine's discomfort) and rightly stressed his famed generosity. The characterisation of a man of 'most lively intelligence, most elegant manners and most eager to please' is borne out by all other sources save the very few who did not find him congenial; as for being 'still young', he was just forty-four.

The next letter, to his father again, gives more details about Drovetti's fortune. He had made 'enormous sums' in Egypt, but had spent them helping Italians and French who came to the country. In Vidua's case, Drovetti obtained for him a ship for his journey up the Nile, and ensured the success of the whole undertaking by obtaining firmans and letters from the Pasha.[124]

On his return to Cairo, preparing to go on to Jerusalem, he was taken by Drovetti to see Ishmael Pasha and the Defterdar (Mehemet Ali's son-in-law). Soon he knew 'the whole family'. Everyone spoke of 'Drovetti taer' (good Drovetti) and said that he was 'bakseis ketiri' (very generous). Even in Nubia Vidua heard of him, and when Drovetti travelled in Upper Egypt, he reported, salvoes of artillery were fired to greet him (perhaps the echoes of these had reached even the ears of Pillavoine). There never before was a European who had so much influence in a Muslim country.[125] As for the consulship, Vidua believed that Drovetti would like to be reappointed, but if this were so, it had to be admitted that he did not reveal it. Vidua was kind enough to report that the Inspector of Consuls in the Levant, Felix Beaujour, had visited Egypt, complimented Drovetti, and stated that he must be reappointed.[126]

At the very end of his stay, in August 1820, Vidua summed up his new friend in the following words:

In this country, Drovetti is omnipotent. I am glad to see Egypt, so to speak, ruled by a Piedmontese. He was consul for France, and is now unemployed, but he is the Pasha's favourite: he consults him about everything.[127]

A briefer visit was made in summer 1820 by a leading diplomat, the comte de Marcellus. A royalist and protégé of Talleyrand, he was now secretary of the French ambassador at Constantinople, and making a tour of the eastern stations. On his way to Egypt, we may note, he had found an example of classical sculpture which he thoughtfully sent back to Paris: it was the Venus de Milo. Although Drovetti was not at the time a French representative, Marcellus met him in Cairo:

> M. Drovetti placed complete trust in me from the outset; I found in him a deep understanding of our political interests and that calm and reflective reason, the result of a long stay in the East, that Mehemet Ali was able to appreciate so well, and expert information about the works and monuments of ancient Egypt. Our reciprocal and sincere friendship which began in Africa continued and strengthened later in Europe; it survived on both sides of our offices and our public duties.[128]

Drovetti could hardly have asked for a warmer tribute, and this published nearly twenty years later. Such 'sincere and reciprocal friendship' could bridge the considerable political differences between the two men. Here also was further powerful support for Drovetti's reappointment. The assessment is given even more point by the contrast with the description of the incumbent consul, Pillavoine, as 'an old bachelor, and a bit of a rogue' ('un vieux garçon, quelque peu malin').[129] Although he visited only Alexandria, Cairo and the Pyramids, Marcellus left Egypt with a small collection of antiquities – given, of course, by Drovetti.

The Prussian government also sent an archaeological mission to the country in 1820. It was led by baron Heinrich von Minutoli, an army general, who was accompanied by his wife, the baroness. They arrived in Alexandria on 7 September, 1820. As soon as they entered the harbour, he reports, Drovetti came on board and told them that everything was ready for their reception at the house of his trading partner Tourneau. The baroness wrote her own account. She confirms the meeting with Drovetti, 'so well known in Europe for his refined taste, his indefatigable researches, his fortunate discoveries, and kind hospitality'. The baroness mentions being entertained in his own house, and assures her readers that she did not go out much in society, 'finding in the conversation of the amiable and sensible persons who formed our little circle, all the pleasure that might be expected in the most select companies in our capitals.'[130] It is most unfortunate that she does not tell us who were the members of this amiable and sensible group. It presumably included Tourneau and Mme Drovetti. In the following swift sketch of Drovetti, she asserts that he might have had any important post in the administration or the army of Egypt.

Drovetti gave Minutoli letters of introduction to Buccianti[131] and Anastasy, respectively the Prussian and Swedish consuls, and organised an audience with Mehemet Ali, to which he accompanied the baron and the Prussian officials. While she awaited her husband's return, he then proceeded to escort the baroness around the harbour.[132] Since the baron was anxious to visit Siwah, where Drovetti had been so recently, he had every reason to consult him. One could not, however, in all the above reception and protocol have a more striking proof of Drovetti's continuing to act not only as a consul, but even as the doyen of the consular corps.

After the visit to the oasis, Minutoli returned to Cairo before proceeding to Thebes. On the way he found Father Ladislaus, the man John Hyde had mentioned the previous year, excavating for Drovetti at Abydos, and he noted that at Dendereh Drovetti had excavated (or caused to be excavated) a small temple consisting of eight columns, of which two had already disappeared. In addition, Rifaud had excavated an avenue of sphinxes at Apollinopolis, and he notes that many years before, Drovetti had found a 'beautifully worked Typhon in a wall at Athribis in the Delta'. His collection of papyri currently numbered 180 rolls.[133] There is nothing incredible in this; for in his own short stay, Minutoli collected no fewer than fifty-three.

These excavations at Abydos now under way were long remembered – at least in certain quarters. St John, who visited Egypt in 1832 and 1833 mentioned the discovery in the tombs of a fine statue or sculptured sarcophagus, removed for Drovetti by Ladislaus.

> The ravages committed by this brutal monk and others among these ruins by order of Drovetti, who has obtained from the ignorant and unreflecting Pasha a firman for the purpose, would in any civilised country have condemned the perpetrators to the galleys. The robbers of graves in England have poverty and the interests of a useful profession to plead, but the persons engaged in these equally disgraceful transactions, conducted with the most wanton contempt of every feeling of taste and humanity could be actuated by no possible motive but the most inordinate and sordid love of money.[134]

The contrast between the pictures left to posterity by the Prussians and the Englishman is enormous, and the latter's defence by contrast of English grave-robbers is intriguing.

On his return north, Minutoli vouchsafes us two very important things. The first is that he had found the entrance to the Step Pyramid. This was with the help of an Italian engineer, Girolamo Segato. Drovetti and Salt had both visited the pyramid.[135]

The second matter was a most important episode in Drovetti's own life. Minutoli intended to go on to the East, and Drovetti wanted to accompany him to Jerusalem, Baalbek and other places. They intended to take an Austrian ship, but the war between Austria and Naples which broke out over the revolution in Naples made that unsafe. They next purposed to use a Greek ship, but then the Greek war of independence broke out and the situation of Christians in Syria would have been most unsafe.[136] This was far from the end of Minutoli's adventures before he finally blessed his good fortune to set foot again on European soil in August 1821. It was, however, the end of Drovetti's plans to visit Syria.

Apart from all these eminent visitors who relied on him so profoundly, those in the highest places in Europe thought that he could obtain for them what they wanted, and they did not hesitate to ask. Wilhelm of Wurtemburg decided that, as a man who had almost everything, he lacked only four Nubian horses. He wanted two stallions and two mares, all to be completely black – or white, at a pinch. Drovetti could see to it. The German prince was not the only one to receive a Nubian steed. Drovetti also sent one to the Prince of Carignano, 'a cultured young prince and zealous protector and friend of arts and sciences.'[137]

The year ended brilliantly for him. On 6 November, the king of Piedmont awarded him the cross of the Order of Saints Maurizio and Lazzaro. The citation mentioned the post that he had held in 'difficult times', the upholding of the Catholic religion in Egypt, and the help that Drovetti offered to all Europeans who visited Egypt. The same letter went on to make him a formal offer for his collection of antiquities.[138] The king conferred the decoration in 1820, but it was not until 1826 that the patent was issued.

The order was founded in 1572, by the restoration of the Order of S. Maurizio (originally founded in 1434) and its union with the very old hospitaler Order of S. Lazzaro. The new regulations of 1816 divided it into two groups: by right for the nobility, and by merit for others.[139] Members of the second category, to which Drovetti belonged, had to satisfy eight conditions. He made a declaration before the Austrian Consul in Egypt that he could not undergo the proofs personally in Torino, and appointed Baron Lorenzo Bianco as his procurator, who appeared before Count Galeassi, the Royal Chamberlain, and Vincenzo Cavaradossi, Captain of the Royal Carabiners. The four witnesses were Francesco Gaudina, Royal Treasurer, Domenico Pedemonte, a landowner, Antonio Drovetti, another landowner, and obviously some relative, but that is not specified, and Domenico Chiesa, the Royal Physician. The conditions to be satisfied were: that he was of legitimate birth; a Catholic; not guilty of lèse majesté or any 'atrocious crime', including murder (!); that he was not a bigamist (ie. married only once); that he was sound of body and mind (the reply was that he was Consul of France); that he was at least seventeen years of age (the witnesses answered variously 50, 49, 47: he was, in fact, 48); that he was not personally subject to anyone; that he was not a debtor (it was answered that he possessed a considerable patrimony). The proofs were held on 15 November, 1825, the habit and cross were conferred the next day, and the patent was issued on 11 April, 1826.[140] It is interesting that Drovetti had to ask permission of his sovereign Charles X to take the oath of obedience to the King of Sardinia.

The conquest of the Sudan

In the same year as this conferring began one of Mehemet Ali's most brutal conquests. The reasons for this expedition (1820-1822) were many: mainly the prospect of gold and negro recruits for the new army, but also trade, and the fact that some of the Mamelukes had fled to Dongola. The commander-in-chief was Mehemet Ali's twenty-five years old son, Ishmael.[141]

There was little resistance until Dongola, then two battles were fought in November and December 1820. Ishmael made a triumphant entry into Sennar in June 1821, but disease then struck the army and it was immobilised until the end of the year. Egypt meanwhile was to be embroiled in the Turkish war with both the Greeks and Persia. Ibrahim joined his brother, and the plan was that he would ascend the White Nile and Ishmael the Blue. Ibrahim, however, fell ill and had to return to Cairo. Ishmael continued south, meeting fierce resistance. There were few slaves to be captured and little gold to be found. In February 1822 he returned north, reaching Tomat.

The campaign was marked by the most appalling and senseless destruction, with enslavement and massacre of the peaceful natives and wanton burning of their villages. Cailliaud, who was sickened by what he saw, paid Ishmael the best compliment he could:

> Certainly he must have been endowed with great courage, perseverance and even genius to have been able, with a weak army of four thousand men, poorly paid and malnourished, to have overrun in all directions barbarous and savage regions, to have invaded in less than two years four hundred and fifty leagues of country, conquered twelve provinces and a kingdom, and fought unceasingly against a host of warlike tribes.[142]

What little glory he won, he paid for with his life. As he was returning to Egypt, at Chendy in October 1822, he became careless, attended a nocturnal banquet, and the old king Nemr and his men set fire to the house in which he slept.

This terrible war has a very close connection with Drovetti. In his collected correspondence, which claims our attention on so many counts, there is probably no letter which leaves as indelible impression on the reader for its drama and pity as that addressed to him in September 1820 by three Italian doctors on their way south to join the expedition.[143] They found themselves in a world of utter corruption and terrifying intrigue. They had not so far been paid. All their medical equipment had vanished (sold by the chief doctor, Demetrio Bozari):[144] dressings, ointments, instruments. Rossignoli asks how he is to operate on someone whose hand has to be amputated. As if that were not enough, he has good reason to believe that there is a plot to poison him. A young Greek has a bottle of prussic acid and is uttering threats. The three (all Piedmontese) had decided to return home, then realised that such a move could easily be misinterpreted, and that it would damage the reputation of their countrymen. They begged Drovetti to see to their replacement. Rossignoli sent him 600 piastres to send to his wife if anything happened to him, keeping only fifty for himself and his two colleagues. Now the troops had embarked, but were almost without provisions.

G.A. Gentili, a chemist, died of obvious poisoning.[145] Six months later, in summer 1821, Rossignoli was dead of fever – was he also poisoned, as he had feared? These two men whose profession dedicated them to the care of others both lost their lives. Their sacrifice reminds us more forcibly than any other what risks Europeans ran in taking prominent service in Egypt in these times. Drovetti himself was in fear of his life at about the same time.

The Dendereh Zodiac

It was the French expedition, and particularly Denon, which had first brought to Europe's attention the fascinating relief in the ceiling of the temple of Hathor at Dendereh.[146] It naturally excited great interest; for it was considered by some to be a major key to the 'wisdom' of the Egyptians which had haunted Europe since the Middle Ages; more especially it was very evocative for those who imagined themselves as initiates of the Egyptian 'mysteries'. Now one of the most infamous actions of vandalism was to be committed against this piece of Egyptian art, and indeed against the whole structure of which it formed such an important part.

The man who masterminded this action was Sebastien Saulnier, deputy in the French parliament and collector of antiquities. He calmly despatched Jean Baptiste Lelorrain, a master mason, to detach and transport to Paris the stones showing the relief. They were 12 feet long, 8 feet wide and 3 feet thick, and weighed sixty tons. Lelorrain left France in October 1820. On arrival in Egypt he obtained a firman to carry off antiquities. By March 1821 he was at Dendereh, but the presence of English tourists there made his task impossible, given the rivalry among the antiquarians. He continued to Thebes and returned to Dendereh in April. Three weeks' frenzied labour was required to cut out the stone and another two weeks to drag it to the river. When the news was revealed by an American, it was Salt and Bankes who felt particularly cheated. These two were just about to remove the zodiac for themselves.

It reached Paris in January 1822 and, thanks to enormous publicity, was acquired by the King for the Royal Library at the enormous cost of 150,000 francs. It was transferred to the Louvre in 1919.

When Lelorrain arrived, Pillavoine was Consul.[147] At the end of May 1821, Pascal Coste met Lelorrain at Girgeh as he was carrying off the zodiac and they spent an evening together with much gaiety.[148] Girgeh is about two days from Dendereh. Saulnier published an account of the whole operation, and the only mention of Drovetti is a passage abusing him and Salt for assuming 'exclusive rights' over all antiquities.[149] We know that Drovetti was outraged by this account.[150]

Champollion published a letter on the removal of the zodiac in the *Revue encyclopédique* in October 1821.[151] He stressed that the temple had previously been intact, and declared that this action of Europeans imitated the Persians, Greeks, Romans and Arabs. He asked what had been the point of the removal of the zodiac, wrenching decoration from its vital context: could a cast not have been taken? Champollion realised that these sentiments would be those of an educated minority, and so suppressed his identity as their author. It is, then, interesting that Jomard wrote to Drovetti a little later, in January 1822, expressing his horror. He, in fact, had recommended Lelorrain to Drovetti, quite unaware of the true purpose of his visit. In many respects, Jomard's letter is identical in sentiment to that of Champollion, but he stated that all French travellers were horrified and asked Drovetti what was the reaction in Egypt.[152] Given the wholesale removal of antiquities from Egypt by notable collectors of all nations, but especially the two consuls of England and France, these sentiments have a rather hollow ring. The episode of the Dendereh zodiac was, in fact, to have more influence on the fate of Drovetti's own collecting than he perhaps realised at the time.

Reappointment, as Consul-General

There is a gap in the official correspondence for the first six months of 1821. On 20 June, Drovetti was named Consul-General with a salary of 20,000 francs.[153] He was forty-five years of age.

It was precisely during this gap in the correspondence that an event occurred which marked the passing of an age, not only for Europe, but especially for Drovetti. On 6 May, 1821, late in the afternoon, a small man with a disproportionately large head, delicate limbs and pale skin gave four last sighs and was no more. On a tiny island in the middle of the southern Atlantic, at the age of 51 from a chronic ulcer and cancer, died the man who for so many years had both galvanised and terrorised Europe. His career was based on the fatal error that war was man's highest employment. How extraordinary that half a million men had perished in a Russian winter, while the general who had led them astray died in his bed on a tropical island. It was also ironic that within a month of the death of the man who had appointed Drovetti to Egypt for the first time in 1803, he would return to that post in the service of the restored Bourbons.

A great number of people sent him congratulatory letters: Luigi Gandolfi, Apostolic legate in Syria; Admiral Halgan of the Levant fleet; Auban, French Consul in Rhodes; Allary, Commissioner of Police at Marseille; and David, French Consul at Smyrna.[154] The most memorable note was instantly penned by Asselin de Cherville in Cairo: 'We will now be delivered from the oppression of the wicked, the stupid, and the imbeciles under whom we have suffered for so long.'[155]

The *Epistolario*, in fact, reveals much of why Drovetti was reappointed, despite the fact that he was not French by birth and was a known Bonapartist. One of his most fervent supporters had long been the comte de Forbin, the powerful Director of Museums, who had been so impressed with Drovetti when he met him in 1818. He negotiated especially for the purchase of the antiquities collection for France, and it was accepted that a result of this would be Drovetti's reappointment.[156] Another very influential figure was Edme Jomard of the Institut, who was constantly recommending Drovetti to Dessolle, the Minister of Foreign Affairs, to the comte de Cazes, Minister of the Interior, to baron Cortal, and to Deferre, Keeper of the Seals.[157] Not least influential must have been the declaration of Allary, Commissioner of Police at Marseille, that no French captain returned from Egypt without declaring that, although no longer consul, Drovetti obliged them in every possible way, was deeply attached to France, and that nothing would please them more than to see him naturalised and appointed Consul-General.[158]

Another fervent supporter was Roussel. He wrote to the comte d'Hauterive, a councillor of state, and the letter is highly interesting for its revelation of the arguments being used against Drovetti's reappointment.[159] It was urged by some, in the first place, that Drovetti would be a merchant in competition with French traders. Roussel simply stated that he had never heard this from any of these people themselves. While out of the office, Drovetti had given some money to a trading friend and had obtained a job there for one of his relatives. He would not continue such actions if reappointed. As well, he would be a strong protector of any French with business in Egypt. Second, Drovetti was a foreigner. Roussel answered that he was 'naturalised' and known for his devotion to France. Third, his character was held against him: too lively and emotional. Age, rejoined Roussel, was moderating this, and it was offset by his 'natural obligingness', ability to win favour, military experience, and his standing as an adviser with Mehemet Ali and his sons. Fourth, he was blamed for inducing the Pasha to take over all land and set up a monopoly of both internal and external trade. As for the first, Drovetti himself claimed that he had orders to see to this from the French government because of plans for a second invasion (now the truth could be told!); as for the monopoly, this was occasioned only by the Pasha's greed, and the same system existed throughout the Ottoman Empire. As a final argument, Roussel offered some more remarkable facts and logic: he claimed never to have been intimately connected with Drovetti (this naturally depends on the definition of 'intimate'), but noted that Drovetti owned the French *okel* at Alexandria. If he became consul for another power, a post which had been offered to him, the new French Consul would have difficulty finding lodgings!

Further support from diplomatic sources also came from the Vice-Consul Thédénat-Duvent. In 1822 he published a small book entitled *L'Egypte sous Mohamed Ali*. In it he stressed the 'general wish' for Drovetti's reinstatement, and admitted that he was always praising his old chief to both the Minister of Foreign Affairs and the French Ambassador at Constantinople. By the time the book appeared, his wishes had been granted, as a footnote recorded.[160]

There is finally an undated letter to the Minister of the Interior from the government-sponsored mineralogist Frédéric Cailliaud.[161] He stressed the great standing of Drovetti with Mehemet Ali, and the fact that all Frenchmen who came to Egypt, and even all Europeans, wished to see him reinstated. As a further incentive, Cailliaud also mentioned the matter of his collection of antiquities, stating that the reappointment would be a way for France to acquire this unique cabinet. An interesting note in the letter asserts that since 1815 Drovetti had been doing everything possible to be naturalised. As it happened, France recovered Drovetti's services, but missed his first and best collection. That, however, was no fault of his.

His six years out of office had been a trying time. He had toyed with the idea of returning to Europe, but he was obviously too well acclimatized in Egypt. He found that his position as a private citizen did not greatly alter his political influence, especially not during the administration of the more congenial Roussel. With the appearance of Pillavoine, the text-book bureaucrat determined to make a purge, things were much more difficult, and it seems clear that Drovetti used all his considerable connections to fight back and to undermine the paranoid and pretentious consul. On the personal side his affairs suffered greatly in the financial sense, but he more than compensated for these losses by the three major expeditions in which he participated, to the Second Cataract, to Dakhla Oasis, and to Siwah. With freedom from consular duties, he was able to devote himself wholeheartedly to his collecting of antiquities, but it was bad luck that precisely in this period there appeared on the scene his greatest rival, Belzoni, with whom after a friendly enough beginning relations soon deteriorated very badly. It must be admitted, however, that even the sophisticated and easy-going Salt found Belzoni impossible, and had equally difficult relations with him.

The support of all the very influential people in Drovetti's reappointment was one thing. There is another major consideration. Drovetti was by birth a citizen of the Kingdom of Sardinia. By annexation in 1799, he became a French citizen. The Kingdom of Sardinia regained its independence on the fall of the Napoleonic empire, and Drovetti was replaced as Consul in Egypt. In 1817 he had been told by his successor, Roussel, to take French citizenship, and according to that same person, a not lightly to be rejected witness, when he wrote in his support in 1820, he declared that Drovetti was naturalised.[162] Two other very interesting pieces of evidence accord with that statement. In 1820, when Drovetti was awarded the knighthood of SS Maurizio e Lazzaro, he had to ask the permission of Charles X before accepting. And in 1826, in the famous letter regarding the best place to send Egyptian students who were coming to Europe, Drovetti described himself as 'Italian by birth and very affectionate towards my old country' ('italiano di nascità e affezionatissimo alla mia *antica* patria') (my italics).[163]

By his own statement as well as by the testimony of others, he had taken French citizenship. If there are any not yet convinced by this startling and hitherto unrevealed fact, Drovetti is described in his will as 'naturalizzato francese'. Drovetti, claimed as Italian by his compatriots, was in fact French for the greater part of his life![164]

IV   Drovetti restored: Consul-General (1821-29)

It is ironic that despite an amazingly unrestrained campaign of vilification against Drovetti throughout 1820 by Pillavoine to the duc de Pasquier, Minister of Foreign Affairs, it was that same minister who reappointed Drovetti to be Pillavoine's successor.[1]

Drovetti wrote to Pasquier on 17 August, 1821 that he had formally taken over as Consul-General the day before.[2] He took the opportunity to offer a word at last in his own favour: France's enemies had gained great advantages in the last few years, having powerful friends with Mehemet Ali. Drovetti, although devoted to France, had had no position, and thus could not block them. He admitted the destructive monopoly on raw materials, industry and trade, but asserted that Egypt was still the best governed country in Africa or Asia.

A Levantine consul's duties

There is nowhere in Drovetti's writings, voluminous as they are, a description of the duties of a Levantine consul at this time. We are fortunate, then, in having a lively letter from his counterpart, Henry Salt, to his niece in September 1822.[3]

> You must know, that the office of Consul in Turkey is very different from what it is in Europe; for every stranger, in civilised countries, being subject to the laws of the state he lives under, the Consul has nothing to do but sign passports, regulate ships' papers, and use his interference with the local government in cases where the terms of the treaty are not complied with; while, on the contrary, in these barbarous regions the Consuls are a sort of King. Every Consulate here is a little Government, and all those residing in the country are considered to be under its exclusive protection. Once in a way, indeed, the Pasha does presume, on any enormous crime being committed, as killing one of his officers, or such like offence, to cut off a European's head; but otherwise, he leaves every thing that concerns our subjects (for so they are always called) to our wiser jurisdiction; so that we have to try causes for murder, assault and robbery; and to

decide between contending parties, where hundreds of thousands of piastres (a piastre is about fourpence halfpenny in value) are concerned.

I have at Cairo about three hundred of said subjects, Maltese, Ionians &. and there are about as many more at Alexandria, who principally are under the rule of the Consul, Mr Lee, but who have the right to appeal to my superior 'worship' (as Dr. Richardson in his Travels, calls me) at Cairo. It is a strange system, and one that was certainly never in the contemplation of the Government at home, so that no regulations nor proper rules for our guidance have ever been laid down.

The complexities and powers of the French Consul-General's position must have been very similar; certainly the same lack of guidance was obviously a major concern.

An interesting English visitor appeared in Egypt about the time of Drovetti's reappointment. This was John Carne, who although meticulous about days and months, gives no year for his travels. He left England, in fact, in March 1821,[4] and so was in Egypt from August to October of the same year. His main information about Drovetti relates to Thebes. He was well received at Luxor by a Frenchman employed by Drovetti, who must be Rifaud. At Karnak he described a lofty granite gateway at the end of the avenue from Luxor, presumably the tenth pylon. Fifty yards further on was a smaller temple which Drovetti had been excavating. This must be the temple of Amenhotep II, on the eastern side of the courtyard between the ninth and tenth pylons. It is remarkable for the elegance of its long porticoed facade, and the fineness of its reliefs.[5] One hopes that it was not Carne's nationality and his friendship with Salt which led to the following charge:

> Drovetti is quite inexcusable in having caused one of the most beautiful obelisks at the entrance to the temple of Karnak to be thrown down and broken, that he might carry off its upper part: such an act is absolute sacrilege.[6]

There were no obelisks at the 'entrance', as we now know it. The main obelisks in the complex were a pair belonging to Tuthmosis I between the third and fourth pylons (of which one remains), and two of Hatshepsut between the fourth and fifth pylons (one intact, the other lying broken by the Sacred Lake). In addition, in the 'Temple of the Hearing Ear' at the eastern extremity was a single obelisk, now at S. Giovanni

Laterano in Rome; and a pair between the seventh and eighth pylons, one of which is now in Constantinople. The mention of beauty by Carne makes one think of the obelisks of Hatshepsut above all others, and precisely one of hers is broken—it is however the upper half which is still at Karnak! He speaks, however, of the 'entrance' to the temple, by which he means on the Luxor side.

Of the obelisks of Tuthmosis I, Richard Pococke stated that they were both still standing; the *Description de L'Egypte*, however, shows the same obelisks upright as now. If Pococke was right, then the obelisk of Tuthmosis fell between 1728 and 1799. As for the broken obelisk of Hatshepsut, no evidence can be found as to when it fell, or whether any human agency was involved. Given the prevalence of earthquakes at Thebes, which shattered pylons, none would be necessary. The obelisk seems to have been moved to near the Sacred Lake only recently. No-one other than Carne blames Drovetti for any damage to an obelisk at Karnak, and given the number of his rivals, their silence is important. His charge may be dismissed as a confusion.[7]

The outbreak of the Greek war

Mehemet Ali was certainly nervous about Egypt's fate in international affairs. He believed that Europe would make war on Turkey and dismember the empire, allowing Egypt to fall to the English. He went so far as to call in Salt and tell him that he had won Egypt by the sword and would not lose it otherwise. Drovetti instantly saw a chance to regain his old position as a trusted adviser, and explained the European situation to the Pasha to calm him. Further French advances came in September 1821 when the Pasha saw the visiting French warship, the *Jeanne d'Arc*. It had come at Drovetti's urging, in order to carry money to the Sultan for Mehemet Ali. The Admiral of the Levant fleet, Halgan, described the frigate as being first class, 'which one can show with confidence to strangers'.[8] Little did he realise how true were his words. The Pasha instantly decided that he must have two ships exactly the same. Drovetti had then to write to Pasquier supporting this request on two grounds: it would be a boost to French industry, and it would deprive the English of the contract, which they were anxious to have.[9] The first hint of the Greek war came, in fact, in September in the official correspondence: the Sultan ordered Mehemet Ali to send troops to Crete, under the command of Hassan Pasha.[10] War also broke out between Turkey and Persia, and the latter with a European trained army soon won great successes, capturing Baghdad.

Among the European visitors for whom Drovetti had instantly to care on resuming duty was the naturalist Wilhelm Hemprich, who had come with baron Minutoli. Having reached Upper Egypt without making any interesting discoveries apart from a few plants and insects(!), he asked Drovetti to extend his firman to take in the newly conquered Kordophan. In February the next year, he sent Drovetti an account of the plants, animals and minerals which he had found in the Dongola. Drovetti did indeed arrange for his firman. New plants were discovered—one named Drovettia in gratitude—new fish, and new birds.[11]

And Drovetti was involved in a most difficult dispute about antiquities concessions at Gizeh between Caviglia and Louis Jumel in November. The famous explorer of the pyramids was brawling with the founder of the Egyptian cotton industry over the possession of granite statues found at Gizeh. Caviglia appealed to Salt, Jumel to Drovetti. The outcome is, unfortunately, unknown.[12]

On 25 November, Drovetti was appointed acting Russian Consul, as Pillavoine had been before him, a post he held until 20 May, 1827, when he was succeeded by Malivoire. Most of Drovetti's despatches concern the Greek war, and are duplicates of those he sent to the French Foreign Minister.[13]

The new Foreign Minister, the duc de Montmorency,[14] illustrated some of the results of the frequent changes in this vital portfolio. In his first correspondence with Drovetti he asked for an historical précis of the reign of Mehemet Ali! He also told his consul that he did not like his 'bulletins': instead of the usual formal letters, Drovetti had been sending a monthly summary of events. One might have expected the minister who demanded an historical précis to appreciate the merits of a more analytical summary – but no, it was too unusual.

By February 1822 it was reported that Hassan Pasha was going to Crete with 6,000 men, and another commander was to proceed to Cyprus with 1,500. This was the only hope the Sultan had of keeping control. A fleet of thirty-two ships was to take the first contingent across. Thus began Egyptian participation in the Greek war, which was to have momentous repercussions on European and eastern relations.

It naturally took some time for the request for two frigates to be considered by the French bureaucracy. It was not until the end of March that Montmorency replied to Drovetti, expressing great concern that a foreign power should have two ships modelled on France's best. He had not even mentioned it so far to the King, but was awaiting a 'better moment'. He did not understand that the English would be rushing to fill such an order. In June, however, he informed Drovetti that the French would indeed build the two frigates.[15]

The year was marked for Drovetti by another of those galling internal episodes which dogged the lives of all consuls in the Levant: the Adda affair. Jacob Adda was a Jew, who on being punished by an Egyptian court claimed to be a naturalised French citizen. The situation was complicated by Pillavoine's judgement. He had advised that French protection be denied to all but French citizens. This sounded logical, but put the French Consul at a considerable disadvantage, because other consuls, notably the British, offered protection to people other than their own. Drovetti accused Pillavoine of simply wanting to avoid discomfort, which, he observed, consuls were paid to suffer. On investigation it then transpired that Adda was in fact a French citizen. His case was therefore taken up, and Mehemet Ali assured the consuls that 'although he favoured all nations equally, he had a predilection for France and the French'. Just as everything seemed sorted out, however, another source of tension arose, this time between Drovetti and his assistant, Thédénat-Duvent. Salt showed Drovetti a letter which he had received by courier on the Adda case. Drovetti was furious with Thédénat: he had heard everything from the other consuls, and when his colleague finally did send him information, it was by ordinary post. How seriously would the freedom and safety of a Frenchman need to be threatened before Thédénat would send a courier? The complaint to Mehemet Ali was seven days late. In the end, Drovetti gained agreement from the Pasha that Adda would be compensated for his injuries.[16] Perhaps Thédénat's age and health were much to blame. Drovetti admitted that he had given thirty-five years' service, and needed rest and retirement. This is the last heard of him.

The first evidence we have for Drovetti's reaction to the Greek war is in July 1822,[17] when he was intervening with his colleague David at Smyrna, who had contact with the Turkish admiral, on behalf of the Greeks at Patras. David spoke of Drovetti's 'philanthropic wish' to free Greek slaves.[18] Then came news of the capitulation of the Acropolis at Athens with its Turkish garrison and the massacre by the Greeks. Voicing obviously Drovetti's thoughts as well as addressing him, David asserted that the 'lack of faith since the institution of their government is going to dishonour the cause of the Greeks completely'.[19] Later in the same year David was heavily sarcastic, knowing that his colleague would appreciate it: 'The Europeans who return from Greece do not give me a very grand idea of Leonidas' successors: they have again lost Thermopylae and Corinth'.[20]

In the midst of these events which threatened the peace of Europe and the great eastern empires, Drovetti was approached by the archaeologist Felix Lajard of the Marseille Academy. Drovetti had been elected a corresponding member of that body in April.[21] He had many friends in the city and had made gifts to the museum there.[22] Lajard had received fourteen fossils from Drovetti. He explained to him the great studies being undertaken to trace now vanished fauna of the earth, and urged him to devote the same zeal to this subject as to the collection of antiquities. His own interest was oriental archaeology, and he mentioned his unrivalled collection of cylinder seals and amulets. These small items were vital in documenting relations between Egypt and Asia. He heard that Drovetti had some Persian or Babylonian cylinders, and asked for plaster casts or drawings. This was just one of Lajard's many requests: could Drovetti also send him some samples from the mineral mines, and some shells from the canals, and some fresh grains of wheat, and so on.[23] As if the Consul-General had nothing to do! What was the result? From his own collection Drovetti sent him five cylinders and three 'talismans', not to mention three packets of seeds for Professor Delile of Montpellier. This only led to the last's asking for sycamore plants, with special directions for making slips, as well as Rosetta onions. And the palaeontologist Jean Cuvier looked forward to Drovetti's inducing the Arabs in the Libyan desert to bring in fossils.[24] The Consul was thus performing vital services for leading French archaeologists, botanists and anatomists.

In 1820 Mehemet Ali had begun the war to conquer the Sudan. Cailliaud, who was with Ishmael, sent an account to Drovetti in August 1822.[25] The limit of the expedition was fixed at 10 degrees latitude, given the 'miserable' state of the army. Ishmael had used 'rolling fuses' to terrify the enemy. In this letter he praised Mehemet Ali's son as courageous and intrepid. The country was described as mountainous and wooded, with many streams to cross, trackless, beset with wild animals, and an enemy who gave no respite. Within two months Ishmael was burned to death.[26]

Cailliaud was also feuding with Linant de Bellefonds about antiquities. The latter claimed to have discovered Meroe. Cailliaud himself had been to the kingdom of Bertat. He described the antiquities of the region for Drovetti. He correctly identified Meroe with Atbaral and Nepata with Barkal.[27]

Typical of Drovetti's seemingly extra-political duties, but with grave political repercussions, was the appeal to him by the Custodian of Terra Santa to intervene with the French Ambassador to Constantinople against attempts by the Greek Orthodox to take over the Catholic sanctuaries in Jerusalem, notably the Tomb of the Virgin.[28]

Champollion breaks the code

The year 1822 is immortal in the history of Egyptology. On 22 September, Jean-François Champollion (ill. 23), aged thirty-one, sent his *Lettre à M. Dacier*, the Secretary of the Académie des Inscriptions et Belles-Lettres. In it he set out his solution for breaking the code of Egyptian hieroglyphs. After millennia of silence, at last the monuments of Egypt would speak with their own voice. Within six years, just as Drovetti was leaving his consular post, Champollion would arrive in Egypt to vindicate his discoveries on the spot in a triumphant survey of the classical monuments from Cairo to Abu Simbel. It is highly significant that within a few months of his momentous discovery, Drovetti provided Champollion with new sources. Of the five cylinders which he sent to Felix Lajard, one allowed Champollion to read a royal name also found on an obelisk at Karnak, and to show – as Champollion always delighted to do – that once again the *Description de l'Egypte* was inaccurate.[29]

In September there arrived in Egypt yet another traveller, the German Gustav Parthey, classicist and Copticist, book collector and philanthropist, who was to compile the standard Coptic dictionary and to be admitted to the Berlin Academy. At this time he was only in his early twenties, but Drovetti introduced him to Mehemet Ali, and advised him also to consult the governor of Alexandria. It was during the audience that Parthey provides us with one of the most delightful vignettes of Drovetti and his relations with the Viceroy. The Consul was, Parthey tells us, 'very susceptible to draughts'. A breeze was coming in. Mehemet Ali motioned with his hand. Drovetti thereupon put on his great Consul-General's hat. Thanks to his patronage, Parthey was able to travel to Dongola and back, and the career of one of the leading scholars of the age was much facilitated.[30] In December 1822 Drovetti had the great pleasure of seeing his old friend Chateaubriand return as Foreign Minister.[31]

In all of Drovetti's *Epistolario,* there are only a couple of letters in English. The one dated January 1823 might be evidence that the Consul understood that language; for its writer seems to assume as much, in his subject and tone. The letter came from Boston and no less interest attaches to its author: George Bethune English (1787-1828). Drovetti can hardly ever have met anyone to equal him. He had graduated from Harvard in 1807, studied law for a few months, failed to gain a commission in the army, then taken an MA from the School of Divinity at Harvard. He first came to public notice with an attack on the New Testament. Finally through John Quincy Adams he obtained a commission in the marines and toured the Mediterranean. At Alexandria he resigned, converted to Islam and joined the Egyptian army. 'After attempting unsuccessfully to revive the use of scythe-bearing chariots', he also joined Ishmael's expedition to the Sudan. The letter to Drovetti came after his return to America, and recalled the Consul's hospitality, 'friendly deportment' and the pleasure of his society. He was now to be appointed American secret agent (what else?) to Constantinople, but the mission failed. English is said to have been a marvellous linguist, passing for a native Turk. In his letter to Drovetti, however, he asked him to have a document for the Viceroy translated into that very language![32]

23. Jean-Francois Champollion,
by Leon Cogniet, 1831

Other visitors reveal to us that the antiquities trade had not been overlooked in these years. Drovetti was busy forming his second collection, and the old rivalries continued. Moyle Sherer described the scene at Thebes:

> Nothing is more difficult than to procure here any little antiques of value, to carry away with you a memorial of your visit: the Arabs, indeed, bring you little mummy ornaments, such as little termini of wood or pottery, which are always found in the tombs; also scarabaei, rings of wood or pottery, scraps of papyrus, a variety of trifles which I cannot name: but these are seen to be the mere refuse of the privileged collectors, and of the many sharp-witted nondescripts in their service. The ground is regularly parcelled out on both sides of the river: here England may dig, there France; this is Mr Salt's ground, that Mr Drovetti's; here lord Belmore made excavations, there an American traveller. The Arab fellahs get their twenty paras a day, and work as little as possible for the money. French and Italians generally in Turkish costume, that is, in a sort of half and half dress, are their task masters.

Sherer watched one of these parties and heard its director speak to Rifaud in French: he was a deserter from the French army. Sherer was, in fact, shown around Thebes by no less a person than Rifaud, and he leaves an interesting picture of Drovetti's agent as a 'polite little cicerone', 'with the air of a condescending savant'.[33]

A new commander of the French navy in the Levant had been appointed in 1822: Henri Gauthier de Rigny. One of his first letters in January 1823 was to Drovetti.[34] He expressed his regret at the death of Ishmael in the previous October, but more to his present purposes protested against Greek piracy, and noted with astonishment the fall of Nafplion the previous month. De Rigny expressed his devotion to Drovetti and looked forward to meeting him. It was, indeed, the beginning of a long and close cooperation. Under George Canning, the new English Foreign Secretary, however, English policy diverged from that of France, and David and Drovetti discussed the possibility of Europe being in flames once more.[35]

A general revolt in the Sudan on the death of Ishmael was crushed by the Defterdar. The organisation of the new Egyptian army was progressing well, trained by Sève. By April there were ten battalions in Upper Egypt. The institution of a poll-tax and the incidence of conscription, however, brought a not-unexpected revolt, and Mehemet Ali had to go to Manfalut. The most vivid description of the appalling oppression in the south by Ali Cachef, the governor of Girgeh, was sent to Drovetti by his agent there, Ladislaus, who, as well as being in charge of a hospice, collected antiquities for him. The main stimulus to the oppression was the search for contraband cloth: people, including women, whose clothing did not bear the government mark, were stripped by the soldiers. Mosques and churches were also despoiled. Some suspected that this robbery was to raise contributions for the new army. Those adjudged guilty of contraband were executed, mutilated or beaten.[36] Then another blow struck the Viceroy. After the loss of his son, he now suffered the death of his most trusted lieutenant and son-in- law, Hassan Pasha in Crete.[37]

In straits of a different kind, people turned to Drovetti. The noted Italian geologist Giambattista Brocchi (1772-1827) found his services not appreciated. After graduating in law at Padova, he soon turned to botany. After some years teaching natural history in secondary schools, he had been appointed Inspector of Mines in northern Italy 1809-1818 and Keeper of the royal collection of Natural History. In this capacity he travelled all over Italy, studying natural history and geology; his *Conchiologia fossile subapennina*, 1814 made him one of the founders of modern palaeontology and won him a European reputation. For political reasons, he lost his post as inspector in 1818 (he had been, like Drovetti, a supporter of the French and did not show the proper respect to the restored regime). In 1822 he was thus brought to Egypt by the scientist Giuseppe Forni to survey ancient mines (his first book in 1792 had, in fact, been on Egyptian sculpture). As a government geologist, Brocchi's problem was simple: he could not invent reports of fabulous riches to be found in Egyptian mines. He visited lead and silver mines and found them to be iron; he advised caution with the emerald mines of Sacheto and Zabaia, and similarly with the gold mines. Although he had worked harder in three months than in a year as inspector of mines for Napoleon, he had 'lost both the lye and the soap'. Added to Mehemet Ali's rejection of his exact mineralogical survey which indicated the economic uselessness of the mines, Salt, out of jealousy of the rival French company, induced the Viceroy to survey deposits of fossil carbon in Syria.[38] Brocchi obviously hoped that Drovetti could intervene on his behalf with the ruler.

Yet another traveller found himself in trouble. This was the unfortunate Jean-Raymond Pacho, who had originally intended to be a botanist. He came to Egypt because his elder brother was a merchant there, and undertook travels under the patronage of the industrialist Louis Jumel. The latter died, however, in June 1823 and Pacho sought another patron. He hoped that the Swedish Consul, Giovanni Anastasy, would assume this burden and asked Drovetti to raise the matter for him. We know that this was not to be. He did obtain a new sponsor, but that was Guyenet; either Drovetti did not think it appropriate or advisable to approach Anastasy to help a Frenchman, or the wealthy Armenian refused.[39]

The same month a most elaborate and expensive testimony was offered to Drovetti's political and cultural standing. The King of France gave him a copy of the *Description de l'Egypte*: ten volumes of text and fourteen of plates. The same gift was made to other political and academic figures. It transpires that Drovetti's old supporter, the comte de Forbin, was the instigator of this tribute to him.[40] The whole edition had not yet appeared, so the beneficiaries could receive only the instalments so far in print, with the others to follow. It would not be until January 1826 that Jomard could announce to Drovetti the completion of the work, which had required sixteen years (1809-1825).[41]

In October 1823, Drovetti received an interesting request on behalf of Ibrahim Pasha. The Consul was asked to see to obtaining from France quite a collection of military equipment, including two hundred of the best rifles, cartridge pouches and bayonet sheaths. The most amusing item on the 'shopping list' is 'one infantry captain, even if he is a little old, of the Napoleonic Guard'.[42] These materials and this person may have been for the new style army or in preparation for intervention in the Greek war.

Mehemet Ali went to Upper Egypt in November to review the troops. He asked Salt and Drovetti to accompany him. It was in connection with this journey that Drovetti received his only mention in the famous diary of

Henry Westcar. The two consuls travelled separately, and at Minieh Salt, accompanied by Westcar, learned that his French colleague was two days ahead of him.[43] One of the places which Drovetti visited was the military hospital at Manfalut, on which he later received a horrifying report from one of the French doctors.[44] It was while absent that he was further importuned by the Custodian of Terra Santa to become embroiled in religious controversies. The Orthodox and Catholics were still bickering over their respective privileges in the church at Alexandria: where they were to sit, whether they were to have 'national altars' to celebrate national festivals, and what part, if any, the Greek Orthodox were to have in the church.[45]

Shortly after his return from the south, Drovetti wrote to Chateaubriand on 1 February, 1824, that the new army numbered 30,000 negroes and peasants under Turkish and Mameluke officers; it was trained by the French. One need not be in doubt over Salt's reaction: with some satisfaction, Drovetti reported that he had not been pleased. The French Consul's own stocks were high. Mehemet Ali had been named the Sultan's commander-in-chief (Seraskier) against the Greeks, and had hopes of being named Pasha of Syria. In that case, he had asked Drovetti to accompany him on a tour, and he had accepted.[46]

In January, 1824 the first great Drovetti collection had finally been sold to Torino.[47] As a recognition of his patriotism in rejecting the offers of various other European museums, on 18 March Drovetti was elected a Corresponding Member of the Torino Academy of Sciences.[48] Along with him were elected Gaetano Marre and (Louis?) Durante. The other corresponding members were of the highest eminence: in 1823, for example, Angelo Mai, the Vatican Librarian, and Barthold Georg Niebuhr, the great German historian of Rome; in 1825 the two Champollions; in 1827 Dr Thomas Young, Henry Salt, and Gustav Seyffart; in 1828 Jomard himself (the last four all 'Egyptologists').

Excavations at Hawara

The Consul's interest in antiquities continued unabated. A series of a dozen letters from his agent Rifaud about these undertakings is, however, less than informative. Rifaud was virtually illiterate and mainly occupied in self-justification – a difficult combination for the modern reader seeking to make sense of events. Attempts were being made at this time to open one of the Fayum pyramids, namely that of Amenemhet III at Hawara.[49] One detects also that Drovetti believed that he was being robbed of finds which belonged to him, and that he was being duped in some speculation. It is striking that he is quoted as saying that 'these cursed antiquities have caused me many troubles'. Work was still going on around the pyramid until the end of March 1824, when the harvest meant that no workers could be spared for archaeology. Rifaud, accompanied by Pacho, took the opportunity to survey lake Qaran, including a search for the Labyrinth. He was already looking forward to excavating a temple in the Fayum. It is a great shame that the details of expenses for the work for five months which Rifaud attached for Drovetti do not survive – unless they have been omitted by the editors of the *Epistolario* – in order to have some idea of the scale of the work being carried out for Drovetti at this time. These costs, we know at least, were being defrayed by the sale of the excavated material, including 9,000 baked bricks and 6,000 broken ones! The end of the story comes in October, when Rifaud reported the abandonment of the opening of the pyramid, his own pennilessness, and great dissatisfaction on the part of Gastaldo, apparently another of Drovetti's agents, against whom Rifaud sided with the Consul.[50]

In view of these important operations, it is not without interest to find the following description of the pyramid in a modern guide:

> Well preserved down to the Graeco-Roman era, this was one of the great tourist attractions of ancient Egypt. The mortuary temple, with its numerous chapels to the nome gods of Egypt, was so extensive and complex that it was known to the ancients as the 'Labyrinth' (Strabo, Geographica book 17.1.37). So complete is the destruction, however, that it is only with an effort of the imagination that these buildings can be visualised against the pyramid's south face today. The pyramid itself, built of mud brick, has lost its limestone casing, and the interior – designed with considerable ingenuity to foil grave- robbers – is inaccessible.[51]

In one of the most remarkable stories in the annals of Egyptology, Petrie found the entrance and funerary chamber of this pyramid in 1888-1889.[52]

By March, Drovetti's new colleague, the Vice-Consul at Cairo had been appointed: Felix Mengin; he arrived in May. Chateaubriand took the opportunity to present Mehemet Ali with a landau and harness for four.

There were military developments on two fronts. Ibrahim, the Pasha's eldest and almost only surviving son, aged thirty-five, was appointed to command the expedition to Greece. And in Arabia, 25,000 Wahabites were defeated by 4,000 Egyptians who had been trained by the French. Counterbalancing disaster, however, struck in Egypt. On 22 March, fire broke out in the Citadel in Cairo, and the powder magazines exploded, destroying the arsenal and wreaking havoc in the city. Four thousand lay dead. It was suspected that the fire was deliberately lit by the 'old' troops, furious at being displaced by the new army.[53] As well, a peasant revolt broke out in Middle Egypt around Esneh, but was soon put down by the army. One thousand fellahin were killed. The new army had survived its first crucial test: the peasant soldiers loyally put down the uprising of their own class. The plague then raged in Cairo.[54]

The death of Byron (19 April 1824) did not escape notice in Drovetti's correspondence. His colleague David at Smyrna said that he was reported to have died from a stitch in the side. His body was to be sent back to England in a barrel of rum. The versions of his death were endless: strangulation, poisoning, apoplexy. The truth was much more prosaic: he had caught a chill out riding and was then weakened by over zealous bleeding and purging by doctors. His body was, however, crudely embalmed, and the coffin was placed in a cask of 180 gallons of spirit to be transported back to England for burial in the family tomb at Hucknall Torkard near Newstead on 16 July.[55]

It seems that Drovetti's own health began to show the signs of deterioration which led to his retirement five years later. He complained first about eye problems. David attempted jokes in response: at Smyrna, people were losing only their hair and their teeth. The only consolation for loss of sight was Homer's lyre or Milton's harp. 'Tell me soon that you have no need of these instruments', he chaffed Drovetti.[56]

As so often there were honours to compensate for pains. On 6 May Drovetti was decorated with the Order of Knight of the Holy Sepulchre for his support of the centres of Terra Santa and the religious who cared for them and the hospices and convents.[57] By another letter of the same date as the one congratulating him from Bastiani, the Custodian of the Terra Santa, Drovetti found that the honour only entailed new and delicate duties. He was asked to intervene against the Father-General of the order, Cirillo Alamedo, who was issuing orders favourable to the priests of his own nation and causing strife between them and the Italians. Drovetti was urged to use the name of the French King to remind the superior of his duties.[58] In short, the protection of the French was sought for the Italian priests of the Terra Santa order. The dispute was over, amongst other things, the control of alms received by them.

A new French Ambassador to Constantinople had been sent out at the very end of 1823. Armand- Charles Guilleminot was just two years older than Drovetti and had served in all the major Napoleonic campaigns, including Italy, Russia and Waterloo, obtaining the rank of General. He instantly established close relations with Drovetti and informed him of a plot to overthrow Mehemet Ali by Silkim Pasha of Monastir in June.[59] The plot aimed to replace Mehemet Ali with Mahmoud Soliman Pasha of Trebizond, brother-in-law of the sheik of Mecca. The difficulties of diplomatic correspondence are illustrated by the fact that in such critical times a letter of Drovetti to Constantinople via Crete had taken two months.

Guilleminot was also able to tell Drovetti of the preparations of the Turkish fleet for the invasion of Greece, anticipated in August. Much was hoped of the Egyptian contribution, and the whole rebellion, it was thought, would be over in a year, but Guilleminot admitted that he did not think that the Greeks would be so easily overcome, even with Egyptian intervention.[60]

The Egyptian expedition sails against Greece

As preparations for the invasion of Greece got under way, Mehemet Ali asked that Ibrahim be appointed Turkish admiral, but the Sultan refused. The admiral was to be Khosrev, the old Viceroy of Egypt! A fleet of 150 ships was to carry 12,000 men, but that meant hiring them from the English and the Austrians. One of Chateaubriand's last actions was to approve of Drovetti's accompanying Mehemet Ali to Asyut to review the army, and even his going to Syria.[61]

With the dismissal of Chateaubriand in June 1824, the French government revealed a much more severe attitude to its overworked Consul. Villèle, the Prime Minister, blamed him for not sending more detailed and frequent reports, and for a general lack of conscientiousness – although it was admitted that this was caused by Drovetti's conviction that the government was not interested in him.[62] It was, indeed, only now with Egypt entering the world stage that such interest was suddenly being evinced. Drovetti had, in the meantime, not been omitting his customary acts of kindness to those who were interested. The mayor of Lyon thanked him for sending no fewer than eight stelae to the museum there.[63]

By the middle of 1824 Crete had submitted to the Egyptians, allowing them to turn their attention to deal with pirate raids on Damietta and Alexandria. The main expedition waiting to sail for Greece was detained in camp by the plague, unrest and lack of money. In all, there were 15,000-16,000 men, including 2,000 cavalry, sappers and fifteen pieces of artillery. The medical service was headed by an unnamed Frenchman. Drovetti, thinking that he was still writing to Chateaubriand, informed him that Mehemet Ali was hoping that the war would quickly be over through conciliation, or 'clemency and philanthropy' as he said a fortnight later.[64] He rightly stressed the enormous drain on Egypt, with men needed also in Upper Egypt, Arabia, Ethiopia, Crete and Cyprus. Ibrahim finally sailed on 19 July.

In September, at the end of his excellent report on the Egyptian cotton industry, Drovetti indulged in very bitter protestations on the uselessness of his sacrifice for France in Egypt over twenty-one years. He asked for leave to recover, if possible, his ruined health. The answer came in November: he was asked to defer his request.[65] He had been talking again to friends about his ills, again to his ironic friend at Smyrna. The Consul at Salonika, Botta, had just had sick leave in France. David replied that the ills of the 'sick man of Alexandria' were not as obvious as the rheumatism and gout of Botta, and that he might be accused of laziness. Guilleminot also pressured him to stay.[66] Events in the Levant were making Drovetti's absence less and less possible.

The first news of the Greek expedition was wildly vacillating. The Turkish admiral was said to have been seriously defeated at Samos, but then it was claimed that Ibrahim had destroyed 32 ships at Isara. A true account came only with a report from a French officer with Ibrahim, which Drovetti received in November.[67] After leaving Alexandria on 19 July, Ibrahim met the Turkish fleet at Bodrum at the end of August. In up to four engagements, the Turkish fleet and its admiral did not perform courageously and Ibrahim saved the day off Kos (5 September) and Samos (10 October). Already the famous Greek tactic of the fireship was in evidence.[68] The fleet finally sailed for the Morea on 6 November.

It was in 1824 that one of the most amazing international political hoaxes was played, on none other than Pope Leo XII, famous as a reactionary and missionary. A letter was sent to the Pope, purportedly by Mehemet Ali's 'Agent-General' on behalf of his Secretary and Interpreter John Saracini, requesting the sending of an Apostolic Delegate to Egypt to appoint bishops, principally with the aim of converting the Copts back to the Roman Church. Totally duped, Leo consecrated a Copt aged twenty-two, 'without talent or character', as 'Archbishop of Memphis', equipped with decorations as specified by the Viceroy and accompanied by proselytising priests. They all arrived in Alexandria on 28 September, and were sent packing by Mehemet Ali, whether in amusement or rage is not clear. The Pope was subject to 'the ridicule of all Europe', declared the delighted Salt: let us hear no more of papal infallibility! He could not imagine how the papal court contained not one person who could unmask such a blatantly implausible story as that the ruler of a Muslim country would invite Christian missionaries to deal precisely with one of the most dangerous elements of the population and to obtain their loyalty to a foreign power in addition. It is said that Drovetti's intervention was crucial in limiting the possibly enormous political damage to relations with Catholic powers such as France.[69]

The death was announced in September of Louis XVIII, to be succeeded by Charles X. Drovetti made the appropriate noises for his detested Bourbons: he told the Minister that he felt 'the most keen grief'. There was probably no-one who still remembered the famous incident of the flags nearly a decade before. Another death, seemingly much more modest, was to have far greater repercussions in Egypt. Peter Lee, the English Consul at Alexandria, died in this same month, September. As incredible as it may seem, his replacement, John Barker from Aleppo, did not arrive until October 1826. For two years, Drovetti's counterpart, Henry Salt, was pinned down in Alexandria, attempting to preside over the vital English maritime affairs at the port, and at the same time exercise his influence at the court when the Viceroy was in Cairo. Drovetti's ascendancy with Mehemet Ali was ensured by his ability to follow him as he moved between the two centres.

The engagements of the Turkish and Egyptian fleets with the Greeks in September were discussed in correspondence between David and Drovetti.[70] The former enlightened his colleague with the information that the ships captured by the Turks were only fire-ships, but that one of them had blown up the pride of Mehemet Ali's fleet, the frigate *Africa*. The Greek war took a decidedly personal turn for Drovetti when his nephew and a friend became involved and nearly lost their lives. They seem to have wanted to serve the Greeks; the friend, Berton, claimed that he wanted to be colonel of a cavalry regiment. The Greeks, however, thought that they were spies, and the governor of the island of Syra ordered the arrest of Drovetti the younger and his despatch to Nafplion. He was saved only by the French agent there, who packed him off back to Egypt. Drovetti thought his nephew a fool.[71]

At the end of November there arrived in Egypt two French generals to assist with the training of the Egyptian army, Boyer and Livron. The details of their disastrous mission will be treated in detail in a later chapter. Suffice here to note that Drovetti was diplomatically embarrassed. Boyer had brought with him five hundred rifles from the King for the Viceroy, who was delighted with the public presentation at this delicate moment. Drovetti told Damas, the Foreign Minister, that a little more 'circumspection' would have been desirable. Dumas had, in fact, sent Drovetti instructions on 8 November, but they did not arrive until much later. The government had not wanted any publicity. It was beginning to be thought in Paris that Mehemet Ali was plotting his own independence. Drovetti urged his obedience to the Sultan in the expedition against the Greeks as the best evidence that such suspicions were unfounded.[72] Boyer, on the other hand, conveyed his generous first impressions of the Consul: he is very capable, and enjoys the respect of the Pasha, who calls him his great friend. No other consul is on this footing. He also noted that Drovetti had recently found solid gold ornaments of a 'royal mummy' at Sakkarah (this information almost certainly came from Drovetti). Boyer was in general alarmed at the control exercised by Italians in Egypt, as he saw it: as military instructors, professors and writers of textbooks.[73]

Youssef Boghos had not always been on the best terms with Drovetti. The famous secretary of the Pasha and now Minister of Trade, was now, however, becoming more pro-French; Drovetti detected this change, under the influence of his master, from his previous pro-English attitudes. Drovetti therefore asked the Foreign Minister to make him a present, and he suggested a set of porcelain. The Consul himself had received a portrait of the new king, Charles X. As soon as Mehemet Ali saw it, he took it for himself. Drovetti asserted that he was inconsolable!

At the very end of 1824, more precise details are forthcoming of the illness plaguing Drovetti. He was 'tormented by sciatica'.[74] There were, however, plagues other than physical: Terra Santa. Cozza da' Luzzi, Vice-Prefect in Cairo for two years, was to be transferred as Parocchial to Jerusalem. He believed that this was all a plot by two enemies, a Maronite and a Copt, and turned to Drovetti not only for advice but even declared that he would obey his orders as 'father in common of the whole Terra Santa Custodia'.[75] Again, Drovetti's application for leave was rejected: 'objects of greater importance' were in the air, requiring his perseverance, Damas told Guilleminot. By the New Year he seemed, in fact, to be much better.

Drovetti does not appear in his letters or those to him by his friends as a man haunted by self-doubts. A rare exception is the visit of Commander Drouault at the beginning of 1825. Drovetti wrote to his friend David at Smyrna that he was very nervous about the impression he had made. David went to some lengths in sincere reassurance; for Drovetti imagined that one of his ex-dragomans, whom Drouault had brought with him to Egypt, was defaming him to the captain.[76] The same month a scandal broke at Constantinople. A nephew of the Sultan was having an affair with one of his uncle's most beautiful wives. He was to be exiled to Kurdistan, but instead spirited the lady out of the harem and was said to have set sail for Egypt seeking asylum there. It seems that there really could be an *Entführung aus dem Seraglio*! Guilleminot put aside even the news of the Greek war to devote a letter to Drovetti to this topic.[77]

Probably on the advice of Drovetti, Mehemet Ali sent presents to the new French king, Charles X: four horses each for him and the Dauphin, as well as an elephant. The matter of presents caused Drovetti to write to Damas about their importance in Egypt. One of the most constant concerns of a diplomat in the Levant was the incessant demand for recognition of every kind of occasion. The gifts, of course, had to be proportionate to the status of the person concerned, and with someone like the Pasha the expense was enormous. This was not yet chargeable to the

Ministry of Foreign Affairs, but came out of the consul's own pocket! His burdens were eased greatly, however, by the appointment finally of a new Vice-Consul in Cairo, Malivoire. This was in February and his salary was 10,000 francs; he was being transferred from Tunis.[78] Relations with his new subordinate were not, however, to be as comfortable as with Asselin de Cherville and Thédénat-Duvent.

The noted Italian botanist Giovanni Battista Balbis was yet another scientist who called on the Consul's help. He asked Drovetti for Egyptian specimens and told him how to gather and preserve them (pressing them in paper under a weight). Realising that Drovetti perhaps had more important things to do, Balbis assumed that someone else might be called in to help, and even suggested young Dr Cani, but he was too busy with vaccinations.[79]

In April, Drovetti described his own position as 'ever more critical and delicate'. His rivals, the English, kept him on his toes with their intrigues and traps to embroil him with the Pasha, who, despite all this, continued to show the French great favour.[80] Yet another example was provided at the same time of the increasing amount of work connected with his knighthood of the Holy Sepulchre. He received news from Guilleminot that the Sultan had given permission for the rebuilding of the monastery on Mt Carmel; Drovetti was thanked for 'useful co-operation' in obtaining his favour.[81]

By May 1825, Ibrahim was attacking Navarino, which he captured in June; he then began to move inland.[82] A combined Egyptian and Turkish fleet had disembarked 5,000 Albanians to join Ibrahim. Misitrea, capital of the Maniotes, had been burned. Drovetti in July declared the fate of the Morea sealed.[83] Both sides committed atrocities in this war, but those of the Greeks were intolerable to Drovetti. When Greek pirates began taking Turkish passengers from French ships in order to massacre them, he declared: 'Such excesses can scarcely be conceived when the European powers, and perhaps France especially, are adopting measures to ameliorate the fate of the Greeks.'[84]

The French military instructor, General Boyer, reported in July the amazingly frank interviews he had had with Mehemet Ali, who told him of his ambitions and his optimism, and his dream of building a strong and vast kingdom on the ruins of the Ottoman empire, a realm extending to the Euphrates. Boyer also recorded the vital French assistance to the Greeks given by Roche and Fabvier, who had been successful against Ibrahim at Nafplion. Ibrahim's reputation in Greece had been besmirched by his massacres. He was in danger of being cut off by the Greek fleet, and a disaster would be fatal to Mehemet Ali. Drovetti tried to reassure Boyer about Egyptian successes in Greece, but Boyer noted that these were contradicted by reports from Hydra and Zante. And of 2,000 horses sent to Ibrahim, only 400 arrived, because there were no proper transports and the majority perished.[85]

Becoming bolder, the audacious Greeks next attacked Alexandria harbour on 10 August. There were no fewer than 150 European ships in the port when the Greeks launched a fireship. Disaster was narrowly averted. Mehemet Ali was so enraged that he set off himself in pursuit. He was away for one week, reaching Karamania on the southern coast of Turkey.[86] In his absence, the Turkish admiral arrived, much to everyone's consternation. With the Morea 'subdued', Mehemet Ali demanded the title of Grand Vizier, second only to the Sultan.

The Greeks, meanwhile, had made an appeal for English protection. Drovetti was able to obtain a copy of this letter, which he sent on to Damas on 6 September. It is interspersed with his own commentary. He fulminated against Greek insults to the French flag during four years of 'robberies and atrocities', and claimed that European officers who had gone to help the Greeks were so maltreated that they came over to Mehemet Ali. And the appeal was such a paradox: the Greeks regarded the English as the only strict neutrals, but it was they who had given all the arms to Egypt which were now being used against them.[87]

In the midst of this international turmoil and the most delicate diplomacy a letter was sent to Drovetti from, of all places, St Petersburg. Count Romanoff did not know Drovetti, but he was a merino breeder. He merely thought that he would like to have five fine Nubian sheep in his flock – 'I mean the white sheep with horns' – and five or six ewes of the same breed. They were to be sent by sea. At least Drovetti was to be paid, and 2,000 roubles were put at his disposal. As well, the Count requested quantities of the best Egyptian grain, rye, oats, millet and beans.[88] The source of this resort to Drovetti was, in fact, Count Sekowski, of the Russian embassy at Constantinople; Drovetti had sent him papyri.[89] Two months later, the Director of the St Petersburg Imperial Botanical Garden, Friedrich Fischer, wrote to the Consul. He wanted samples of sycamore, fig and date. He also sent instructions for their packing: in a little barrel between layers of earth, to preserve the 'germinative force'. On matters of quarantine, however, he had to rely on Drovetti's experience.[90] These are telling examples of the way Drovetti's services were constantly called upon on all sides, and the way his generosity to one person led to a whole chain of requests.

In September 1825, two more regiments were about to sail, one for Crete and one for the Morea. New soldiers were being constantly pressed. The progress in training was remarkable. 24,000 troops were already away, and another 12,000 were in training. When the Greeks accused a French brig of breach of neutrality in firing on a fireship in Alexandria harbour, Drovetti recommended the young officer in charge of the ship for the Légion d'Honneur: the captain had been dining at the time with the Consul![91]

Mehemet Ali gained his wish. In October he was elevated to the rank of Grand Vizier and promised the Pashalik of Damascus. His army now numbered 40,000 and would soon reach 60,000. He held the fate of the Ottoman empire in his hands. It was at this juncture that General Livron paid Drovetti the highest compliment:

> I would not be able to say how great are the services rendered by M. Drovetti in Egypt. He has the complete confidence of the Viceroy, and it is to him that the predominance which France enjoys in the country is owed. It is much to be desired that his very ruined health allows him to exercise his functions as Consul-General in Egypt for a long time to come.[92]

The depredations of the Greek fleet at Santorini called forth the Consul's condemnation: the Greeks did not exhibit a 'tolerance worthy of all the wishes of Europe for the emancipation of these co- religionists.'[93] One of the many reports to Drovetti from those taking part in the war is the letter from Brunetti, instructor with the 8th Regiment in Greece.[94] After a crossing in which no enemy ships were sighted, some battalions had landed at Navarino, to march overland with Ibrahim to Missalonghi, while the fleet sailed around to Lepanto in the Gulf of Corinth. Brunetti had hopes that Missalonghi might fall within a month (it was to take another five).

The Russian Emperor Alexander died on 19 November, and Boyer discussed with Drovetti the possible repercussions. His successor Constantine was not 'patient', and there was a heightened possibility of war with Turkey, but all other European powers wanted to keep the sword in the scabbard. The two agreed that Constantine might be more pro-Greek, but that Alexander's brothers might dispute the throne. Everything depended on Ibrahim's siege of Missalonghi.[95]

At the end of the year, the Sardinian government was sending its first consuls to Egypt. The appointment to Alexandria as Consul-General was Domenico Pedemonte, Drovetti's own son-in-law, and to Cairo a man named Magnetto. There certainly had been moves to have Drovetti appointed to such a post, but his long services to France might have counted as much against him as for him, and his notorious Bonapartist sympathies would not have been attractive to the restored house of Savoy. We may be sure, however, that the appointment of Pedemonte was not a coincidence.

The English obviously felt their influence slipping behind that of the French. According to Drovetti, they went so far as to criticise Mehemet Ali for having French officers in his army. The Viceroy's reply seems very sophisticated, but is certainly bien trouvé: without the support of the French, he would be in the same position in Greece as Lord Byron. Further diplomatic moves saw Salt having a long conference with the Pasha, offering to arrange a peace. Mehemet Ali replied simply that he would not negotiate with rebels.[96] France was, however, being compromised in Constantinople, as the Sultan made arrangements at the end of the year to step up efforts in Greece, with money and men. The Turks lacked artillery, and France had now gone back on an earlier agreement to provide it. At the same time it was predicted that Russia and England would intervene. The former was ready to invade Turkey, and England viewed events in Greece with increasing alarm. The French admiral de Rigny was very angry about Greek piracy and the failure of his government to provide him with enough ships to escort merchants. He characterised the Greeks as 'ranters drunk on money and power'. It is no wonder that in all of this, Guilleminot frankly admitted that he did not know what to think or what direction French policy was taking. Drovetti's information about affairs in Greece was therefore of the highest value to the Ambassador. One special humanitarian question was close to the Consul's heart and Guilleminot asked him to protest to Mehemet Ali against the use of Egyptian or Turkish ships to carry off Greek slaves and to warn him that the French navy would use force to stop it.[97]

It is against the background of this struggle between French and English diplomacy that we have a most amusing picture of Drovetti from a most partisan source. Dr Richard Madden arrived in Egypt in July 1825 as 'medical man' to Henry Salt, in whose house in Alexandria he lived. He could hardly be expected to be favourable to 'foreign consuls':

Unfortunately the foreign consuls are so wrapped up in their own importance, that they affect to be worshipped as little demi-gods by their subjects, and are ridiculed as foolish persons, doting on their gold lace, and dressed only "in a little brief authority", which renders them conspicuous but not respectable. Most of them are the devoted servants of Mohammed Ali; the interests of their governments are of minor importance to them; the Pacha knows their price. When he has any object in view, either to banish a Frank merchant (for this takes place in defiance of Frank treaties and is winked at by the Consuls), or to settle a dispute with a Christian captain, about damaged rice or ill- stowed cotton, he gives one Consul a cargo of beans; he gives credit for his produce to another; to a third he grants permission to dig for antiquities at Thebes; to a fourth at Memphis; and to M. Drovetti, he allows the pay and privileges of a privy counsellor. The latter (sic) has more influence over him than any other European.[98]

The reference to the banishment of merchants is explained by a footnote: when some had been appointed to arbitrate between the government and an Austrian captain, and decided in his favour, they were banished, save two Frenchmen, who terrified their Consul with the threat of a process against him. The claim that the interests of his government were 'of minor importance' to Drovetti is quite the opposite of the view of that government, which refused so long to grant him leave, and the idea that only 'foreign consuls' had excavation rights when Salt also formed three collections of antiquities is hardly fair.

Madden left us an unforgettable picture of Drovetti at this time, for all its malice:

> Mohammed Ali was now firmly fixed in his government, and it was evident that something more than Turkish wisdom preserved him in it. Telegraphs were established from Alexandria to Cairo; and every insurrection which begun (sic) was disconcerted in the space of a few hours. The Mamelukes deemed his agents supernatural, but his only agent was M. Drovetti, the French Consul. This gentleman still holds the office of Consul, and he it was whose prudence and dexterity seated Mohammed Ali on the throne. Every measure of the latter was his planning; and the Viceroy well knows that to him the success of his ambition is wholly due. Drovetti is the most perfect courtier in his manners and appearance I ever met; the elegance of his address is only surpassed by the depth of his dissimulation and the skilfulness of his subterfuge. There is, however, something terrible in his countenance; and as he stalks along the plain of Alexandria every evening, muffled in his white bernous, the Franks are seen to retire with a sort of deferential horror, and whisper, as he passes, "Make way for Catiline".
>
> What share he had in the destruction of the Mamelukes, I know not; but in his quality of privy counsellor, it is to be presumed the bloody business was not transacted without his knowledge.[99]

This truly is a stunning testimony to Drovetti's reputation. Some fifteen years after the 'Cairene Vespers' the Irish doctor still portrays him as the Grey Eminence behind the Viceroy's throne and credits him with masterminding the appalling massacre. The evocation of Drovetti in his great hooded cape is worthy of a Gothic melodrama. It presumably drew something from the ambience of the good Henry Salt and reflected a certain inferiority complex.

Excavations at Tanis

The Mediterranean might well be in turmoil with a war threatening to engulf the whole of Europe once again, but Drovetti still found time to correspond with his agent Rifaud, who by the middle of 1825 had moved to the great Delta city of Tanis (ill. 24). The relevant correspondence is not easy to follow. Drovetti himself characterised Rifaud's communications in a way that the reader now can only agree with wholeheartedly: 'more designed to confuse matters than to clarify or facilitate them'.[100] The day after beginning the excavations Rifaud dug up a superb seated statue in grey granite (size unspecified) and another of the same material more than twenty feet high. He also spoke of a sarcophagus, the extraction of which was causing considerable difficulties. A little later Rifaud revealed that one of the statues in pink granite (sic), three times natural size, was broken in two but that it could easily be repaired. Another was a 'masterpiece', also in pink granite, twice natural size, and depicted a king with crossed arms holding a sceptre and the 'key of the Nile' (an ankh sign?), but was unfortunately acephalous. In all he had found eleven statues, of which six were very valuable. He was working under great difficulties, but hoped to find, 'other prizes' within the month which would form 'another museum' (in other words, the second Drovetti collection). Rifaud especially asked for wheels from gun carriages in order to transport his finds.

Drovetti promptly sent off money, provisions and five chariot wheels; for Rifaud reported that he spent a fortnight unable to pay his workers and living on bread and water. The excavations in course had commenced in September, and he found again a magnificent group in pink granite of two standing figures, one with hands on the shoulders of the other in front, but both acephalous. Rifaud hoped to bring the finds to Alexandria by the end of the month, but the sarcophagus could not be moved yet, for the site was flooded. The missing head turned up in October, but the great difficulty was still to get the finds to Alexandria, which depended on the hire of boats and information on the time of the Nile flood and the opening of the canals. Rifaud himself was at Basta (Zagazig), the crossroads between Tanis and Alexandria. This letter was really a restrained rebuke to Drovetti, whom he accused of having left him without money or instructions for a long time. He had, however, managed to obtain a firman for excavations from the local sheik.[101]

It is undoubtedly in the light of all this that General Boyer complained to his colleague Belliard in June about the French consuls (sic),

135

who devoted themselves to making rich collections of antiquities thanks to generous firmans, and who served the Pasha's interests but not those of France, because they did not see the danger to commerce from Mehemet Ali's control of the Mediterranean.[102] There were, it must be noted, personal reasons for animus between Boyer and Drovetti; for the soldier was a philhellene. It was, however, he who was totally to discredit France by his actions.[103]

1825 was one of the most rich in honours in Drovetti's life. On 18 March he became an honorary member of the Imperial Society of Naturalists in Moscow at a meeting presided over by Prince Andrew Oblensky.[104] His enormous work for Russian science noted above was being rewarded. On 21 May he was made a corresponding member of the Musée Académique of Geneva. This was in recognition of various gifts which he had made to the museum, including an ostrich and various antiquities.[105] The very next day in Paris he was promoted from Chevalier to Officer of the Légion d'Honneur.[106] And in August he was awarded by the Emperor Alexander I, just before his death, the Order of St Anne of Russia, second class. The decoration was set with diamonds. This award was made for his services as Consul for Russia during the war with Turkey, and was initiated by the Russian mission in Constantinople.[107]

European sympathies in the Greek war

Drovetti realised, of course, that his attitude to the Greeks was not shared by most Europeans, and this division made his position very difficult. When French ships called at Egypt, they declared that all Europe, especially France, was pro-Greek. Needless to say, this thoroughly ruined France's credit with Mehemet Ali. The English, of all people, Drovetti reported to the Foreign Minister, were stressing French support for the Greeks, precisely in order to discredit French standing with the Pasha. Support for their claim was, however, provided by the fact that some French officers and munitions had been sent to the Greeks. Drovetti did his best to convince visiting French ships that Greek independence would benefit principally the English and the Russians. Mehemet Ali was so put out that he wondered whether it would be better for young Egyptians who were to be educated in Europe to be sent to Italy instead of to Paris. Drovetti visited Cairo to try and undo all the harm to French influence, and asked if he might offer the French government as an intermediary in negotiations with the Greeks. Mehemet Ali began, however, to realise that the English, despite their supposed neutrality, were much more committed than the French to the Greek cause.[108]

It was in January 1826 that Mehemet Ali was granting three hour interviews to General Boyer, in which with his usual frankness the Pasha

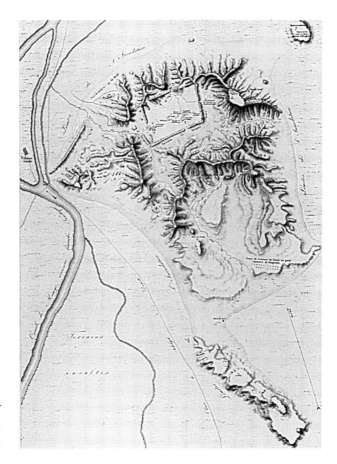

24. Tanis, site of
one of Drovetti's
major excavations

spoke of raising a navy of 20,000 men with three triple-deckers, ten of 74 guns and fifteen frigates. He proposed to invade Syria with his army. He had sent spies to Persia and found that they had only 40,000 men in a defensive militia organised by the English traders. His only fear was England.[109] All this was changed by the English admiral Hamilton, who declared to the Greeks that England was their great protector, and that France was on the side of the Turks. Into the bargain, Salt had told Mehemet Ali to evacuate Greece immediately! Drovetti and Boghos were summoned to Cairo urgently for talks with the Viceroy.[110] Much of this recovery was, however, undone in February when there appeared the first sign of the terrible feud among the French military instructors, which was to lead to a débâcle.

The battle for Missalonghi, begun in February 1825, now entered its last phase. Two thousand bombs were thrown into the city in twenty-four hours, and the weakness of the Greek position was revealed by the slowness of their batteries. Ibrahim chased away Greek ships attempting to relieve the garrison. Although such visits always affected his health, Drovetti was again in Cairo in March having interviews with Mehemet Ali. The English also offered to mediate in the war: the Pasha told them to deal with Constantinople. When Drovetti suggested to him that the Sultan was anxious to end such a disastrous war by granting concessions to the Greeks, he replied prophetically that the Porte would never agree to foreign interference. He also feared the effects on the modernisation of Egypt:

> I cannot make headway against the rebels, but I think that my friends would not wish me to be reduced to that extreme necessity where all my plans for the organisation and civilising of Egypt would fail completely.[111]

In fact, this year Mehemet Ali sent away from Cairo all his chief administrators, despatching them to the provinces to oversee reforms, especially the situation in agriculture. This meant that the Pasha himself had to stay in Cairo to run the central administration almost single-handedly, assisted by his devoted secretary and a few others.

To offset the problems of the French, Drovetti was doubtless delighted to hear that the English were in danger in India. The source of this information was the visit to Egypt by Sir Charles Colville, the governor of Bombay. It is a testimony once again to the French Consul's intelligence sources that he was able to provide the French Foreign Ministry with pages of the most detailed information on British forces in India.[112]

In March 1826 Drovetti was alerted to the imminent arrival of a very important figure, Count Alexandre Laborde, famous for his *Voyage pittoresque et historique en Espagne* (4 folio volumes), 1807-1818, an amazing survey of culture in Spain with 900 engravings, from the Roman period to modern times. He was also an educator, who had gone to England to study the Lancaster method of educating the poor; he was as well, since 1822, a member of parliament for the centre-left. He would have had much to discuss with Drovetti, and his arrival was announced by none other than the comte de Forbin. The count was in fact accompanying his son, Leon, as part of his education, on a tour of the East. Owing to the climate, the father soon returned to France, but the son went on to tour the Fayum.[113]

We have seen Pillavoine's claims about the state of the French consular residence in Alexandria, although that was stimulated by his intense antipathy for Drovetti.[114] From 1826 we have a description of similar conditions for the consular representative in Cairo. It is astonishing how ill-equipped the French diplomatic corps was. Malivoire wrote to Damas explaining that there was no official residence for the Consul in Cairo! He simply rented part of a house at a very high rent. That house belonged to none other than Felix Mengin, one time Vice-Consul. The accommodation was described as rather a *pied à terre*. The French quarter in the city was very small, and all the houses were occupied. Now an inn was for sale, at 20,000 francs, and it would require a further 5,000 for repairs. It consisted of two floors, with good rooms and a garden. Malivoire strengthened his case by pointing out that he could not, in present circumstances, offer even a room to Drovetti if he came to Cairo.[115] Where did Drovetti stay, then, on his frequent visits? No wonder such visits were uncongenial.

Animosities on the world stage were reflected at a more parochial level. As Knight of the Holy Sepulchre, Drovetti received a letter from the Cardinal Prefect of the Propaganda in Rome regarding the endless disputes between the Melchite Greeks and Catholic Copts for control of a church in Cairo. The squabble this time was over the respective hours during which each should be able to use the church for services. The complaints of the Greeks were upheld by many European diplomats. It was Drovetti, significantly, who was shown the high trust of being asked secretly to verify the claim and to suggest means of conciliation.[116] As well, there was uproar in the Order of Terra Santa, with ambitious monks vying for power. Father Liberato, called variously Superior or President, asked to retire, and there had been moves to remove him, but Drovetti agreed with the Custodian that too frequent changes at the top were undesirable. A much younger monk, Dionisio, was anxious to have the position. Drovetti was also here taken into the Custodian's confidence, and his advice sought.[117] These appeals to Drovetti were nothing in comparison to that made to him by the Custodian of Terra Santa to use all his influence with Guilleminot, Ambassador at Constantinople, to have a long series of important sanctuaries in the Holy Land restored to the Catholic monks. They had lost the Holy Sepulchre to the Greeks in 1818, the Tomb of Mary to the Greeks and Armenians, the Grotto of the Shepherds in Bethlehem to the Greeks in 1821, and the Sanctuary of the Crib to the Armenians.[118]

Still attempting to protect French influence with Mehemet Ali, Drovetti noted that the besieging army at Missalonghi contained no French and few Italian soldiers. This was because Ibrahim wanted all the glory to fall to the Egyptians alone. French newspapers favourable to the Greeks were, however, being received in Egypt, and because some few educated Egyptians were beginning to read newspapers, French interests were being harmed once again. We know that Egyptian successes in Greece gave Drovetti pleasure. He wrote to Noureddin, Egyptian Chief of Staff, informing him of news he had received in March.[119] This was presumably the capture on 9 March of fort Vasiladi which controlled the entrance to Missalonghi.

The fall of Missalonghi

At this crucial juncture, Missalonghi fell on 22 April. It is remarkable that only one letter of Drovetti is preserved in the official correspondence between 15 April and 8 July, 1826. For the news of these events we must rely on Malivoire and Saint-Sauveur in Crete. Eyewitness accounts of the last days of the town describe the Greeks starved into surrender by the winter-long blockade and the siege by thirty thousand. A plan to break out and join up with another Greek force of nearly one thousand nearby was discovered, and the Greeks found that the force which they expected to be their own was in fact Turkish. They were caught in an ambush and massacred. The town was then taken in desperate street-fighting, with the inhabitants blowing up many sections. Five thousand perished and six thousand women and children were taken as slaves.[120]

At the same time the army in the Morea was for its part desperate for supplies. A convoy of eighteen transports and three escort vessels sent from Navarino was nearly destroyed by the Greek navy and had to take refuge in Suda Bay in Crete. It had to wait for a stronger escort to rescue it. Crete itself was almost blockaded by Greek pirates.

As if all that were not enough, a dreadful dispute broke out in Cairo between the French and Sardinian Consuls, the so-called Marengo affair. It is strange that the official correspondence has nothing from Drovetti about this, events which must have caused him grave discomfort, since the Sardinian Consul was his own relative. The episode shows that the Europeans were in danger not only from fanatical Muslims but even from fellow Europeans. A Sardinian named Marengo who was about to be arrested by the Sardinian Vice-Consul, Magnetto, took refuge in a French pharmacy. The French Vice-Consul, Malivoire, thus became involved, and told Marengo that he must give himself up. Despite this, the Sardinian Consul became very abusive of his French colleague. Colonel Rey, head of the Pasha's arms factory, then came to advise Marengo, who was still in the pharmacy, whereupon Magnetto's men, believing that Rey was trying to get rid of Sardinian workers in his factory, stormed the pharmacy, stabbed Rey and carried off Marengo. The last had, however, claimed that he was a convert to Islam, whereupon Mehemet Ali ordered that he be surrendered to him. Marengo confirmed his conversion, whereupon Mehemet Ali ordered Magnetto out of Egypt for attempting to coerce one of his subjects. He also set about trying to track down those who had attempted to murder one of his leading European assistants.[121]

Rey, in fact, recovered from his stabbing, but the would-be assassins promised to try again. The result of this extraordinary fracas was the issuing of orders by Mehemet Ali in June that all 'seditious and incorrigible' Europeans and those without support were to be expelled, and that all workers in Egyptian factories were to be subject to the local police.[122] Malivoire admitted that many Europeans came to Egypt simply to make their fortunes, especially Maltese, Genovese and Sicilians, and that they were very undisciplined, assaulting Egyptians and blaspheming against Islam. The Pasha had appealed to the various consuls to control their nationals, but in vain. The new regulations were the result, and significantly it was the doyen of the diplomatic corps, Drovetti, who was chosen by the Pasha to circulate them among all the consuls at Alexandria. The French cabinet, it must be stressed, had no objection to the new rules, since everyone was given a choice: accept them or leave.

Although the official correspondence does not contain Drovetti's reaction to the Marengo affair, documents in the *Epistolario* do. There is his letter to Malivoire, in which he simply represented to him the complaints of Pedemonte over Malivoire's 'imprudent insolence' in not handing over Marengo to the Sardinians and his contravention of all diplomatic conventions in giving asylum to a person against his own consul, when the various diplomats always required mutual support. The letter is signed 'your affectionate colleague'. It seems clear evidence of a conflict of interests. He also passed on to Malivoire two letters of the Sardinian Consul, one of which concerned Malivoire's complaints against the young vice-consuls in training. Magnetto was taking the matter further, and Drovetti advised Malivoire to inform the French Foreign Minister in order to anticipate trouble between Torino and Paris. And a week later, obviously in response to Malivoire's expression of reluctance, Drovetti urged upon him the necessity for France to be the first consulate to enforce the Pasha's new regulations for Europeans. Malivoire thought that the new rules would induce most European workers to leave Egypt, but Drovetti assured him that there was no fear of Oriental-style punishment such as the bastinado, but only imprisonment or loss of salary. Drovetti had in fact suggested to Boghos that each factory should have a European overseer to see to such punishments. He described the workers as unruly, drunken and immoral.[123]

The Greek war dragged on. Although there was disunity within the Greek government at Nafplion, Ibrahim was unable to subdue the Maniotes, and when the Captain Pasha attacked Samos, thinking that the enemy were occupied at Hydra and Nafplion, thirty Greek ships instantly appeared. An interesting light is thrown on all this by a letter to Drovetti from Admiral de Rigny.[124] He had spent three hours on board the Turkish admiral's ship. The latter was terrified of the fireships and was waiting for the Greeks to be more obviously at a disadvantage in the Morea. De Rigny, for his part, could not understand how with 'two vessels or five to six frigates' he did not annihilate the forty Greek ships opposite! De Rigny and Drovetti sympathised with Mehemet Ali: the European liberals could not see that all he wanted was to withdraw his troops from Greece, since there was nothing to be won and grave risks to be run.

As for Drovetti's own military career, in the middle of 1826, he was granted the rank of lieutenant- colonel in the French army.[125] The highest rank he had attained in the army before his appointment to Egypt in 1803 was cavalry major, but officers with ten years' service in a particular rank about to retire (!) could be given honorary promotion to the next grade. This was, of course, to increase pension entitlements. A letter from Drovetti stated that someone had made this request on his behalf and without his knowledge. That request had been for the rank of full colonel (Maréchal de Camp).

It was in 1826 that arrangements began to be made for the most important visit to Egypt by a European during the whole of Drovetti's consulate. The Consul replied to Jacques Joseph Champollion-Figeac, brother of the decipherer of the hieroglyphs, saying that he had done everything to facilitate the visit of Alexandre Vaucelles, who arrived in February. He pointed out that the time of Champollion's visit was not the 'most propitious', but offered no further explanation: he would seem to refer to the general instability caused by the Greek war. If Champollion wished to come, however, Drovetti declared himself entirely at his service, 'convinced in advance of the precious results of this journey'. He was most anxious that it should be 'certain, easy and pleasant' and had been in correspondence with Artaud in Lyons about it.[126] This is a vital letter, given the changed situation in 1827 and the charges which have been levelled at Drovetti's honesty.

As early as October 1824, in fact, Drovetti's son-in-law and soon the Sardinian Consul in Egypt, Pedemonte, was urging Champollion, who was at the time in Torino, to come to Egypt, 'seeing that the possibility of this journey depends on a bad cup of coffee which can be administered to the Pasha any day'! It was also in 1826 that the acquisition of the Salt collection by the Louvre induced Champollion to speak out about the relations between the French and English Consuls: he described relations between them as like those between 'the Popes of Rome and Geneva.' A colossal sphinx was to be transported from Alexandria, and Champollion declared that Drovetti was quite capable of being careless about it out of jealousy. One wonders who put this view of the Consul into his head, since he had never met him, and his only connection with him was the collection which he had esteemed so highly in Torino.[127]

The answer to the letter to Figeac is preserved in the *Epistolario*. In November 1826, he replied to Drovetti that his brother contemplated visiting Egypt at last. After spending two and a half years in Italy, he had been appointed Curator of the Louvre in May, and foresaw that it would

142

take a year to arrange that collection. Egyptian antiquities were no longer merely objects of curiosity since the decipherment of hieroglyphs. Figeac went on to make the extraordinary suggestion that the Viceroy might make Paris his centre for antiquities, and send everything there for twice-yearly auctions![128]

To complete the dossier on relations between Drovetti and Champollion before the latter's arrival, in another letter of March 1827, the Consul urged him to come to Egypt before too late, since so many monuments in the south were being turned into sugar mills.[129] This letter indicates even more than that of 1826 the genuine interest on Drovetti's part – despite Champollion's suggestion that he was motivated by rivalry with Salt – in the French scholar's visit.

The two brigs and a corvette built for Mehemet Ali in France arrived in July 1826. Another corvette and a frigate were still to come. The story of the last was a saga in itself.[130] The appalling bad luck and incompetence in the attempt to launch it were a clear omen of what was to come. It was at this time that mention was made by Drovetti of the possibility of Lord Cochrane's coming to the Levant, to aid the Greeks. He was described by Mehemet Ali as the 'fireship' of the English. Thomas Cochrane was one of the most remarkable sailors in English history. He had terrorised the Spaniards and French from 1800, was an indefatigable critic of abuses by the Admiralty, had been court-martialled for exposing his admiral's incompetence, was falsely implicated in a swindle on the Stock Exchange, and was appointed in succession admiral of the Chilean (1817), Brazilian (1823) and now Greek (1825) navies.[131]

The dissensions of the French officers came to a climax with the departure for France on 15 September of General Boyer, along with a number of others whom he induced to resign at the same time. This scandal gave the English a great advantage, and various visitors had interviews with the Viceroy, including the secretary of the Marquis of Hastings, later Governor of India. Salt was reported to have said in conference with the Pasha that he hoped that the batteries built at Alexandria by the French would become English. As Drovetti remarked, he was himself in the most difficult situation, combatting not only the English and the Italians but also the French because of their indiscretions. The Pasha in fact decided that the French could not train his army and sent to England to enlist officers. Drovetti worked tirelessly to convince him that it was not an official plot, but simply a private squabble among officers. Just how seriously new political alignments were taking shape is revealed by Salt's report of his confidential interview with Mehemet Ali. The Viceroy revealed his desire to act in unison with England. He assured Salt that the Sultan would never accept that power's mediation in the

Greek war. The question was, what was England willing to do for him? He referred to that country's designs on Egypt ('an idea always pressed upon him by the French Consul-General', Salt suggested, revealing one of Drovetti's main cards). Mehemet Ali concluded by stating that he was awaiting a British offer – or command of the Turkish fleet, which would allow him to compel the Greeks to surrender.[132]

The construction of more ships was undertaken in Europe. After being delayed by a fire which destroyed six thousand uniforms, an Egyptian fleet left for the Morea at the end of November, taking clothing, food and money for the winter. Ibrahim was, however, essentially holding his position until the Sultan's intentions became clearer; that is, whether he would make some compromise with the Greeks.

At the end of the year Drovetti was thanked by the Minister of the Royal Household for his present of a male and female antelope to the King. An oryx which he had sent to the Prince of Carignano unfortunately arrived dead; it was donated to the natural history museum.[133] His health had again been troubling him. He wrote asking for leave to Guilleminot who passed it on to Damas. He granted the leave but asked Drovetti to wait until the arrival of an interim replacement, Regnault from Jean d'Acre.[134]

A giraffe in Paris

It is hard to imagine that, in the midst of these international crises, the French Consul-General in Egypt was much concerned with a giraffe. At the end of 1825, in the Sudan, two young specimens had been captured and sent to Mehemet Ali. Drovetti had recently been instructed to try to obtain animals to send to the zoo in the Jardin des Plantes. He instantly applied for the giraffes as a gift for Charles X. Not surprisingly, Salt almost simultaneously asked for them for George IV. The Pasha fortunately had two, so that they could each have one, only one was decidedly healthier than the other. Exhibiting the wisdom of another Oriental ruler, he allowed the two consuls to draw, and Drovetti triumphantly announced that the lot had favoured France. 'Our giraffe is sound and vigorous, while the one which fell to the king of England is sickly and will not long survive.' He was right: it died at Windsor in August 1827.

Drovetti was instantly deluged with questions by the Museum of Natural History concerning the habits of the animal, what it ate and drank, and its temperament. It was even suggested that the Consul should accompany it to France. His own parlous health might not win him a speedy reprieve, but a giraffe might serve as a passport! Drovetti provided the essential information that the giraffe lived on milk, between twenty and twenty-five litres a day. To satisfy this, three cows were to be sent with it by sea. And to care for it, the Consul deputed one of his own servants and three Sudanese. The ship on which the animal was embarked, the Sardinian brig the *Due Fratelli*, was not large. The giraffe, although young, was four metres tall. A hole was therefore cut in the deck in order to allow its head to project. The captain signed a contract with Drovetti and was paid 4,600 francs.

Early in October 1826 the ship left Alexandria. General Boyer, returning to France, was another passenger. The *Due Fratelli* arrived in Marseille on 23 October. The subsequent history of the giraffe was even more extraordinary. It was walked nearly nine hundred kilometres to Paris by Geoffrey St-Hilaire, Professor of Zoology, along with its cows and attendants, and dressed in a fantastic proofed coat when it rained. The journey took five weeks, and they all arrived at the end of June, 1827. 'Giraffomania' swept Paris for a year or so: mementos, music, drama, political satire, and fashions. The giraffe died in 1845, aged 21, and was preserved in the National Museum in Paris. It may still be seen in the museum at La Rochelle, where it was sent in 1931.[135]

In his own archaeological research, 1826 also brought further trouble with Rifaud, whom Drovetti accused of complaining about him to Salt and to the Swedish Consul, Anastasy. Rifaud admitted that he had dined with Salt and that the British Consul had visited his house, and that there had been some probing questions about Rifaud's relations with his employer. As for Anastasy, Rifaud had offered his services to him to transport his collection of antiquities to Europe. Drovetti had furthermore blamed Rifaud for not taking better care of the antiquities in store during an absence in Turkey. Rifaud's defence ended with an outpouring of a more lyrical and philosophical character than one might have expected. He described Egypt as a country where not only people's morals collapsed, but where also slander and calumny were rampant, where people imputed to others what was true of themselves, and where those who tried to do their best were discredited and dishonoured. He concluded with hopes that one day Drovetti would realise how much he had wronged him, and by stressing the sacrifices he had made and his right to the rewards of his labours.[136]

The dispute between Rifaud and Drovetti was over money. It had been agreed that the former would receive 10,000 piastres (12,500 francs) for his discoveries at Thebes. By 1826 he had received 6,000, which he claimed he had spent on expenses. Out of the remaining 4,000 piastres he had to pay considerable debts and his passage back to France. He would obviously have little to show for all his labour in Egypt. He had even been selling off his collection of natural history specimens to make ends meet. Much of this collection had been destroyed by insects, and now he was suffering from hydrocele (the same ailment which killed Edward Gibbon), and had to return to Europe for an operation. His greatest grief was that his youngest son had died. All these afflictions had struck within a year, and he threw himself on Drovetti's charity and honour.[137] If the situation was as Rifaud represented it, one can only hope that Drovetti responded with his usual generosity. The souring of relations between the two men is disquieting.

One of the most persevering visitors to Egypt in these years was Robert Hay (1799-1863), who arrived in November 1824 and stayed into the next decade.[138] He met most people of importance in the European community, and gives the most unforgettable picture of Osman, the Scotsman who stayed behind in 1807 and converted to Islam. Hay travelled with Burton and Bonomi, and met Wilkinson, Maddox and Lane at Thebes. He showed Sir Hudson Low, Napoleon's jailor, around Thebes in one day, which set a record for lightning tours. He witnessed the destruction of the temple of Hermopolis in 1826, and the blowing up of the 'catacombs' at Asyut for stone. He does not mention meeting Drovetti, although it is almost inconceivable that he did not, but recorded that he had heard that Mehemet Ali intended to introduce the Napoleonic Code on his advice.[139] He is, however, among the most instructive sources on Drovetti's agents. At Girgeh, early in 1826, he met Piccinini, the excavator of mummies and bitter enemy of Yanni (Giovanni d'Athanasi), who were 'continually fighting about the division of the ground.... Such has been the case ever since the time of Belzoni ... bribes upon bribes given in all directions rather than lose their prize.' And near Manfalut he met another of Drovetti's friends, Antonini, who collected for him, and who among other things had a very fine scarab. Hay tells how a dishonest traveller named Kennedy agreed to the high price of $12 asked for it, which was only meant to discourage him. He was foolishly allowed to take it away, and then never sent the money.[140]

It is pleasant to read of the recognition of Drovetti's services in January 1827 by the attorney Chayolle in Paris, writing to Damas. The Consul's position was made very difficult, he noted, by the 'sentimental exaltation' of the Greeks. France's favourable position with Mehemet Ali was owed solely to Drovetti, and the personal dangers to which he was subject were not imaginary: his life was threatened. The English had induced the Arabs to assassinate French officers going to India during the American war, Chayolle asserted. Now Drovetti's health was very bad, and trips to Cairo made it worse. On top of that, there were the endless expenses, notably caused by French visitors, whether private travellers or naval officers. Chayolle stated that Drovetti had never been repaid by their relatives or the English government for the expenses he incurred to save soldiers in 1807. He concluded by noting the grant by the King of the rank of lieutenant-colonel, and contrasted this favour with the behaviour of the Ministry of Foreign Affairs which never did anything for their representative in Egypt.[141]

Drovetti had written to Chayolle about the scandal involving the French military instructors, pointing out other unpleasant implications. His deputy, Malivoire, was involved with Boyer against Drovetti. He was ambitious to succeed him as Consul-General, as is proven by his applications in the consular correspondence. By the end of the previous year, Drovetti had described his position to Chayolle as more unpleasant than anyone else's, 'assailed by liberalism and philhellenism'.[142] Just as he had forecast, however, early in 1827, Mehemet Ali softened his regulations for foreign workers, in order to prevent a mass exodus of his factory work-force. The indispensable ones were assured that they would not be subject to the local authorities.

The clash of command in the Greek war between the Captain Pasha and Ibrahim was also settled when the Sultan appointed the latter as commander in Greece. Mehemet Ali's long complaints against the Pasha of Crete were also answered by his replacement. The Viceroy reviewed 12,000 new troops and was very pleased with their discipline, rewarding the European instructors with a month's bonus.[143]

The road to Navarino and Drovetti's leave

In February 1827 the Sultan gave Mehemet Ali carte blanche in Greece, and he announced that he would personally lead a large fleet with many disciplined troops in an attack on the Greek islands. He ordered new levies of 10,000 infantry and 5,000 sailors. The new governor of Crete, Soliman Pasha, arrived in Cairo bringing the Sultan's firman for Mehemet Ali's command, but at the same time asking him not to leave Egypt. It was obvious that Ibrahim would continue as the Egyptian commander. The news that Lord Cochrane was commander of the Greek navy, however, caused Mehemet Ali to attend once more to Alexandria's fortifications. Two corvettes built in Europe arrived, and the French frigate was awaited. The expenses of all these were, of course, enormous, and Drovetti reported that the Pasha had sent an agent to Europe to raise a loan.[144]

By April Drovetti's leave had been granted and Regnault of Sidon was to replace him, although he was trying desperately to avoid it. This caused Malivoire to write depressed letters to the Minister suggesting that all his efforts to make a good impression over the last two years had been in vain. He would, he asserted, be despised; for the Egyptians respected a diplomat to the degree that he was valued by his own government (Drovetti had made the same point before). Although he was only going on leave, Drovetti was given a beautiful horse, a sabre decorated with gold and a shawl of great value by the Viceroy. He was also to take back four of the best Arab horses as a gift for the King.[145]

The long-awaited French frigate finally arrived. In his last letter from Egypt before he left, Drovetti reported that for the first time Mehemet Ali had declared that he wanted the European negotiations in the Greek war to succeed. He admitted that the most efficacious way would be the threat of united action against Egypt if she persisted in attacking the Greeks.[146] The Viceroy thus began to suggest ways in which he could be forced to extricate himself from a position that he also found intolerable. When the Captain Pasha was elevated to the most prestigious rank of Seraskier (Lieutenant to the Sultan), thus making Mehemet Ali once again his subordinate, the latter complained to his old friend the Consul that it was the lack of gratitude from the Sultan which had decided him to cooperate with France and to free the Greeks. He confided this message to Drovetti to be conveyed to the French government.

For the first time in twenty-four years, therefore, Drovetti left Egypt, embarking on the *Hecla* on 20 May, 1827. He handed over to Malivoire in Cairo and Clairambault in Alexandria.[147] The Consul was not fond of sea voyages, but the crossing, given the season (it was almost summer), should not have been boisterous. He was still in quarantine (one month) at the end of June. Jomard wrote to him in July, counselling him not to compromise the reaping of the rewards of his labours by indicating too soon his intention of retiring. This would indicate that Drovetti was considering not returning to Egypt. For more than a year, Jomard informed him, the European powers had inclined towards the Greek side, but it was still only a 'vague intention to intervene'.[148] It would seem that he did not know of the Treaty of London, to be signed the very next month.

The momentous events in Drovetti's absence can be simply told. Athens had fallen to the Turks, but on 16 June a Greek fleet of twenty-two ships appeared off Alexandria. After various feints on both sides, the Greeks sailed off and Mehemet Ali, who had rushed to the defences, relinquished the idea of pursuit. The entire situation in the Greek war was then changed by the signing of the three-power Treaty of London on 6 July between France, England and Russia, demanding autonomy for Greece. Egyptian naval confidence mounted, however, when the new frigate, the *Guerrière*, lived up to her reputation in the pursuit of Greek pirates as far as Rhodes. There had been much criticism of the French shipwrights, and the Viceroy had threatened never to use them again; now he asserted that he would always ask them to build his ships! Another two Egyptian frigates out of Patras ran across the Greek flagship, the *Hellas*, tried to board her and forced her to retire. Mehemet Ali overwhelmed the captains with praise.

The new Egyptian fleet sailed for Greece on 5 August, a total of 89 vessels, half of them warships, the rest transports and fireships. Sixteen were Turkish, four Tunisian, five Austrian, the rest Egyptian. Well might Malivoire wonder how Egypt could support this vast expense; as well as the fleet, five million francs were despatched to Ibrahim for the army. 'The whole weight of this ruinous war is now supported by Egypt.'[149] Just at this moment another omen occurred: the Minister of War, one of the Pasha's longest and closest associates, died.

It was only now, early in August, that an English envoy arrived in Egypt with news of the Treaty of London, ordering Mehemet Ali to desist. He was told to consult the Pasha's sovereign in Constantinople. Mehemet Ali repeated the same view, that he was only the servant of the Sultan, in an interview late in August with Salt and Major Cradock from Corfu. He expressed surprise at the treaty and asked how it would operate: would the powers actually move against the Turkish-Egyptian fleet? The English officer replied that he knew nothing about that. The Pasha did, however, know the character of the Sultan better than the Europeans did: he declared that the Porte would not accept foreign intervention. The real content of what passed in these negotiations is revealed, of course, only in the English record. Mehemet Ali revealed that he was willing to risk losing his whole fleet if offered the Pashalik of Damascus by the Sultan, unless the Allies guaranteed his independence. By this time only 17,000 troops were left to hold Egypt, and his control of Arabia and the Sudan was imperilled as well. Salt was, however, insistent on the need to conciliate him; for as he rightly stressed, his fleet was his 'ruling passion', and it had never been acquired with any thought of using it against the Greeks. The English Consul-General went even further: he informed his government in June that Mehemet Ali wanted to be forced to withdraw from Greece.[150]

The delicate situation in the Levant is demonstrated by an invitation received by Drovetti this month to dine with the Minister of the Navy.[151] Within four days of the proposed date of this diplomatic consultation, however, the Minister of Foreign Affairs informed Drovetti that 'the interest of the King' necessitated that he return to Egypt immediately. He was promised that when 'the interests of the service' allowed, he would be granted leave again. Meanwhile, he was given a gratuity of 12,000 francs. For reasons only half explained, however, Drovetti was not to set foot again in Egypt until January of the next year. When news came of the death of Regnault at Smyrna, Malivoire again asked to be appointed Consul-General until Drovetti returned.

At this delicate moment, the Wahabites recommenced hostilities. The war which the Egyptians thought they had won flared up again, and the garrisons fell back on Mecca. Mehemet Ali could raise another regiment, but money was the problem. His troops were owed ten months' pay, and the expedition would have to be fitted out as well. The only solution was an advance from the Europeans against the next harvest.

The Egyptian fleet reached Modon in Greece on 1 September.[152] Malivoire suggested that everything indicated that Ibrahim would not listen to the European admirals' pacific advice, although the Greek fleets had accepted an armistice. It was, in fact, on the very day of the battle of Navarino, 20 October, that Malivoire reported to Damas that a French ship had arrived in Egypt on 6 October for secret consultations with the Pasha. The terms he had managed to discover. Ibrahim had attempted to sail out of Navarino against the Greek islands. The French admiral, de Rigny, had forbidden him to do so, and he had returned to the harbour. He was thereupon allowed to send messages to both Constantinople and to his father. Mehemet Ali gave him the not very helpful advice to avoid trouble with the French and English admirals, de Rigny and Codrington, but – at the same time! – to obey the Sultan. Egypt continued in blissful ignorance of what had finally happened, and when Malivoire saw him at the end of the month, Mehemet Ali said that he feared that the blockade would lead to a rupture between the Europeans and the Porte! He was at the same time behaving very graciously to various French captains, urging them to come back often because their visits were always welcome.[153]

Drovetti, in the meantime, had been very active in Europe. On 24 September he was invested as Chevalier of the Order of St Louis by the King,[154] and on 11 October his second collection was sold to the Louvre for 150,000 francs, and his ideas on African education were published in the *Bulletin de la Société de Géographie* in Paris.[155] He was also conferring with Damas on the organisation of the diplomatic service in Egypt. The result was major changes.[156] The consulate at Cairo was to be suppressed. Malivoire was to be transferred to Aleppo, to replace Matthieu de Lesseps (the colleague of Drovetti twenty-four years before in Egypt), who was to go to Tunis. Malivoire, to his chagrin, again missed out: he was only temporarily to be Consul-General; for the post was to be regraded as a consulate, since the other consuls on the Syrian coast were to become independent, instead of being subordinate to the Consul at Aleppo as before. As for Egypt, Damas made clear that Drovetti had suggested the new arrangements there. Only one French representative was needed, in either Alexandria or Cairo, depending on where Mehemet Ali was residing. When that Consul was absent from Alexandria, there was to be a subordinate there to look after commercial matters (Clairambault) and an agent at Cairo. Drovetti was reappointed as Consul-General in Cairo at his old salary (24,000 francs), plus half the salary of the suppressed consulate (6,000), making a total of 30,000.[157]

There was another event that also changed Egypt fundamentally for Drovetti. His old friend and rival, the handsome and indefatigable Henry Salt died, at the age of forty-seven at Alexandria on the last day of October, from a liver complaint. He was buried in the city.[158] Although there is no reference in all his correspondence, we may be sure that Drovetti sincerely missed Salt and that he made a visit to his grave one of his first duties on his return. Just when history had made allies of the English and French, his old rival had gone. Salt's successor as Consul-General was John Barker (1771-1849), who had been Consul at Aleppo (1799-1825) and then at Alexandria from 1825 (he arrived in 1826). He was to serve until his retirement in 1833.

It is clear that all these arrangements for the French consular service were made before either Damas or Drovetti knew anything of the battle of Navarino, because of the panic they were thrown into when they did learn the news. Drovetti's return to Egypt was, in fact, delayed when the news reached Paris, because French relations with Egypt were uncertain. Egypt, more remarkably, did not find out until 2 November.[159] It was only on 6 November that Malivoire wrote to Damas with the news, and we must assume that he would have written to his Minister immediately, suggesting that he was not among the first to know. It was only now, nearly two weeks after the event, that Egypt learned that the Turkish-Egyptian fleet had been blown out of the waters of the bay of Navarino, and that Egypt had lost three frigates and three corvettes, the pride of her navy and the very ships that had cost so much to build in France and Italy. Fifty ships in all had been burned or sunk in three hours.[160]

What was the reaction of the old Viceroy to this disaster, which must have struck him like a thunderbolt? The diplomatic correspondence allows us to see his real feelings at this great crisis of his reign. The instantaneous and unanimous report was that Mehemet Ali's reaction was incredibly one of utter calm and courtesy. General Livron reassured Damas that the Viceroy's attitude to the subjects of the three powers involved had not changed, and that neutrality was still vital to Egypt's commerce.[161] There was no danger to any European living in Egypt from the government. The population was another matter, and steps were taken immediately to station police and troops, and to disarm the Turks. How could one possibly explain Mehemet Ali's reaction? He stated simply that the blame lay with the ministers of the Sultan, who as late as 29 October (sic, a week after the battle), were still suggesting that their policy might change. And by the end of the year he was blaming the English, not the French, for the loss of his fleet.[162]

Now Drovetti's return was indispensable. Damas gave his instructions. He was to tell the Viceroy how much the allies regretted the union of his fleet with the Turks, and that they were aware of his advice to the Sultan, presumably to end the war. Drovetti was to convince him to withdraw from the Morea. It would be a disastrous and dangerous position for Ibrahim were he cut off among a hostile population. He was finally to reassure the Viceroy that France would continue to assist his programme of modernisation in Egypt. And with the death of Salt, the French Consul was to protect the English in Egypt also – as if John Barker had not been appointed to succeed Salt.[163] Remembering the many times he had been left without adequate instructions, Drovetti had the foresight to ask Damas what answer he was to give Mehemet Ali if he sought allied protection for his evacuation of the Morea, given that this action would constitute disobedience to the Sultan.[164] By Christmas Day, 1827, Drovetti was waiting at Marseille for the *Lancier* under Captain Vigoroux to convey him back to Alexandria. Perhaps he knew that his last tour of duty would be short – eighteen months, in fact.

Drovetti's return

He arrived back in Alexandria on 6 January, 1828, to great acclaim. This was just after the return of the remnants of the Egyptian fleet from Navarino, on Christmas Day. In his own words, there was almost a holiday for his return.[165] He set about his basic task, reconciling Egypt and France. This was almost instantly undermined by news of a Greek attack on Crete. Mehemet Ali was very upset at the allies' failure to make the Greeks respect the frontiers: this had produced the Sultan's intransigence and undermined his own arguments for a compromise. Drovetti had a hard time to win over the Viceroy, but his success was spectacular. French warships and merchantmen alike were granted unlimited access to Egyptian ports, and even in the event of war, merchants would be protected. And Mehemet Ali promised to treat for evacuation of Greece, even though the Sultan had just granted him the Pashalik of Damascus. He had, however, learned a lesson: he stipulated that these undertakings were not to be published, unlike those Drovetti had taken back to France in 1827 and which had been published by the English, forcing him to send his fleet to Greece to prove his loyalty. The Viceroy asked, indeed, to be kept informed by the allies of their negotiations with the Sultan; in return he would give them information about Constantinople. He was as good as his word: he again asked the Sultan to accept the French proposals, and renounced his coveted pashalik. The Porte, however, ordered all European consuls in the Empire to cease their functions, with the exception of those in Egypt. The French consuls in Syria were all to return to Europe via Egypt.[166]

It would have been difficult to imagine a worse time for the mounting of a major scientific expedition to Egypt. On 11 February, 1828, however, from Paris Ippolito Rosellini, Professor of Oriental Languages at Pisa and

'Director of the literary expedition of Tuscany to Egypt' wrote to Drovetti.[167] Apart from the correspondence going back to 1826, Rosellini had met Drovetti recently in Paris, where the matter had obviously been discussed. The 'uncertainty of political events' alone was impeding the project, Rosellini admitted, but now that Drovetti had been restored to his post, his advice was sought about the proposed departure date of the expedition at the end of the coming summer (i.e. mid 1828). A week later, Champollion himself wrote.[168] He thanked Drovetti for all his kindness; for he also had met him in Paris. He noted that Drovetti agreed with him on the need to undertake the expedition 'promptly'. What Champollion referred to must be the protection of the Viceroy, which might not be extended forever, or more likely, the patronage of Drovetti, whose plans for retirement had been made known. The changed political conditions had, however, thrown these calculations into confusion, and Champollion suggested a date in August for his arrival, if politics did not forbid it. He recognised that the major problem was the *interior* of the country, since he proposed to journey at least as far as the Second Cataract. He thus relied on Drovetti alone, as he told him, to inform him of the help or obstacles which the Egyptians far from the control of the capital might provide. Drovetti's presence would, he concluded, be an assurance of success.

It seemed that always in the worst political crisis there would be further trouble for Drovetti from Terra Santa. In March, the Custodian, Tomasso da Mont'Asola in Jerusalem, informed him of further upheavals, this time financial. The Spaniards, who had previously contributed two-thirds of the expenses, while the Italians made up the other third, insisted now that both should contribute equally. The French contribution of 2,000 francs for the Holy Sepulchre was, furthermore, to be shared. And thirdly, a convoy from Naples had been robbed and tortured by pirates, and another from Portugal would not set out. Terra Santa was on the brink of financial collapse, with only 2,000 *talaris* in the treasury, 'hardly enough to satisfy the Turks in the next Ramadan'. Drovetti was asked to intervene with the Minister and the Admiral of the fleet in the Levant.[169]

Despite the critical situation in Greece, Mehemet Ali made a tour of inspection in March in Lower Egypt, and Drovetti accompanied him until April. The French were now blockading the ports of the Morea, and the Viceroy was very angry at the lack of respect for the honour of the Sultan and of Egypt, notably Ibrahim and his troops. He had, however, refused an order from the Sultan to strengthen the garrison on Cyprus, in order to hasten a settlement. The Sultan thus became increasingly suspicious of his vassal, and friends of Mehemet Ali in the Divan told him that a voluntary evacuation of his army would be disastrous for him. The Defterdar, in fact, was going to Greece with money and ordering all Ottoman governments to help Ibrahim, but his father wanted him to be allowed to withdraw to Roumeli. When the English threatened to blockade Egypt, Mehemet Ali told Drovetti that this would be disastrous only for European trade; for he would live off the land as the French army did in 1798.[170] In all of this, the French had an enormous advantage over the English, thanks to Drovetti's presence and sympathy with the Viceroy. The English demanded immediate replies when they asked if Mehemet Ali was joining his fate to that of the crumbling Ottoman Empire; they showed no diplomatic formality, as he complained to Drovetti. The French, on the other hand, were ready to give guarantees by April. The Foreign Minister assured Drovetti that the allies would protect Mehemet Ali from the Sultan's vengeance. Turkey was very worried about war with Russia, and Ibrahim had no chance of survival if the Greeks cut off his supplies. Even the French were considering a blockade of Egypt to force some action, but Drovetti was to reveal to Mehemet Ali that the French would claim to the Sultan that they were ready to bombard Alexandria.[171] The situation entered the realm of melodrama when letters fabricated by Egypt to defend Ibrahim from charges of negotiation with de Rigny and of causing the disaster of Navarino were intercepted by the Greeks. Drovetti again discussed the possibility of a blockade of the Morea; the Viceroy told him that the Sultan had already replied to this by promising to supply Ibrahim by land or withdraw him to Roumeli. Drovetti discovered, in fact, that Mehemet Ali had told his son to obey the Sultan unless forced to do otherwise by the 'last extremity', but that he did not expect to see his son again very soon. An alternative to pressure on Greece was a Russian invasion of Egypt: the Viceroy told Drovetti that he would imitate General Rostopchin in 1812, ravage Lower Egypt and retire to the Thebaid.[172]

These most intimate consultations of Drovetti with the Viceroy were cut short by the Consul's forced return to Alexandria in early May for health reasons. It may have been owing to hopes of an improvement in the political situation or simply his absence from this city and the usual unreliability of communications with Europe which meant that a most important letter was not written until 3 May,[173] a reply to the above mentioned letter from Champollion of 18 February. Drovetti regretted to say that he could not encourage the proposed expedition, because of the animosity in Egypt towards Europeans. Were everything dependent on the Viceroy there would be no difficulty, but the Pasha himself was a victim of this same antipathy. Mehemet Ali was not, therefore, able to guarantee the members' safety when Drovetti asked him about it (and remember that the Consul had just spent much time in discussions with the Viceroy). If, on the other hand, there was a change in relations between the allies and Turkey, then, Drovetti assured Champollion, he could set out without further notice (a clear condition, note). This letter has been used as the vital evidence for some kind of treachery on Drovetti's part towards Champollion. It is necessary to point out that their relations had so far been most cordial ever since the scholar had been working on the Torino collection of antiquities, that until a year ago, Drovetti had been encouraging the expedition, that this answer was not Drovetti's own opinion but that of Mehemet Ali whom he had consulted, that far from inventing obstacles, they were on the contrary very real, and that finally Drovetti left completely open the possibility of the expedition's taking place if the conditions he cited were seen empirically to have changed; indeed, he encouraged him in that case to set out.

It is opportune here to examine further the matters raised. This letter finally reached Paris and was then sent on to Champollion by his brother on 28 July. Had it arrived, Champollion admitted that he would not have set out.[174] Here is his own admission that the arguments were convincing. The dangers for Europeans at this time are confirmed by Pascal Coste, who was leaving just after the news came of the fate of the Egyptian navy at Navarino. The whole population of Alexandria was up in arms, the military guard had to be doubled, and orders were sent all over Egypt that no European was to be harmed.[175] When the expedition arrived in August, moreover, at the first meeting with Drovetti, the Consul added the further consideration on the Viceroy's part that it would be compromising to allow such a numerous expedition from a country at war with the Sultan to have access to Egypt. By this time, however, the treaty for the evacuation of the Morea had been signed; conditions had thus improved.[176] In a letter to the Foreign Minister, Drovetti had to explain what had happened. He stated that Mehemet Ali was very angry when the expedition arrived, believing that Drovetti has disregarded his advice.[177]

On his return to Alexandria, Drovetti was again concerned with the fate of Greek slaves; he found that his intimacy with Mehemet Ali since his return was exciting adverse comment. Guilleminot assured him that Egyptian ports were to be blockaded and supplies cut off to Ibrahim, and Drovetti consulted the English Consul Barker on the matter. Mehemet Ali was putting a bold face on things: 'Let the blockade begin so that I do not have to tolerate these discussions', he cried.

As an example of the French government's sang-froid, a most inopportune arrival in June 1828 was baron Isidore Taylor in connection with a very important state mission. He was sent, incredibly, to negotiate the gift of an obelisk to commemorate the Napoleonic expedition, and to see to its transport back to Paris! It is not surprising that he failed and that a second mission was required two years later in 1830. This ended with the arrival of the Luxor obelisk in Paris on 23 December, 1833 at a total cost of an amazingly modest 17,000 francs, so that Taylor brought back 83,000 of the 100,000 francs granted him. In recommending Taylor, Felix Lajard passed on to Drovetti the compliments of two famous French orientalists, Abel Remusat and Jean Saint-Martin, whom he must have met in Paris when on leave.[178] It is surprising that such an official visitor to Egypt says so little of Drovetti. He only notes the Consul's house in Alexandria as one of the most remarkable in the city, and most interesting for its memories, because it had been occupied by Napoleon during the expedition. There are, otherwise, only allusions to Drovetti's trips to Siwah and Abu Simbel.[179]

Mehemet Ali finally in June announced his intentions to Drovetti: Ibrahim would be recalled, but a garrison would remain in Greece, and the Greek slaves would be surrendered as long as, to save face, it looked as if they were being exchanged for Egyptian prisoners. Drovetti noted that the Viceroy was obviously relying on the protection of the allies against the Sultan.[180] The Foreign Minister informed Drovetti, however, that his government was sure that a blockade would not be enough to effect an evacuation, that an invasion of Greece would be needed, and that Mehemet Ali, in fact, favoured this in order to give himself a pretext. England was now prepared to support this, even if it did not participate. Twenty thousand troops were to sail from Toulon in August. The key man in all of this plotting and pressure was Drovetti, who had to keep Mehemet Ali informed and make him understand that it was – in part, at least – to save his honour and to prevent Ibrahim trying to occupy the Roumeli, which would have been a brilliant stroke.[181] The vital agreement for the evacuation was gained from Ibrahim in July, just before an envoy from the Sultan ordered him to retire to Roumeli. Mehemet Ali was now in precisely the dilemma he had wished to avoid, faced with disobedience to his overlord. Drovetti (and Barker) had the difficult task of convincing him to send his fleet to bring back the army.[182]

The convention of Alexandria

The vital step of a formal agreement for the evacuation of Greece signed by Mehemet Ali was now to be taken. This was just in time; for there was much allied naval activity and their squadrons were blocking the ports of the Morea.[183] The English Admiral Codrington arrived in Alexandria on 1 August, the Viceroy two days later. On 6 August, Drovetti accompanied the Admiral to an audience. The discussions were naturally drawn out. The result was, however, that Mehemet Ali asked Drovetti to draw up a convention which would be the least compromising to his government. The French Consul was therefore the key person in drafting the Convention of Alexandria, and acted precisely as protector of the

156

Viceroy in one of the most delicate moments of his career. It is a striking coincidence that Drovetti's role was so crucial in 1828 shortly before his tour of duty finished, exactly as it had been in 1807 when he had not long arrived.[184] The convention was signed on 9 August, and the first division of the Egyptian fleet set out for the Morea just four days later to bring home the Egyptian army.

The Franco-Tuscan expedition

Meanwhile, on the last day of July, the *Egle* had put out from Toulon early in the morning. On board were the fourteen members of the Franco-Tuscan expedition (ill. 25), led by Champollion and Rosellini.[185] They arrived on 18 August. Champollion at least was installed by Drovetti in a 'delightful' apartment in the consulate, and the whole expedition dined at Drovetti's 'sumptuous' table. Then at 8 a.m. on 24 August Drovetti drove Champollion and Lenormant in his calèche to present them to Mehemet Ali. Champollion admitted to being spoiled by everyone, especially Drovetti, and this despite the latter's terrible suffering from pains in the joints caused by dengue fever.[186]

There was only one thing which caused Champollion alarm. Before he left Cairo he had to obtain not only safe conducts, but also firmans for excavations; for he had been charged by the King to conduct excavations in order to bring back treasures for the royal museum – despite the fact that he had been denied any funds for such work![187] When told that Drovetti and Anastasy alone had such rights, Champollion penned a memoir threatening an international incident, and citing the permits granted to Belzoni, Passalacqua, Laborde and Rifaud solely for sordid commercial exploitation. His motive, by contrast, was to further science, and he was, moreover, an agent of the French King. Drovetti knew the East better than the young scholar. He did not send Mehemet Ali the memoir. Instead he suggested to the Viceroy that he and Anastasy should cede their rights to Champollion. The matter was thus resolved, thanks to Drovetti's skills and generosity. In Champollion's mind, however, the episode was a formative one: he came to believe that the attempt to dissuade him from coming to Egypt in the first place had been motivated by selfish concerns.[188] The expedition left Alexandria for Cairo and the south on 14 September.

In August two envoys also arrived from the French King, namely Saint-Leger and Gros, who had come especially to liberate as many Greek slaves in Egypt as possible. Mehemet Ali advised them to be as discreet as possible when they were presented to him. The delicacy of their task may be imagined, but they were not the first visitors to Egypt under such conditions to rely on Drovetti, who 'knows so well and has known for so long the means of success in this country'. He immediately suggested

25. The Franco-Tuscan expedition in Egypt. All members of the expedition are shown: Champollion is the seated, bearded figure, Rosellini the figure standing centre

enlisting the help of the Patriarch. Gros was already sure that the number of Greek slaves in Egypt had been greatly exaggerated in Europe but that it was clear, on the other hand, that the Viceroy would do nothing to help. The two envoys soon came to rely on secret Greek agents to draw up lists of owners of slaves and their addresses.[189]

At this vital juncture, another alarm was sounded about Drovetti's health. In September he had to go to the country for eight or ten days. We are fortunate that the report of the three doctors has been preserved.[190] On 28 September doctors Vernoni, Imperiale and Roubio signed a certificate that Drovetti was suffering the third attack of a long and painful illness which he had had since 1825. It was caused by the 'repercussions of a herpetic humour' along with chronic gastro-enteritis, and he had suffered as well from sciatica for seven years. The doctors therefore recommended his prompt return to Europe, or at least a rest of several months. This severe condition is confirmed by none other than Champollion, who agreed that Drovetti had to escape from Egypt or he would be dead within a year. Not least depressing was the strong impression made on his mind by the reflection that everyone else who had been there as long as he had was no longer alive.[191]

By the end of September, Champollion was at Cairo, had visited Sais, and was about to see Sakkarah and Gizeh. He sent best wishes for Drovetti's recovery, and thanked him for his kindnesses: obviously excellent wine among other things, in which a toast had been drunk to him at Sais. Champollion took the opportunity to urge Drovetti to acquire a trilingual stone in a mosque at Cairo which Lord Prudhoe had shown him. The letter ended with a desperate plea for the sending on of any correspondence which had arrived from Europe: the expedition had not received any for two months.[192] When Bibent left the group next month for reasons of health, Champollion sent him back to Cairo with a letter asking Drovetti to obtain a passage for him back to France.[193]

The first division of Ibrahim's army returned at the end of September, and the commander himself in October, with 18,000 veterans.[194] Drovetti's illness meant that Saint-Leger and Gros had to accomplish their very difficult redemption of Greek slaves without his help. After one month they were disgusted. They had found no honour, they said, in any Greek, slave or free. They were being hoodwinked at every turn by both categories, simply interested in extorting money. Priests presented slaves for ransom who were already free, and pocketed the proceeds. Women who told harrowing stories were found to have escaped with enormous sums in cash and jewellery. Greeks pretended to be master and slave and then divided the ransom payment. Hospitals where the freed slaves were maintained thought only of profits. By the middle of October, only 120 had been freed at a cost of 60,000 francs.[195]

Some weeks later, the novelist Jane Porter wrote to Drovetti from England. She was a close friend of Sarah Belzoni, 'who seemed to live only for the memory of her deceased husband', and who especially wanted to see Drovetti and reconcile the living with the dead. In the meantime, however, she was preparing the publication of her husband's greatest discovery, the tomb of Seti, and was asking both Champollion and Drovetti as the two greatest antiquarians to give her their support.[196] The help was certainly granted by Champollion; of Drovetti's response we are in ignorance.

By the end of November, nearly three hundred Greek slaves had been freed. Lists of all those owned by Greeks (sic) were being drawn up, and they were being brought to a monastery for interrogation. Almost all the freed slaves elected to remain in Egypt. Drovetti had hired two ships to take those who wished back to Europe. He himself repatriated at his own expense thirty-seven to the Cyclades; for this the Greek government issued him with three certificates.[197]

The strain of all this activity exacerbated the breakdown of the Consul's health. The Foreign Minister was convinced, and the major questions of Egyptian politics had been solved. On 28 November, 1828 de la Ferronnays wrote to Jean François Mimaut, Consul at Venice, appointing him temporary replacement as Consul-General in Alexandria at a salary of 30,000 francs.[198]

Diplomatic problems may have been solved, but Egypt's crisis deepened. The enormous burden of the Greek war was not lifted; for the Sultan immediately demanded compensation in food, money and troops. No fewer than seventy ships laden with grain sailed by the end of December, four million piastres were sent off, and a force of 20,000 men was being raised by conscription.

In the same month the wish of Drovetti's friend Artaud was finally fulfilled. The Consul was elected an Associate of the Lyons Academy. The delay might suggest that not all members supported his admission, but the truth was more simple, as Artaud explained. The rules of the Academy required that the candidate express a desire to be admitted, and Drovetti had not made a formal request.[199] Also of interest in the cultural and scientific sphere are the three letters addressed to Drovetti at the end of 1828 and in the first months of the new year by Charles Mirbel, Administrator of the Garden of the King of France, looking forward to the setting up of a botanical garden in Egypt in order to extend the famous system of exchanges with the Paris garden. It was only natural that Mirbel should turn to Drovetti to ensure the success of the scheme.[200]

It was also in 1828 that Drovetti made one of his most important introductions to Mehemet Ali of a European who had come to serve Egypt, the veterinarian Pierre Hamont. On leaving the audience, Hamont met Osman Bey, the Scottish soldier (in fact, Donald Thompson) who had come to Egypt with Fraser in 1807, been converted to Islam and spent the rest of his life there until his death from dysentery in 1835. Hamont asked him if there were many Europeans at Rosetta where he was to be posted. Drovetti instantly intervened, looking at him hard, and said: 'Do not worry about that; seek the company of Turks: it is preferable to that of Europeans in Egypt.'[201] This is the only mention of Drovetti by Hamont, but the story is very telling, indicating his disenchantment shortly before his departure.

The new year found him and his English colleague John Barker in close consultation with Mehemet Ali, who was very angry. British ships had been blockading Crete, preventing him sending aid to his troops there, and the Greeks had responded to his neutrality towards them by attacking his grain fleet to Constantinople. He saw the European powers as increasingly hostile to him.[202]

It was on 20 January, 1829 that the royal envoys sent to free Greek slaves returned to France and made their final report. Despite claims that there were up to 12,000 Greek slaves in Egypt, they were convinced that

160

the true figure was closer to 8,000 or 9,000. They were owned by all nations except Arabs. Many had converted to Islam, but then they could no longer be slaves by law, and might expect to rise to positions of power, rather like the slave dynasty of the Mamelukes. Most of those held by fellow Greeks had been ransomed. Women had been the hardest of all to find, for they had naturally for the most part entered harems. There had been endless deceit in order to profit from the ransoms. In all, three hundred had been returned to the Morea, but they had been unwanted, there were not preparations to receive them, and there had even been a plot to wreck one of the ships.[203] In all this saga, Drovetti had played a leading role, as the envoys declared.

The repercussions of the Russo-Turkish war were now beginning to be felt in Egypt. Pezzoni, Consul-General for Russia, departed in January and the next month Russian ships attacked Egyptian convoys heading for Constantinople. This happily gave Mehemet Ali a pretext for not acceding to the Sultan's demand that Ibrahim be sent to command the 20,000 men despatched. As always, Drovetti was a key figure in negotiation and communications; after all, he had represented the Russians before. The Russian admiral Heyden accused the Viceroy of preparing for war against his country. Drovetti gave the admiral's letter to the Viceroy and conveyed the latter's response to the admiral.[204] Drovetti's own allegations were clearly spelled out to his Foreign Minister: he deplored such hostilities against the only Islamic prince whose intentions had always been pacific. Another incident of the same time, but with very serious ramifications, reveals rather a contrary picture, and certainly the strength of Drovetti's character. In March the second officer of the Egyptian ship the *Fulminante* deserted. Drovetti urged that he be given asylum on a French ship, saying 'We are not the gendarmes of the Egyptian government.'[205] If this account is true, the incident must have caused some friction with Mehemet Ali.

The earliest months of 1829 were also remarkable for the letters from Champollion. The expedition spent ten days at Abu Simbel: 'we are carrying off the whole of Abu Simbel in our portfolios'. In their folders the artists had copies of all reliefs and inscriptions in detail and in colour. The like had never been accomplished before. Now they were to return down the Nile, planning to be at Thebes in February and Champollion assured Drovetti that he would be delighted to meet him there. It would have been indeed a most striking combination: the excavator who had known Thebes so well now for at least seventeen years, and the young philologist who could read all the texts, but it was not to be. Drovetti missed one of the unique chances of his life. Champollion's last request was typically for political news: he wanted newspapers, however old![206] Another letter a month later, from near Ombos, thanked Drovetti for letters and for the generous provisions which the Consul was sending. Champollion for his part was helping Sarah Belzoni (as Jane Porter had requested) with information about the tomb of Seti. He also entered into a little plot with Drovetti. The French government had asked him about the possibility of transporting an obelisk to Paris. Champollion urged Drovetti not to discourage it, but to induce it to undertake the project; for once having begun it, it would not give up, even if difficulties later arose![207] By March, the expedition was at Thebes and, thanks to Drovetti, 'swimming in plenty'. Thebes was 'a little Paris, a sojourn of pleasure and indulgence'. Hearing that Drovetti was about to leave Egypt, Champollion regretted the loss of a 'zealous friend as much as a protector in this strange land'. Now they would have to rely on their own 'star' instead of on his providence. Champollion was still busy on the tomb of Seti, but hoped to see Drovetti in Europe at the end of the year to express his gratitude.[208] They did indeed meet at Toulon in January 1830. The vital contribution of these letters is the cordial relations which they attest as existing between the two men after some initial misunderstandings, and despite some contradictory views to which Champollion was to give vent later.

Drovetti was not, of course, to escape the endless pesterings of the Terra Santa in his last months. The Custodian sent him a dossier of requests in March with the claim that the only hope for some action was through Drovetti's representations in Rome or Paris. We do not have the list, but from the accompanying letter we may deduce that a shortage of priests was a major concern; that there was some plan to free the organisation from 'bullying' by Greeks and Armenians; and that some solution was needed to the bickering between Greeks and Copts.[209]

Drovetti continued to facilitate the exchange of Greek and Egyptian prisoners. The Greek government sent back the crews of captured Egyptian ships, while Greek women handed in lists of missing relatives who were thought to be in Egypt. The French chargé d'affaires in Aegina, de Valmy, informed him, after the arrival of a cargo of repatriated Greeks, that providing for those who had no family was a heavy burden and suggested that preference in ransoming slaves might be given to those sought by their families! Drovetti was also asked to intervene in the case of a Greek woman who had traced one of her sons to a British agent, who immediately handed him over, but another was held by Selim Bey, who refused even to sell him; the mother was sure that a daughter was in the harem of Ibrahim.[210] Of great concern to Drovetti also was his own condition. It was becoming too late in the season for him to be able to take advantage of the baths and mineral waters which the doctors pronounced as essential for his health.[211]

La Contemporaine sails in

Just before Drovetti's departure from Alexandria, another ship arrived in June 1829 carrying one of the most infamous women of her time, the French journalist, 'La Contemporaine'. Elzelina van Aylde Yonghe (c. 1777-1845) was the daughter of a Russian father (the self-styled Count Tolstoy) and a Dutch mother. She married at thirteen and divorced the next year, to become mistress of Marescot, Moreau (whom she accompanied to Italy), Talleyrand and Ney. She later changed her name to Ida de Ste Elme, and tried to enter the Théâtre Française. Failing there, she went to Italy with one of Napoleon's suite. Now she was touring Italy and the East, on which she wrote memoirs. After later becoming involved in defamation and forgery suits, she retired to Brussels where she died.[212] If only Drovetti had known that she was to become one of his most unrelenting critics and that his name would be attacked at every opportunity in the account of her travels, in no fewer than six volumes! She regarded his whole term of office as a proof that one should never appoint a foreigner as French Consul; she was, on the other hand, utterly charmed by his successor, Mimaut, a man of merit, 'without impetuosity or fits of passion', who would 'by the simple contrast between dignity and caprice and hauteur' soon make everyone forget Drovetti![213]

She began by giving a totally new explanation of his retirement. This was occasioned not by sickness or exhaustion after twenty-six years in Egypt, but by embarrassment. There had been a struggle over consular rights between the French Vice-Consul Clairambault and the Austrian Consul, Acerbi. According to La Contemporaine, Drovetti was a friend of both these 'transalpines' and antiquarians, and feeling himself unable to take sides, he quickly left Egypt! Not only that, the consulate was left in total disorder. She tells that it was located near the Hotel of the Three Anchors. Drovetti was accused of having removed important papers. What was the source of all this? None other than Mimaut. The story, at least as an explanation for a hasty and necessary abandonment of his post, is not flattering to the journalist's intelligence. The only credit granted him is the admission that along with the support of Murat, he was appointed because of his 'undeniable talents'. This was, however, immediately undercut by sneers at the Consul's supposed own statement that he had ruined himself in French service. La Contemporaine asserted that he retired with a yearly income of 40,000 francs, in other words, far in excess of his full salary.[214]

Another way to damage Drovetti was by association. He was a friend of the Tuscan Consul Rosetti, who, claimed La Contemporaine, was a crook and even a slave-trader, as was the agent at Rosetta, Lanzoni. Drovetti's own nephew at Alexandria was another slave-trader.[215] All this seems to have been devised to undermine Drovetti's reputation for his help to Greek slaves in the recent war. It was claimed that his horror of slavery did not extend to those of a different colour. Mimaut was the only European in Egypt who did not use slaves, she asserted.

Then there was his 'frenzy for excavation' (rage de fouilles) as she put it. This activity was not, 'as had been falsely claimed', for the benefit of French museums, but for his own advantage. She contrasted this with the work of the French Consul in Greece, Fauvel, who devoted thirty years to research and intended to donate twenty cases of antiquities to the nation. This was prevented only because they were seized by the Greeks during the war.[216]

As if all this were not enough, Drovetti had not forwarded one of La Contemporaine's favourite projects, the housing of the Egyptian peasantry à la européenne, that is, in little houses made of wood! To heighten his crime in not bettering the lot of the fellahin, she suggested that, although he could speak Arabic and Turkish without an interpreter, he was just like all the other Europeans in Egypt, interested only in flattering Mehemet Ali and obtaining antiquities.[217]

What lay behind this unrelieved attack on the Consul, published only long after he had returned to Europe and whom she had not even known in Egypt? It seems that it was Drovetti who had induced La Contemporaine to come to Egypt in the first place.[218] He made every effort to persuade her to come, then said publicly that he did not know what she could do there, that everything had already been said about Egypt, and that it was not a country for a woman.

There is also a variety of valuable incidental information. Drovetti had a nephew who was a landowner in the Fayum, and who arranged for the sale of his furniture when he left. She also mentions Iousouf Cachef who supervised Drovetti's excavations, and on her way to the Valley of the Kings she saw the remains of his vegetable garden in Thebes. The Pedemonte family was not only mentioned by her, but she knew them very well and provides, alone of all sources, the vital missing link for the reconstruction of Drovetti's family tree: Pedemonte was indeed, as others say, his son-in-law, but by the daughter of Mme Drovetti from her previous marriage. She states that Mme Drovetti lived in Paris, but owned the Palais de France (the French consulate) at Alexandria, which, although unfit for the residence of the national representative, brought in a good rent, as she hastens to emphasise.[219]

La Contemporaine was, in fact, in total agreement on one major matter with the man she despised so much: the Greek war. She did her best to stress the tolerance of the Turks and the Greek atrocities which had motivated the reprisals. She praised Ibrahim's mercy during the siege of Navarino in contrast to the Greek massacres of the Turkish garrisons which surrendered, recounted the treacherous attack on the Egyptian fleet at Navarino according to the details given her by General le Tellier, and described how the Greeks had used women as human shields in the sortie from Missalonghi. In short, the Europeans had misplaced sympathies for 'the Christians of the East'.[220]

Farewell to Egypt

Drovetti's departure was dramatic. Knowing that Mimaut was on his way, and anxious not to miss a whole year's cure, Drovetti sailed out of Alexandria on 20 June, 1829 on board the *Acteon*. He had not gone more than a few leagues when the ship carrying Mimaut was sighted making for the harbour. The two vessels hove to, a dinghy was launched, and Mimaut was carried across to the *Acteon*. He was thus able to greet his predecessor, who apologised for not having been able to remain to welcome him. He had left Clairambault in charge, who was now to be posted to Tripoli. The two Consuls-General thus conferred for half an hour until a fresh wind sprang up and they had to part. The *Acteon* continued on its way, bearing the fifty-three years old Drovetti from the land where he had spent almost every day of the last twenty-six years of his life, for most of them the most powerful European in the country. An era had ended.

Whither was he bound? Thanks to Mimaut's first letter to the Foreign Minister, we know. He must have been told by Drovetti during that brief meeting on the *Acteon*. This ship would put in at Naples. Drovetti was appropriately to take the waters in the land of his birth. Little did he know that in his long and active life almost as many years lay ahead of him as he had spent in Egypt, which he was not to see again.[221]

V   Private citizen once more
1829-1952

After an almost uninterrupted residence in Egypt of twenty-six years, Drovetti had a European reputation for not only his diplomatic career but also the fame of his two collections of antiquities in the Torino and Louvre museums, not to mention the bonds both professional and personal formed with travellers of all nations through his famous hospitality. Whether he knew it or not, unlimited possibilities for activity opened up for him. Retirement he was not to have.

The first event in his new life would have been the dreaded quarantine. Those who arrived in France from places like the Levant spent a month either on board their ship if it were staying in harbour, or in the wretched quarters of the quarantine station. The weather by this time would have been becoming perhaps unpleasantly warm, but this at least was preferable to the freezing conditions endured by Champollion at the end of the same year which contributed to his tragically early death.[1]

The world to which Drovetti returned must have made him feel as if he had been dreaming. Much had happened since the fall of Napoleon, but it was for the most part as if the clock had been put back to before the French Revolution, to the politics and society of Drovetti's youth.

The clock turned back: the Concert of Europe

Twenty three years of war ended with the Congress of Vienna, supported by the Holy Alliance of Russia, Austria and Prussia, the policemen of Europe. The continent enjoyed, with the exception of some short and local wars (notably the Crimean and Franco-Prussian), a century of peace. On the other hand, absolute monarchy had been restored wherever and as far as possible, a system of international intervention had been set up to crush all attempts at liberalisation, and this was bolstered by censorship and forces of secret police. The system broke down for the first time through Canning's 'leadership of European liberal and romantic opinion in favour of the Greek war of independence'.[2]

The restored Bourbons in France under Louis XVIII 'kept the social organisation of the Revolution, and the administrative organisation of Napoleon'[3] but reimposed on these two foundations a monarchy with very wide powers. Louis was clever enough to maintain the essential balance between extremists and moderates, but with Charles X (1824-1830), much less politically skilful, the forces of reaction became predominant. In Spain, following the extreme democracy of the 1812 constitution, the Bourbons were restored under Ferdinand VII (1813-1833). The Napoleonic wars allowed the Tories to maintain their domination of English politics and this continued for the next fifteen years as well, until 1830. The thirty-eight states of Germany, mostly autocratic, in 1815 explicitly formed 'a confederation to prevent a federation'[4] with an impotent assembly, but the country was, for the most part, politically quiescent. The most ramshackle state in Europe was the Austrian Empire, composed of eleven nationalities ruled by Francis II (1792-1835) and Metternich, Foreign Minister 1809-1848.

In Italy, Austrian control was almost universal. Lombardy and Venice were directly governed; Tuscany was under the Emperor's brother, Ferdinand; Modena under Francis IV; Parma under Maria Luisa. Ferdinand of Naples had to sign an alliance with Austria. Only Piedmont retained a nominal independence. The fall of Napoleon also saw the revival of Catholicism: Pius VII was a hero; the monarchs abandoned their antagonism typical of the Enlightenment towards the Church; the educated returned to the faith; and the Jesuits were restored.

In Drovetti's native Piedmont, a most reactionary regime was reestablished in 1815. The constitution of 1770 was essentially restored; the Napoleonic Code was abolished along with equality before the law, the right to a fair trial, and religious freedom; patriarchal and ecclesiastical privileges were reinstated.[5] Genoa was given to Piedmont by the Congress of Vienna, and the kingdom, with a population of $3^1/2$ millions, now had an interest in the sea.

The position of the younger liberals – people like Cesare Balbo, Luigi Provana, Santorre de Santarosa – was now complicated:

> for Balbo and his friends dynastic loyalty, wishfully identified with Italian patriotism, remained overriding. Sharing the Lombards' romantic vision and their belief in a moderate constitution as a guarantee of liberty, these Piedmontese nobles retained a distinctive pride in Savoyard destiny. The house of Savoy was exalted not just as the only true Italian dynasty, but because of its military traditions.... The Napoleonic military epic retained its appeal for those young noble officers.[6]

Drovetti was on intimate terms with many of the moderates such as Cesare Balbo and Federico Sclopis, not to mention the Prince of Carignano. These Piedmontese nobles were also zealous Catholics, as Drovetti was increasingly to become, but, unlike him, closed to 'the most modern and progressive currents in Europe'. The ex-consul was in contact with the broadest European influences, as his extensive travels after 1829 show.

The apparent calm had been shattered as early as 1820. A military revolution broke out in Spain, forcing the King to restore the constitution of 1812. The revolution quickly spread to Portugal and Naples, and to Piedmont in the next year. In Naples it was led by the army and the *carbonari*, the secret societies whose members dreamed of liberal institutions and Italian independence. The King granted the constitution, but then internal divisions broke out, and no preparations were made to resist an invasion. In March 1821, the army under General Pepe was defeated by the Austrians at Rieti, and the revolution collapsed.

In Piedmont, there was sharp conflict between the radicals and moderates, which was further complicated by dynastic loyalties. In January 1821 student unrest was crushed by the army, but in March democratic officers at Alessandria proclaimed the Spanish constitution, and the moderates joined them. Vittorio Emanuele refused to grant the constitution and abdicated in March, nominating Carlo Alberto (the Prince of Carignano) as regent. He accepted the new constitution, but refused the main aim of the movement, war against Austria. Accused of being a counter-revolutionary, he fled. Conflict then broke out between the democrats in Alessandria and moderates in Torino. These discussions were terminated by another Austrian invasion, victorious at Novara (8 April), and followed by executions, many imprisonments, and the dismissal without trial of hundreds of officers, civil servants and teachers. Austrian armies had thus restored the kings in both Naples and Piedmont. They had been able to capitalise, however, on major dissensions among the liberals.

The new King was Vittorio's brother, Carlo Felice (1821-1831). His reign has been described as 'simply repressive', characterised by 'Jesuitical bigotry, and a system of absolute immobility and opposition to any proposal for change, even if only administrative'; the army was turned into a police force. The Austrians were the bulwark against any revolutionary ideas, but even they were concerned that repression would produce only a worse explosion. As for the King himself,

> the ardours of religious rapture combined with rancour against his old liberal allies, who were now most bitter enemies, and perhaps also the need to substitute a new faith for the old ideals of glory and nationality, had acted on his closed and complicated character, driving him to a kind of politico-religious mysticism of reactionary inspiration, which in time assumed almost superstitious form, and which finally coloured his entire policies, both internal and foreign.'[7]

It was to this world that Drovetti returned in 1829. On the surface, this Europe was little different from that of 1815, but the cauldron which had bubbled over in 1820 and 1821 was still seething. Drovetti himself, however, was for some time to remain deeply involved in African politics.

The Algerian crisis and the Drovetti Project.[8]

In April 1827 the ruler of one of the three 'Regencies' on the north African coast, the Dey of Algier, committed the famous insult against the French Consul of hitting him in the face with his fly-whisk. Along with Tripoli and Tunis, Algier was formally a vassal of the Sultan but in fact in revolt against him. The Regencies caused considerable offence to the European powers by being centres of slave-trading and piracy. France was at the time, however, powerless to avenge her insulted honour because of the Greek war and then the Russian war with Turkey. A diplomatic solution was attempted in 1828, but the ship bearing the French envoy was fired upon.

It was on his return to Egypt from leave in 1828 that Drovetti became increasingly excited about his plan to settle the whole affair to the benefit of many parties. He even so far overcame the customary reticence between French and English diplomats as to discuss his ideas with the English consul, John Barker. When he was granted retirement in 1829, however, he made formal representations to the French government in the person of the sympathetic Minister of Foreign Affairs, Polignac. His remarkable proposal was that Mehemet Ali should be deputed by the French to punish the Dey of Algier. His reasons were simple: a French expedition would be too difficult and costly and would excite jealousy, mainly from the English. Egyptian troops, on the other hand, were used to the desert, the Sultan would approve of his leading Pasha's reducing rebellious vassals to obedience, the Viceroy would win the gratitude of the European powers as well by crushing such unattractive regimes, and everyone would be delighted at the end of Barbary piracy. Charles X approved this proposal in October. The French Ambassador in Constantinople, Guilleminot, was then to obtain the Sultan's approval, and his aide-de-camp, Huder, was sent to Egypt to assist Mimaut, the Consul-General, in negotiations with Mehemet Ali.

Huder arrived in Alexandria on 16 November. The Viceroy immediately accepted the proposal, but was concerned over the attempt to obtain a firman from the Sultan: he would immediately suspect French-Egyptian collusion. Mehemet Ali's favourite son, Ibrahim, was as usual appointed commander-in-chief and given a force of forty thousand men. What was the Viceroy's price? He asked for a loan of 4 million talaris (20 million francs), to be repaid within four years, and the gift of four warships of eighty guns each. At this, the negotiators drew back, whereupon Mehemet Ali stated that Drovetti had assured him about all of these terms.[9] It seems that, indeed, before leaving Egypt, Drovetti had assured the Viceroy of complete French support, and Mimaut also knew about such conditions. Huder decided, however, to return to France for further instructions.

Guilleminot had meanwhile been negotiating in Constantinople. The Porte did not forbid the project, but said that it was more difficult than the French imagined, and that Turkey was fully occupied with the Russians. The French Ambassador threatened European intervention, which would mean a presence in Africa as colonists. The Prime Minister finally offered to send Taher Pasha to Algier to negotiate. This man was a mortal enemy of Mehemet Ali; the Porte, more importantly, informed the English Ambassador, Sir Robert Gordon, of a French plot in collusion with the Viceroy.

On Huder's reporting to Polignac, the Minister accepted the Viceroy's conditions. The problem was, how to win over his colleagues in the Council of Ministers. They refused point-blank, especially the Minister for the Navy, Haussez, to hand over any ship that had once flown the French flag. As a compromise in January 1830, they offered 8 million francs as a *gift*, so that Mehemet Ali could buy four ships or have the French build them for him, and also an interest-free loan of 20 million francs.[10] Drovetti left Paris immediately to go to Toulon to convey these terms to Huder and 'any other advice which his understanding and experience could offer'.[11] Polignac told him that, after that, he could go on to Italy for the sake of his health! There was one major difficulty which Drovetti instantly saw: the French government wanted the Viceroy to begin the campaign against Algier instantly, but the money would not arrive until a month later. He suggested an immediate advance of two million francs; Polignac saw the point and agreed.[12]

The Drovetti Project had thus led to concrete proposals by the French government, and by this time everyone knew what was afoot. The English Consul in Egypt, of course, knew – Drovetti had spoken to him as early as 1828 – but so did everyone else in the East. The last man to find out seems to have been the English Ambassador in Paris, Lord Stuart de Rothesay. He had, however, noted Drovetti's frequent meetings with Polignac, and an article in *Le Constitutionnel* of 8 October, 1829 about Egypt, reputedly written by Drovetti. He had in fact questioned the ex-consul, but obtained no satisfaction. When French newspapers published news of the expedition, even Rothesay could no longer remain unenlightened.

He confronted Polignac in December, and was told that this was the first that the Minister knew of any French backing for the Viceroy's expedition against Algier! The wily Metternich had, however, intercepted Polignac's despatches to Constantinople. The English saw the whole scheme, naturally, as an extension of French influence in Africa, but based their case on the lack of approval by the Sultan. Confronted by the evidence, Polignac wrote a long note of explanation to London on 18 January, 1830. The French Ambassador there, Laval, also tried to allay suspicions by claiming that the whole plan was simply to return the Regencies to the control of the Sultan.

As opposition increased in European circles, so that of Polignac's colleagues revived. What if Mehemet Ali should fail? How could French honour be upheld by a Turkish vassal if he succeeded? Most important of all, Prussia finally vetoed French plans for redrawing the map of Europe on the expected demise of the Ottoman Empire, so that French armies were now freed from that theatre for operations in Africa.

The turning-point thus came at the end of January 1830. The French government did a volte-face, and approved a totally different plan. The French would avenge their own honour in Algier; Mehemet Ali would be their ally, and subdue Tripoli and Tunis. The earlier offer to the Viceroy was completely changed: he now needed no money for ships, and the loan was reduced to ten million francs.[13] The situation was a farce. Huder returned to Egypt on 8 February and began negotiating on the basis of the terms offered in January. The Viceroy agreed to let his son Ibrahim decide what to do. Ibrahim and Huder were on the point of agreement when the new terms arrived on 17 February.

It is extraordinary that Mehemet Ali did not react more violently at the total disrespect with which he was being treated. Everything indicates, however, that he was totally calm – as after Navarino – and simply by the end of February definitively rejected the new terms.[14] He thus had the last say, and left France in the very unpleasant situation of having to deal by herself with a most difficult problem. The main reason he always gave with endless patience to the French diplomats was that he could not, as 'the hero and hope of Islam', ally with a Christian power. The real reason was perhaps revealed in an interview with Barker, the English Consul, on 7 March, when he turned to offer England his help in the East, especially against Russia.[15] The appalling clumsiness of the French had thus fundamentally changed the political sympathies of the Viceroy. The great scheme conceived by Drovetti had come to nothing. It is significant, however, that such a momentous shift in Egyptian foreign policy followed immediately after Drovetti's departure from Egypt. One cannot help thinking that such a fiasco would not have occurred had he remained as Consul-General. The French were forced to solve their own problems in Algier, with repercussions both at home and abroad which still have their echo to this day.

Rendezvous with Champollion

It was on his return to France at the very end of 1829 that Champollion in his correspondence finally gave vent to his real feelings about Drovetti. This was caused partly by a perceived contrast with his successor Mimaut, who showed Champollion a 'true affection' which he had not, in his view, received from his predecessor. Mimaut was everything to him that Drovetti should have been, he stated. Champollion went so far as to link Drovetti with Jomard as the two major advisers to Mehemet Ali in the ruination of Egypt! The most bitter attack came in a letter to his brother of 14 January, 1830: Drovetti had been responsible for the problems over the firman for excavations, which had to be extracted from him by resort to higher authorities. Champollion admitted, however, that he had at the time wished to continue to appear the Consul's dupe in this matter, and to maintain every appearance of harmony, even though he had not the least confidence in him, and despised his behaviour in Egypt. Drovetti thought only of his own interests and those of the Viceroy, and cared nothing for the Europeans whom he was paid to protect. In sum, Champollion asserted, all the French in Egypt curse him![16] There is, unfortunately, more than a little hypocrisy here on Champollion's part, in flattering someone he despised, and that was one of his least typical traits. And in such judgements on Drovetti's lack of care for Europeans in Egypt, Champollion was quite alone.

What is our surprise, then, to learn that when he came out of quarantine on 23 January 1830, someone was waiting for him and had been so longer than anticipated. That person was none other than Drovetti. The two men spent the next two days with each other, before Drovetti left for Nice and Champollion for Marseille.[17] The latter offers no explanation to his brother for the ex-consul's visit, nor does he here indulge in any injurious comment. The reason for the meeting was to discuss the raft which Champollion proposed for the transport of the Luxor obelisk to France. Accompanying Drovetti were officials of the French navy. They were apparently completely won over. The project was then neglected through the influence of Champollion's enemy, Haussez, the Minister for the Navy, and a ship was sent off with Baron Taylor to bring back one of the two obelisks at Alexandria, which had been given to France through Drovetti's efforts. The mission was a complete failure. One of the Luxor obelisks, as in the original proposal, was finally removed by Apollinaire Lebas and brought to France on the special raft, the *Luxor*, and set up in the Place de la Concorde in 1836.

'A man honoured by the whole of Europe'

It took some time for Drovetti's friends to realise that he was no longer in Egypt. Jomard was still writing about the schools in August

1829.[18] Early in 1830, Drovetti was in Paris being solicited by the vicomte Doncour to visit him, but he needed to seek warmer climes, such as Nice, for the sake of his health. He was to spend much of the succeeding years here.[19]

One of his old Levantine colleagues, d'Amandy, the French agent at Moka since 1824, now in Cairo, wrote begging Drovetti's pardon. He had already written various letters and received no reply. He explained why he accepted the demands of a Greek ship in the Red Sea which had come to ensure the neutrality of Arabia in the war between Greece and Turkey. The ship was the famous *Hellas*, flagship of the Greek navy. He had been imprisoned by the Arabs, had written to the Consul-General in Egypt seeking instructions, and after waiting five months had been willing to accept the offer of an English captain to attempt to free him. Relations with Drovetti were obviously very chilly; he thought that d'Amandy was trying to avoid repaying large debts: that was all a calumny, the latter assured him. The agency at Moka had now been suppressed, and d'Amandy was at Cairo, but desperate to clear his name. For this very purpose he now wrote again, referring to the ex-consul as always his generous protector and benefactor. There is a further letter on the same theme from June 1831. D'Amandy had now left Egypt in March and returned to Italy, but had still not received any answer to his letters and had to believe that they had been lost. He again fulsomely begged for Drovetti's continued esteem, but it seems clear that the other regarded his conduct as having severed their friendship. This is one of the rare cases where Drovetti is known to have acted with such intransigence. It is, at the same time, curious that he kept the letters for the rest of his life.[20]

His more characteristic generosity to his friends is demonstrated in correspondence with Nota, who addressed him as 'most dear' (*diletissimo*) and thanked him for the gift of a cornelian which he found on his return home to San Remo.[21] Drovetti had obviously visited him and not found him there. The first of many appeals to return to his family and friends in Torino begin to be heard, first from his old friend baron Bianco di Barbania, to whom he had sent Moka coffee. Family matters are also more prominent in the correspondence, as one might expect. The baron mentioned paying over some 6,000 francs to Drovetti's younger brother, the priest Luigi, for his establishment in his parish and to clear a debt.[22] And another old friend was not neglected. This was Huder, the aide-de-camp of the French ambassador at Constantinople, whom we have seen acting as envoy in the Algerian affair. He wrote of his 'inviolable affection' for Drovetti and of the latter's repeated proofs of most noble feelings. The two had, in fact, known each other since Huder came to Egypt in 1824 with General Boyer.[23]

By June 1830 Drovetti was in Vienna. A friend with whom he stayed in Trieste on the way, Jean Sartorio, referred to him as 'a man honoured by the whole of Europe'. The visit to the Austrian capital must have been in connection with the Egyptian education programme; for in 1832 he advised Jomard to send one of the Ethiopians there.[24] Among his correspondents at this time also was General Macdonald, the famous Napoleonic soldier, but the letter has unfortunately not survived. The onerous burdens for Terra Santa did not cease with Drovetti's departure from Egypt: how could he imagine that they would? The Custodian wrote bemoaning the immediately felt effects of his retirement, and revealing a scandal. It was claimed that the organisation was selling the use of its flag, and that it was being exploited even by the Greeks. Drovetti was importuned, as the last resort, to deny these allegations with the ambassador at Constantinople. The Custodian asserted that everyone knew that any donations made to Terra Santa for the right to use of their flag were completely spontaneous![25]

The same year, 1830, Drovetti was elected a member of the Royal Society of Antiquaries in Copenhagen.[26] His European fame is further illustrated by the only thing we know of him in the next year, when he was consulted in November 1831 by the Health Commission of Torino on quarantine. An international conference in Paris was considering the question. Drovetti was asked a number of basic but technical questions: had there, in fact, not been a case of bubonic plague in the Levant for twelve years? Was it transmitted only by people and not by goods? Was the incubation period a maximum of fourteen days?[27] The knowledge and experience of a consul in the East were obviously thought to embrace even advice to medical authorities. Drovetti spent the summer in Switzerland, presumably at a spa.[28]

The rocking of the foundations

There is paradoxically no hint in the *Epistolario* as it survives of the momentous events shaking Europe in 1830 and 1831. The 'nationalist risings led by military groups' of 1820 were replaced by 'liberal revolts led by broader elements of the wealthy middle classes'.[29] In July 1830, having lost the elections, the French royalists dissolved parliament, the Republicans set up barricades, Charles X abdicated and Louis Philippe was proclaimed King. In August, the Catholics, French and Flemish in Belgium rose up against the Dutch, and on 4 October, Brussels proclaimed its independence from Holland. A conference of five powers in London in November recognised Belgium. The Dutch invaded and were victorious, but were then forced by the French to withdraw. The same year, the Liverpool to Manchester railway was opened, inaugurating the end of man's dependence on the horse. Hector Berlioz composed his first masterpiece, the *Symphonie Fantastique*, and Stendhal published his novel of the Restoration, *Le rouge et le noir*.

The next year the revolution moved to Italy. In February 1831, governments fell from Emilio Romagna to the Papal States. The proposals for action were as usual beset by endless divisions, especially among the exiles in London and Paris. Was Italy to be a constitutional monarchy, a republic or a federation? Such rivalries and the resultant inability to organise military defences led again to defeat when the Austrians invaded.

In 1831 Carlo Alberto, the discredited hero of 1821, came to the throne in Piedmont. He was 'the paladin of every Catholic legitimist cause in Europe'. It was only in 1847 that he was to make 'a half-hearted conversion to the national cause'.[30] He had, of course, to contend with both the extremist Republicans and the neo-Guelphs. By the time he became king he was a reactionary, but the demand for change had infected the enlightened aristocracy and the professional and middle classes.

In the same year, Giuseppe Mazzini launched his 'Young Italy' society, Victor Hugo published *Notre Dame de Paris*, and chloroform was discovered. At the same time a cholera epidemic began to spread over western and central Europe which was to kill vast numbers. Twenty thousand died in France, including the Prime Minister.

As if nothing had happened, early in 1932 Drovetti was undergoing treatment in Torino, and a letter from one of his doctors is preserved.[31] It is highly revealing and extraordinary in that it is one of the very few in the whole *Epistolario* in which anyone spoke harshly of Drovetti. The doctor, Costantino Bosio, was by his own account young and independent and he admired his patient's 'gifts', but had apparently been ill-used by him (he 'refrained from baptising' the manners and words of the ex-consul). He thus wrote to refuse any further medical assistance. It may be that Drovetti's medical problems were causing him much distress, and that, as has happened in many such situations, there was a misunderstanding between doctor and patient.

More characteristic is the following letter, from Mehemet Ali's secretary, Etienne Abro, on his way from Florence to Vienna for an eye operation. He made a detour via Torino, in the hope of seeing there the man who had 'heaped paternal affection' on him.[32] Drovetti was taking the waters in the summer. A major concern of the year was still the education programme of the young Egyptians. This is demonstrated by two letters from Jomard, and Drovetti's advice and action were both indispensable.[33]

The English had finally to feel some effect of the trends shaking Europe. The First Reform Bill was passed this year, the first fruit of the new

Whig government which had at last come to power. The bill abolished the Rotten Boroughs and extended the franchise to the upper middle classes, doubling the electorate. It constituted therefore as much of a revolution as events in Paris in 1830. The greatest figure in German culture, Goethe, died in Weimar. Events in which Drovetti would, however, have been more personally interested were threatening the dissolution of the Ottoman Empire.

Mehemet Ali's first Syrian War

In December 1832 Ibrahim was advancing on Constantinople at the head of the victorious Egyptian army. The war found its cause perhaps for the most part in personal antagonisms: a continuation of the old feud between Mehemet Ali and Khosrev Pasha. The Viceroy did, however, also covet the four Syrian pashaliks, for their resources in men, money and timber. They had been promised to him after the Greek war, but because of Khosrev had not been granted. Syria was also a refuge for the unfortunate fellahin who were fleeing conscription and agricultural misery.

In November 1831, therefore, an army of 9,000 infantry and 2,000 cavalry moved against Jaffa, and Ibrahim commanded the fleet. Acre fell in May after a six months' siege. The Sultan responded by issuing a firman replacing Mehemet Ali as Viceroy of Egypt with Hussein Pasha, although Khosrev himself desperately wanted the position: he had been Mehemet Ali's inveterate enemy for some twenty-five years. When he was also refused command of the Turkish army, however, he decided to wreck the whole resistance to the Egyptian invasion.

Damascus fell in June, and the Turkish army was defeated at Homs on 8 July. Ibrahim entered Aleppo on the 15th. Syria had been conquered within seven months. Hussein was clearly a failure, and was replaced in the Sultan's firmans by the Grand Vizir, Reshid. He fared no better, being overwhelmingly defeated at Konia on 21 December. It was thus that Ibrahim advanced on the capital at the head of 30,000 men.

The advance was halted by order of his father. The Russians sent an envoy demanding withdrawal in January 1833, and the Captain Pasha arrived with terms on the 21st. The first war thus ended with a firman granting Mehemet Ali the four pashaliks as well as Crete. The total tribute was fixed at 30,000 purses.

Early in 1833, precisely while these events were taking place, Drovetti seems to have been contemplating a visit to his son-in-law, Pedemonte, the Sardinian Consul in Alexandria, and was needing assurances about the reception he would receive.[34] During his famous tour to display the new graduates of the Egyptian medical school, Clot looked for him in February, but obviously failed to meet him.[35] In April, in fact, Drovetti was in

Naples, where he met the eminent antiquarian and most famous cicerone to all English visitors to the Kingdom of the Two Sicilies, William Gell:

> Drovetti has just left us for Turin. He is an amiable, well-informed person who has been consul in Egypt for twenty-five years, and is quite devoted to Mehmed Ali and Ibrahim.[36]

The characterisation of Drovetti provided by the Englishman, himself most amiable, is a precious judgement. It is a great shame that we do not have more details of what passed between the two men.

As Gell said, Drovetti was leaving Naples for Torino. In June Carlo Botta wrote to Giovanni Giordano there, that he had forgotten in his last letter to send greetings to 'il nostro mirabile Drovetti', and to give him a copy of Botta's *Camillo* and news of his son Paolo Emilio, travelling in Egypt.[37] This son was later to become the famous Assyriologist. The *Camillo o Veio conquistato* was originally published in Paris in 1815 but was now reprinted in Torino. This was an epic poem in twelve books in the style of Homer and Vergil on the first great war conducted by Rome in Italy, for the conquest of her nearest Etruscan neighbour, Veii (406-396); the hero of the final victory was Camillus. At the end of the year negotiations were in progress through Baron Minutoli for the purchase of Drovetti's third collection by Germany.[38] The winter was spent at Pisa, for health reasons. Torino was very cold this year.[39]

Ferdinand VII of Spain died in 1833, and was succeeded by his daughter Isabella. The succession was contested by her uncle, Don Carlos, and civil war lasted until 1839. The constitutionalists and Isabella were supported by England and France. Events closer to home would have alarmed Drovetti. In mid 1833 in Piedmont, a network of Mazzinians was uncovered, based in Genova. The plan was for an uprising and the return of exiles with French Republican support. Piedmont was then to attack Austria in Lombardy, which was to be the signal for revolts in central and southern Italy. The revolutionaries were hunted down by a special commission, and many were executed. Carlo Alberto was seen as the arch reactionary, and liberal opinion all over Europe was horrified.[40]

In 1834, Drovetti heard again from an old colleague in Egypt, with whom he was to have many communications in the next years. Clot Bey, head of the military and naval health service, wrote to reassure him that, after all Drovetti had done for him, he was not one of the 'many ingrates'. It was said, Clot noted, that with the water of the Nile one drank oblivion of services received, and the African sun exercised a 'fatal influence' on the brains of both Egyptians and strangers who came there. Clot had achieved, if not everything he ought, at least everything he could.[41] The letter was an expression of gratitude to Drovetti, who had been his patron, and highly gratifying it must have been when other initiatives for the modernisation of Egypt, notably the education programmes, were not flourishing.

The same year there was an outbreak of cholera in Torino. An attempt was naturally made at first to conceal it. A doctor friend referred to Drovetti's 'philanthropic health instructions', which, although judged excellent by all the experts, he had not been able to get published; only manuscript copies were circulating.[42] These notes must have been those he had compiled on the basis of his experience of contagious diseases in Egypt. Perhaps they were the notes which he had prepared for the Health Commission in 1831.

The ex-consul could be pursued for more trivial reasons. He had known the Piedmontese political figure Ferdinando dal Pozzo since 1800, and in Egypt in 1824 he had recommended some young patriots to him. Like Drovetti, dal Pozzo was a lawyer who had served in the Provisional Government; he had gone on to be a member of the French government in Rome (1809-1814), and been Minister of the Interior during the Regency, but then spent the rest of his life in exile in London and Paris. His restless policies seem to have alienated all parties. He had in 1830 married for a second time, an English woman young enough to be his daughter. Drovetti and he met in Milan, and the former mentioned Caroline Murat, then living in Florence. Dal Pozzo now sent him a letter begging for an introduction to the one-time queen of Naples; his English wife was desperate to meet all 'respectable' people![43]

At some earlier time, Drovetti had visited Dresden. He now presented the Royal Library there with a Greek manuscript. The librarian, Karl Falkenstein, added to his letter of thanks a request naturally for information on the provenance but, more remarkably, on the date of the manuscript, confessing his ignorance of such matters – as if there were no German scholars who were experts in the field. He asked Drovetti also if he might spare for the library some autographs of famous visitors to Egypt.[44] As always, it seems, one act of generosity simply led to requests for more. And his old friend Cesare Balbo was editing the letters of the traveller Carlo Vidua, who had visited Egypt in 1819-1820 and had died in 1830 in the East Indies. He asked Drovetti to give him any information he could about Vidua.[45] The *Lettere* in three volumes appeared this year and are full of references to Drovetti.

1835 was Drovetti's sixtieth year. Further correspondence with Jomard showed the despair of the great Orientalist. He fought a constant battle to maintain French influence in Egypt, and was appalled at the inertia of his country's politicians. Mehemet Ali sent him letters and gifts in recognition of his help to Egypt, but it was to Drovetti that Jomard paid the highest tribute: 'without you, I could not have succeeded; without you, the Pasha would have dared nothing, would have dreamed nothing.'[46]

Carlo Botta, in exile in France since the time of Napoleon, had been in touch with Drovetti through their friend Giordano in 1833. He now wrote directly, giving news of his health and his sons. Although the two had seen very little of each other since the heady days of the revolution in Piedmont thirty years before, their relations were intimate. 'I wish you all the happiness you deserve', was Botta's closing sentiment.[47] Drovetti had been at Yverdun in Switzerland this year, presumably taking the famous sulphur springs.

In 1836 the third collection was finally sold to Berlin.[48] There continued to be crises with the education of Egyptians in Paris, and Jomard corresponded with Drovetti about this and the Syrian situation and the problems of the Egyptian economy. He hoped that more peaceful conditions would allow resources to be returned to agriculture. Jomard had written a pamphlet on this to be distributed to the French parliament. He especially sought Drovetti's views: 'there is not on this matter a single opinion which I value as much as yours.'[49]

A personal upset occurred in the same year. Drovetti's son-in-law, Pedemonte, ceased to be the Sardinian Consul-General in Egypt. His father-in-law referred to the matter as a 'disgrazia', which may mean either 'misfortune' or 'disgrace'. The case was called an 'injustice' by Clot Bey in 1840, and he did what he could for Pedemonte while in Italy, but was not able to mention his name in an audience with the King.[50] The dismissal of Pedemonte also threw Drovetti's own son Giorgio out of employment in the consulate. His father therefore recalled him to Europe to find another career. Before he left, however, he was to make arrangements about a farm in the Fayum which his father had given him. Drovetti now wrote to the new Consul seeking his assistance, explaining that family circumstances made it necessary for him to resort once more to Mehemet Ali's kindness. Drovetti's brother, the lawyer Giuseppe, was now dead, after having dissipated a good part of Drovetti's capital as well as his own inheritance, and leaving debts to be paid and a numerous family, for whose education and sustenance Drovetti now had to provide.[51] Few letters better illustrate his generosity.

Drovetti had served in Egypt for twenty years spread over two periods. His successor Mimaut, two years older than his predecessor, took leave in 1836 and died in Paris at the beginning of the next year. Until the middle of the century French influence in Egypt was henceforth to be plagued by a series of very short-term consuls. In England a young woman came to the throne who was to give her name to the rest of the century, and in the United States Samuel Morse filed a patent for the telegraph. If only

Drovetti had had telegraphic communications while he was Consul-General in Egypt, instead of waiting months for correspondence to travel between Alexandria and Paris.

As we have seen, one of Drovetti's most faithful correspondents of the years of his 'retirement' was Jomard. He gave, in his own words, 'three quarters of his soul' to Egypt, in the hope that France might receive some benefit. As well as the cultural programmes, he was vitally interested in politics, and consulted Drovetti as someone who shared his ideas. They both hoped that the enmity between the Sultan and Mehemet Ali might be brought to an end by means of diplomacy. (This was to happen in 1841 in a way that probably neither of them foresaw). Only the English would profit from the continuing strife, Jomard lamented. The second French war in Algeria (1835-1837) further stimulated his regrets and he again mentioned Drovetti's plan for the use of Egyptian auxiliaries. In that way, Jomard agreed, 10,000 men could have done what now 30,000 could not.[52]

Carlo Botta thought continually of Drovetti. Writing to the marchese Felice di S. Tommaso in March, he asked him to embrace Drovetti on his behalf. In this year, 1837, the Marquis' work on the history of Philosophy from ancient to modern times, *Saggio sulle rivoluzioni della filosofia dai tempi di Talete sino al principio del secolo XIX*, was published in Torino, and dedicated to Drovetti.[53]

The famous doctor Etienne Pariset had visited Egypt in 1828, intending to accompany the Franco-Tuscan expedition. He had been sent by the government to study diseases there, as he had in Spain in 1819 and 1821. He must have become acquainted then with Drovetti, and they had become close friends. In 1837 Pariset wrote to him about plans for a trip together through Italy, Sicily, and Malta to Egypt, Syria and Lebanon, in the course of which the foundations of a hospital at Beirut would be laid. He sent Drovetti a copy of his 'little yellow book', which he suggested might be translated into Italian if the other liked it. This was Pariset's *Mémoire sur les causes de la peste*. It was in fact translated into Italian in the next year by Dr de Rolandis, and obviously at Drovetti's urging. Pariset echoed Jomard's sentiments: if what he had done gained Drovetti's approval he was content. He declared that he loved, cherished and honoured his friend, and that there was a veritable cult of Drovetti among his circle in Paris.[54]

Yet another friend dedicated a work to Drovetti. Giuseppe Baruffi was a fellow Piedmontese, but a generation younger. Although a professor of mathematics at Torino University, he was, like Drovetti, much interested in the revival of Piedmontese agriculture. He was most famous, however, as a traveller. In October 1837 he dedicated one of his letters of pilgrimage, that on Vienna, to Drovetti. It is instructive for the ex-consul's interests at the time. It is one of the longest in the *Pellegrinazioni autunnali*, 1841 (no 24), some fifty pages. It eulogises the cultural life of Vienna (libraries, galleries and museums), its palaces, schools and hospitals, its gardens, streets and shops, not to mention special areas of education such as institutions for the blind and deaf and dumb, and the Polytechnic, and agriculture. The only blot on the city's copybook was the obvious one for the priestly visitor, its immorality: 12,000 foundlings a year were given to the hospitals! Baruffi referred to Drovetti's collections and travels, but admitted that he himself had not had time to visit the Egyptian museum. Drovetti replied with gratitude, recalling his time in Vienna and agreeing with Baruffi that it surpassed all other European cities for its 'numerous magnificent public and private scientific and philanthropic institutions'. He expressed the hope that Baruffi's letters would be read by those on whom 'depended the future of human happiness'.[55]

A short and enigmatic letter of January 1838 shows Drovetti to be in Torino or nearby; for he had dealings with the marchese di Barolo over some pictures.[56] What is important is not the content but Drovetti's connection with the Marquis. Carlo Tancredi Falletti, married to a French wife whom he had met when a page at the court of Napoleon, was a famous philanthropist, best known for his establishment of schools for poor children in his Torino palace, and a free school to teach art to poor children. His salon was the centre of the Piedmontese aristocracy and culture. There were thus many mutual interests between the two men, and they had many friends in common. What is most remarkable, however, is that the letter was written by none other than Silvio Pellico, one of the most famous figures in Italian culture of this time, and a martyr of the Risorgimento. As a young man, he had come under the influence of Foscolo, Alfieri, Manzoni and other liberals and romantics, had joined the *carbonari*, and then been imprisoned by the Austrians for ten years (1820-1830). The result was one of the most influential works of the Risorgimento, *Le mie prigioni*, 1832. He addressed Drovetti in this letter in the most intimate terms.

In 1838 there begins a series of letters from a very old and devoted friend, Pietro Giordano in Parma. Two years older than Drovetti, Giordano was born at Piacenza, studied law and then taught Latin and Italian at the University of Bologna, and published a panegyric on Napoleon in 1808. The letters began with his passionate gratitude for a present: Drovetti kept sending him chocolates anonymously! He protested that he would much prefer a brief letter.

He had been seeking Drovetti constantly in Torino, only to be told that he was in Livorno.[57] In August, however, Drovetti was in Paris. This is clear from an invitation from Jomard to dine with him and the director of the port at Alexandria. The ex-consul's presence was required as 'the man who was the first to give the stimulus for Egypt's improvement'.[58] This was one of several visits Drovetti made to Paris, to see his old and powerful collaborator in all matters affecting Egypt's progress. For the sake of his health, however, as usual Drovetti returned to milder climes for the winter, to his well loved Nice.

Other friends from Egypt did not forget their Consul, even though nearly ten years had elapsed since his departure. One of the Italian doctors who had come to serve Mehemet Ali in the 1820s, del Signore, never forgot Drovetti's 'generous and kind friendship', and always sought news of him, from whatever source. After an interval in Aleppo, he had returned to Egypt as Medical Inspector and member of the General Council of Health. He had also supported the widow of one of his medical colleagues for a year, but was now thinking of retiring to Europe.[59] Here is a worthy example of the professionals Drovetti had brought into Egypt's service, who had long remained there and reached some eminence, and who were inspired by the same ideals of generosity.

One of the most interesting correspondents of Drovetti this year was the sculptor Charles Marochetti. Although he was to become a naturalised Frenchman in 1841, he was born in Torino in 1805. His masterpiece is the equestrian statue of Emmanuele Filiberto of Savoy (now in Piazza San Carlo in Torino), but he sculpted as well one side of the Arc de Triomphe, the main altar of the Madeleine, and the tomb of Napoleon. In 1838 he wrote to Drovetti, asking him to stay a few days with him and his family, obviously relying on a long and intimate friendship.[60]

Only four letters from Drovetti survive from his years of retirement. The most important of them dates from February 1839.[61] Such letters would be preserved in his *Epistolario*, of course, only in the exceptional circumstance that he kept a copy. He was still at Nice when Cailliaud arrived, bringing him a letter from Jomard. He had been, he admitted, cut off from news about Europe and Egypt. This was just at the beginning of the second war of Mehemet Ali with the Sultan. Drovetti agreed with Jomard that the situation was not very favourable and that England and Russia might combine to settle the Persian and Indian questions, perhaps to the detriment of Egypt. Mehemet Ali ought to devote himself, Drovetti asserted, to the improvement of his country. He need not worry about the mines in Ethiopia; one had only to scratch the soil of Egypt to reap treasure. Drovetti was most concerned that a man of the Viceroy's age should expose himself in the war to such privation and danger. Trade could easily be encouraged with Ethiopia; the Darfur caravans unfortunately now rarely came to Egypt, but preferred to make for Tripoli, because of high taxes. Here we have the clearest statements of Drovetti's concerns for

Egypt in a time of crisis, and his priorities for Egypt's prosperity: she should rely on agriculture and trade.

The second Syrian war (1839-1841)

Syria constituted the 'cockpit of Europe'. England especially was convinced that any further Egyptian advance would serve only as a pretext for the Russians to intervene and begin a war involving all the European powers, or to bring about a change in the balance of power, which would soon lead to the same thing. Mehemet Ali refused to withdraw or to cease his reorganisation of the Syrian government or conscription. This outraged the European consuls, who had made enormous profits from previous Turkish corruption, but won the support of European merchants, because their operations were much facilitated by the new orderliness. The Viceroy was increasingly frustrated by Turkish refusals to recognise his dynasty in Egypt.

He cannot be accused of impatience – it was six years now after the first war – or of aggression. With Russian encouragement and German training, the Turkish army crossed the Euphrates in April 1839. After restraining his son for two months, Mehemet Ali allowed him to confront the Turks at Nabiz on 24 June. It was a total rout. And on 1 July, Sultan Mehmed died, to be succeeded by his sixteen years old son, Abdul. Learning that he was to be sacked by Khosrev, the Captain Pasha Ahmad Mushir sailed the Turkish fleet to Alexandria and surrendered it to Mehemet Ali. At this point, to avert Russian intervention, the European powers – including Russia! – intervened to prevent any independent action by either Turkey or Egypt.

On 15 July, 1840, the four powers (excluding France) offered Mehemet Ali hereditary status in Egypt and southern Syria during his lifetime. The Viceroy refused to be overawed. The European consuls were recalled from Egypt in September. On the 11th of that month, English and Turkish forces under Sir Charles Napier landed at Beirut. On 10 October Ibrahim was defeated, and the city fell, to be followed by Acre in November. Napier went on to Alexandria and signed an agreement with Mehemet Ali on 27 November for the evacuation of Syria in return for recognition in Egypt. This was ratified by the Sultan by firman on 1 June, 1841.[62] Mehemet Ali had failed to realise his dream of empire, but he had gained independence guaranteed by the European powers.[63]

In 1839 meanwhile Baruffi took the opportunity of a visit to Nice by the Secretary to the King in his capacity as Grand Master of the Order of SS Maurizio e Lazzaro, to which Drovetti belonged, to send him a letter with news of his many friends. 'Who does not always remember, who could ever forget that most likeable of men, Drovetti', when so many acquaintances and friends heartily desire to have his happy company, asked

Baruffi.[64] A further remarkable testimony to Drovetti's continued reputation is the letter written to him in May 1839 by de la Rue, French agent in Vienna from 1816, who was charged with the enforcement of the various conventions following the fall of Napoleon, notably that which reimbursed the beneficiaries of his donations in Illyria and Lombardy, which had now naturally been lost again. It was partly Drovetti's expressed interest in the course of these negotiations which occasioned the letter, but also de la Rue's assertion that only intervention by the government of Sardinia could force Austria to fulfil her obligations.[65]

By now a decade had passed since Drovetti had relinquished the consulate in Egypt, and his Piedmontese friends were becoming impatient. The painter Count Cesare Benevello jokingly accused him of being ungrateful for all this affection, in not wishing to settle among so many friends who desired and appreciated him. Climate could not this time be a motive, Benevello assured him, for the winter of 1839 was really 'African'.[66] Those who know Piedmontese winters will understand Drovetti's scepticism! In this year Charles Darwin published his *Voyage of the Beagle*, to be followed by the *Origin of the Species* twenty years later. Giuseppe Verdi's first opera (Oberto) was performed. Fox Talbot produced the first photographic negative, and Charles Goodyear invented vulcanisation. The world was changing at an ever-increasing pace in Drovetti's old age.

Touring Italy at this time to observe health practices was Clot Bey. He wrote a long letter to Drovetti describing his travels. In Bologna he had been presented to the Duchess de Berry, but he stressed that he had not sought this honour, since he was not a 'party man'; for him, the Duchess was simply 'an historical personage'. The disclaimer is significant. Drovetti would not have been impressed with Clot's seeking out the widow of Ferdinand of Bourbon, son of Charles X. She was one of the Neapolitan Bourbons who lived to see the unification of Italy. On the other hand, Clot dared to suggest to Drovetti that Francesco IV of Modena, the ruthless Austrian, was not the devil that he was made out to be in Europe. Closer to Drovetti's heart must have been the account of Clot's kind reception at Parma by the Archduchess, none other than Maria Louisa, the widow of Napoleon. In Torino, Drovetti was able to give Clot letters of introduction, and when he met the King there was talk of the ex-consul and his work. The French doctor did not need to give Drovetti news of Florence in late 1839; for he had been his guest there, for which he thanked him fulsomely. We discover also that Drovetti gave him a cheque for 1,000 francs, should he need any money in Torino – but we should not now be surprised at his unending generosity to friends.[67] In his memoirs, Clot did not publicise these personal matters, but stated that he was well acquainted with Drovetti and very proud to be so.[68]

The ex-consul could not ever escape his Egyptian connections, and the *Epistolario* attests to his constant support and protection of those who resorted to him. Etienne Abro, the secretary-interpreter of Mehemet Ali, somehow found himself in trouble and had been sent off to Smyrna, but thanks to Drovetti had been recalled to his post. His English father-in-law was now trying to destroy his marriage, and he again sought letters from Drovetti in his support.[69]

In the summer of 1840 Drovetti was again as usual taking the waters, at Loch at the southern end of what was obviously for him a favourite spot, Lake Constance. His agent in Livorno, Morpurgo, took out a subscription in his name to an English paper published in Malta, so that he might have news of the Levant. Morpurgo himself admitted that he could not read English: the clear implication of the whole episode is that Drovetti could.[70] Clot Bey was still on leave from Egypt in August 1840 when he wrote again to Drovetti, announcing the publication in Paris of his *Aperçu sur l'Egypte*. He admitted that it had been written in haste and needed revision, but declared that no-one could be a better judge of it than Drovetti, and sought any observations which he cared to make for a second edition.[71]

Returning south in September from lake Constance, Drovetti passed through St. Moritz in southern Switzerland, where he missed seeing an old friend, Giuseppe Bertalazone, who had much to tell him.[72] Bertalazone had been attending the second of the famous Italian scientific congresses, this year in Torino. These meetings were part of the great intellectual and emotional ferment pressing for Italian unification and propagating liberalism. The first had been held at Pisa in 1839 under the patronage of Leopold II of Tuscany, despite the opposition of the Austrians and Pius IX: the Duke was even threatened with ex-communication, and scientists from the Papal States were forbidden to attend. This event of 'extraordinary political importance' was the 'first time the unity of the country was solemnly asserted', in the presence of 421 Italian and foreign scientists. The most striking speech had been that by Giovanni Rosini, in honour of Galileo and denouncing his trial. Apart from the more obvious political manifestations, the inestimable value of the congresses was the opportunity they provided for all the leading Italian thinkers and activists to meet.[73]

Bertalazone described the 'spirit which animated this truly Italian meeting' in 1840. He noted the extravagant applause for the Prince of Canino, Napoleon's nephew and a naturalist. The President of the congress was Marquis Alessandro di Saluzzo. Despite the high emotions, the congress in Bertalazone's words 'concealed the fire under the ashes'; the only untoward incidents occurred in mathematics and medicine! It had also been decided that the third congress would take place in Florence in 1841. Drovetti was thus informed of political developments in Italy by an old friend. He himself did not attend, as far as we know, any of these congresses. There may have been a conflict in his mind: he was on the one hand a progressive who had joined France in his youth, thinking that he could thereby assist his country, and he had favoured all manner of modernisation in Egypt; on the other hand, certainly as he grew older, he became more pious and conservative. The congresses were perhaps too politically radical for his taste; yet Bertalazone had given him a full and committed account, obviously on the assumption that he was communicating with someone sympathetic to the cause.

Another fellow-Piedmontese and a most famous one was Luigi Canina. He had moved to Rome in 1818 and had become the architect of the Borghese family. By the 1830s, he was also making his name as an archaeologist, with justification. Now he thanked Drovetti for those two delights which he distributed with such generosity: Moka coffee and Torino chocolates. The gifts bespeak an established intimacy. Canina had, however, a more practical reason for writing, apart from his thanks for these presents. In February 1839 Gregory XVI opened the Museo Egizio in the Vatican, by gathering together items from various Roman collections. He was naturally anxious for further acquisitions and in 1840 three ships sailed for Egypt where Mehemet Ali had promised alabaster columns and other antiquities. Canina now asked Drovetti if he had 'any object of some interest' which he might donate.[74]

In all the great upheavals in the Levant over the conflict between Egypt and Turkey, the European powers had never ceased attempting intervention and arbitration. Jomard as usual lamented the clumsiness of French policy here and told Drovetti in February 1841 that he had attempted to have the government call on Drovetti's services as an envoy. The Ministry of Foreign Affairs for many years had had no expert in Egyptian affairs, Jomard asserted. England would reap the fruit of so many French sacrifices![75] In March, there was talk of Drovetti's being sent to Malta. Pedemonte was returning to Egypt, to rejoin his family. He was in very poor circumstances, and Drovetti gave him half the cost of a steamboat passage at the time, but to save money he was taking a sailing ship. When he arrived he was able to send off a small consignment of antiquities (a child's mummy, two embalmed crocodiles, and two fragments of papyrus): the old collector's urge was as strong as ever with Drovetti, it seems. On the domestic front, Pedemonte was estranged from his wife, Drovetti's step-daughter, who was in Cairo with the daughters, while Pedemonte stayed in Alexandria.[76]

It was now twenty years since Frédéric Cailliaud had left Egypt after his second visit. He was in considerable legal trouble of some kind, serious enough to require a judgement by the Royal Attorney. His reputation was also being sullied in the various European academies by another naturalist. As always when those who had ever known Drovetti were in trouble, they turned to him for help. Cailliaud remembered his first visit to Egypt in 1815, where Drovetti had said to him simply at Asyut: 'I will make you the Pasha's mineralogist' – and so it had happened.[77] Cailliaud obviously hoped for a similarly effective utterance on his behalf in his present straits from his old protector.

In 1842 a Society for the Promotion of Fine Arts was established in Torino. Drovetti bought three shares. 'It is impossible not to find you where something fine and useful is under consideration', wrote the secretary, Benevello.[78] For the first time Drovetti is attested as having returned to Barbania. His friends were often a generation younger than himself. Federico Sclopis was an outstanding lawyer and politician, Attorney-General to the Sardinian senate, one of the authors of the constitution of 1848, member of the first constitutional ministry, and member of the Academy of Torino from 1828, where Drovetti must have met him. He was the author of over seventy works on history, jurisprudence, politics and literature, in Italian, French and Latin. In April 1842 Drovetti sent him some tobacco, 'a sybaritic delicacy'. In return Sclopis sent him a copy of a little book he had recently published, which he had discussed with him while it was 'still on the loom'. The work in question was *dell'autorità giudiziaria*, over which as a lawyer Drovetti may well have cast an eye. It is tantalising to know also that in this year Drovetti was corresponding with George Gliddon, the United States' Vice-Consul in Egypt.[79] The correspondence does not appear in the *Epistolario*, so we have no evidence of what concerns the two diplomats had in common.

The last decade at Barbania

One of the most important publications of the Risorgimento was Vincenzo Gioberti's *Del primato morale e civile degli italiani*, 1843. Although a priest, Gioberti was a liberal, who was forced into exile for his political ideas in 1833, when he went first to Paris and then to Brussels. He was, like Mazzini, anti-monarchist, but founded his vision of a united Italy on the Church, a federation under the leadership of the Papacy. The work naturally called forth criticism from most sides. We know that Drovetti discussed the book with a friend at Barbania after the autumn of 1843, and from the tone of the friend's response, Drovetti's reaction was favourable.[80] It seems, indeed, that Drovetti gave a priest whom he knew the 18 *lire* to buy the work. The resultant influence of 'neo-guelphism' seemed to be epitomised in the election of Pius IX, but not for long.[81]

At the same time, Jomard, his old friend, offered one of his most generous testimonies, assuring Drovetti that he considered him exceptional, and that he was 'the most constant, faithful and warm of his admirers'. He went on to contrast him to his successors as consuls in Egypt, 'not one of whom came up to the level of your knees'. (These were Jean Mimaut, Ferdinand de Lesseps, Adrien Cochelet and Gauthire d'Arc). Jomard offered a most instructive list of qualities which in his view made an outstanding consul: true diplomacy; 'elevated views'; nobility of sentiment; regard for duty more than for the wretched, changeable bureaucracy; willingness to instruct the government instead of apathetically awaiting ignorant, blind and cowardly instructions; and especially the virtues of generosity and sacrifice. In short, Jomard thought of Drovetti as always his fellow-Frenchman, who could never abjure his glorious memories. Jomard assured him that he would never cease writing and speaking about how much Egypt and France both owed to Drovetti. He was, in fact, preparing an 'iconography gallery' of the new civilisation in Egypt, and he sought Drovetti's portrait for the book.[82]

Before leaving at last on his travels in Egypt in August 1843, Giuseppe Baruffi attempted all means to reach Barbania, but in vain. Either horses were not available, or if they were, the road was not known.[83] This reminds us that, although seemingly not far from Torino, to reach Barbania towards the middle of the nineteenth century was not always easy. Baruffi described the route as 'out of the way side-roads'. However tucked away Drovetti was, influential friends never forgot him. Canina was now staying with Count Filiberto di Colobiano at the castle of Aglie, and invited Drovetti to lunch.[84] This fine building, some thirty-five kms from Torino in the Canavese, had been constructed in 1775 and was the residence of the Duke of Genova. When Canina left Aglie to return to Torino, he stayed at the palace for a few days. Since Drovetti had not accepted the luncheon invitation, Canina hoped to see him there.

Someone else, even though he came to Torino, missed Drovetti, because he was at Barbania.[85] This was none other than Jomard, in September. No-one knew, he lamented, how much he would have given for that meeting: he would have been able to talk of men and matters, while Drovetti could have 'consoled him for everything that had happened, maintained his courage, and guided him in what remained to be done'. There was also the disappointment of seeing the 'Drovetti museum' without its creator, although Jomard was sorry that more was not being done to exhibit the collection properly; the Academy of Torino needed to show more interest. Jomard had put himself at the disposal of Drovetti's son in Paris, but he asserted frankly that he would rather have been at the father's service, despite his own poor health. He assured Drovetti of his eternal affection and devotion.[86]

What had taken Drovetti back to Barbania, as inaccessible as we have seen it to be, after so many years of restless wandering in Europe? The answer is not difficult. By 1843 he was 67. To this year is to be assigned his foundation, along with the lawyer Flandino, of a society for the women of his home town, with the aim of visiting and helping the poor and their children, especially women in childbirth and newly-born infants. They were to be assisted with clothing, medicine and food, and given medical attention. There were no fewer than forty-eight families eligible for this attention in Barbania and surrounding villages – a telling indictment of conditions in Piedmont in the middle of the nineteenth century. It is a tribute to Drovetti's humanity that he realised such a society was necessary. Even more interesting is the way he conceived the society fulfilling its heavy burdens: by involving all the women of Barbania, regardless of class.[87] His great concern with reforms in Egypt was now being put into practice in his own Piedmont.

Jomard's rheumatism made him, perhaps, melancholic. In June 1844 he explained to Drovetti, the man to whom he had always ceded first place whenever he himself was given credit for reforms in Egypt, what was happening there. In so doing, he revealed his own varying estimate: in 1840 he had thought that Egypt was lost to England, in 1842 he had been more hopeful in view of the attention being given to agriculture, 'the true gold-mine of Egypt' (and we know that Drovetti agreed with that estimate), but now he saw reasons for fear. Finance was collapsing; and so the schools were being deprived of funds and the European teachers were being sent home. There was one ray of hope: an old pupil, Artin Bey, had just become Minister of Commerce. After expressing his fervent wish to see Drovetti in Paris or in Piedmont next year, Jomard urged him to attend the unveiling of a monument at Annecy to Claude Berthollet, the great chemist who had been one of the savants with Napoleon in Egypt so long ago.[88]

By the beginning of the very next year, 1845, Jomard had more positive and concrete proposals, that Drovetti should return to Egypt as a kind of independent ambassador, accompanying the Viceroy everywhere, with the right to 'counsel, speak and act'. This plan was obviously motivated by Jomard's usual despondency over the results of all his efforts and his conviction that the French government showed no interest in the civilising and educational projects in Egypt.[89]

Agricultural reform in Piedmont: the Biellese oration

Apart from the charitable foundation mentioned above, another positive way in which Drovetti put his reforming ideas into practice locally was the inaugural speech he made in 1845 to the Biella Society for the promotion of Arts, Crafts and Agriculture.[90] Biella lies about forty miles

NE of Torino, at the foot of the Alps, a small episcopal seat divided into an upper and a lower town. This was the eighth year of the society. The subject was one of Drovetti's lifelong passions: agricultural reform. We have here a rare insight, given the scarcity of his own publications, into his theories on economics and society. The speech reveals a certain rhetorical elegance in his own language, after he had spent most of his life writing diplomatic reports in French.

Illustrative of his own religious convictions, Drovetti began with allusions to the ideals of doing as one would have others do, and charity. He then turned to those who earned their living by the sweat of their brows, the farmers and artisans who allowed others to enjoy a 'calm, comfortable, even sumptuous existence', and the obligations of the last to provide work for the able and comfort for the weak. The greatest benefactor of society, he asserted, was the man who provided work, in order to increase society's riches. Drovetti admitted his own horror at seeing men pleading for work, while land remained untilled and roads were impassable. Often the idle were forced to emigrate, and – here was the point – returned home with minds 'contaminated by the false and disturbing principles of communism and by immoral ideas absolutely contrary to religious, political and civil order'.

Drovetti praised the initiatives of private citizens such as agricultural associations, at whose instigation all Europe was being covered with canals and metalled roads. These examples were drawn, however, from England, France, Belgium and Germany, not to mention the great British trading empire of 100 million inhabitants. The same progress, Drovetti sadly admitted, could not be seen in Italy. A society set up to drill wells in Piedmont a few years before had been dissolved at the first difficulties. He was led so far as to criticise Italian fondness for 'dolce far niente' and susceptibility to loss of heart when faced with any problem. Not to be discounted, in addition, was the influence of the selfish and of opponents of progress.

The province of Biella was already noteworthy in Piedmont for its industry and manufactures, Drovetti reassured his audience, but now had to cultivate its soil better, paying special attention to the growing of mulberries for the silk industry, to free Piedmont from the disgraceful tax paid over the Alps. Agriculture was for Drovetti, as we know, the main source of a society's wealth, and he illustrated the point with an example. Despite the complete collapse of French society and economy with the Revolution, her territorial resources allowed France to survive all her crises in a less exhausted state than England and the allies.

Drovetti praised the establishment of the Agrarian Institute of Sandigliano, a centre for study and experiment to discover the 'axioms of agrarian economy'. There were academies and writers even in Piedmont devoted to this, but they lacked study and practice. Such agrarian institutes were common in Europe and their contribution was enormous, but Italy was, Drovetti admitted, little inclined to associations. The agrarian committees, composed of owners who were wealthy enough to experiment and teach their peasants, filled the gap, distributing prizes and equipment to peasants who would use it. He looked forward to the use of capital in such a way that 'ruthless usury' could be abolished, that 'daughter of greed and insatiable thirst for money, consumer of the sweat and tears of the small farmer, the peasant and the abandoned artisan.'

Quoting Isiah's prophecy of the end of war 'when honour and glory will consist no longer in spilling human blood', Drovetti called on the nobility to lead the way in founding establishments of public usefulness, especially to protect agriculture. In this he realised that he had to combat certain snobbery against interest in agriculture by the very people who were the large landowners. Among the ancient Romans, 'first nation of the world', war and agriculture were equally honoured, and Drovetti drew other examples of attention to agriculture from the Greek and Persian worlds. He called for the establishment of model farms imitating those at Pollenzo, Lesegno and la Veneria. One stimulus to the nobility's activity in this regard he saw as the improvement in the lot of their peasants.

Misery abounded in the countryside, Drovetti admitted, caused by the peasants' ignorance, inadequate rewards, unemployment, poor harvests, illness caused by wet farming (notably rice, of course), and the total lack of care for the sick. The peasants were thus reduced to extremities. Complaints about theft were universal in Piedmont and the prisons were full. The best insurance would be to provide work. The major help, however, according to Drovetti, was to be provided by the clergy, on whom he placed a major burden in education. The priest's main advantage was that he belonged to all classes of society, but the results were somewhat uneven, as all faithful such as Drovetti have been forced to admit: the priest urged the rich to despise luxury and to be generous, but the poor had to resign themselves to privation and misery. Drovetti looked to the priesthood also to see to the sanitary conditions of their community, to be enlightened in the working of their parochial lands, and to conduct workers' education classes on Sundays (there were now two hundred of these schools in Lombardy).

This small address is invaluable for the insight it provides into Drovetti's most sincere convictions towards the end of his life. Although worried by some radical political philosophies which were emerging, and obviously a member of the Church, he was at the same time a firm believer in the improvement of agriculture, both as a science and as the foundation of society at that time and the livelihood of the majority of the population. The stress on the need to improve the lot of the peasant is insistent, and the burden was placed squarely on the more privileged classes. Much of these sentiments stemmed from Drovetti's experience over so many years in Egypt. It is finally not without interest that the young man who had thrown himself with such fervour into war and revolution on the side of the French now sought different ideals and looked forward to an age of peace.

The situation of Italian agriculture was indeed serious. After the opening up of larger markets and the increase in private property during the Napoleonic years, which had led to an increase in productivity, there was a slump in the 1820s and 1830s. This was compounded by the problems of the absentee landlord, minimal capital investment and the peasants' squalid living conditions, without equipment and weighed down by enormous debts. Those in debt often became vagabonds or brigands. Diet and housing conditions were appalling, although more attention was given to possible amelioration in the north. There was an outbreak of typhus all over Italy 1816-1818, and of smallpox in the cities of Piedmont and Liguria 1829, and a cholera epidemic 1835-1837. A feature of the north was the share- farmer, subject to increasingly exploitive contracts. The small proprietors teetered always on the brink of disaster, dependant on the size of the farm, and whether a balance could be maintained between working bodies and mouths to feed, as well as being hostage to natural disasters. There were disastrous famines in 1812, 1816-1817, and 1846-1847. In sum, 'the evidence for the worsening conditions of the rural population is continuous from the mid-eighteenth century through the nineteenth century'.[91]

There were thus many debates over agricultural reform, especially in Tuscany in the 1830s; for example, Gian Pietro Vieusseux's *Giornale agrario toscano* (Florence) 1827-. The need was recognised for increased capital investment, new technology, and education of peasants, and there was considerable argument over the relative merits of agriculture and industrialisation. Even closer to home, one must mention the Piedmontese Agrarian Association (1842), which contained some of the most prominent nobles, as well as members of the bourgeoisie and professionals, and was soon split between the conservatives who wished to confine the association to technical questions, and the liberals who wished to widen the discussion to include the obviously related political programmes which alone would make reform possible.[92] In his 1845 speech, then, Drovetti was participating in one of the most important debates of the time. His knowledge of another agricultural nation must have given him a wider perspective than most of the other contributors. What is uncanny, however, is how closely his programme accords with that of the more conservative government circles:

le gouvernement ne favorisait que l'agriculture; il ne désirait pas qu'un peuple, auquel le sol pouvait donner encore d'utiles moyens d'existence, devient industriel, il en calculait les dangers pour les moeurs et le courage, et il ne croyait pas devoir sacrifier à la richesse les avantages d'une population vigoreuse, morale, sobre et tranquille.[93]

In this same year Austen Layard began excavating at Nineveh, thus revealing the civilisation of the Assyrians and a rival to the splendours of ancient Egypt. Drovetti would surely have been interested. And Alexandre Dumas completed his most famous novel, *Le comte de Monte Cristo.*

It was in 1846 that Drovetti founded at Barbania a society of young farmers, who on holidays worked for the sick, widows and orphans.[94] This was the second initiative of this kind by Drovetti, and it was again consonant with contemporary trends. There were movements afoot in Piedmont now as we have seen for popular education, kindergartens, and general charity. Leading figures in such initiatives were aristocrats such as the marchese di Barolo, an old friend of Drovetti, members of the bourgeoisie, such as Roberto d'Azeglio (brother of Massimo), and anti-aristocrats such as Lorenzo Valerio. Such movements revealed a new stirring of conscience, caused partly by international European influences and by a new concept of the relations between classes, but also, as Cavour admitted, they were necessary in order to reconcile the lower classes to their less fortunate lot. The most natural supporters were, of course, the moderate liberals, and the movement was opposed by both reactionaries of church and government and by the more radical democrats who understood its political uses.[95]

While Drovetti paid attention to those less fortunate than himself, there was very unpleasant bickering within his own family over the Fayum estate in Egypt. Pedemonte wrote from Alexandria in November, reminding his father-in-law of the 10,000 francs which he had promised to his god-daughter Emma (and also his granddaughter) as a dowry. Pedemonte urged him to pay the money, which was to come from the Fayum property. He feared that the Egyptian government was going to resume it, and therefore suggested that Drovetti sign it over to his granddaughters.[96] The letter is, in fact, most unpleasant in tone, and can almost be described as verging on blackmail.

In Rome the papal conclave pinned its hopes on the liberal bishop of Imola, Count Ferreti, who took office as Pius IX and was to reign longer than any other Pope. Lord John Russel established his liberal ministry in England (1846-1852). Cesare Balbo published his *Sommario della storia d'Italia*, a powerful rallying-call in the Risorgimento, Emily Bronte published *Wuthering Heights* and Dostoevsky published his first novel. Henry Rawlinson deciphered Persian cuneiform. Another of the great ancient civilisations was yielding up its secrets.

A most strange episode occurred in the next year, 1847. Ibrahim Pasha was by now regent for his failing father, Mehemet Ali. His own health was, however, cause for concern, and he came to Europe, even to Italy. Too long in the damp of Lower Egypt had given him a kind of dysentery and lassitude (in fact, chronic bilharsia). He sailed from Egypt, only to be affected by constipation! After quarantine in Malta, he wanted to go to Italy, and especially asked that Drovetti should come to be with him. The latter was, in fact, invited to join him in Malta. The letters flowed in a steady stream from Ibrahim's servants, but without reply. Ibrahim was in Malta in October, in Livorno at the end of the same month, and Pisa in November, and he went to Naples for the winter. Four letters or more received no reply, until Drovetti responded from Rome towards the end of the year.[97]

This confirms the tradition that this year Drovetti had an audience with the new Pope. His biographer uses this incident as the excuse for a eulogy of the man whose accession to the Papal throne raised so many hopes, and recalls Drovetti's admiration of him.[98] In this year France was finally victorious in the long Algerian war which so interested Drovetti, and Liberia was the first African state to gain independence.

Drovetti did in fact meet Ibrahim, and his father. Mehemet Ali, suffering from cerebral arterio-sclerosis, was sent to Italy in 1848 to seek medical help, and came to Naples. From a letter to his son Giorgio, we learn that Drovetti was in Naples in March to see the father and son re-embark for Egypt.[99]

1848: the great revolutionary crisis

Europe was shaken as never before since the Napoleonic wars. It was indeed, the end of the 'system' established in 1815. Metternich and his friends finally left the stage. In February 1848 the Communist Manifesto was first published, in London. On 22 February the barricades went up in Paris in favour of parliamentary reform. Two days later Louis Philippe abdicated, and a provisional government of moderates and radicals took over, led by Lamartine. With an electorate increased from 200,000 to nine millions, in April a moderate government was elected, and the radicals were dropped from the ministry. The result was that on 15 May, the Paris mob invaded the Assembly, which was dismissed. The next month, in the 'June days', barricades went up in the streets, but the movement was crushed by the army and the National Guard. In November the constitution was established for the Second Republic, and in the following elections Louis Napoleon became president. These elections in France in 1848-1849 by universal manhood suffrage were epoch-making, albeit short-lived: 'For the first time in history Western Europe experienced the working of a full democracy.'[100]

On 13 March there were demonstrations in Vienna which forced Metternich to resign. On 17 March barricades went up in Berlin and a liberal government was established. In May the German parliament met in Frankfurt, representing all states. It sat for a year and argued about the definition of Germany, and who was to lead it. In June a workers' and students' revolt in Prague was crushed by the imperial army and in December Francis-Joseph became Emperor of Austria, to rule until 1916. The Austrians invaded Hungary to crush its independence.

Events closer to home could hardly have failed to concern Drovetti. On 12 January there was a revolt in Palermo of the urban masses supported by the peasants against Ferdinand II of Naples. Constitutions were speedily granted in Sicily, then in Tuscany, Piedmont and even Rome. These constitutions were based on the French one of 1830: the members of the upper chamber were nominated by the ruler, while eligibility for the lower house depended on wealth. There were varying degrees of freedom for the press. The first Prime Minister of Piedmont was Massimo d'Azeglio.

Then in the famous 'Five Days' of Milan (18-22 March), an uprising forced the Austrian army to withdraw. On 22 March an independent republic was set up in Venice. For once in his vacillating life, Carlo Alberto seized the reins. He intervened in support of Milan and Venice. On the other hand, in an infamous declaration of 29 April, Pius IX dissociated himself from the war. This action finally shattered the illusions of the neo-Guelphs such as Gioberti. Ferdinand of Naples also withdrew support, so that generals Durando and Pepe led contingents of rebels and volunteers. In a series of plebiscites, however, the various regions of Italy (Regio-Aemilia, Lombardy and Venice) voted to join the kingdom of Sardinia (May-July).

Carlo Alberto had intervened in Lombardy out of fear of democracy and French intervention. The campaign was pathetic: poor supply-lines, inadequate officers, divisions among the generals, and the bungling by the King as commander in-chief. The Piedmontese did not try to cut off General Raditsky or to join the Papal or Venetian troops. More fundamentally, the intervention was contrary to the army's own reactionary principles, and was mistrusted by other states as having imperialist motives.[101] The victory of the Austrians at Custoza (23 July) forced Piedmont to an armistice.

Revolution was lost by enmity between democrats and moderates, the latter obsessed by fears of anarchy, and fundamental divisions over the priority of independence or political reform, and what constitution the latter would embody. Lurking behind all of that in Italy lay widespread suspicions of the territorial ambitions of Piedmont, despite the fact that Carlo Alberto was the only possible dynastic leader of an Italian war of liberation. The votes in the plebiscites had reflected the vote of the poor against the rich: they sought protection under a monarchy. The Piedmontese army, for its part, felt betrayed by the withdrawal of Rome and Naples.

These momentous events are discussed in two letters to Drovetti by a fellow-Piedmontese, Michele de Negri, in February and May 1848. Drovetti had met him in Rome, and finding that he was involved in some religious litigation, had lent him 20 scudi. De Negri was delighted with General Durando's appointment: 'the reign of the reactionaries is almost over'; he spoke also of the opposition of prelates and Jesuits to Pius' reforms, and divine punishment for those who have forgotten the Gospels and devised 'blameworthy plans'. De Negri presumably expected Drovetti to share his views on the fall of Louis Philippe, that it was caused by his restrictions on the Church.[102] Drovetti was at this time in spring 1848 taking the waters at Acqui. The briefest allusion is made in these letters to the other great revolutions of the year: the recall of the Neapolitan troops from Bologna and the flight of the deputies from Naples, the bad impression made by the Pope's famous renunciation of war against Austria (29 April), the quarrel of Mons. Corboli with the Pope, the embracing of Mazzini's proclamations in Genova, the awaiting of Gioberti – 'the only one to put sense into heated heads', and of the attempt to discredit Durando by Ferrari.[103]

There was continued resistance by Venice and Bologna, and Mazzini called for a people's war. Events then took a very different turn when the Roman Prime Minister, Pellegrino Rossi, was murdered. Pius fled to Gaeta (24 November), and on 8 February 1849, a republic was declared in Rome. The next day a republic was also declared in Tuscany, and Duke Leopold fled. In March Carlo Alberto moved again. He rejected the truce with Austria, but was once more defeated, at Novara (23 March). He abdicated and retired to Portugal where he died four months later. In May, however, Ferdinand conquered Palermo, and Leopold, who had been recalled by the moderates in April, returned with Austrian support in July.

Pius IX, who could not declare war on the national enemy of his country, could meanwhile declare war on fellow Italians. His reputation lay in tatters. The armies of France, Austria, Spain and Naples intervened to overthrow the Roman Republic. There followed the siege of the city by the French, who attacked from the Janiculum; the defence was organised by Garibaldi. The heroes who gave their lives laid the foundations for the events of 1870. When all was lost, four thousand men and Anita Garibaldi accompanied their leader on one of his most legendary feats, the retreat to San Marino.[104] Venice surrendered to the Austrians in August. Pius returned to Rome in April 1850. The moderates were entirely compromised by their trucking with restored monarchs. The democrats had failed, but had created an invincible legend.

Apart from the overthrow of the monarchy in France and the return of 'Bonapartism' with the election of Louis Bonaparte as President of the Second Republic (one wishes there survived the reactions of Drovetti to this pale imitation of the uncle), in Egypt the older order of which Drovetti had been so much a part, in the creation of which, indeed, he had played such a leading role, was slipping away. The hope of the dynasty, Ibrahim, died on 10 November, 1848 at the age of 59. He had succeeded his brother Tusun as commander in the Arabian war in 1816 in which the Wahabites were defeated; he had then assumed command in the Morea (1824-1828), forcing the capitulation of Missalonghi; his final campaign was in Syria (1831-1841), where he won victory after victory over the Turks. He was, then, the main architect of the international power of Egypt, and his death left open the way for his cousin Abbas Hilmi to succeed Mehemet Ali.[105] The end of the Drovetti era in Egypt came, indeed, with the death of the Viceroy himself on 2 August, 1849.

It is characteristic that one of Drovetti's most constant tasks was the despatch, as we have already seen so often, of Torino chocolates to various friends. Consignments were still going off in 1849, to Littardi in Toulon.[106] The letter regarding this dilates on Italian politics, and one may again assume that his friend Reyneri, a lawyer, was writing to a sympathetic Drovetti when he complained of Bourbon despotism in the south, and of Republican movements in central Italy and even Piedmont, when the war against Austria was the main concern. Once again the name of Gioberti was discussed, and his fall from popular favour following his removal from the ministry.[107] His fears for Piedmont in government and war were seen as a bad omen. Reyneri assured Drovetti that it was the 'universal opinion of the clear-sighted' that it would be a blessing for Italy, and Rome especially, if the temporal power of the Papacy were surrendered, now that Pius, 'from whom so much had been hoped', had shown that that temporal power was incompatible with spiritual power. Did Drovetti agree with this view? The problem was to be solved in 1870, and no-one was more aggrieved than Pius.

Some time in 1849 the Torino Museum received a most eminent visitor, none other than the Curator of the Louvre Egyptological collection, Emmanuel de Rougé. He was the Frenchman who did most to put Champollion's decipherment into practice, and he was at this time visiting major collections in Europe (also Berlin, Leyden and London). It seems from his letter that he was, like so many others anxious to meet the ex-Consul, destined to be disappointed. He had a thousand questions to ask, but limited his letter to the most important; where did Drovetti find the colossus of Sebekhotep of the XIII dynasty?[108] It was in October this year, when Cavour became First Minister in Piedmont, that there arrived in Egypt the man who was to transform the treatment of Egyptian antiquities, and ensure that the collections of people like Drovetti would never again be possible: Auguste Mariette, later founder of the Service des Antiquités, who soon made his first sensational discovery, the Serapeum at Memphis.

Drovetti's grandson gave him family news the next year, in 1851, as well as announcing plans for railways in Egypt, to be built by George Stephenson. And an old friend, the Consul-General of the Netherlands in Egypt had just died. This was Pierre Ambroise Schutz.[109] He had been treasurer to his embassy in Cairo since 1825, was Consul at Alexandria 1827-1834, and Consul-General 1834-1851. Drovetti and he had known each other much longer even than that: Schutz replaced Briggs as British pro-consul at Alexandria in 1811. They had obviously remained in contact since his departure more than twenty years ago.

The last letter we have from Drovetti's hand is one of the saddest he ever wrote.[110] One year and a day before his death, he wrote from Barbania to his son Giorgio, now nearly forty. The letter begins with fulminations against almost all his relatives, who 'under the names of liberty, equality and fraternity' have espoused 'subversive principles of every kind in society and the family'! On top of this, Giorgio had completely undone all that his father had tried to do for him financially,

26. The hospital of S. Salvario, Torino in which Drovetti died

27. Drovetti's tomb in the
cemetery, Torino

by trusting a 'brigand' named Dizier. This man had robbed Giorgio of most of his fortune, by helping him withdraw from the Rothschild bank a capital of 216,000 francs in order to travel to Turkey and Persia. Giorgio had given his father his word of honour that he would never touch this capital, from which he drew interest. Drovetti now told his son bluntly that, given his intellectual weakness and physical indisposition, it was unthinkable that he should ever marry: this would only make a woman unhappy and produce children with his own infirmities. His father proposed, therefore, to make a life annuity out of the monies still left to his son in Paris, and what he himself could spare from his own annuity, government pension and sale of his patrimony in 1847. In this way his son might have an income of 8,000 francs. Drovetti was clearly in despair: this was the last chance for Giorgio to save something from the wreckage, and even that had to be protected legally by every means. Despite all his efforts, however, Drovetti admitted that he did not expect any gratitude or that his son would reform his ways.

At the same time, Drovetti made generous donations to the Torino hospitals for the treatment of the poor.[111] He then donated his copy of the great *Description de l'Egypte*, given to him by Louis XVIII, to the Academy of Torino, as well as Gau's work on Nubia.[112] This was in December 1851, as if he had a presentiment of his death, although he spoke only of poor health. The letter of thanks was written by the Vice-President, Giovanni Plana. In the same month by a coup d'état Napoleon overcame the four years' limit of the presidency of France, arresting eighty leaders of the opposition and 27,000 others.

The dissolution

Finding medical help in Barbania insufficient, Drovetti went to the house of his dear friend in Torino, Giovanni Battista Cossato.[113] His last known action is dated 3 March, 1852, when he admitted himself to the hospital of S. Salvario in the capital, near the modern railway station (ill. 26). Six days later he was dead; he passed away at 9 p.m. on 9 March. The hospital records show the cause of his death as dropsy (anasarca). He was 76 years old.[114]

Two days later, on the 11th, he was buried in the cemetery of Torino. His will was opened on 13 March.[115] In the declaration that he was of sound mind and therefore able to write a will, it was noted that he had been suffering from some 'strangeness, from imaginary fears', but had been perfectly rational in his replies. He appointed as his executors Giovanni Battista Cossato, Carlo Mosca and Carlo Cagnone. Drovetti's last wishes are sufficient to show that he was not mentally impaired; they accorded with his life-long principles. He asked that the remains of his parents should be brought from Barbania and placed in an appropriate monument beside his own. It might have been thought that his natural resting-place was beside them in Barbania; this was the obvious solution.[116] On the sale of all his property, both real and movable, his first care was the establishment of a life pension for his son Giorgio, 'at present travelling in Ethiopia'. Then all the remainder of his wealth was to be divided: that in Piedmont among the institutions and charitable works most useful for the poor there; that in France, with the consultation of Canon Vandenek, Vicar-General of the diocese of Versailles, for the benefit of similar institutions in that diocese. Drovetti must, like so many other people in the past, have been concerned about being too hastily judged dead: he specified that after his death, his body was to remain for twenty-four hours, and that then an autopsy was to be performed by doctors other than those who had cared for him; perhaps at the end he was possessed by memories of how many times his life had been endangered in Egypt by intrigue. The will is dated 23 February.

Drovetti now lies in the General Cemetery, in the first portico on the right, where his tomb was set up by Cagnone and Mosca. This explains the error in his birth-date as given in the inscription.[117] This records that 'he was doctor in both ecclesiastical and civil law, held the ministry of war, was an officer and Consul-General of Napoleon I in Egypt, where he promoted progress and collected precious monuments, from which was created the Egyptian Museum, the major ornament of this city. He died as he lived, a benefactor, making the poor his heirs.' The tomb is decorated by Drovetti's bust on a plinth (ill. 27). It is in the classical 'herm' form, and of a generally romanticising style. Drovetti is shown with long curly hair. The sculptor was Giovanni Albertoni, pupil of the great Bertel Thorwaldsen.[118]

VI The transformation of Egypt during the reign of Mehemet Ali: Drovetti's contribution

The enigma of Mehemet Ali

It is appropriate that, before discussing the major areas of Egypt's transformation in which Drovetti played such a leading role, some attempt be made to summarise the government of the Viceroy. This is far from easy; for the judgements offered have been very varied, and it is obvious that there were special reasons, both personal and national in particular, for the assessments presented. A review of some of the more notable will be, nevertheless, instructive.

One of the most detailed descriptions of the man himself is offered by the Irish traveller Richard Madden, who was in Egypt between 1825 and 1827 and again in 1840. Mehemet Ali was 5´6″ tall, of a ruddy complexion, with light hazel eyes, prominent eyebrows, thin lips, and agreeable features when in a good mood. He was 'frank, amiable and highly intelligent' with 'well-bred' gestures. His only language was Turkish, but his conversation was 'sprightly, courteous and intelligent'. 'On every subject he gave those about him the impression of a shrewd, penetrating right-thinking man.' In religion, Madden accounted him a liberal, which he ascribed to European influence. As for his standing in the country, we are instantly confronted with the telling contrast: he was enormously popular with his officials and Europeans, especially merchants, but Madden heard his name everywhere execrated by the fellahin.[1] The broadly favourable view offered by this Irishman suffers from the usual limitations of a visitor to a country who attempts to summarise basic conditions, but his picture of Mehemet Ali as a person is invaluable.

Someone who had long acquaintance with Egypt at the highest level was Thédénat-Duvent, the French Vice-Consul. In his *L'Egypte sous Mehemed Ali* he asked a fundamental question: was his government preferable to its predecessors? All scholars and artists agreed that it was, he assured his readers, the consuls were happy, as were the foreign traders and manufacturers, but agriculture and commerce were in bonds and industry and the arts were stagnant.[2] This is a striking summary, given that his book was dedicated to the Viceroy. It may be taken, then, as perhaps a combination of warning and exhortation.

Another Frenchman who spent many years in Egypt was the veterinarian Pierre Hamont. He classed Mehemet Ali as a skilled politician but a poor administrator, which seems to be another indisputable key. In his favour, he was indefatigable and affable, captivating most visitors, so that most accounts of him which were sent back to Europe were favourable – as we have seen, for example, with Madden and therefore to be used with caution; Hamont also stressed his religious toleration. On the other side, the Viceroy was very jealous and would sack any subordinate who was praised too highly, was taken in by liars and hypocrites, allowed informers to flourish, and was surrounded by Armenians and Turks who lacked the skill and knowledge to advise him.[3] This attempt at balance by Hamont is all the more striking because he is, in general, a severe critic of almost every aspect of the regime. He was, moreover, a bitter enemy of the next witness.

Clot Bey, Surgeon-General to the Egyptian army from 1825, gave a lively picture of the Viceroy whom he knew so well. His struggle with first the Mamelukes and then the Porte was a matter of life and death. 'He knew that if ever he faltered, the Sultan would not hesitate to send him a rope or a successor.' Clot emphasised that he had been forced by his overlord to fight the Greeks, and that he had not persecuted them in Egypt. He had also refused the Sultanship after his victories in Syria in 1832, although it had been offered him by 'all the muslim populations'. (This is extremely naive; it was again European intervention to prevent disturbance of the eastern balance of power which curtailed Mehemet Ali's ambitions, not any reticence on his part.) Clot even went so far as to make the incredible claim that he was 'incapable of treachery'! His tastes were simple, and his courage bordered on rashness: these two matters are well documented. Clot tells us, however, something more revealing: that the Viceroy was obsessed with his posthumous reputation; it is little wonder that he was engrossed with the lives of Alexander and Napoleon![4] Clot's statements are an extreme example of the eulogistic strain in European accounts of the ruler of Egypt.

An English traveller who wrote on contemporary Egypt was James St John. He had been an associate of James Silk Buckingham on his radical *Oriental Herald* and visited Egypt in 1832, where he went about on foot, before writing his *Egypt and Mohammed Aly*, 1834. He praised the Viceroy for 'perseveringly, though quietly, proceeding with the destruction of all those stupid prejudices which interrupt the free intercourse of Turk and Christian.' The distinguishing features of the reign were, in his view, 'strict impartiality of justice and equal protection of all nations and religions.'[5] This was high and discriminating praise.

So much for those who knew Mehemet Ali personally. At the end of the century Donald Cameron, a diplomat who was a judge in Cairo from 1889 to 1897 and was later to be English Consul-General at Alexandria (1909-1919), suggested that judgements on Mehemet Ali reflected a national divide: the English were unanimous on the Viceroy's tyranny, while the French tried to gloss over it. We have already in the above brief survey seen that this kind of simplification is quite erroneous. Cameron himself relied especially on the very negative report by Bowring in 1833 (a parliamentary blue book, 1840). 'While he was always a great man, we can scarcely speak of him as a good man' will certainly not be contested in its second part, but might be in its first. Cameron's final judgement is based on the fact that Mehemet Ali's own grandson Abbas undid all his work: abolishing the monopolies, freeing trade, reducing the army, closing the factories and dismissing the Europeans. His work, in the last analysis was, then, all for nothing.[6] The fact that a successor undoes all another's work does not, however, mean simply that the reviser is right and the initiator wrong, and there are few who would agree that Mehemet Ali's reign left no lasting mark on Egypt.

One of the most expert and understanding assessments of the Viceroy was provided by Henry Dodwell, professor at the London School of Oriental Studies, 1922-1946. He properly stressed the oriental context of Egypt with its different traditions of administration from those used in Europe, and the overriding controls on Mehemet Ali as a vassal of the Sultan. He was, however, able to credit him with high ideals, many reforms, and no small amount of success, despite the almost total lack of sound administrators. In so many ways he was a Turk, 'a vigorous but exceedingly unenlightened ruler, who would shrink from nothing for the attainment of his personal ends.' Along with this, however, he was unique among Turkish rulers in absorbing new ideas. Although concerned with the maintenance of his own power and that of his family, he was distinguished by 'a sense of the forces by which states are built up and broken down, a ceaseless struggle for improvement, a never-dulled consciousness of the defects of his administrative machinery such as no Oriental ruler had shown since the days of Akbar. His government marks a great turning-point in the history not only of Egypt but of the Near East as a whole, for he led the way in adapting western political ideas to eastern conditions.'[7]

In a more recent assessment by Helen Rivlin, she sees nothing to praise in Mehemet Ali's government: it was oppressive and corrupt, the Viceroy was surrounded by sycophants, bribery was rampant and officials were unpaid, yet huge sums were extorted from them when Mehemet Ali himself was in need.[8] There is no gainsaying any of these facts, but they are based on a study of what is universally recognised as the most unpleasant, and yet most fundamental department of the administration, namely agriculture.

On the other hand, a modern Egyptian historian, Abdel-Malek, interested primarily in the education policies of Mehemet Ali, for all their shortcomings, ends with a generous overall view:

> objectivement, le Vice-Roi n'aura pas fait qu'édifier un Etat autonome, une industrie moderne et une puissante armée: son action suscite la formation et la montée des premières générations d'intellectuels révolutionnaires et modernistes en Egypte.[9]

What can we make of all these contradictions? The European visitor to Egypt was obviously for the most part very favourably impressed with Mehemet Ali. Most foreigners, indeed, such as diplomats, merchants and manufacturers, are said to have been favourable. Of far greater importance than these, however, were the millions of the Viceroy's own people, and their condition was, as we shall see, nothing short of slavery in the most grinding poverty.

Mehemet Ali had undoubted qualities: he was a masterly politician, and combined ruthlessness with circumspection, calculating exactly what was possible at any moment. He must also be given considerable credit for his relative 'liberalism'. Whatever his own qualities, however, there was hardly another person in the country who could serve him with competence or honesty. The entire administration was notoriously corrupt. The inescapable limitations upon him, however, must never be forgotten: he was not a European constitutional ruler; he was an Oriental despot, who by his own ruthlessness had gained control of one of the most difficult countries to rule in the world (in terms of geography alone), and he was always technically the vassal of the Ottoman Sultan. He believed, nevertheless, that the way forward for Egypt was through the adoption of European techniques, although they were in so many ways, as we shall see, totally unsuited to his country.

Despite all this, he began the process which transformed Egypt from a mediaeval backwater of the Ottoman Empire into one of the leading countries of the Arab world. Had he not been restrained he would have crushed the Greeks' bid for independence and then overthrown the Ottoman Empire. Certainly not a 'good' man, he may not even have been a 'great' one, but without contradiction he was one of the most important and influential figures of the first half of the nineteenth century. And in most of the reforms a leading role was played by Drovetti.

Education

The most striking of all programmes to bring Egypt into line with modern European civilisation with all its dramatic advances in the nineteenth century was the one to send leading young Egyptians abroad to be educated, so that, as in modern study programmes, they might return to benefit their own country by the exercise of their professions. Here, perhaps, above all other examples, Drovetti played an exemplary part.

The first mention of the programme is in 1821, when Cesare Saluzzo, director of the military academy in Torino, wrote to Drovetti about Elie Sabbagh and Raphael Misabiki who were studying chemistry and mathematics respectively at the Collegio delle Provincie, where Drovetti himself had been a student. They were making good progress, and had been looked after by a man called Morosi, but apparently Mehemet Ali was not providing for their expenses. Their professors were Gioberti and Plana. They and Count Balbo, Minister of the Interior, and Abbot Avogadro, the Rector of the college, all supported the programme. Drovetti was asked to intervene with the Viceroy to see to the students' expenses.[10]

The background to this study programme abroad, involving two students, is unclear. It seems to have been very ill-planned, and if the Viceroy agreed to it, he hardly supported it. The sending of the students to Italy, especially to Torino and the Collegio delle Provincie, is highly suggestive of Drovetti's involvement. This is perhaps the scheme to which Jomard later referred in November 1827, when he regretted that the Viceroy seven years earlier had not followed Drovetti's advice and Jomard's ideas in setting up a school in France on the same lines as the Collège des Irlandais.[11]

The *Epistolario* is then silent until October 1825, when Jomard wrote to Drovetti, noting the departure of Etienne Abro, nephew of Youssef Boghos, from France after a year there. He asserted that 'nothing could be more useful for the maintenance of relations between Egypt and France than the despatch of the young people whom Mehemet Ali proposes to send to Paris.' Jomard went on to recommend Joseph Agoub[12] to teach the young Egyptians French language and literature, to replace Ellious Boktour whom he had in mind when the plan was first proposed 'some years ago', but who had died. He was uncertain about the Viceroy's intentions. Were the young students to be put into a royal college or a special house? Jomard preferred the latter. He spoke of a group of twenty.[13]

As so often is the case, such schemes have precedents, and context is required. Early eighteenth century missionary programmes had included sending Egyptian children to France. The Salle des Arméniens had been established in Paris in 1720 for the training of the dragomans. As he left Egypt, Napoleon suggested to Kleber that five or six hundred Egyptians should be sent for education to France. The first educational mission to Europe from the country in fact dates from as early as 1809, and the students went to Italy to study military science, ship-building, printing and engineering. Twenty-eight students were abroad from this year until 1818, but the records were lost in the fire on the Citadel in 1820. The most famous participant was Osman Noureddin, who studied in Italy and France, 1809-1817.

On the other hand, training schools had already been established in Egypt. One for Mamelukes was on the Citadel under Hasan Effendi in 1816, and taught Turkish, Persian, Italian and military science. This was followed by the 'Palace School', also on the Citadel, teaching mathematics, for students drawn from almost all nationalities except Egyptians. Most important was the School of Geometry at Bulaq in 1821, to train surveyors, staffed mainly by Italians.[14]

By 1826, the much expanded programme had begun. Youssef Boghos, private secretary to Mehemet Ali, wrote to Drovetti asking his advice whether students from the high school at Cairo should go to Italy or France to complete their education. Drovetti's reply[15] tells much about himself and his principles and is one of his most interesting letters. He began by stating that as an Italian by birth it would be easy for him to prefer his old country, but the matter was too important to be judged on such simplistic grounds. The first question was language. Drovetti was sufficiently acquainted with current teaching to know that intensive tuition could impart a language in a few months, and Paris had famous schools in Oriental languages, so that Egyptians could learn French easily. In Italy, on the other hand, since the 'revolutionary events of 1821', all education was subject to 'rigorous vigilance and inspection by the police', and must conform to governmental ideas. Religious and political toleration, he admitted bluntly, was unknown. Muslims would therefore be at a severe disadvantage, whereas there was no educational difficulty for anyone in France.

Drovetti then turned to the principles of such education abroad for the young Egyptians. They should not devote themselves to one subject, especially if they were to become administrators; rather they must read all sorts of books and newspapers, frequent all the most capable educators, mix with all classes of society, and learn as much as possible about politics and military institutions. How could all this be possible without freedom of the press and of expression? Foreseeing objections that men of principle must exist also in Italy, Drovetti stated that they would not be able to educate young people without grave danger to themselves. It was thus Paris to which the Egyptians must go: the 'centre of the civilised world', seat of one of the greatest administrations, but where there was freedom to think, speak and write; in sum, it was the great theatre to observe and learn about men, their passions, politics and government. For some subjects, such as law, medicine, theology, physics, Latin and Italian, Italy might be preferable, but Paris was the place to send students of diplomacy, military science and administration, in short, those who wished to become statesmen. Here, then, at the crucial stage in the setting up of the great overseas' education scheme, Drovetti was consulted on the most fundamental choices – and his advice was followed.

By the middle of 1826, forty-two Egyptians were going to Paris, not all young.[16] They included Abdi Effendi, the Muturdar (Keeper of the Seal), Mustafa Mukhtar Effendi, the Defterdar or Finance Minister, and Hasan Effendi. Another letter from Drovetti[17] alerts us to the crucial people at the other end. They included the professor of Arabic at the Royal Library, the Egyptian Agoub. Apart from him the organisation and supervision of the students fell to Jomard, member of the Napoleonic expedition, geographer and antiquarian, and editor of the *Description de l'Egypte*, soon to be appointed Keeper at the National Library. The Paris school was to be a lifelong passion with him, and he and Drovetti were the two main-springs of its creation and continuation, in all its difficulties. Pierre Hamont supplies other vital information. Among the specialist teachers were Macarel (civil administration), Olivier (engineering and artillery), and Gauthier de Chaubry (chemistry).[18]

The second preserved letter of Jomard relating to the school also dates from the middle of this year.[19] He accepted his main role in the project, despite its difficulties, because of the benefit to both countries, even deferring a holiday for his health to which he had looked forward after his twenty years of work on the *Description*. He was inspired by his devotion to the cause of universal education, and the 'initiative which he himself had taken before in proposing a project of this kind' to Drovetti. The latter had persuaded the Viceroy[20] and had been instrumental in having Jomard appointed director of studies (Agoub was 'inspector of studies'). He proposed that the students should stay in Paris for five years. A major concern was a stable location for the school. Jomard proposed the purchase of a building for 250-300,000 francs. He devoted special attention to the alternation of different kinds of instruction, such as manual and intellectual. He had also been in touch with the President of the Council and various ministers, with the result that the French government was very favourable. Jomard realised, of course, the delicate question of the religious practices of the students. He assured Drovetti that they could maintain these under the supervision of the Muturdar, but that some punishments and other practices should be modified to accord with those of French students, 'since it was a matter of civilisation', that is, that the Egyptians were expected to learn about European ways. The next month, Agoub wrote to Drovetti expressing his gratitude to him and Boghos for his appointment. The school, he asserted, was 'almost completely organised and quite ready to receive us'.[21] The location of the school was first in the rue de Clichy, then in the rue de Regard (no.15), in the Latin Quarter near the Luxembourg Gardens.[22]

Much interest was aroused in Paris by these exotic students, from satirical magazines to a comic opera (*La Girafe* of Theaubon) to mock epic (*La Bacriade ou la guerre d'Alger* by Barthelemy and Mery). On the other hand, we have some precious notes from one of the students recording his reactions to Paris.[23]

Drovetti arrived on leave in France in the middle of 1827. Jomard reported to him immediately on the latest progress. The language problem was being overcome, that is, the students were learning French, and now their progress could be more rapid. There were other difficulties, however, including the fact that he had received no instructions from the Egyptian government for a year. The young people had been spread around in pensions. Jomard warned Drovetti against 'false reports', and assured him of his own untiring efforts in the previous year.

In August Jomard was still very depressed, and spoke of being 'tormented' and 'persecuted', but Egypt was being civilised and France was winning laurels more lasting than those of war. He spoke, however, of abandoning the work, such were the obstacles, if he encountered the least disagreement or lack of confidence.[24] In November there was still dispute, it seems, about who would be in charge of the school. It had been suggested that the three senior students should head it. Jomard was outraged: how could people who had such need themselves of discipline impose it and a scholastic life on others? The youngest of the Egyptian chiefs was testing him. Although not named, this would seem to be by exclusion the Defterdar; for Hasan is named as going to a naval school, and the Muturdar showed promise of the best results.[25]

Notice had been taken of the school from the beginning by the Society of Geography.[26] The fruit of Drovetti's leave was published under the name of Jean Pacho in October 1827, a proposal for a much grander and more idealistic scheme, and this is ascribed solely to Drovetti.[27] The Consul had noted the 'rare intelligence' and 'native sagacity' of young Africans. If individuals were so intelligent, why, he asked, were Africans as a nation so torpid? Climatic explanations had long ago been discounted; the human race was the same everywhere. The barrier of the Sahara cut off the Africans from the Mediterranean, and even in antiquity no civilised nation which occupied the coast had penetrated to the interior. In modern times, however, a 'commercial nation' (England) was exploiting the continent, and the natives had been enslaved. Now Europe had declared the Africans free,[28] but this was counterbalanced by the spread of Muslim fanaticism. Drovetti believed that the social status of the negro could be improved only by creating a 'chain of relations' between Africa and Europe. He now proposed, therefore, to send Africans there to be educated, an extension of the Egyptian mission. On their return their new ideas would spread from tribe to tribe and oasis to oasis, he asserted, like a message arrow. This plan had been conceived by the Consul in 1811, but the political crisis (that is, the coming collapse of Napoleon) had prevented its implementation. He now offered to send young negroes to Paris at his own expense. Pacho called on learned societies to obtain entry to the various schools for these new students. Here was a project for the education of not only Egyptians, but also negroes from places such as the Sudan and Ethiopia, perhaps inspired by Mehemet Ali's attempts to build a new Egyptian army from such men.[29]

Early in 1828 Jomard published a very favourable report on the progress of the schools.[30] The students had in February undergone public examinations in French, mathematics and art before a most imposing jury representing leading members of the law, University, Institute and army, presided over by the comte de Chabrol, member of the Napoleonic expedition and now Prefect of the department of the Seine. The results had been very encouraging. The students could write well in French and solve basic mathematical problems. They were now to be divided into fifteen courses for special study: civil administration, military administration, navy, diplomacy, hydraulics, mechanics, military engineering, artillery, armaments, engraving, chemistry, medicine, agriculture, natural history and mining, and translation. In a private letter to Drovetti, however, Jomard expressed many concerns, notably about prejudiced and unjust people, who were, he stated, very numerous in Paris. Jomard had, in fact, refused any salary for himself as overseer of the whole programme, not least to avoid any hint that it was a speculation on his part. He trusted that Drovetti would approve of his action; we can be sure that he did. Jomard revealed his own attachment of special importance to geography; he hoped to teach that subject himself.[31] The young Egyptians, meanwhile, were progressing in chemistry; the three sailors were doing well at Brest; the others at Nancy were soon to have examinations. Most of them responded to Jomard's efforts, but a few caused worry by their lack of discipline.[32]

Drovetti's plan to extend the educational programme to negroes was put into practice. In January 1829 he announced to Jomard the sending to Paris of six young Ethiopians. The latter instantly set about preparing for their arrival, asking various bodies for help. The Society of Geography declined; the Ministry of the Interior did nothing, that of Education sent him to the Navy, which finally agreed to look after two; the Society of

Education took the other four. They were to learn French, natural history, drawing, mathematics and Arabic.

For the Ethiopians, Jomard aimed at producing men who could carry back to their own country some idea of European arts and sciences, so that they could make exact observations there and enrich science by their discoveries. They had to learn French, and geography was to begin with the example of Ethiopia.[33] It was Drovetti's generosity which had 'redeemed them from slavery', and Jomard was happy to cooperate in this 'philanthropic project'. They arrived in Paris in May 1829. The contribution of the Society of Education turned out to be a miserable 800 francs, which would assist four of the six for only six months.[34]

Jomard's next letter was written after Drovetti had returned to Europe for the last time, in June 1829. The students were beginning the new school year, and the naval cadets were being delayed by the Ministry which had not yet sent them to a naval school or put them on board a ship. The others, studying administration, chemistry, agriculture, medicine and mathematics, were progressing well.[35] For the Ethiopians, however, tragedy struck. The following winter was too severe for one of them, despite the care taken of them by the married couple who conducted the pension, and he died of consumption. Jomard was understandably worried over the reaction of the Egyptian government; he had received no reply as usual to his letters. The financial help from the Society of Education had ceased. Jomard was in the meantime paying the board for four of them.[36]

Drovetti's silence in correspondence (probably letters lost rather than not written) so disturbed Jomard that he wrote a progress report in January 1832.[37] Twenty-eight students sent in 1826 had by now returned to Egypt with their studies complete. Of these, Jomard estimated that ten could be teachers, and the others good 'practitioners'. Twelve of fifteen were still studying, and thirty-four new students had arrived. Jomard was still, however, fulminating against 'egoists, intriguers and lazy charlatans'. He had managed to present the leading officials among the students, the Muturdar and the Defterdar, to the King, but the French newspapers had reported the matter clumsily. There was still, Jomard lamented, no serious attention by the French government to Levantine affairs.

By September of the same year, another Ethiopian had died. Three of the remaining four had learnt French, and the eldest had distinguished himself in natural science and could take up medicine. One was, however, not a success, and Drovetti suggested that he might be sent to Vienna. He was to be consigned to the Russian ambassador, and an official letter from Drovetti was required.

Of the Egyptians, the Defterdar had been brilliantly received on his return to Egypt, because of his education and his manners. Even Mehemet

Ali was impressed. Hasan Effendi had been given command of a warship. Abdy Effendi, on the other hand, to Jomard's amazement, had not returned to Egypt at all, but had gone off to Livorno, Rome and Naples! Of the more ordinary students, eight or nine had been placed in charge of the teaching of their specialisations, but Jomard was concerned at the inactivity of the others. Everything had been upset by the Syrian campaign. Now, however, some students from Clot's medical school were also to be sent to France.[38]

Three years later, by 1835, the schools of mines and canals, and of civil administration had been set up in Egypt. Jomard's pupils were professors and directors. His most brilliant product was the Defterdar, Murtar Bey. Jomard spoke of his own enormous sacrifices, but asserted that he would do it all over again. He then turned to Drovetti and paid him one of his highest compliments: the honour was all due to him. 'Without you, I would not have been successful, without you the Pasha would not have dared anything, would not have considered anything.'[39]

Then suddenly, in January 1836, all Egyptian students in Paris were recalled. Jomard must have been amazed, and later found that it was a misunderstanding and that some students might return.[40] The last reference to the great project in Jomard's preserved correspondence with Drovetti came in 1844. He thought of the educational programme as he cast a more hopeful eye over Egypt's position at the time, recalling one of his most important students, Artin Bey, now Minister of Commerce.[41]

In summary, then, a plan had been conceived for European education for both Egyptians and Africans as early as 1811. A start had been made with the former in Italy a decade later, but it seems to have been short-lived. It was in 1826 that the first contingent was sent to Paris, and the first negroes followed in 1829. Dozens of the former, including some very highly placed officials, and six of the latter received education in France in languages, science, mathematics and geography. The support of the French political and scientific bodies was paltry, and initially the Egyptian government did not understand the costs involved.

Who had conceived this plan? Jomard's letter to Drovetti in June 1826 is clear. Jomard, stimulated by his devotion to universal education, had proposed the scheme as early as 1811, but it was Drovetti who had convinced Mehemet Ali to set it in motion and to appoint Jomard as director. In keeping with this was the compliment he paid him in 1835, stressing Drovetti's vital part in convincing the Viceroy. He was furthermore instrumental in the choice of Torino for some students in 1821 (we may be sure) and more importantly of Paris in 1826. What is most interesting on his part, however, is his idealism. The letter of 1826 is illuminating. It was the repressive political conditions in Italy which convinced him to prefer France as the location for the school. Italy suffered in the comparison from many points of view: religious prejudice, lack of books, and limited opportunities to learn about European society. The failure of the first attempt in his native Piedmont must have been the final argument. The article of 1827 set forth his belief in the intelligence of the Africans, and the need simply to break down their isolation to bring out their potential.[42] Jomard, on his part, was the Director of the Ecole Egyptienne in Paris, who set up the whole school, devised the entire curriculum, taught geography there, and had to combat critics from every side. For all this he received no salary.[43]

What were the aims of the programme? For Drovetti and Jomard, they were the continuation of French influence which had begun with the Napoleonic expedition, and a desire to allow France to exercise its 'civilising mission' in modernising Egypt, as well as a strong wish to see reforms in Egypt. For the Viceroy, on the other hand, the purposes were purely practical: to educate servants who could modernise Egypt, to provide the technical and educational personnel needed, above all, for the creation of a modern army, and to free Egypt from her dependence on imported educators.

As with every other initiative in Egypt at this time, even the education programme had its critics and, even worse, its belittlers. Pierre Hamont devoted a good part of his book to this subject. He admitted that the sending of Egyptians to Europe was necessitated by the inadequacy of European teachers in Egypt. From 1826 to 1842 he calculates that about one hundred students went to France. Every effort was made by Mehemet Ali, he asserts, Jomard was full of zeal and devotion, and great changes were expected in Egypt from the importation of ideas. The illusion was shattered in 1832, when the students returned. The Viceroy declared them useless; he wanted only doctors and soldiers. There was a famous story that he placed the students into areas totally different from their studies, and Hamont gives examples: Mouktar Effendi and Akmet Effendi, who had studied military science, were sent to civil administration, Mammouth Effendi (naval studies) to finance, Estefan Effendi (diplomacy) to education, and Mohammed Beyoumi (hydraulics) to chemistry.[44] A more recent scholar also admitted that Mehemet Ali made little use of the specialists whom it had cost so much to educate, and stated that such qualified people met unchecked and open hostility from the bureaucracy.[45]

The results were, however, far from negligible. The brightest did in fact complete the highest grades in French education, and many went on to be the most eminent ministers in the government. Among the outstanding products were Moukhtar, Minister of Education, Hasan, Minister of the Navy, and Artin and Estefan, Ministers of Foreign Affairs.[46]

The effect on the minds of dozens of Egyptians from their years in Paris was of incalculable importance, and Drovetti had been the man who had made it all possible.

Health

The greatest contribution made by Drovetti to the well-being of the Egyptians was his sponsorship of widespread vaccination programmes. This began in 1822, and many of the doctors performing the first vaccinations and instructing native assistants were Italians. Clot estimates the death-toll before the vaccination at 50-60,000 children a year.[47]

The earliest mention of vaccination in May 1822 was occasioned by an outbreak of the plague in Dahmanur. Drovetti recommended a French doctor, and Mehemet Ali gave orders that all children were to be inoculated. The Viceroy's secretary also wrote to Drovetti to make all the arrangements.[48] At the same time the Consul was consulting the controllers of public health at Marseille about measures to be taken in Egypt. They replied that a hospital was necessary to isolate anyone who had been in contact with victims, in order to protect Europeans at Alexandria. Drovetti thus attempted to enlist French governmental support by appeals to the duty it had to protect its nationals in Egypt.[49]

The vaccination programme was well under way by 1824, and Drovetti received many reports from the various doctors administering it. Dr Francesco Massari was at Mansura in the Delta in September. There was, of course, considerable resistance from the Arab population, which thought that this was some method of marking boys for conscription or slavery. Massari assured Drovetti that 'one day his good advice would be followed, always to the advantage of the Egyptian population.' By the end of the year he reported some success: in a month he had vaccinated twenty-five villages, without the slightest trouble. Drovetti's plan would thus have a happy outcome. The doctor suffered, however, from irregularities in pay, and asked the Consul to see that he was paid monthly rather than quarterly.[50]

Others did not have so easy a time. Dr Daumas was also in the Delta, at Zephta. The local chief brought along many children. As soon as they had been vaccinated and returned to their parents, however, they rubbed the vaccine off their arms. A plot was then formed by some soldiers to destroy the village. This had nothing to do with the vaccination, but was caused by a dispute over pay. Daumas' life was in danger, and he had to flee. His limited financial resources were also running low. He naturally turned to Drovetti, asking what he was to do, and if he could obtain an increase in pay from the Viceroy.[51]

Similar financial difficulties were experienced by Dr Ailhaud, who arrived in July 1824. By November he had spent 150 talaris (750 frs) for

214

food, lodging and travel. In order to survive he had had to sell some medical equipment and undertake some private practice. He wrote to Drovetti seeking daily expenses of 5 francs, his salary since September, and reimbursement for the cost of his voyage and quarantine (500 frs).[52] The great hopes of a medical programme staffed by European doctors were obviously not being supported by the Egyptian government.

Dr Celestino Cani reported to Drovetti in December of the same year from Samanud in the Delta. He was training two assistants, and his interpreter could also vaccinate perfectly. He asserted that he would be nothing without Drovetti's protection.[53] This was followed by a long report in which he noted the lack of willingness of the population to undergo vaccination and the way those so treated interfered with it to make it fail by washing it off and other means. In winter, smallpox was epidemic and it often happened that those vaccinated caught the real disease, so that the programme was harmed. To overcome all these problems, Cani suggested to Drovetti that the religious leaders should be made to support the programme, that district heads should be forced to vaccinate from door to door, omitting no woman or child, and that revaccinations up to three times be performed. He had discussed these new regulations with the local Cachef, and now he sought Drovetti's approval, presumably to win over Mehemet Ali.[54]

Daumas had not, it is pleasing to note, been forced to give up. He had been working since December at Tanta in the Delta in the presence of Ibrahim Cachef, and winning over the peasants. He was training assistants in accordance with Drovetti's orders. Cani saw his work in his province lasting until August, and had perfected a way of making the vaccination easier and surer. He thanked Drovetti for a loan. It transpires, indeed, that it was Drovetti who ensured that doctors were paid monthly by the provincial chiefs. Massari was able by February 1825 to report the first real proofs of the campaign's success: smallpox was raging in neighbouring provinces, but was virtually unknown in that of Mansura. And in July Cani spoke of the extension of the inoculations to Damietta after the success in two other provinces which had saved so many lives. He foresaw the extension of the programme to the whole of Egypt. It is significant that he applied to Drovetti to vaccinate in Damietta.[55]

Things took a turn for the worse in the second half of the year. When Cani left Fua, the cachef stopped the inoculations by his assistants, and the doctor was unable to obtain more vaccine even in Cairo. Massari was in the same situation. In October, in fact, Cani asked Drovetti to allow him to resign in order to seek the post of chief surgeon or even to return to his own country. Massari was at Asyut in November, but the vaccine was of poor quality. He asked Drovetti to help him obtain better, and also to use his influence with the new provincial governor to gain his support for the work. The same misfortune affected Cani in the Fayum. He wrote to Drovetti that he had bought bad vaccine from a Greek in Cairo. In Middle Egypt things were not going well for him. The provincial governors were not helpful, they produced only two or three children as sufficient for the vaccination of a whole village, and so the advantages did not become obvious. On Cani's arrival, in fact, the mothers had all fled with their children. If Drovetti and the Viceroy (a significant conjunction) wanted universal vaccination, the present methods would not do. As Cani had suggested, many assistants had to be trained and sent out two to a province; they could succeed within a year, he estimated. In January 1826, Cani in fact asked to be given the direction of the whole operation. In a further letter of the same month, Cani offered, if he obtained such a position, to import vaccine at his own expense from Syria or another country outside Egypt. He implied that the division he suggested would leave Massari in charge of Upper Egypt, and stated that the number of assistants he needed was forty, and that they would be able to pass an examination within two months.[56]

Drovetti obtained better vaccine for him, and Cani was by March at Beni Suef, 120 kms south of Cairo, anxious about the monthly pay of his assistants (45 piastres). The last letter from him, unfortunately undated, was written perhaps in 1826. It has the air of a final note to Drovetti, to whom he sent six 'quills' of vaccine, and promised to send a copy of the instructions in Arabic which he had drawn up for the assistants. His operations were now finished.[57]

From Drovetti's *Epistolario*, therefore, it is clear that he was the driving force behind a programme of inoculation against smallpox which began in Egypt in 1822 and reached its climax in 1826. The vaccinators at this early stage were, of course, Europeans, and unless the correspondence is misleading, the major medical agent of the consul was Celestino Cani, along with Francesco Massari. There were also Frenchmen such as Ailhaud and Daumas. Attention seems to have focussed on Lower Egypt, although much was also done in Middle Egypt. The European doctors were able to leave the continuation of the work to Egyptians whom they had trained in great numbers. The story is striking for the idealism and practicality of Drovetti, the devotion of the doctors and their constant resort to him for leadership, help and protection, and the great native superstition which they had to overcome.[58]

Apart from the vaccination programme, the other great medical initiative was the establishment of a medical school in 1827, under the direction of Clot Bey. We will not be surprised to learn that the director in April 1828 sent Drovetti a report on the first year of its operation. He did the same in March 1829.[59] A further letter was dated March 1834.[60] Clot wrote to Drovetti, now of course back in Europe, of the intrigues of both Egyptians and Europeans and of his pride that the school had already trained three hundred officers for the army. He had, furthermore, taken a dozen of the best students to France and England, and had been showered with honours. On his return to Egypt, Mehemet Ali appointed him Inspector-General of the Health Service. Clot was fulsome in his gratitude to Drovetti and anxious to be of any service to him.

It is strange, then, to turn to Clot's own published account, his *Aperçu général sur l'Egypte*, 1840, in which he claims that he did not know Drovetti very well, since he arrived in Egypt only in 1825![61] At this time each regiment of 4,000 men had only a chief doctor, four aides and two pharmacists.[62] Clot devised a career for the medical corps, with promotion from lieutenant (aide) to battalion commander, with the same pay and uniform as the regular soldiers. He was able to diminish the mortality rate very considerably.

The medical school, established in 1827 as we have seen, had to endure great opposition, especially from the Muslim horror of dissection. The textbooks were naturally in French, which the students could not read, so translators had to be employed. A system of monthly examinations was used to stimulate competition. In 1832 the twelve best students were sent to Paris for further study, so that they might return as teachers, and also to offer them for independent assessment, to counter calumny. A list of the teachers includes Davigneau, Bernard, Barthelemy, Perron and Scisson; Celesia and Figari; Pruner and Fisher (Bavarians), Gaetani (Spanish) and Pachtod.[63]

It was not, however, until 1949 that Clot's own memoirs were published, which give us the most complete account. He was recruited for service in Egypt by the French agent Tourneau in 1824 for a period at first of five years with a salary of 8,000 francs and a colonel's rations. He admits that it was Drovetti who advised Mehemet Ali to enlist Europeans to help bring Egypt out of its barbarism.[64] Clot duly arrived on 11 February, 1825, and immediately dined with the French Consul.

What needs to be stressed here is the varying versions given by Clot of his relations with Drovetti. In his published account he was at pains to minimise those connections, on the grounds that he knew him for only four to five years. It seems that Drovetti did not have a direct hand in recruiting him for Egyptian service, but when he arrived he found his most natural supporter and protector in his own consul, and his letters to Drovetti show his keen anxiety to report to him and to impress him with the success of the school. Given the detailed documentation of the Consul's part in the vaccination programme, it is obvious that he gave equal support to any other improvement in the medical condition of the Egyptians, no matter how far short the medical school fell in the attainment of its goals.

The health service in the army was established in the same year, with hospitals at Alexandria and training camps at Abu Zabel and finally at Khanka near Cairo. The mortality rate was appalling. Appeals to Mehemet Laz'oglon, the Minister for War, for supplies were disregarded. When the chief chemist was beaten, Clot resigned. He succeeded, however, in winning over the Minister, who then became his protector, notably against the pretensions of General Boyer.

The first examinations were conducted before Osman Bey, commander-in-chief, and the consuls of France, Holland, Russia, Sardinia and others. The costs of entertaining all these dignitaries for five days was, he admits, enormous, but it was considered politic to gain such eminent supporters. Since the students spoke only Arabic and the instructors French or Italian, interpreters were employed who became specialists in particular areas. Clot himself devised many different methods of explanation and demonstration, notably tutorial groups of about ten students. Although teaching was in the native language, it was realised that the doctors would have to learn European languages in order to keep abreast of technical advances. The results of the first examination in 1828 were 20 firsts, 38 found sound to satisfactory, and 43 deemed unsatisfactory, hardly an indulgent pass-rate, we may note. The examinations of the second year, in 1829, again before various officers and distinguished Europeans, resulted in 20 firsts, 26 seconds and 21 thirds.[65]

In 1830 the Veterinary School was established under Hamont, whom Clot described as 'brutal, ambitious and greedy'.[66] He goes so far as to claim that he was dismissed, and then tried to have Clot assassinated, for which he was imprisoned for a month.

Perhaps the most striking medical innovation of the time was the establishment of a maternity school for midwives under Mlle Palmyre Gault. It began with negroes, then trained sixteen Egyptian girls. Clot sent them on holiday, asking them to tell of their experiences and recruit others. The school thus jumped to sixty students![67] The course lasted an amazing six years and was unique at the time in the Muslim world.

For his bravery in remaining in Cairo during the cholera epidemic of 1831 (there were 35,000 victims), Clot was given the title Bey. He returned to France on the death of Mehemet Ali in 1849. In his memoirs he especially thanked the two French consuls whom he had served, Drovetti and Mimaut, for their friendship and support.[68]

It is only proper that Hamont, Clot's closest colleague, be given a chance to speak. He declares an invention Clot's claim that great opposition to the school by the religious leaders had to be overcome; they denied this when Hamont interviewed them. Hamont agrees with others that the examinations in the school were fraudulent, in that the students knew the questions, but he surprisingly defends Clot's actions: otherwise the school would have been closed. Much more damaging is his statement that the graduates of the school were found incompetent, and Ibrahim forbade them to practise in Syria, so that resort had to be had again to Europeans. The school thus cost enormous sums but produced nothing. The most surprising verdict is the final one, that Clot was not to blame: 'he was given a task which he could not fulfil'. Nor was the Viceroy to blame; for no other project had such full government support.[69]

Heyworth-Dunne summarises the medical school, along with the other military schools thus: they were

> essentially intended for special training, mainly naval and military, but even those that were not actually providing officers and men for active service were intended for some auxiliary service connected with the supply and demand of his forces, either directly or indirectly. Not a single institution was set up philanthropically or for the sole purpose of improving the intellectual outlook of the people.[70]

One can hardly gainsay this harsh judgement, but at the same time, given Egypt's situation, one could hardly expect anything else.

A third medical matter is the enforcing of quarantine. As early as 1814 in response to an initiative of Drovetti, Boghos invited all the consuls to consult about its establishment in Egyptian ports. The English were singled out as especially failing to observe any regulations in this regard. Drovetti was to assist the Viceroy in the organisation of the quarantine. He replied with at least four letters and a list of regulations for the quarantine station, consisting of 34 articles. Boghos accepted these, save for toning down some prejudice against Turkish warships. Drovetti was then given the right to nominate a doctor in charge.[71]

It seems that nothing was done, and this is ascribed to Muslim superstition. Quarantine was opposed by the religious leaders as contrary to the Koran and Muslim ideas of fatality![72] Then in a plague Europeans had been the main victims. Sailors with nowhere to take refuge had been murdered sleeping in the streets. The consuls in 1817 therefore took up a subscription, and ships were each to pay 10 piastres as a levy, and patients who could afford it were to pay.[73] The establishment of quarantine on Drovetti's advice is noted by Johannes Bramsen, who had visited Egypt in 1814.[74]

An interesting sequel was revealed in 1823. Boghos wrote to Marseille, trying to obtain a plan of their quarantine station and copies of the regulations. His agents reported that there were no plans and that no regulations had ever been printed, and that the administration was in the hands of merchants who ran it in secrecy. It was thus left only to write to the French government. Drovetti was, of course, the obvious person to do this. He did write to the Minister of Foreign Affairs, Chateaubriand, in December. The Minister replied in June 1824 that the Ministry of the Interior was drawing up plans for the Egyptians.[75]

The fate of the lazaretto in later years is interesting. When James St John arrived in 1832, all was not as could be desired. An Englishman was confined there with smallpox and nearly died. He had no bed, and almost no medical attention, and was kept awake all night by the 'entertainments' of the other inmates.[76]

Drovetti was thus the major European initiator of the establishment of quarantine regulations and a lazaretto in Egyptian ports. He personally drew up regulations for it, and later was the intermediary in obtaining copies of French government rules.[77]

Egyptian agriculture

At the end of the eighteenth century, some three hundred Mamelukes controlled two-thirds of the cultivatable land in Egypt.[78] Combined with this monopoly, their extortions reduced Upper Egypt to anarchy for the last third of the century. The French had therefore attempted reforms: they proposed that the large leases be abolished, with compensation. General Menou in 1800 suggested a single land tax based on area and quality, to be reduced in years of poor flooding. The fellahin were to be given their own land.[79]

In 1806, Mehemet Ali began to reduce the power of the large land leasors and the sheiks, and to take over control of the taxes in Lower Egypt. By the next year, the tax on land was 1400 paras per *faddan*, in contrast to 270 under the French. In 1811, following the destruction of the Mamelukes, Ibrahim was appointed Governor of Upper Egypt, carried out a survey of all lands, and gained complete control over the revenues of the south.[80] The finances of the Pasha were then undermined, however, by the Arabian war and the loss of trade with England when she resumed relations with Russia.

The situation in Egypt by 1812, according to some observers, was deteriorating badly under the strain. Taxes on the land had increased four-fold, there were endless requisitions of animals, and the passage of armies caused grievous hardship to the peasants. It was calculated that one third of the population had been conscripted, and much of the land was no longer irrigated. At the same time, however, 30,000 olive trees were being planted in the Fayum.[81]

A survey was undertaken of all lands in 1813-1814. They were classified according to their crops and quality. The lands of the religious corporations were taken over, amid enormous upheavals. The old system of tax collection was also abolished. The result was the conversion of most of the country into a 'huge government farm under the direct administration of the government hierarchy'. The reorganised revenues brought in 70 million Turkish piastres, the equivalent of 70 million francs. The agricultural changes were far-reaching. All land left uncultivated was to be worked for the Pasha. All taxes imposed by village owners were removed.[82] Mehemet Ali was the richest Pasha in the Ottoman Empire. Further adjustments were made in 1822, when the Viceroy reclassified all land in eleven grades, which paid taxes varying between 2 and 22 francs per acre.[83]

Such are the main changes introduced by Mehemet Ali into the agricultural life of his country. Contemporaries and modern scholars have been, however, virtually unrelieved in their criticisms of the system and its results. One of the most memorable comments came from none other than Belzoni, who noted that, when the general pay for a day's labour in 1819 was 20 paras, a peasant could not afford even a cup of coffee, which cost 5 paras.[84] James St John, writing in 1834 on the condition of the peasants, stated that their cottages 'exceed in filth and meanness the cabins of the Irish and they themselves are generally covered with rags.' He offered two most telling statistics. The Mamelukes' tax per *faddan* had been 12 *patah* (27 piastres) for rich soil, 6-8 for inferior; under Mehemet Ali it had risen to 26. He claimed, indeed, that no notice was taken of the quality of the soil (imitating the East India Company!). Second, wheat was bought by the government at 25 piastres per *ardeb* in Upper Egypt, then sold in Cairo for 120. And a tax on houses was equal to one month's rent; income tax equalled one month's income.[85] Richard Madden joined the chorus of condemnation. He heard the Viceroy's name universally execrated by the fellahin, who lived in misery. There were by the 1830s hundreds of abandoned villages. One third of the land was out of production, but revenues had doubled, because of the cotton crop. He calculated the land tax at an average of 50 piastres an acre, double the rate under the Mamelukes.[86] From the same era came the acute and documented account of the veterinarian Pierre Hamont. Everyone was fleeing the corvée and conscription; the latter had cost so many lives and was disastrous for agriculture. There were endless exactions and requisitions. Much land had been taken from food crops to grow cotton. The state domains (*chifliks*) owned by the Viceroy and his family were ruled in ignorance from Cairo, worked by forced labour, and lacked rations for both humans and animals. The estates of Ibrahim were an exception. State domains in some provinces accounted for two-thirds of the land. The picture Hamont paints of the peasants is one of total poverty and oppression. There were famines (for example, in 1830), disease was rampant, and anyone not living by the Nile lacked even decent water. Any attempt to help these poor wretches invited dismissal of which Hamont cited examples. In short, in his opinion, the fellahin were better off under the Mamelukes. An agricultural school was established in the Delta. Its first director, Grandjean, resigned in frustration, and was succeeded by an incompetent Armenian; when Hamont made criticisms, it was handed over to him! The Ministry of Education opposed him at every turn, demanding that he pay the staff from the sale of produce. Hamont's veterinary school, on the other hand, was, by his own account, an overwhelming success, but even his great enemy Clot praised his work in the face of the greatest difficulties.[87]

The outstanding modern study of Egyptian agriculture at this time agrees with the above criticisms and adds telling detail. Helen Rivlin states that the new survey of 1813-1814 introduced the standard *faddan* of 4,400 sq.m., and established tax according to quality. No notice was taken, however, of the very unstable conditions: poor floods in 1817, 1824-1825, 1837, and disastrous floods in 1829 and 1840-1841. To this were added the enormous losses from the bubonic plague in 1835 and a cholera epidemic in 1842. To survive oppression and starvation, the peasants killed their animals for food and fled the land.[88]

Perhaps worst of all, however, was the monopoly of agricultural products introduced by Mehemet Ali. This began with grain in Upper Egypt and rice in Lower Egypt in 1812. The peasants were underpaid at the prices set, they did not receive cash payment but only tax credits, they were cheated in the valuation of their crops, they were charged for their transport to the government centres, and they could not even retain portion of their crop for their own use. The entire crop of the staple beans was bought up in 1816, for example, and then resold to the peasants at inflated prices. All this was designed to produce exports, which only resulted in food shortages at home. If peasants fled, those who remained were responsible for the village taxes, and where the peasants had to pay in goods or cash, the government paid its debts with promissory notes which could be redeemed only at a loss.[89] The reader acquainted with other periods will recall the almost identical tyranny of the Roman empire in the third and later centuries.

Everyone is agreed that the agricultural policies of Mehemet Ali were a disaster. What part did Drovetti play in their formulation and implementation? The question is important, because even French sources have accused him of being the instigator of the Viceroy's land monopoly.[90]

To the contrary, we have no doubt of his opposition to these agrarian policies. As early as 1812, he spoke out in the official correspondence. By this time, he stated, the Pasha owned most of Upper Egypt which he had inherited from the Mamelukes. This defied the theory of the circulation of the blood, Drovetti grimly joked: it had all gone to the head. The Consul declared that he had never seen such misery in all classes.[91]

Even in his years of retirement, Drovetti never ceased to stress the importance of agriculture. Jomard wrote to him in 1835 about matters on which the two men clearly agreed.[92] Egypt was essentially an agricultural country, and her prosperity depended on the soil. It was now time for development of irrigation and canals; enough had been spent on the army. Everything that the two had tried to do for Egypt would remain unfulfilled if the soil were not exploited; this was the only means to consolidate what had already been achieved. And as late as 1839, Drovetti wrote to Jomard,[93] criticising the Viceroy's continuing search for resources in the Ethiopian mines, instead of reclaiming 'the richest and most fertile soil in the world', where the commonsensible Murad Bey – an unwonted compliment by Drovetti to a Mameluke – had already said that it was necessary only to scratch the ground to find treasures.

Apart from his general interest in agriculture, Drovetti was associated closely with one of the most important farming revolutions in Egypt, the introduction of the European merino. This took place in 1825, and the story is told in the *Epistolario* by Marquis Benso di Cavour, father of the more famous politician.[94] Since the merinos were to be imported from Piedmont, Drovetti acted through the Consul for that kingdom. The Marquis was the sole owner of a fine merino flock imported from Spain by Vittorio Amedeo III, twenty years earlier. Drovetti asked for thirty sheep, and the cost was 1,500 francs; Cavour made a gift of another six sheep to his compatriot. He also sent information on their care. The only problem was to find two shepherds to accompany them to Egypt, a journey naturally terrifying to most of these people. Cavour finally found two brothers named Fruchiero to undertake the voyage, and special care had to be taken of their diet. They detested oil, and lived on onions, rice and bread. The most interesting aspect of the whole operation is perhaps the manner of payment. Cavour asked for coffee: first class Moka, to be sent insured and well packed. The Marquis was worried that the captain might change it for another quality en route! And so Egypt founded its merino flock on the very best Spanish merinos via the royal flock of Piedmont, through the agency of Drovetti and his connections with his leading compatriots. The King himself added another hundred sheep as a gift to Mehemet Ali, who sent an elephant in return![95]

The fate of these sheep was not very pleasant. They died, but produced a great improvement in the quality of Egyptian wool. Sheep farms were established in the Delta, but it was too damp, and the animals were not properly cared for. Hamont was appointed director in 1837, but because of local obstruction, the sheep still died of starvation and disease, if they were not stolen by the fellahin or the sheiks. Despite all this, the flocks increased and the wool improved. By 1836, there were 7,000 merinos in Egypt.[96]

Industry

The French government was, paradoxically, little interested in the development of Egyptian industry, although it was to have a major influence on the French economy. The diplomatic correspondence does, however, contain periodical reports, not least because immigrant French workers played a leading role in setting up the new trades in Egypt, and Drovetti as Consul was often instrumental in inviting and then caring for these European workers.

In 1812 Drovetti reported the beginnings of the silk industry, set up to free Egypt from its dependence on Syria for this commodity.[97] Following this, there is considerable reference to industry during the years of Drovetti's absence from the consulate. In 1816 the Pasha decided to establish a plant for pickled fish. This was a project in which Drovetti had always had an interest. When the decision was made, therefore, Boghos turned to him, although he was at the time only a private citizen, asking him to nominate two Europeans who might be placed in charge of the factory.[98] By the next year, saltpetre factories were being set up at Cairo and at Asyut, and ten million mulberries were being planted at the latter with Druses employed in the silk production.[99]

European workers were now needed, especially for cloth manufacture. An ex-pirate was reputedly recruiting them in France, but England had refused to send any. By December 1817, seventeen silk-workers arrived from Livorno, and another sixty were said to be on their way. On 25 January, 1818 a frigate arrived from Marseille with a hydraulic engineer, four blacksmiths, three women cotton- spinners – and a fencing master. The Pasha was giving up linen in favour of silk and cotton. The attention to the last crop is revealed by the striking increase in its yield: 40,000 quintals (4,000 tonnes) in 1818, 70,000 in 1819. And the *Epistolario* contains a very important letter from Giovanni Baffi, in charge of the nitrate factory near Sakkarah. In spite of working in a ramshackle factory which had been flooded by the Nile for three months, he was able to produce powder in various grades equal to even the very finest English. Baffi was rewarded with a *pelisse* and the promised 100,000 talaris, and the factory was to be modernised. It was to none other than Drovetti, his 'great patron', that Baffi hastened to write this triumphant report in 1819.[100]

These notes tell some of the steps in the attempt by Mehemet Ali to introduce European-style industries to Egypt and to employ European workers in establishing them. The Viceroy was, however, in all things, an extremist and his policies were bound to fail. There is no doubt about Drovetti's reactions, because we have clear statements by him about these policies. In a report in July 1822 he was brutally frank: the attempt to favour industry at the expense of agriculture he condemned as absurd, and this view he conveyed forcefully to the Viceroy. To employ Europeans, he said, would make the cost of the final product too high; Egyptian workers, on the other hand, could never compete on European markets. In sum, the factories were simply theatres for Mehemet Ali's diversion.[101]

The programme went ahead, of course. In the early 1820s, there were factories for cloth under Morel from Chambery, for cotton under Jumel at Bulaq, for nitrate under Baffi and Dussap, for silk at Wadi Tumulat. There was a gunpowder factory on Roda island directed by a Turk educated in Europe; a printing-press at Bulaq under Mesabichi who had studied typography for four years at Milan, and which could print in Arabic, Turkish, Italian and Greek; the arsenal, whose director Gonau had recently died, was staffed by well-paid Europeans; there was a dyeing works at Benesuef and a sugar factory at Radamon.[102]

Drovetti's views are again clearly before us in the report on the Egyptian cotton industry which he sent to the French government in 1824.[103] This had been founded by Louis Jumel, director of the factory at Bulaq. He had discovered Mahon cotton, but the French merchants did not want it. Mehemet Ali thereupon gave it to English and Italian companies. The crop in 1824 was 200,000 quintals (20,000 tonnes) and Drovetti suggested that it would double the next year and be one million quintals in three or four years. One sixth of Egypt's arable soil was to be devoted to it: 50,000 *faddans*, and Americans were being sought to care for this crop. It was virtually a government monopoly, but any 'approved' European merchant could buy it, and the English were getting an advantage, Drovetti warned. Egyptian cotton was therefore available to the French, and might have been cheaper than American but for the Pasha's greed. The main problem was that French industry needed 200,000 quintals (the entire current crop), and French imports to Egypt could hardly pay for this. Mehemet Ali had promised, however, to reserve the next crop for France at 15 talaris per 50 kgs. Drovetti expressed himself against giving privileges to any one French company. Here, then, is clear advice from the Consul to his government to abandon its previous apathy and take advantage of a new Egyptian product. He himself was obviously instrumental in obtaining special terms from the Pasha for his government. We must note, on the other hand, that the report contains typically optimistic estimates of the size of the crop. The highest export in fifteen years was precisely in 1824 and the hopes for the five-fold increase never materialised. Drovetti's report was motivated by the offering of Egyptian cotton on the world market in order to raise money for the costs of the Greek war. The British and Swiss were enthusiastic over the first production of Egyptian cotton, which was of excellent quality, but the French had thought it inferior and so were being surpassed by their rivals.[104]

Concerning Drovetti's attitude to the conflicting demands of agriculture and industry in Egypt at this time he has so often been misunderstood – or, more accurately, misrepresented – but his preference and sound judgement could not be clearer. Jomard in 1825 quoted him.[105] There was much discussion in France about all the improvements in Egypt, but the one most needed, as Drovetti specified, was to multiply agricultural products, and with this Jomard was in perfect agreement. Indigo, cotton, sugar, coffee if possible, cochineal, dyes, medical supplies, rice, wheat and so on would be more profitable for Egypt than spinning and weaving mills.

In November 1825 Ducotet, a cloth manufacturer from Sedan arrived, but was unable to set up because of lack of workers. Another arrived from Carcassonne with six others, but was very old-fashioned. A major problem in the establishment of such industries was the Muslim prejudice against receiving instruction from a Christian![106] Mehemet Ali pressed on. At precisely this time, Drovetti received a letter from Cadeldevans, the manager of a weaving factory and paper manufactory at Cairo, whose establishments had been visited by the Viceroy. He was highly impressed, needless to say, and promised to extend both operations, saying that he was a 'manufacturing prince', and not just a simple manufacturer![107]

It was the very next year that the mixed success of such industry, especially woollen cloth, was revealed. The factory was well equipped, with a French director, but the material was poor and the workers unskilled. The manufacture of cotton thread, on the other hand, was fairly successful, and satisfied local needs, with even possibilities for export. And the production of printed cloth, managed by a Genevan, was successful: the cloth was of good quality and modest price. The cotton crop for 1826, however, was poor. A more important problem was that the cotton was dirty and Alsatian manufacturers preferred that from Louisiana, of lower quality but cleaner.[108]

Drovetti's antagonism to the unbalanced favouring of industry remained strong. In 1826 he asserted roundly that it had been favoured for years at enormous expense, without producing any benefits. He described the building of factories as 'madness', and tried to induce the Viceroy to exploit agriculture. The cost of industry in this year alone he estimated at 20 million francs.[109]

James St John wickedly summed up by saying that Mehemet Ali was persuaded that 'with the aid of certain French and Swiss adventurers, it was possible to render Cairo a second Manchester'. He revealed that the workers were appallingly treated and responded by damaging the factories. A mill was burnt at Khend-el-Merood in 1832 with £35,000 damage. Half the raw materials were wasted, and the thread was worthless when spun. The wages were theoretically too high, but the workers were endlessly robbed. In all, the Pasha was duped by 'unscrupulous adventurers', but was himself too impatient and impractical. In more general terms, Pierre Mouriez stressed that in order to set up European-style industries, the native ones such as cotton, linen and silk were destroyed. The natives obviously could not work sophisticated imported machinery, and the machinery itself was totally unsuited to the Egyptian climate and the intrusive sand.[110]

A more recent assessment by Helen Rivlin notes Drovetti's opposition to these policies, but the overriding of his advice in 1814 through the influence of Bokhty, the merchants, and the mercantile consuls. The recruitment of foreign workers was not very successful: the English prohibited migration, and the French were not very favourable. The largest response came from Italy: the silk and cotton workers. These industrial operations cost Mehemet Ali 100 million piastres before he had any return, and by the 1840s Egypt was increasingly importing manufactured products from Europe. The reasons for the failure of industry on the European model were various: the sophisticated machinery was unsuited to the Egyptian climate and conditions, and could not be maintained; there was no steam power, only oxen(!); and the peasants preferred to work in the fields, despite the apparent privileges of the factories. The removal of forty thousand peasants from agriculture for industry was, in fact, a disaster.[111]

Commerce

French diplomatic sources begin in 1811 to tell of the attention directed to Egyptian trade. The most active informant in the beginning was Saint-Marcel, Consul at the port of Rosetta, but Drovetti also made major contributions, and again it is important to set out his views clearly; for he has as usual been accused of instigating disastrous policies.

Egyptian commerce certainly expanded dramatically under the rule of Mehemet Ali. In 1811 the price of grain was high (80 piastres for 21 bushels), and the Austrians wanted 420,000 bushels and the English

600,000 in these crucial times of the Napoleonic wars. The Pasha in return looked forward to the importation of European goods. Communications had to be improved, notably the reopening of the Ramanieh canal linking Alexandria with the Nile, and the port of Alexandria itself was destined for marked improvement: walls were to be constructed on the model of those of General Menou, and a royal palace constructed; for Mehemet Ali intended to divide his time between here and Cairo.[112]

That same year the first mention was made of the Pasha's obsession with obtaining a trading monopoly: a 30% tax was established on commerce, and the government established a commercial agent in Malta for trade with that island, Sicily, Spain and Portugal. All Egyptian imports and exports were to go through this agent. The main stimulus to these grandiose economic dreams was the desperate English need for supplies for its bases, armies and fleets in the Mediterranean. In the middle of the year there were forty-six English ships taking on grain in Alexandria. Prices sky-rocketed: 100 piastres for 21 bushels of wheat, 10 piastres for one kilo of coffee, and shortages arose. And when imports of American coffee undermined the high prices set by the Pasha for Moka coffee, he banned the American.[113] Drovetti desperately tried to stop trade with the English, of course, but this was precisely the Pasha's answer to his economic crisis. A state monopoly in the grain trade supplying the English fleet would bring money, goods and arms to Egypt.[114]

Customs income reached 8 million piastres in 1811. The plans for commercial monopoly soon, however, went astray. The Pasha's agents in Malta, Spain and Portugal actually competed with one another and the price of grain fell. Mehemet Ali decided, Drovetti reported, to restrict himself in future to an agent in Malta (Keun and Co). As well as that, the warehouses were full of goods at low prices. With so many Egyptian troops absent in the Arabian wars, a major category of consumers was lost. And the attempt to ban imported American coffee induced some speculators to mix it with Moka, ruining the Egyptian market in Asia. As if all that were not enough, the end of the Mamelukes meant that there was no more vogue for Venetian cloth and gold and silk.[115]

English rapacity for grain induced the Pasha to begin the construction of two hundred small ships to transport grain on the Nile and in the Delta. In the first quarter of 1812, grain exports were again worth 1,390,000 francs, and imports from Malta were valued at 1,237,000. The Pasha even began to talk of trade with France, whereupon Saint-Marcel informed him of the difficulties of the 'Continental system'. Undaunted, Mehemet Ali proposed an amazing innovation for the Ottoman empire: a maritime insurance company. The French Vice-Consul declared roundly that it would not work.[116]

In his June 1812 bulletin, Drovetti reported sales of grain to the English and Spanish valued at more than three million piastres. The English were soon the only nation trading in Egypt, and the result was that Indian cotton became the major import.[117] A poor harvest increased the tax on exported grain, but the English continued to buy it. The total for all exported food stuffs including rice and vegetables Drovetti calculated at 10 million piastres, and the land tax would bring in another 30 millions. The Consul declared that Mehemet Ali was the richest pasha in the Ottoman empire. One export deal was known by December: the English would buy 10 million measures of wheat for 3,600,000 francs and the provision of a waterpump (valued at 400,000 francs) to keep water in the Cairo canal, otherwise dry for eight months of the year. English officers were also arranging for the purchase of 2-3,000 horses. Apart from Indian cloth, the other major import to balance all this was arms: the Pasha bought 3,000 rifles from England.[118]

With news of Tusun's victories in Arabia early in 1813 and the conquest of Medina and Mecca, Mehemet Ali told Drovetti that he thought of establishing commercial agents on the Red Sea coast at Jedda and Moka. With the resumption of Arabian trade, certainly, the price of coffee dropped: 25 piastres for 40 kilos. The English were still loading grain in March, paying 95 francs for 20 bushels. Two major blows then fell: the plague devastated Egypt, and the Black Sea was opened again, which meant that the Maltese market was flooded with Russian grain. It was the Pasha, however, who ruined everything. By early 1814, commerce was suffering from exorbitant taxes, and foreign money was disappearing from the country.[119]

Within a year, Drovetti was replaced as Consul. The story resumes under his successor, Roussel. He reported that the Swedish navy monopolised the carriage of Egyptian grain; there were nearly one hundred of their ships in Alexandria in a year, and the French could not compete with their low wages and small crews.[120] Mehemet Ali's methods became more ruthless. He would let contracts for grain to Alexandrian merchants, payable within four months. When the price of grain rose in Europe, he decided to ship 70,000 *ardebs* of grain directly, and at the same time to demand payment from the merchants, two months ahead of time. There was uproar, even among the English. Egyptian exports to France had been ruined by the customs dues. Contraband was entirely confiscated instead of incurring double taxes. Trade with Europe was thus being destroyed, mainly, Roussel claimed, through the advice of 'greedy Armenians' (obviously Boghos!).[121] English interest in Egypt continued, however, and Salt accompanied Mehemet Ali to Suez while the Indian fleet was at Jedda and Moka. The Pasha soon bought a ship of 600 tons for the Red Sea. The Darfur caravan also resumed after many years, bringing slaves to Egypt. This was of vital importance for the new army.[122]

It was Thédénat-Duvent's turn to write a report on French trade in Egypt in September, 1817.[123] In sum, it had completely collapsed since the Revolution. Coastal trade had been lost to the Greeks and Turks. Once 90% of ships in the Levant had been French; now they were 10%. French goods were still sought, but their declining quality had allowed the introduction of, for example, English and German cloth. With their Indian empire, the English were now trading in grain, sugar, cotton, wool, natron, saffron, leather, coffee, incense, myrrh and ivory. A fatal blow had been struck at even French soap-making by the prohibition of the import of Spanish and Sicilian soda and English natron, so that soap factories had been established in these other countries. Thédénat alerts us to what serious damage could be done by even the smallest bureaucratic reform. The consuls in Egypt had the right to charge a tax of one or two percent on all goods entering port in their own vessels, no matter what the origin of the goods. Except in the case of the Spanish and French consuls, this income served as their salary. The French government had abolished this tax, with the result that foreigners used French ships in order to avoid it, while the French used foreign ships, paid the tax and passed it on to the consumers in higher prices! There were, Thédénat reported, incredibly only seven or eight French companies in the Levant: their numbers should be increased, and their control, he urged, should be left to the consuls.

Allusion has already been made to Mehemet Ali's methods in his trading monopoly, the forced distribution of goods to merchants to be paid for within a fixed time. On the other hand, Roussel reported, if the Pasha owed the merchants anything, he paid with grain, 15% of it ruined, and if there were any complaints, the bad grain was actually mixed in with the good. The trading monopoly had other unfortunate results. Mehemet Ali was surrounded by adventurers who wanted to gain advantages for themselves, and some made vast profits. When rising prices forced merchants to seek goods elsewhere, such as the Crimea, the Pasha forced them to buy grain from him on credit. Cheaper goods from the Black Sea and the Levant, on the other hand, pushed prices down in Europe, not to mention Mehemet Ali's undercutting of his own agents by selling all over the Mediterranean in order to pay his armies. Egypt was by this time groaning with imported goods and again the Pasha turned it to his account, by selling them forcibly at fixed prices. The result was that cash disappeared, and the price of beans, staple of the Arab population, jumped 60% in three days. Late in 1818, Mehemet Ali revalued the 'strong piastre' and gold by 10%. Faced with protests, he could not understand why after so many victories he did not have the right to make fiscal arrangements in his own country! There were $2^{1}/_{2}$ million hectolitres of surplus foodstuffs in store by 1819 because prices in Europe had tumbled.[124]

Shortly after Drovetti's reappointment, he made another report on the Egyptian economy in July 1822, and it contains some fascinating history.[125] He had never had a good word for the Mamelukes, and even at this remove characterised them as two dozen rapacious, tyrannical, unjust and incompetent warring chiefs. Before 1790 there were only two consuls in Cairo, representing France and Venice. Bourriez was assassinated and the main French seat was transferred to Alexandria. Trade was confined to that with the interior of Africa and Arabia. There were only about twenty European companies in Egypt, and many went bankrupt.

The regime of Mehemet Ali, Drovetti noted, began in reality in 1812 after the crushing of the Mamelukes and the Bedouin Arabs, and the gaining of control over the ullemas and the Coptic scribal class, and with the encouragement of agriculture and industry. Now the whole system was collapsing. He predicted that exports would fall to one-sixth of what they were in 1816 and that revenues, recently 60 million francs, would halve to the 1790 level. The Consul stated that it would be a great advantage if Mehemet Ali gave up the monopoly of cotton, linen, sugar and saffron, but the Pasha claimed that this was his guarantee against a fall in demand. Perhaps more influential was one of his favourite maxims: a government should take a long time to make a decision, but once taken, it should never go back! The policy of giving large credits to merchants also backfired: Mehemet Ali recovered only 10% of the debt and to five or six French merchants he lost two million piastres. On the other hand, there had been no falling off in imports: arms, cloth, hardware, furniture and wines.

This was Drovetti's most exhaustive analysis of Egyptian commerce. In 1825 more ambitious schemes were contemplated. Italian engineers were to blow up the navigational obstacles between Sennar and Aswan to allow twenty-four armed warships to protect commerce and communications. It was anticipated that a vast quantity of timber could be brought down to Egypt. Other Italian engineers were digging a canal to supply Cairo with running water all year.[126] At the very same time, in May, Drovetti wrote a stiff letter to Boghos, reminding him that Mehemet Ali had promised France half the cotton crop, about 200,000 quintals. The Nile floods were very poor, and navigation was difficult, and someone was trying to extricate himself from the agreement. Drovetti stressed the obligations of the French traders to ships' captains, and strongly supported their demand for part of what they had been promised, as well as alluding to the displeasure of the French government. The French trading companies were, in fact, all concentrated in Alexandria. It was easy to sell cloth, silk, wool and cotton to Europe but it had to be sent to Cairo. By the beginning of

1826, Boghos had been appointed Minister for Commerce.[127] All this while Egypt was a province of the Ottoman Empire, paying a yearly tribute. This is specified in 1826 as amounting to 300 cases of silver, which were taken to Constantinople by an Austrian ship.[128]

The cotton crops in 1824 and 1825 had been very small, precisely when exports were most needed, because of the crippling expenses of the Greek war. The crop for 1826, however, was excellent, with similar hopes for silk, indigo and saffron. Cotton was fixed at 13 talaris (66 francs) a quintal. Mehemet Ali, however, still made the old mistakes. The cotton crop was destined for Europe, but many French companies were disappointed to find that the government had a monopoly which controlled the whole market. The Viceroy was convinced that he could make the same profits as these European merchants.[129]

As with his agrarian and industrial policies, there are few commentators who have defended Mehemet Ali's practices in commerce. One is Guémard,[130] who stresses that the monopoly was designed to stabilise the markets and protect farmers from exploitation. We may reply by suggesting that one system of exploitation was simply replaced by another. Guémard suggests, however, that the proof of success, at least for some, is that by about 1820 there were thirty-five foreign trading companies in Cairo and Alexandria, twice the number under the Mamelukes (but again this may simply demonstrate that now Egypt was much more open to the outside world in general). The effects on the Europeans were very varied. The supplies of grain to the British in 1810-1811 allowed them to stay in Spain and made a vital contribution to the decisive campaigns there, as Drovetti perfectly understood: hence his active opposition. And the imports of goods from Europe were especially damaging to French trade with the Levant in cloth and silk. The English, on the other hand, received the enormous privilege of having their Indian trade pass via Egypt for only 9% tax. This was organised through Briggs and Company. In 1836, a few years after Drovetti's departure, Jomard estimated the main trading partners of Egypt as Austria (10.3 million francs), England (5.5), Tuscany (4.8), and then France (4.6).[131]

As with everything else which went wrong in Egypt, Drovetti was blamed by some. The trading monopoly was no exception. He was 'an adherent to the Bonapartist economic philosophy favouring monopoly and protectionism'.[132] We have already seen his opposition to the monopoly, however, in his report of 1822. Of even greater interest, in an undated letter in the French archives, which dates from the interregnum between the two periods of his office, apparently September 1816,[133] Drovetti describes Mehemet Ali's trade in commodities as 'the most despotic system one could imagine', and notes that people have written from Marseille to Paris accusing him of being one of the promoters of the resulting damage to European trade. These people, he replies, are liars and imbeciles. He was the only person in Egypt who dared to make strong representations to the Pasha, and he still did so. Drovetti's further explanations then become, it must be admitted, rather oscillating. He states in the first place that when the monopoly was introduced, French trade was non-existent, while that of 'our enemies' was superior, so that to protest against the new system would have been to assist the enemy. It was when he saw the 'dangerous results ... in general' that he began to protest. The other consuls remained silent, and so did he on occasion out of consideration for political reasons. When circumstances allowed, however, no one contributed more, for example, to the abolition of the tax on merchandise coming from Africa such as natron. On the matter of giving advice, Drovetti then stresses that the Viceroy indeed takes notice of that given by him, but that he would be 'entirely ignorant of political economy' if he advised him to ruin his country! In addition, Mehemet Ali, he stresses, has to be treated carefully once he has adopted 'a certain tone of sovranty': detours rather than direct statements are needed to bring ideas to his attention. Drovetti admits that raising the subject of commerce with him is usually ill-advised. When Drovetti complained about the unprofitability of natron, he was informed that the problem was not the price in Egypt, but the tax on its entry into France. The Viceroy had actually talked of abolishing all taxes on trade with the exception of customs, but Drovetti realised that this was only a whim. The letter concludes with reference again to the calumnies and inventions by enemies of honest men. A postscript states that one should be frank and even proud in order to silence such critics. In that light, he reveals that in 1815 Mehemet Ali offered him a post in the Egyptian government, but that he refused precisely because the Viceroy had confided in him his intention to make a monopoly of all Egyptian trade, which Drovetti had always opposed.

As a complement to this highly revealing letter, we may add the remarks quoted by Roussel in a letter of November 1820.[134] Drovetti stated that the trading monopoly was simply the product of Mehemet Ali's greed, but that since the same system existed elsewhere in the Ottoman Empire, how could it be avoided in Egypt?

The Mahmudieh canal

The first mention in the French diplomatic correspondence of Mehemet Ali's intention to reopen the old canal linking Alexandria with the Nile, and therefore with Cairo, occurs in March 1817.[135] Drovetti reveals, in fact, that he had raised the matter with Mehemet Ali through Boghos at the end of the previous year.[136] The first reaction from the Pasha was that this canal would be equally useful to an invading army, and that it would be better to continue building forts and palaces at Alexandria.[137] The clearing of the canal began, nevertheless, in July 1817.[138]

The main labour was carried out in 1819. Thédénat-Duvent noted that 60,000 fellahin were employed in February; by March there were 300,000. The Turkish engineers, however, were not worried about the levels. The French engineer, Xavier Coste, had to be called in, and as the harvest approached, the fellahin had to be sent home.[139] In September, another problem arose: the clearing somehow cut off the water-supply to Alexandria for its cisterns, and it had to be brought in from elsewhere. Continuing difficulties with the levels led the Viceroy to call in other Frenchmen, Jean Nicolas Huyot and Lachaise from Cairo.[140]

When completed, all was not well with the canal. Pillavoine complained that the sea water came in, and that in the inundation the canal would be joined to lake Mareotis. It was not, in fact, until May 1820 that the canal was announced as being in operation.[141] It was named after the Sultan, Mahmud.

A contemporary visitor, the comte de Marcellus, states that the workers numbered 250,000, each paid one piastre a day, in contrast to the European engineers paid 1000 piastres a month, with 2,000 bonus. The total cost was 40 million francs, and work occupied January to October 1819. By contrast, Thédénat-Duvent denied that there were ever more than 100,000 workers.[142] The cost in lives is variously estimated between 12,000 and 100,000.

The motives for the construction were varied. Rosetta was not a satisfactory port for trade, and goods often had to be carried overland to Alexandria. Rosetta was also vulnerable to Turkish invasion. The result was disappointing. The canal was never a success, because of the faulty levels. It continually silted up. The banks were also too high, so that either boats were sheltered from the wind or it caught the tops of their sails and overturned them.

> The construction of the al-Mahmudiyah Canal was the principal public work undertaken and completed by Muhammad Ali. Its history personifies the history of almost all the major public works which he undertook – a brilliant conception, although not an original one, badly planned, badly executed, and carried on at great cost and suffering to the Egyptian people. It serves, in fact, as a case history of energetic, ambitious and amateurish despotism.[143]

It seems that Drovetti was among the promoters of the canal.

After relying on his own Albanians since his rise to power, in 1820 Mehemet Ali sent his son Ishmael to conquer the Sudan in order to provide negroes for a new Egyptian army. The expedition failed in this respect, and it was thus that the Viceroy decided to raise an army from his own fellahin. By the end of 1823 there were six regiments of infantry, some 23,000 men. More than slight interest attaches to this subject in a biography of Drovetti. As General Boyer described him in 1825, 'you are the main instigator and adviser of the regular army of His Highness.'[145]

It was, in fact, in 1819 that probably the most famous European military instructor arrived in Egypt. This was Joseph Sève, who had had an illustrious but turbulent military career. When Ibrahim returned from Arabia in 1819 and the new army was to be built, he was appointed instructor, and played a leading role henceforth. He converted to Islam and was known as Soliman Pacha.[146]

By 1823 a military hospital had been established at Manfalut. Drovetti visited it during his tour of Upper Egypt with Mehemet Ali at the end of the year. A French doctor sent him a report in January 1824, stating that conditions were such that many more soldiers died than should have, had they received proper care. The fundamental problem was lack of medicines; as well, the Turks knew nothing of medical hygiene, and the food for the sick was appalling. The hospital held 2,400 patients(!), and the doctors were Dussap, del Signore, Pasquali, Canova, Espanelle, Terra Nova and d'Andre, half of whom were themselves ill.[147]

The most detailed account of what happened during Mehemet Ali's visit to Manfalut accompanied by Drovetti and Salt, and one of the most vivid of all contemporary sources on the army, is the report by the English Consul to his government.[148] He gave the highest praise to the work of Sève, which required 'great courage, perseverance and patience', but denounced his famous conversion: 'he is a fool for his pains', he declared, having 'sold for preferment his birthrights.' The training had succeeded better with the Mamelukes than with the negroes, however; for they died in great numbers when they fell ill. Only 3,000 survived of the 20,000 Sudanese 'cruelly torn from their country'. It was now, Salt revealed, that the Viceroy's 'chief adviser on this occasion' – undoubtedly Drovetti – suggested conscripting the fellahin.

Colonels were well paid, receiving 100,000 piastres per annum (£1,500), but ordinary soldiers received only 216 piastres, with uniform and rations. Salt praised the great courage and devotion of the ordinary soldiers, but agreed with every other observer on the parlous state of the medical service, with only six assistants. By this time, Mehemet Ali had 15,000 men ready.

The cleverness of the Viceroy was apparent to Salt: he was paying great attention to both him and Drovetti, who, in fact, had tents in the camp next to one another: Salt appended a splendid plan of the camp to illustrate its disposition. He also had summoned all the cachefs to the camp, as well as three tatars (couriers) from Constantinople – all to see the army. Salt described the masterly manoeuvres which he witnessed, 'en petite guerre', and the war games of the commanders with lead soldiers in Mehemet Ali's tent. 'The formation of this army the Pasha openly attributes to chevalier Drovetti, most of the officers having been recommended by him and he having been consulted throughout, but as I imagine without the consent of his government.' It is no wonder that the unmilitary Salt spent only twenty days in the camp, and was thoroughly bored. One can, on the other hand, imagine Drovetti in his element, the old soldier observing and participating in every manoeuvre, with much to discuss with the European instructors, especially if he had been instrumental in bringing them to Egypt, and, on top of all that, basking in his glory as the Viceroy's right-hand man.

Salt ends with a characteristic episode. A conscripted Copt was threatened with one thousand strokes for refusing to serve. After five hundred(!), he consented to convert to Islam, but later repented. He was condemned to die under the bastinado. Salt and Drovetti intervened to save him, and Salt conveyed him back to Cairo.

It was also at the end of 1823 that a group of French officers arrived in Egypt to assist the modernisation of the army. One of them wrote Drovetti several letters about his experiences. This was Victor Besson, who had served twenty-four years in the navy. He was one of the first to find out that everything in Egypt was not what it had been made out to be, or what he had expected. If what was wanted was the formation of a marine corps on the English model, then he, as a sailor, was not the man to create it. It was, as usual, Drovetti to whom any European in difficulties turned. There was also a dispute over Besson's salary. With the rank of captain of a frigate, even as second officer he was entitled to 5,000 francs. His second letter was full of references to discord, apparently among the French officers. Thanks to Drovetti's encouragement ('since the arrival of your first letter, I seem to be a new man'), by January 1824, however, Besson believed that he could build an Egyptian navy and planned to draw up a simple but detailed memoir.[149] Another European officer, also beneficiary of Drovetti's patronage, was Giuseppe Ghilini, employed as Captain Instructor.[150]

A major and most disturbing chapter in the history of the Egyptian army opened in November 1824, with the arrival of Generals Pierre Boyer and Pierre Livron with other officers.[151] The six original regiments of the new army were now employed: the first in Arabia, the second in Nubia, and the other four in Greece. It was thus necessary to train three new regiments. For this reason, a general was sought from France. The Viceroy sent a merchant, Tourneau, to France to find one. He approached General Augustin Belliard, who in turn chose Boyer. Mehemet Ali was somewhat surprised when two generals arrived: Boyer insisted on bringing a friend as well! Unperturbed, the Viceroy granted him 30,000 francs p.a., with a bonus of 6,000 and his expenses while away from Egypt.

The mission opened with another misunderstanding. Boyer and Livron arrived with a certain fanfare, bringing arms from France and being received by Drovetti. Only some time later did the Consul receive a letter from the Minister of Foreign Affairs stressing that the whole mission was unofficial and warning Drovetti not to give any other impression, since it was generally believed that the generals were part of the Viceroy's attempts to make himself independent of Turkey.[152]

Mehemet Ali's instructions to his new instructors were clear:

> Use your methods, apply them everywhere to the organisation of my armies on French lines. I do not want among my troops any other tactics than those of this admirable and great nation. This country is still full of memories of your glory. Help me and we will achieve great things.[153]

Not satisfied with the men who had arrived, the Viceroy in addition asked for a colonel of infantry and three captains.

The *Epistolario* contains no fewer than sixteen letters by Boyer. The first, of December 1824, mentioned the 'perfidious insinuations' of Salt, obviously trying to turn the Viceroy against the French officers as being untrustworthy. Livron was to be stationed at Alexandria, Boyer at Cairo. Livron was sent back to Paris in December, to ask the King's permission to build two frigates on the model of the *Jeanne d'Arc* and a brig like the *Cuirassier*. Boghos' instructions to him, apart from the permission to build the two frigates, were to bring back officers for a naval school, and workers and machinery for the cotton industry.[154]

On his first visit to the camp, Boyer was impressed with the ten battalions and their drill, but stated that the arms, dress and equipment were 'miserable'. He asked Drovetti to obtain more European officers, preferably French of course, but assured him that the good would always be preferred to the mediocre, whatever their origin. Boyer's language to Belliard was more direct: the new regiments lacked everything, and the European instructors were all refugees from Spain, Piedmont or Naples, 'the greatest rabble on earth'. And in January 1825 Drovetti received a letter saying that Boyer found the Italian instructors 'execrable', that there was 'no order, no discipline, in a word no army'. The letter reveals the general's agitation. The army was in chaos, there was no administration, a terrifying mortality rate, the surgeons were quacks, and the arsenal a labyrinth. Drovetti had to come immediately: 'you are the soul and linchpin of my coming to Egypt', Boyer asserted; Drovetti would provide 'coherence and method'.[155] One must admit that these are direct and high compliments to the Consul from a leading general.

Later in the month, Boyer had an interview with Mehemet Ali. They did not agree on what was to be done with the army. Boyer felt like 'the fifth wheel on a chariot'. He complained again about the Italian elements. He had put forward a 'methodical plan' for the army which had been applauded, but nothing more had been done. He felt that his dignity had been affronted, and that he was being moved about like a pawn. He was living in the middle of a 'rabble, the rejects of Europe'. All of this despair and concern for his own status was a bad omen for the future. The evidence he gave for the state of the army, on the other hand, is appalling: the regiments lacked everything, and men were dying at a rate of 12-18 every day. Boyer was ashamed for his country of the French military doctors. In a postscript, however, he took back what he had said about the Italians: some were good men.[156]

Boyer intervened to obtain special conditions for Colonel Gaudin, who sought double the normal removal allowance from France to Egypt of 4,000 francs, since he had come with his wife. This man was soon to play a leading role in events. By February 1825, Boyer reported that his camp had been halved to 7,000 men, presumably by the requirements of the Greek war. That month, Mehemet Ali and his General Staff with many dignitaries visited the camp for a fortnight. All must have gone well; for Boyer received a pelisse and a sabre and was invited to dinner. The general suggested that his honours were bestowed rather late: he should have received them as soon as he arrived! Real problems were, however, the low rates of pay, the promotion of 'blockheads', and unjust dismissals, while an excellent man, Perron, experienced in both the army and the navy, was not taken onto Ibrahim's staff, despite Boyer's recommendation. Perron was to resign in August, after eight months' service, because he was expected to drill one thousand men for six hours a day for 200 francs a month![157]

Despite Boyer's having arrived only in November of the previous year to train the three new regiments, in August 1825 the 7th and 8th were sent off to Greece, heavily supplemented by the 9th, while the last, made up in reality mostly of the 10th, 11th and 12th, was to be sent to Arabia. Boyer managed to hold back the 9th for two more months.[158]

Very serious trouble then erupted. An unspecified number of instructors were dismissed. Drovetti questioned the reasons and was informed by Noureddin that there had been a plot and that they had demanded a separate unit for themselves. Some had, in fact, resigned rather than being dismissed. There seems, as usual, another side to the story. Boyer informed Drovetti a little later that some of the instructors had made their intention to return to Europe clear for months, and that since their leave had expired, they would lose their pensions if they did not return. One, who was a noble from Genova, could not do what he was asked and two others had refused to accompany their regiment. Most of the instructors seem by name to be Italian. One Frenchman, however, was highly praised by Boyer, but had been paid so poorly that he had resigned. (This is obviously Perron.) In general, for their difficult job, they received low pay. Boyer asked Drovetti, as usual, to negotiate increases: 750 piastres a month (instead of 500?) for up to the rank of lieutenant, 1000 for captains, 1500 for majors; as well they wanted rations and two uniforms, and the promise of annual bonuses. Drovetti had supported the officers' request for houses to be built for them in the camp. Regiments were being sent off to serve in Arabia or Crete with very little training and the Turkish commanders were arrogant, Boyer stated, and would bring disaster on their men.[159]

In September 1825 Rey, the artillery colonel, and Cadet Devaux, described as a 'mechanicien chémiste', arrived. The rewards for some Europeans were high. We do not know whether, like Boyer, Rey was installed in a palace, but he was to be paid 15,000 francs, to receive his keep and to wear a magnificent Mameluke costume. The later history of this man is explained only by some remarks of Boyer. In the first place, he was very skilled, but his 'modesty' equalled 'the infernal battery of the imperial guard'. Second, the arsenal was full of Italians, and Rey determined to get rid of them all. The result was, in Boyer's words, that all had sworn his destruction.[160]

Livron late in 1825 provided a list of all European officers in the Egyptian army.[161] It is a fascinating document, and is reproduced as an appendix. Drovetti was continually active recruiting new officers for the army, with results which were not always encouraging. Boyer reported that three Italian officers had arrived. When examined, they had not been able to answer the simplest questions. Only one of the three was successful: he was a captain who had really held that rank. Stricter controls were obviously needed, and being applied, before any European was accepted as an instructor. Boyer also reported on the construction of a military hospital at Abu Zabal, which would house 1,800 sick, and he had high praise for Clot. Drovetti had apparently proposed a hospital closer to the capital, but the problem of desertions made the site unattractive. More evacuations of sick from Greece would make it necessary. Boyer also mentioned the arrival of Dominique Mariani, one of the old musicians with the French army in Egypt, on Drovetti's recommendation; this was the beginning of musical instruction in the army.[162] Another matter in which Drovetti played a special part was caring for the families of European officers who came to serve in Egypt. He had seen the Minister of War to press for pensions to be paid to those invalided and to their families in case they were killed.[163]

By 1826 the military college established the previous year near Cairo, and modelled on French military schools for the training of officers, had 88 students. They were being taught mathematics, drawing, topography, artillery, fortification, encampment, drill and languages (French, Turkish and Persian). The director was the artillery lieutenant Planat, and the courses lasted three years, with a fourth being planned.[164]

A Polish instructor, Faroucki, who was apparently French-trained, arrived in 1826. His forte was drill, and Boyer hoped that he would be employed to teach this, as he told Drovetti. Dissatisfaction with conditions of service was not always the reason, on the other hand, for resignation. The Piedmontese Colonel Cresia resigned the same year – but in order to leave with Mme Jumel, who had come with him. She was the widow of Louis Jumel, and her infidelity had caused him to come to Egypt. She had hoped, in vain, to inherit a large fortune. Apart from such problems with his imported officers, Mehemet Ali was ill-served by other European employees in the army. Frangini was a contractor for supplies, who brought about the overthrow of the Kiaya Bey (Prime Minister) by involving him in some scandal. In 1826 it became known that, having been sent to Europe with 100,000 talaris to buy weapons, he had brought back 50,000 rifle butts and 50,000 plates for cannon, almost not one of which was of any use.[165] The same year seven new officers arrived: five battalion chiefs (paid 10,000 francs p.a.) and two captains (8,000 frs), as well as thirty-two musicians. According to Boyer, the captains were alcoholics.[166]

The major upheaval occurred in the same year. Malivoire in Cairo gave the first alarm. Some of the French officers had fallen out with each other, and the Viceroy called on someone to help. One does not have to guess the identity of the man to whom he resorted. Drovetti was summoned to Cairo and had two interviews with Mehemet Ali. He discovered that General Boyer and Colonel Gaudin were at loggerheads. The Viceroy was threatening to send most of the French officers out of the country. The Consul managed to bring about a reconciliation, but it was short-lived. He saw the very serious implications: the English seized upon the trouble, claiming that it was all a conspiracy against Mehemet Ali. The damage to French standing in Egypt was enormous.[167] It is our good fortune that the *Epistolario* gives the other side of the story, namely Boyer's.

He had at first been so impressed with Gaudin that he had induced the Viceroy to accord him signal honours. Gaudin had then been so carried away as to incite intrigue, discord and pride among the instructors. He was, however, entirely erratic, flattering them one moment and accusing them of incompetence and ignorance the next, and praising those punished by Boyer. The latter's vocabulary was rich: 'vile flatterer and rampant courtesan', 'Tartufe'. What was most disturbing, however, was that the Egyptian officials did not support Boyer in his attempts to discipline Gaudin.[168]

By August Drovetti had unravelled the Boyer-Gaudin story and wrote about it at length to Damas in Paris.[169] He complained that from the beginning the military mission – meaning especially Boyer – behaved suspiciously, as if the members were sent by the French government and preparing for a French invasion! Boyer was more interested in money than anything else. He thus allowed control to pass to Gaudin, an active, ambitious man who had won the confidence of the Viceroy. After eight months, Boyer attempted to resume command. This was in March, when Drovetti had first been called in. Now the quarrel had resurfaced, because Malivoire, Vice-Consul in Cairo, asked Boyer to discipline an officer, who, incited by Gaudin, refused to obey. Bad health prevented Drovetti calming things again. Boyer then dismissed both the officer and Gaudin. Induced by his success to go further, he sought greater powers than before over the other instructors, and when these were refused, he resigned. Drovetti thought that Gaudin might have informed Mehemet Ali of Boyer's 'secret mission'; certainly the last had made very impolitic pro-Greek statements: for example, that within three months there would not be a Turk in the Morea! Drovetti blamed his colleague Malivoire in part, for not being more conciliatory. As the story unfolded, the Vice-Consul's actions could only be described as utterly incompetent.

The soldier who had been the agent provocateur was named Pecoud; this whole story could therefore be called the 'Pecoud affair', a parallel to the 'Marengo affair' of the same year which also showed Malivoire in a bad light. Pecoud was described by Malivoire as an agitator, quarrelsome, and even a spy. He was obviously totally undisciplined, or acting outrageously precisely in order to provoke someone. He took to 'hunting' in the garden of his hotel, a garden surrounded by houses including that of Malivoire. When the Vice-Consul ordered him to desist, he refused and became even more dangerous, firing shots at the consul's windows. Malivoire foolishly appealed to Boyer who did nothing, and then went to Mehemet Ali himself, who dismissed Pecoud and ordered that he be deported.[170]

This was the feud between Boyer and Gaudin, which led to the resignation of Boyer. He forced a number of other officers to go with him, by threatening their pensions. Boyer left Egypt in September. Drovetti laid the blame squarely on Boyer's own impetuosity. Rey also decided to leave. By the end of 1826, Mehemet Ali asserted that the French could not train his army, and he sent to England for new officers. He still wanted French naval instructors, and Livron was to return next spring. Drovetti's position was very delicate: he worked overtime to convince the Viceroy that it was not a government plot, but only a private squabble among officers. It seems very likely that a French plan to take over Egypt had been revealed by Gaudin.[171]

Drovetti's last note on the matter in 1827 was very hostile to Boyer, noting his philhellenic sentiments and the statement attributed to him that he had come to Egypt to acquire dowries for his daughters. On his departure, he threatened to stir up all France against the Consul. Drovetti declared that Malivoire and Boyer had undone twenty years of his own 'work, privation, dangers and sorrows' in order to fill their own pockets. What he held against Malivoire was his incredible mistakes. He had gone to Boyer about Pecaud. Either the man was a French citizen, and therefore subject to the Consul's own authority, or he was a Turk, subject to the Viceroy.[172]

The marvels performed by the European officers can best be appreciated by comparing the transformation of the Egyptian army with what the English accomplished in Persia. By 1826 the Persians had 40,000 men, but they were a militia rather than regular troops; for they came together for only three months each year, then went home. There were only eight instructors, all English, and no artillery or engineering officers, and no military school.[173] By the early 1830s, just after Drovetti's departure, the Egyptian army numbered 150,000,[174] and had only been prevented from crushing the Greeks by European intervention. It was soon to show its capacities in Syria. The military schools were very highly regarded: for infantry at Damietta under the Piedmontese Bolognini, 1822; 'Saint-Cyr' at Khanka near Cairo under the Sardinian Plasso; the General Staff at the same under the Piedmontese Planat; artillery at Turah under the Spaniard de Seguiera, 1829; the engineers at Bulaq, 1834; and cavalry at Gizeh under Varin, 1831.[175]

The negative side of all this is, however, enormous. As Pierre Mouriez so trenchantly remarked, as soon as revenues increased, they were devoted not to the people, but to the creation of an army totally out of proportion to the state.[176] Conscription 'drained the country of its best agricultural workers'. The methods used were brutal, the soldiers being torn away from their families, which were left to starve. To avoid this, the men abandoned their homes and fled to the desert, even migrating to Syria, or inflicted on themselves the most appalling mutilations, for which they were condemned to the galleys; even a regiment of blind was formed. Conscription caused revolts in 1823 and more seriously in 1824 from Isna to Aswan, and again in 1838 at Manfalut. There was no provision made for the families of those killed in the army.

In sum, 4% of the population was taken for the army, an enormously high percentage. There was only one benefit, and that was long-term:

> conscription of the peasants had drawn them out of their state of lethargy, and ... the soldiers as a class inclined towards the European civilisation which had influenced the Pasha.

It was 'an awakening of a kind of national self-consciousness among the Egyptians.'[177]

The navy

One of the greatest innovations of Mehemet Ali's reign was the establishment of a navy, both because of the financial and technical problems in building the ships and because of the enormous challenge of training Egyptians as sailors. The Pasha's main purpose was to challenge the Turkish navy, a formidable opponent. The first ships were built abroad, at Marseille, Livorno and even Bombay. The first navy was lost at Navarino. A dockyard was then established at Alexandria under French management: Lefebure de Cerisy was brought from Toulon. By 1833, the navy again numbered thirty ships, including seven of the line, armed with between eighty-four and one hundred and ten guns, and the budget by 1835 was 73 millions: each ship built cost the equivalent of the revenue of a province! These ships were not, however, used in the Syrian wars, and shortly after Mehemet Ali's death all serviceable vessels were sold to Turkey. The Minister of the Navy, Noureddin, was theoretically in charge, but in fact the navy was controlled by Victor Besson, who commanded the naval school at Alexandria. An earlier one had been established in c.1825 at al-Kubrusli under Hasan Bey, and did excellent work in producing officers. In sum, however, the navy seems to have been even more detested by the Egyptians than service in the army.[178]

Such are the main lines of the naval history of Egypt under Mehemet Ali. The real story is truly amazing, and has been revealed by the researches of Georges Douin.[179] Although there is little explicit mention of Drovetti, we may be sure of his close involvement. The need for Egypt to have its own fleet was revealed by the naval campaigns against the Greeks in 1824. Command was divided between the Turkish admiral, Khosrev Pasha, and the Pasha's son Ibrahim, and the result was a fiasco, due to the incompetence of the former. With the arrival in 1824 of the second general, Livron, it was possible, since he was not needed in Egypt, to send someone of high rank to France to obtain ships.

The stimulus for this was, in fact, the visit in 1822 of the frigate the *Jeanne d'Arc*: her modern features made a very strong impression on Mehemet Ali. Livron was sent, therefore, to obtain two frigates like her, and a brig like the *Cuirassier*.[180] The Viceroy's brilliance was demonstrated in the choice of Livron: he had considerable business experience, and was not too committed a Bonapartist to offend the restored monarchy. The main obstacle was that the ships could only be built in the state dockyards at Toulon with material and workers from the state arsenals. Chabrol, Minister of the Navy, was totally opposed to the scheme. When the King's Council debated the matter in April 1825 a compromise was suggested, that the ships should be built commercially at Marseille by Bruat, Daniel and Company, but with all unofficial help from the French navy![181] This assistance consisted initially of more than nine hundred great planks of oak, and the supervision of Cerisy. If this arrangement was supposed to remain a secret, it was soon discovered by the press. Chabrol was forced to declare that no more material would be supplied by the navy.

The possibility of profit soon brought in other companies, this time none other than the Zinzinia brothers, who asked permission to build two brigantines at Marseille and La Ciotat for the Egyptians. The Zinzinias were, of course, Greeks, whose relatives had in fact perished in Chios; they were now building ships to be used against their own people. Being so sure of permission – or so unscrupulous – they began building immediately, and then permission was refused. They were forced to sell the hulls at a loss to a French company, Rambaud, which took over the work.

The attempt by the French government to distance itself from these activities was again weakened when permission was given to Bruat and Daniel to cast the anchors for the frigates in the naval forges. The delicate question was raised of how to get the completed ships from France to Egypt. It was decided to send them under a French flag, but without too obvious an armament and manned, as far as possible, by non-French crews. A 'sale' of the ships was to be effected when they reached Alexandria. Now, however, naval contracts were superseded by melodrama.

In March 1826 a Greek schooner, the *Spartiate*, arrived in Marseille. The captain, Vitalis, posed as a passenger, and rumours began to circulate of criminal intentions. The two brigs built by Rambaud then left for Alexandria in May, as did one of the corvettes built by Cerisy in June. The situation in Marseille regarding the Greek war was very interesting. There was a very active Hellenic committee, but it enjoyed little support, because most of the population relied on trade with the Levant, especially Egypt.

46,000 quintals of cotton, for example, arrived in 1826; 68,000 in 1827. 'Marseille was thus for the Egyptians and against the Greeks; one could even say that it was at this time violently anti-Greek.'[182] On the night of 13 July the whole city was galvanised by an attempt to burn one of the frigates, the *Amazone*, in the shipyards. No real damage, however, was done. The police were baffled despite their pompous reports. Suspicion fixed on a young man who had volunteered for Greece, but nothing was proven, and he went off to join the war.[183]

Then began a much longer saga, the attempt to launch the other frigate, the *Guerrière*. This was set for 12 August, and a vast crowd assembled. The ship jammed two-thirds of the way to the water. The police suspected a plot to burn or capture the ship instigated by the philhellenes. The second launching was set for 19 August, and was even more unfortunate. The ship entered the water for two-thirds of its length, and then heeled over on its port side when the bow touched the shallow bottom. A famous expert in such crises, Molinari from La Ciotat, was called in. He asked 10,000 francs, and finally in October floated the ship, but repairs meant that it was not ready to sail until the next April.[184] The other frigate, the *Bahira*, was not launched until November 1827, and thus escaped the destruction of the fleet at Navarino.

Marseille was the main port for the construction of the Egyptian navy, but not the only one. Although the main negotiation was so ably carried out by Livron, the support of Drovetti as Consul-General for Egypt must have been crucial. Being Italian by birth, he may also have played a considerable part in placing other contracts in Italy, at Livorno and Venice. At the former, two ships were begun in August 1825: a frigate of 60 guns, and a corvette of 24. Although the builder was Tuscan, the plans were French. The corvette, ominously named *Ville de Navarino*, was ready by early 1827, when Cochrane in the *Unicorn* appeared off the port, examined the ship closely and lay in wait for it to sail. He then, however, sailed off to Greece, and the ship thus reached Alexandria safely. The frigate the *Leone*, followed in July.[185] At Venice a frigate, the *Egyptienne*, of 60 guns was begun in April 1826 and launched in May 1827. It was to sail under an Austrian flag and with an Austrian crew, until the government drew back. The ship was meanwhile driven by wind from its anchorage and ran aground, requiring a refit before it finally sailed in April 1828.

By early 1827 Mehemet Ali had achieved a long-standing aim. He had Khosrev Pasha replaced as Turkish admiral by Isset Mehemed Pasha, who in fact sent a deputy to serve under Ibrahim. A new levy brought 5,000 new sailors. Livron obtained a set of French naval regulations, which were translated by Osman Bey. And six Egyptians went to Toulon to learn naval construction. Of all these European-built ships, including the flagship, the *Egyptienne*, which sailed from Egypt on 5 August, 1827, only the *Leone* returned from Navarino. The first phase of the history of the Egyptian navy ended in disaster.

Conclusion

Egypt was transformed in the reign of Mehemet Ali as never before in its history since the conquest by the Greeks and Romans after three millennia of pharaonic rule. The Viceroy was determined to modernise his country, to make himself rich and independent of the Sultan, and to restore Egypt to the dominant role in eastern affairs which had eluded her for so many centuries.

So much was attempted in such a short time, but success was very limited. The education programme was essential for efficiency in every department of the administration. Thanks to the dedication and idealism of Drovetti and Jomard, the sending of Egyptians to France for education achieved very substantial results. Whatever Mehemet Ali's whims and reactions, those who had seen Europe at first hand for five years could never be the same, and were to exercise a decisive influence on Egypt at the highest levels in the next generation.

The health programme was an unqualified success. The vaccination campaign had revolutionary results for the peasants' well-being. The unsung heroes of this dangerous and very poorly rewarded work were the Italian and French doctors. The medical school for the army was equally revolutionary and beneficial, given the preceding situation and the endless wars in which Egypt was now engaged. Three hundred medical officers had been trained by 1834. Not to be forgotten are the midwifery and veterinary schools, and the establishment of the first quarantine procedures. In all of this again Drovetti's influence was paramount.

The economic history of Egypt tells a very different story. Despite so-called reforms in land-owning, the position of the peasants became inhuman. The monopoly of the Mamelukes was simply exchanged for a much more crushing one in the hands of the Viceroy. Taxes were vastly increased; land was given over to products other than food; many peasants fled the land and left it unworked; disease ravaged the population. The only success was the introduction of merinos. Mehemet Ali was also obsessed with the transformation of Egypt into a manufacturing country: factories for silk, fish, saltpetre, cotton, wool, sugar. The attempt to install, maintain and work sophisticated European machinery was obvious madness. European workers of the right kind were hard to obtain, and the peasants naturally hated factory work. Closely connected with industry was commerce, an even more striking example of the Viceroy's obsessions, because he thought there were fortunes to be made. More monopolies were established, and some success was achieved during the wars when the English were in desperate need of grain. Exorbitant taxes and totally unscrupulous business methods then ruined everything. No-one would buy overpriced Egyptian goods, and many merchants went bankrupt. Against the madness of all these policies, Drovetti raised his voice, but what could he achieve in the face of Mehemet Ali's despotism and concern only for profit?

In comparison with this the story of the new Egyptian army is a relative success. It was formed of the peasantry, but trained by European officers. The arrival of a major group of French instructors in 1824, however, led to a scandal. There were national rivalries between French and Italian officers, and many adventurers who had no training at all tried to pass themselves off as officers. Despite this, the army acquitted itself brilliantly in the very bitter Greek war and in the wars against the Sultan in Syria in the next decades. In the last analysis, however, success was more than overbalanced by the horrendous cost to the Egyptian economy, and the price paid by the Egyptian people, who were mercilessly conscripted and killed and mutilated in the wars.

The crucial role played by Drovetti in the development of the European-style Egyptian army is beyond question. He was instrumental in bringing many of the Europeans to Egypt and was regarded by such officers, from the highest ranks down, as their major resort in any difficulty. He undoubtedly saw the chance for France to exercise a dominant influence in creating the instrument by which Egypt was to overturn the existing balance of power in the Levant.

The story of the navy is very similar, a grandiose attempt to become a major naval power almost overnight. Perhaps the most extraordinary feature is the cooperation Mehemet Ali received, notably in France, although it was obvious that the ships were destined to be used against the Greeks and perhaps to upset the whole balance of power in the East. Again it must be admitted that the Egyptians proved themselves to be splendid sailors, but the cost to the whole economy was staggering. The first navy was lost almost to a ship at Navarino, but the Egyptians here were the victims, caught between the leading European powers and the Ottoman Empire. The great plans of Mehemet Ali must have had the fullest support of Drovetti, and the contacts of the Consul in both France and Italy, as well as his noted anti-hellenic sentiments, were indispensable to successful letting of contracts on such a large scale in those two countries, with even the discreet cooperation of the French government.

VII   Three museums: the Drovetti collections and Drovetti as excavator

The appreciation of Egyptian antiquities and collections before the nineteenth century

The first people to appreciate Egyptian art and even to collect it were the Romans. From the first century AD, there were many temples of Isis in Rome, and the first emperor, Augustus, brought two obelisks from Egypt – a tremendous feat – and set them up in Rome in 10 BC.

Even during the Middle Ages, many Europeans visited Egypt, but they rarely ventured further south than Cairo, where they always visited the pyramids, before hurrying on to the Holy Land. They were in constant danger from Muslim fanatics, often robbed, and sometimes murdered. They gave little thought to collecting antiquities, but usually brought back some souvenirs. The major export, indeed, was mummy, very highly valued for its supposed medicinal uses.[1]

A new era was signalled by the efforts of Sixtus V (1585-1590) in moving the obelisk of St. Peter's and raising no fewer than three others. These pagan monuments were 'Christianised' and became valued urban decorations, marking the main basilicas. By the seventeenth century, important collections of Egyptian antiquities were being formed: by Claude Peiresc (1580-1637), who owned mummies, papyri and Coptic manuscripts; Pietro della Valle (1586-1652), who brought back two mummies from Sakkarah in 1615, which passed to the collection of Cardinal Flavio Chigi (1641-1693); and Athanasius Kircher (1602-1680), who obtained Egyptian material from Peiresc as the nucleus for his famous museum at Rome. Contemporary travellers like Pierre Belon, the French apothecary who visited Egypt in 1610, went out of their way to extol Egyptian 'sublimity and magnificence' in comparison with the Romans. The German Johannes Wansleben made two visits, in 1664 and 1672-1673, in the second instance to collect manuscripts for Louis XIV. He reached Middle Egypt and was impressed by the 'grandeur and vanity' of Egyptian civilisation.

As an example of eighteenth century travellers we may mention the English divine Richard Pococke, who went to Egypt in 1737-1738 and reached as far as Philae. His enthusiasm was such that he described the Hypostyle Hall at Karnak as having 'more of the beautiful magnificence in it than any other building I ever saw'.[2] He also tried to place Egyptian art and architecture in their historical context, as pre-classical. The Egyptians were, for example, the originators of architecture, but with them it was 'stiff and proud'; he gave them credit, however, for inventing a precursor of the Corinthian order. Pococke did collect antiquities such as statuary and smaller objects. It was not, indeed, normal for any respectable collection in Europe to include Egyptian material. The founder of the British Museum, Sir Hans Sloane (1660-1753) bequeathed his collection to the museum: it included some 150 objects from Egypt, none of great importance.

It is the eighteenth century which saw Egyptian art come into its own right for the first time. There was a battle of three titans, interestingly of different nationalities, and the palm goes to the French. In 1764 there appeared Johann Winckelmann's *Geschichte der Kunst des Altertums*. Perfection in ancient art was achieved by the Greeks. The Egyptians for him were merely 'primitives', lacking physical beauty, uninspired by nature, devoted to the mysterious, restrained by traditionalism, and with no understanding or skill in anatomy. The Italian Giambattista Piranesi, the great engraver, on the other hand, championed the Romans against the Greeks. At the same time, he gave credit to the Egyptians for what they taught their successors, and stressed the subtlety and variety of Egyptian art. His *Apologetic essay in defence of Egyptian and Tuscan architecture* appeared in 1769. Piranesi did more, however, than just theorise: he decorated the Caffe Inglese at Rome in Egyptian style in the 1760s.

The greatest champion of the Egyptians was the doyen of French antiquarians the comte de Caylus, who edited his *Recueil d'antiquités égyptiennes, étrusques, grecques, romaines et gauloises* in seven volumes, 1752-1767. For the first time, Egyptian antiquity was given equal weighting with the classical world and took its place in the development of world art. Caylus had the extraordinary intelligence to surmise that the earliest Egyptian art had been lost (it had, in fact, not been discovered). Architecture showed skills which the moderns had lost, and the Egyptians were also excellent metal-workers and jewellers.

> The recognition of Egyptian art as a style with its own laws was the meritorious achievement of the comte de Caylus.... To him, the Egyptians were a wise and enlightened people, in comparison with whose stern and massive buildings the temples of the Greeks were bound to seem like finely decked-out houses of cards.[3]

None of these three antiquarians and art critics had ever been to Egypt! It was from books of illustrations such as Caylus' that famous potters such as Wedgewood in the 1770s and later derived their inspiration for Egyptianising motifs, such as canopic vases.

The conditions which had prevailed in Egypt from the Middle Ages and which made travel there an adventure and more persisted until 1798. A major turning-point is marked by the French invasion of that year. The expedition was accompanied by dozens of scholars of every profession, who set about recording every feature, notably antiquities, and preparing the mighty *Description de l'Egypte* (19 vols), 1809-1828. The most famous account of the expedition was by baron Vivant Denon, *Voyage dans la Basse et la Haute Egypte*, 1802. Thebes seemed to him to be decadent. It was rather Dendereh which inspired him to reflect on the order and simplicity, the rationality and taste of Egyptian architecture, in short, Egyptian 'perfection and sublimity in the arts'. The whole army was besotted at the sight of the temple.[4]

The appreciation of Egyptian culture had come into its own, and now with the overthrow of the Mamelukes and the new era which was to see the establishment of the dynasty of Mehemet Ali, the country was open to visitors of all kinds as it had never been before. This was precisely the Egypt of the first third of the nineteenth century in which Drovetti was to gather no fewer than three major collections. That period would not last forever. In 1858, the Service des Antiquités was established by Mariette, and Egypt would henceforth jealously guard her cultural patrimony. The brief age of the great collectors was over.

The first collection: the foundation of the Torino Museum

The exact circumstances under which the great Drovetti collection was gathered together are not entirely clear. It is most commonly said that it took fifteen years to amass, and since it arrived in Livorno in 1821, that would imply that it was begun at the latest in 1806.[5] Jomard, a very close associate of Drovetti and editor of the renowned *Description de l'Egypte*, stated in 1821 that Drovetti had begun collecting twelve years before,[6] giving a date of c.1809. Another traveller to Egypt, Montulé, in 1818 said that Drovetti had been 'studying antiquity' for seven years,[7] implying a beginning c.1811. The matter is even mentioned in the diplomatic correspondence. Saint-Marcel, Consul at Rosetta, noted Drovetti's departure with Boutin for Upper Egypt on 17 November, 1811, and his return at the end of the next January with a collection of antiquities, notably papyri.[8]

The collection, or what was taking shape as such, was seen by many travellers. The Englishman William Turner saw it in June 1815:

250

In the morning, I returned the visit of the French consul, who showed me his museum, which, though small, is select and contains some beautiful things. He intends carrying it to England, where he hopes to sell it for 5,000 pounds. Among other things, is the head of a mummy, with the flesh and hair still in perfect preservation (though the former is blackened by the embalming drugs) of which an engraving is given in the account of Egypt, published under the auspices of Bonaparte.[9]

Here is vital information. In 1815, the collection was still small, and Drovetti was apparently saying that he would sell it to England.

The Swiss Orientalist John Burckhardt's only reference to Drovetti in his *Travels in Nubia*, 1819, is, in fact, to the collection, which he declared the finest of all in Europe (sic). He saw it while in Egypt between 1814 and 1817. Its strengths were the many 'middle-sized' statues, the 'particularly valuable' papyri, and the innumerable articles of everyday life. He went on, however, to say that 'mercantile and pecuniary interests' had triumphed over the love of antiquity and that Drovetti wanted to sell. Burckhardt thought it 'most desirable' that the collection should come to England. He believed that it had cost about 1,500 pounds to amass, but that it would fetch three or four times that amount.[10]

Another important person who saw the collection in 1816 was none other than the newly-arrived English Consul, Henry Salt. This is one of the few references to Drovetti in Salt's *Life and correspondence* by J. Halls: on Salt's arrival, Drovetti was reported to be in Upper Egypt, 'buying up everything there to complete a collection upon which he had been engaged for some years … it contains a great variety of curious articles, and some of extraordinary value.' Salt is said to have tried to get Drovetti to offer it to the British Museum, but it was too costly (3,000-4,000 pounds).[11]

The talk is always of England, and the value is agreed to be 4,000-5,000 pounds. The situation was completely changed by 1818, when the comte de Forbin, Director-General of French Museums, met Drovetti at Alexandria:

He has a very curious collection of Egyptian antiquities, and the most ardent wish of his heart is to decorate with them the rich museum of Paris. To effect this proposal, he has overlooked many opportunities afforded him of realising property, as offers have been made him which it would be conceived difficult, but which he has dared to resist.

Of the collection Forbin mentions, in fact, only a 'valuable sheet of papyrus'(!).[12] Contrary to Turner's and Burckhardt's hopes, Forbin talked of the Louvre as the destination of the collection. This was only natural, given his position. If Drovetti seemed to acquiesce, was it only politeness, or a consciousness of the possible connection with his restoration as Consul?

The great value of Forbin's account lies rather in the clues he gives for the way the collection was acquired. Forbin notes that Drovetti was constantly approached by Arabs offering him antiquities for sale, and they always let him set the price. 'His just and noble character has merited their universal applause, and they ever departed perfectly satisfied with the prices which he set, and which were frequently to his own disadvantage.'[13] As well as his own researches and those of his agents, therefore, Drovetti let the native population know that he would reward them appropriately for material brought to him. Those conversant with the history of Egyptian archaeology will recall that Flinders Petrie swore by this method of fair payment to prevent theft from his excavations.

Few people knew more about the collection than Carlo Vidua, in Egypt from late in 1819 until August 1820. He declared that it was unique in the world and frankly exposed Drovetti's secrets: no-one else was able to collect so much, partly because of his diplomatic position, and especially because of the favour he enjoyed with Mehemet Ali. More bluntly, 'he has turned Thebes upside down to find statues there.'[14] Vidua was not able to see the collection, which he described in summary as 'the most beautiful, the most complete, and the most extensive made, or ever to be made', because it had already been transported to Livorno.

We may continue to widen the national boundaries of the visitors to Egypt. In 1821 there arrived Johann Scholz, Professor of Divinity at Bonn. His professional interests dictated a more specialised appraisal:

> M. Drovetti ... possesses, among others, eight partly decayed MSS containing the Bible in Saitic dialect, and the wisdom of Solomon in Memphitic dialect, which are probably older than any in Europe. He has likewise a fine collection of historical inscriptions.

He mentioned also some statuettes of Serapis found 250 paces south of Pompey's Pillar in Alexandria 'some years since', and 'now in the estimable collection of M. Drovetti'.[15]

The full story of the acquisition of the collection by the most unlikely purchaser, Piedmont, may be found in the *Epistolario*. As early as 1816, Drovetti's friend Jean François Rignon, a Piedmontese, had been asked to sound out the possibility of purchase by the King or the University, but there was a lack of money. Some of the leading Piedmontese intellectuals had been approached, apparently on Drovetti's own suggestion, but nothing could be done. Count Prospero Balbo, President of the Torino Academy, sighed and had to admit that the Academy was a year behind in receiving its annual 12,000 francs. We may note that at this rate, the total income would have been required for many years in order to buy the collection! Abbé Botta, the King's confessor, was impressed with Drovetti, and suggested some payment in the form of a life pension. Strange as it may seem, Drovetti had not at this stage suggested any price. Rignon summed up very sadly: 'My dear friend, in short, our country is not yet civilised enough to make some sacrifices for these objects which would gain it glory and respect: our ideas are still too restricted.' He mentioned other treasures and other buyers: Drovetti's was not the only collection on the market. Abbé Derossi, librarian at Parma, had offered Torino a very rich collection of Oriental MSS, asking 50,000 francs in cash and a pension of 10,000. Maria Luisa, Duchess of Parma and Napoleon's widow, bought them for 150,000 francs in cash.[16] What is most interesting in all of this is the revelation that while so many were talking of England, Drovetti was already sounding out reactions in Piedmont.

As Forbin stated in 1818, France then had a chance. On his return to Paris in May 1818, he spoke of devoting himself without stint to ways to gain for France all that he had seen.[17] The price had now been set, and it was a little 'frightening'. Forbin was anxious to have Drovetti reappointed as consul, and suggested that he might then 'perhaps feel more keenly than ever the need to enrich France',[18] by ensuring that the collection came there. Another supporter was Frédéric Cailliaud, who returned to Paris in April 1819, and spoke of the collection in the highest terms to Forbin.[19] The Count was negotiating with the Minister of the Interior, the comte de Cazes, in May. By this time matters had reached the stage of asking for a complete catalogue, and whether there were any conditions attached to the price. As a reward, it was now stated that Drovetti was to be named Consul-General and to receive the Légion d'Honneur. Forbin asked therefore for a 'positive and categorical' reply.[20]

Rignon had in the meantime, however, not been idle. He had discussed with Abbé Incisa, the King's Almoner and head of the Collegio delle Provincie, possible ways of securing for Torino University a collection 'announced to the whole of Europe by so many famous travellers and all the public papers'. Incisa had been emphasising to Balbo the glory which he would gain by acquiring such a collection for the state. Rignon asked Drovetti for a catalogue, but admitted that it would be difficult to recompense him for his expenses, despite his 'extreme unselfishness'. He had been in contact with Forbin and had even gone to Paris, and the museum director was sure that France would buy the collection. Rignon hoped, however, that Piedmont would get the first offer. Drovetti's brother assured Rignon that the Prince of Carignano was very active on his behalf, but it was also obvious that only a great and rich government could afford the collection. Rignon ended on a note of great regret and resignation.[21]

The French bid looked even more confident when Jomard gave it his full support. He was a member of the Institut de France, and was constantly lobbying with the Minister of the Interior and the Académie des Inscriptions et Belles-Lettres. He had the advantage of being able to convey to both a catalogue compiled from memory by Cailliaud![22]

The Légion d'Honneur was conferred on Drovetti in 1819,[23] but it was in March 1820 that Piedmont offered to buy the collection, paying in instalments. The details come in a letter from Cesare Saluzzo, luminary of the Torino Academy, to Carlo Vidua. Saluzzo[24] had been consulting the Minister for Foreign Affairs, the marchese di San Marzano, and the Minister of Internal Affairs since September 1819, Prospero Balbo, who gave their support to the proposal, not to mention the King Vittorio Emanuele. Vidua had indicated the price which Drovetti sought, and Saluzzo answered that not even the royal treasury could pay such a sum (it is remarkable that we have not so far ever heard what it was!) although the King was able to confer decorations and honours. It was now Balbo, who 'as head of the University, did what he could not do as a minister': offer Drovetti 20,000 lire per annum, the equivalent of 5% interest on a capital of 400,000 lire. This was obviously the value set on the collection. The capital was to be paid off at 10,000 lire per annum – in another forty years! At this point, another strong supporter of the scheme was revealed, Count Bianco di Barbania, an old connection of Drovetti and one of the Prince of Carignano's staff.

Two months later the young German artist Franz Gau, who had been so kindly treated by Drovetti and who had now returned to Europe, was in Rome and spending much time with Barthold Georg Niebuhr, the greatest historian of Rome of his time. Gau knew the collection well, and obviously spoke highly of it to the great historian and diplomat, who wanted a catalogue.[25] The Prussians, new entrants in the contest, were certainly not to be underestimated, but much more worrying was the acquisitive Prince of Bavaria – soon to become Ludwig I – for whom Gau also sought information in June.[26]

Vidua was the man on the spot in Egypt, negotiating for the Piedmontese. Communications were most complicated. Drovetti was told that Vidua would be receiving a letter from Saluzzo about the offer, but it did not arrive. Vidua's correspondence then takes up the story, in a reply to Saluzzo in July 1820.[27] By this time Vidua was sure that Drovetti would prefer to give his collection to Piedmont above all other countries. He had offered it to France for 200,000 francs in cash and the same in instalments; to sell it to Piedmont on the terms offered would therefore entail a loss, but he willingly undertook that. He had to wait, however, for negotiations with France to be finalised, and had promised to wait until September for a definite answer from that government. The danger from France was obviously great: Vidua noted Forbin's flattery of Drovetti and an article by the comte de Volney in some periodical, and the conferment of the Légion d'Honneur. The French seemed (understandably) to be using the possibility of reappointing Drovetti as another lever. The danger from Prussia had lessened because the king was not rich enough, but a Bavarian agent was in Egypt. Vidua therefore recommended bringing Drovetti to Piedmont to settle the matter.[28]

We have one letter from Drovetti's own hand at this crucial time, apparently to the French Minister of Foreign Affairs, and dated 24 July (obviously 1820).[29] It could not come at a more illuminating time. He pressed France for a decision about the consulate; for in the meantime he was being forced to give 'evasive answers' to another government which was making offers. He declared that he was willing to wait only two or three months, after which he would have to decide both about his own future and about the collection. The offers he had received were very tempting: an annual income of 50,000 francs and a post in Egypt for as long as he wished to stay. Drovetti concluded with a discussion of the details of the contract with France should it buy the collection, thus indicating his preference for that country. Which country was offering him such a high pension and presumably a consulate? The offers cannot, of course, come from England. Piedmont had as early as March 1819 been considering Drovetti as its consul in Egypt, and on his refusal, none was appointed until 1824. Piedmont was offering 20,000 lire as interest and 10,000 p.a. off the capital, and with a consul's salary of c.20,000, this makes precisely c.50,000 lire (francs).

By August, as the time for a decision drew nigh, Vidua saw the crucial key to the negotiations: to bind Drovetti to keep his promise to wait no longer than the next month, September, for the French to make up their minds. 'He is most scrupulous about honour and his word.' Vidua repeatedly emphasised to Drovetti that he had informed Saluzzo of this promise.[30] Saluzzo had been writing to Vidua from at least March, but in September realised that the letters had not arrived and so Drovetti knew nothing. In this month he therefore asked him for an immediate indication of his intentions and the approximate time for their realisation. As has been pointed out, Drovetti's silence must have been critical: it was assumed that he intended to sell to France or that he refused the Piedmontese conditions.

Drovetti must now have replied immediately; for the formal offer from Piedmont came in November 1820 from the hand of Prospero Balbo, Minister of the Interior.[32] He prefaced his letter by assuring Drovetti that his work in Egypt was well known to the King, especially his support for religion (important to the fiercely Catholic Piedmontese) and his generosity to Piedmontese travellers and those of all European nations. Such travellers and eminent and learned men spoke of the 'very great and very rare' collection. In the name of the King, Vittorio Emanuele, Balbo requested it for the University. As proof of the King's esteem, he had made Drovetti a Knight of the Order of SS Maurizio e Lazzaro.

Drovetti formally accepted this offer in December.[33] The abdication of the King in March 1821, and the resultant resignation of Balbo, however, raised new problems. Balbo had been the most eminent supporter of the acquisition.[34]

Despite the fact that the collection had now gone to Piedmont, the French government still nominated Drovetti as their Consul-General in Egypt on 20 June, 1821. Vidua himself returned to Europe in September of that year, uncertain whether Drovetti had sold the collection, and if so, to which government.[35] And that was not all.

The excitement caused by the arrival in Europe of the first great collection of Egyptian antiquities was enormous. The race to break the code of the hieroglyphs was approaching its climax. Drovetti's relations with Champollion are well known,[36] and the latter was soon to have unlimited and vital access to the whole collection. Many obviously hoped that clues such as further multilingual texts might be contained there. How extraordinary it is to find that none other than Dr Thomas Young was at Livorno in September 1821, and saw the collection. In it he found a bilingual cippus, but was not allowed to take a copy.[37] The inscription was not, Young explained, in the catalogue. It was in demotic and Greek, and came from Menuf (Memphis). Both inscriptions were almost illegible, and Young wanted to make plaster casts and squeezes to take to England for study. He wrote to Drovetti, asking permission, offering, of course, to pay all expenses and to make duplicate copies to be kept at Livorno until the inscription arrived safely, wherever the collection was finally sold. Young claimed that Drovetti refused, his 'cupidity' being aroused, but that within a few months other sources turned up which made the poor bilingual worthless. This episode throws an unpleasant light on Drovetti. Young's motives were entirely based on fear that the stone, perhaps vital, might be lost to science. Either Drovetti was more involved than we know in the race between the English and the French to decipher the hieroglyphs,[38] or, more likely, was concerned at the devaluation of this investment for his retirement.

In January 1822 Vidua wrote to Drovetti that he had been devastated to hear that the government had withdrawn from the contract. By March, however, he was able to reassure him that this was all a misunderstanding of something which the King had said. Not the least difficulty was the loss of Drovetti's letters, which did not reach Torino. Vidua had luckily kept those which he received in Athens, in which Drovetti declared: 'from this moment my collection belongs to the University of Torino.' This was the vital evidence that he had kept his word and so the government should respond in kind.[39]

Vidua returned to Torino at the end of March, and immediately saw Roget de Cholex, Minister of Internal Affairs; he also induced his father to speak to him. Great stress was laid by Cholex on Carlo Felice's sense of justice and his promise to uphold Vittorio Emanuele's obligations. To those who claimed that there was no contract, because Drovetti had not replied, Vidua quoted his letter of 3 December 1821. Vidua even had an audience with Carlo Felice. Equally important was the arrival of the catalogue. Not everyone was as enthusiastic as Balbo, simply because of the fame of the collection! Strife between the government and the bishops then intervened, and the King went off to Genova. Vidua thereupon handed over copies of Drovetti's letters and the catalogue to Cholex, who certainly revealed that he was won over by Vidua's arguments. It was in October that the latter was able to reassure Drovetti that all was finalised.[40] It had required all Vidua's prudence, patience and delicacy to prevent the ruin of the entire undertaking.

The return of Carlo Felice was now awaited to draw up the contract. Rignon was Drovetti's procurator. Even so, the whole affair was completely confidential, and Vidua urged Drovetti not to tell a soul. As Vidua noted again, it was only by insisting that Drovetti had kept his word that he finally succeeded in forcing the government to keep its side of the bargain. A further complication then arose in February 1823, with the death of Rignon.

The contract was signed by Drovetti in Alexandria on 24 March, 1823, in the presence of the chief interpreter and chancellor of the consulate, and with Florent Tourneau and Charles Escalon, two French merchants, as witnesses, and Domenico Pedemonte as procurator. The price was 400,000 lire. It was paid in the form of 100,000 lire in cash, and 15,000 lire per annum interest (5%) on the other 300,000.[41]

Giulio Cordero di San Quintino,[42] who was to become curator of the collection, made a summary catalogue at Livorno in October 1823,[43] listing, among other things, 169 papyri, 485 objects in metal, 454 of wood, 1,500 scarabs, 175 statuettes, 102 mummies, 90 alabaster vases and 95 statues. It has been pointed out that, although the price of 400,000 lire was not large, given the size and value of the collection, it was enormous in relation to the finances of the kingdom of Piedmont at the time.[44]

The saga was not, of course, completed by the mere signing of the contract of sale. The collection had then to be transported to Torino. San Quintino wrote to Drovetti in February 1824 that it had arrived safely, without any damage whatever, via Genova.[45] It transpires within a paragraph that the famous colossus suffered slightly in being disembarked at Genova. And another letter of the same month revealed that a door jamb had been broken in two, as was a statue, while the colossus had lost the top of its staff and one of the two horns, although it was found. The great sphinxes had also been bruised, because they had been moved with chains instead of ropes![46] The total cost of the transport by ship from Livorno to Genova and from there on carriages to Torino was 8,000 francs.[47]

Then arose the problem of where to house the collection, which would involve 'not a few difficulties'. San Quintino raised a major question. He wanted to indicate where each object had been found, but how could he do that without gaining such information from the man who had formed the collection? And who was to be the curator? San Quintino confessed ignorance – only some people thought that it might be he! He claimed that he did not deserve the honour and that he had not indicated any desire for it, but as a lover of Egyptology he would not refuse it[48] – a perfect exercise in false modesty.

A small collection of Egyptian antiquities already existed in Torino.[49] These had been brought back by Vitaliani Donati, who had visited the East between 1759 and 1762. His donations have been identified as a mutilated statue of Isis, wearing a solar disc and horns (actually that of an eighteenth dynasty princess), a so-called statue of Osiris, in reality of Ramesses II, and a statue of Sekhmet bearing the cartouche of Amenhotep III. It has been suggested that without this existing nucleus, Carlo Felice would perhaps not have acquired the Drovetti collection.[50] From the above saga of the negotiations, however, we may doubt whether the few existing Egyptian items in Torino had any influence whatsoever on the acquisition of 1824. Almost every museum in the world and every royal cabinet had a few such objects. There was, in fact, an even earlier Egyptian collection, that of Savoy, of almost three hundred items, including the famous Mensa Isiaca.[51]

The main rival of Piedmont for the acquisition of the Drovetti collection had been France, a kingdom much richer and far more culturally self-conscious than the other. How and why did France miss this great opportunity? It was in 1822 that a Frenchman announced that the key to hieroglyphs, lost for centuries, had been rediscovered. Champollion regarded the loss of this collection as a disaster.[52] Some of the most powerful cultural figures in France, such as Forbin and Jomard, had led the negotiations.

The *Epistolario* reveals a variety of convincing explanations. They are scattered about, like pieces of a jigsaw puzzle. François Artaud, director of the museum at Lyon, declared in March 1824 that the 'cursed zodiac' had deprived France of the Drovetti collection.[53] France had paid an enormous sum, 150,000 francs, in fact, for the great zodiac which had been hacked out of the roof of the temple of Hathor at Dendereh by Lellorain, on the assumption that it was a priceless demonstration that classical astrology was derived from ancient Egypt. When it was soon shown that the zodiac was in fact part of a temple dating to between the fourth century BC and first century AD, the outrage was enormous. Egyptian antiquities were ridiculed as costly fakes.

A year later Artaud modified this judgement. The price was not the obstacle; for the King had just bought the Durand collection.[54] This was the collection of Edme Antoine Durand (1768-1835), mostly classical objects, which had cost no less than 480,000 francs. Almost two years later, the same man revealed to Drovetti that it was 'religious scruples' which prevented the purchase: the antiquities were thought to be 'of too great an antiquity'.[55] One has only to recall the grave concerns about Champollion's voyage to Egypt in 1828, with *instructions* not to find anything which imperilled the authority of the Bible, to understand how tenacious and powerful was religious censorship at this time in France under the restored and reactionary monarchy. Such scruples did not, however, prevent the notoriously Catholic Piedmont from buying the collection!

More recent scholars have other suggestions. Marro suggested that Drovetti was a 'good Piedmontese patriot' who never wanted the collection to go to France; this was mooted only as a means to ensure his nomination as Consul-General.[56] Another obvious consideration is that, as a Bonapartist, Drovetti did not have total French support.[57]

It was in June 1824 that Champollion arrived in Torino to study the collection. He had already written his *Lettre à M. Dacier*, on 22 September, 1822, and completed his *Précis du système hiéroglyphique* on 15 April, 1824. The texts of the ancient Egyptians were beginning to reveal their secrets, but one of the greatest triumphs of modern decipherment had met, especially in France, with almost total opposition and ridicule. There were too many others who still believed that they could win for themselves the immortal prize of the decipherment. Champollion had exposed the weaknesses of the members of the Institut, notably by his demonstration that the Dendereh zodiac was virtually a Roman monument, and he was widely feared as 'le jacobin enragé'.

In Torino, on the other hand, he was feted by royal, aristocratic and intellectual circles. This support and admiration were of enormous value to him at this time. Equally important, however, was the chance to study a mass of Egyptian material of which he had the highest estimate, to test his decipherment and to develop his understanding of Egyptian history and every other aspect of that civilisation. He saw in Torino for the first time the masterpieces of Egyptian art which completely revolutionised his understanding of its importance and development. This was, in sum, Champollion's most intensive study of Egyptian monuments and texts before his first – and only – visit to Egypt in 1828. It is no wonder that, despite first intentions to spend only a short time in Torino, he remained there no fewer than nine months.[58]

Why did Drovetti assemble the collection? The documents in the *Epistolario* speak often of his many toils, but offer no further clue. The motive cannot have been patriotism, that is, concern for the embellishment of the state of his birth; for Drovetti was quite willing to sell to the highest bidder.

The most obvious answer would seem to be the unflattering one of monetary gain. It has been admitted that 'he well knew how valued was every product of pharaonic civilisation'.[59] There are a variety of observations which temper this. In the first place, many collections were being assembled at this time by travellers and diplomats and all were being sold for high prices. Drovetti could hardly have been expected to donate his collection. Second, his office of consul was ill-paid and financially very burdensome. Some contemporaries had the decency to point this out.[60] Such antiquarianism was, therefore, a legitimate and customary method of recouping expenses and providing for retirement. Third, Drovetti was very well known for his charity and generosity, to all travellers in Egypt, to friends all over Europe, and most pressing of all, to his family. The heaviest burdens were the family of his elder brother and his own son. He had many calls on a modest private income. Fourth, Drovetti cannot, in fact, by any stretch of the imagination be said to have made much money when he did sell. The price of 400,000 francs for the vast collection was nothing in comparison to the 150,000 francs paid for the Dendereh zodiac. And he did not get the price he asked and upon which agreement was reached. He received only one quarter in cash; the rest came in the form of a small annual payment of 15,000 lire.

To put the Drovetti collections in their true perspective, we have only to consider the three made by his rival, Henry Salt. He had very close relations with Viscount Valentia and his father, the Earl of Mountnorris; for he had accompanied the former as his secretary and draftsman on a long and arduous voyage to India and the Red Sea, 1802-1806. When Salt was appointed Consul-General in Egypt, not unexpectedly these two asked him to gather antiquities for them. More ominously, as the sequel was to reveal, Sir Joseph Banks had urged Salt to collect for the British Museum. Most interesting of all, however, is Salt's frank admission that his salary was very inadequate (1,700 pounds) to cover all the necessary expenses of his office. He mentions three horses and grooms, two janissaries, a steward, a cook, two footmen, a gardiner, various animals such as a camel to bring water and a bullock for the garden, and a secretary. He had as well to rent a house at 50 pounds.[61]

Collecting was in itself not free. Salt's first collection was made possible only by a bequest on his father's death in 1817, and cost him 3,000 pounds. By 1819 he was able to offer this fine collection to the British Museum. The only comparison we have for the cost of a single piece is the head of Memnon, which had cost Salt 350 pounds.[62] This was, of course, exceptional, since it was so colossal, and it was in fact given by Salt to the Museum. In a notorious series of events, complicated mainly by Belzoni's abuse of Salt's generosity, the Museum finally paid him a mere 2,000 pounds; Sir John Soane paid the same amount for the gem of the collection, the sarcophagus of Seti I.[63] The other treasures included statues of the queens from Abu Simbel, statues of Sekhmet, and the head of Tuthmosis III.

Salt's second collection was ready at Livorno by June 1825, and he valued it at 4,000 pounds. It was bought by the Louvre, after Champollion's warm support, for 250,000 francs (10,000 pounds).[64] The third collection was formed shortly before Salt's death, and was valued at 100,000 francs (4,000 pounds). It realised 7,000 at Southeby's in 1835, the majority of the pieces (4,000 pounds in value) going to the British Museum.

There is no doubt whatsoever about Salt's major concerns. His expenses in Egypt as Consul-General were very heavy, and his salary quite inadequate. He was, moreover, unlike Drovetti, not entitled to a pension! He talked of giving the second collection to the British Museum in return for an annuity of 600 pounds. In addition, however, Salt was genuinely interested in Egyptian antiquities. He visited Upper Egypt as far as Thebes in 1817. As well as financing Belzoni, he contributed generously to Caviglia's researches around the Gizeh pyramids. He made a second journey south 1818-1819, and although forced to return because of illness, did much work at Thebes. His third and final tour was in 1822, as far as Aswan.[65] In the great controversy over the decipherment of hieroglyphs, Salt had at first been an adherent of Young, until he was won over by Champollion. He himself published *An essay on Dr Young's and M. Champollion's phonetic system of hieroglyphs, with some additional discoveries*, 1825. Salt was, indeed, a scholar of some accomplishments, knowing Latin and Greek as well as French, Italian and Arabic.

28. Amunhotep II
(18th dynasty)

In Drovetti's first collection, the story of very few monuments has been told. The most famous is the colossus of Seti II,[66] engraved as having been found by Rifaud at Thebes in 1818, and transported to Livorno in the Norwegian ship *Trondheim* by Capt. Richelieu in 1819. The statue was one of two at the main entrance to the Temple of Amon at Karnak (a companion piece is in the Louvre). It weighs six tons, and its transport across the Mediterranean in a sailing-ship of 158 tons was a feat.

The colossus was in Torino by 1824, but owing to shortage of space it then had to stand in the courtyard of the Palazzo dell'Accademia delle Scienze. It was this undignified location which caused Champollion, who came to Torino in June 1824, to compose a satire, 'Petition du Pharaon Osymandias à S.M. le roi de Sardaigne',[67] distributed in the streets in December and which caused an uproar. It also led to the better protection of the statue. The name Osymandias, given to the statue by Champollion, was an error. That name is, in fact, a Greek version of User-maat-re, one

29. Amunhotep and
Tutankhamun (18th
dynasty)

of the names of Ramesses II, but the statue is of Seti II. San Quintino, the curator, accepted the false name and placed the king in the fifteenth dynasty, dating him c.2,300 BC as a contemporary of Abraham! The first scholar to identify the king correctly was Pier Camillo Orcurti, in the first scientific catalogue of the collection in 1852.[68]

The story of the finding of another of the treasures is told by the Prussian traveller Johannes Bramsen, who came to Egypt c.1815:

We visited the elegant collection of antiquities belonging to Mons Drovetti, the French consul, who is well informed, polite and attentive to travellers of all nations. He informed us that some time ago he was out shooting pigeons, which are in great abundance here; he killed one which fell in a yard belonging to an Arab, and while in search of the bird discovered a piece of black stone, the rest of which

30. Princess Redi (3rd dynasty)

was buried in the ground. He offered a Spanish piastre to the Arab if
he would permit him to dig on the spot, to which he gladly
consented. On Mons. Drovetti's digging, he found a most beautiful
block of granite, with a Greek inscription of which I insert the
following translation with which he presented me:

> le peuple Lycien à Ptolomie, chief des guardes du corps et de
> grand veneur, un des premiers favoris de Ptolomie, et fils de
> grand veneur qui à cause des virtus et de la piété permanente
> de son père, rend les dieux satisfaits et propices au roi Ptolomie,
> à sa soeur la Reine, à leurs enfants, et au peuple lycien.

We saw the statue, which is in a perfect state of preservation, and from four to five feet high.[69]

This is the statue of the chief royal guardsman Ptolemy, officer of Ptolemy V Epiphanes (204-180), and apparently dedicated to him by the Lycian community, because he belonged to it by origin. As usual, modern commentaries make no mention of Drovetti.[70]

The Torino collection acquired from Drovetti is particularly notable for the large statuary of the New Kingdom (dynasties 18-20). Outstanding are the figures of Amenhotep I in painted limestone, the enthroned Tuthmosis III in diorite, the kneeling Amenhotep II in red granite offering vases to a deity (ill. 28), Tuthmosis IV in red granite standing under the protection of Amon the ram, Amenhotep III as a sphinx in sandstone, Tutankhamon protected by Amon (ill. 29) (later usurped by Horemhab), and Horemhab with his queen Mutnedmut.

From the later dynasties come various statues of Ramesses II, especially that which is almost the emblem of the Torino collection, the king in black granite enthroned with blue crown and pleated kilt,[71] and the colossus of Seti II in sandstone to which reference has already been made. Statues of divinities are also well represented, such as Ptah of Memphis in black granite, and most famous of all, the lion- headed goddess Sekhmet in diorite, both dating from the 18th dynasty. There is not much that is earlier than the time of the New Kingdom; for little attention was being paid to Old and Middle Kingdom sites at this time. A notable exception is the diorite seated statue of princess Redi of the third dynasty (ill. 30).[72]

Another major strength of the first Drovetti collection is papyri. The most important of all is the so- called Torino Canon, or king-list (ill. 31). This is another neglected saga; where it has been alluded to, it has been only for the purposes of sensationalism or calumny. The most colourful account is perhaps the following, by a brilliant excavator, who should have known better:

> When the papyrus was found by Drovetti, either in 1823 or 1824, it was *apparently* (my italics) complete, and he put it in a jar which he tied around his waist, mounted his donkey, and proceeded to ride into town. The joggling which the jar got along the path was disastrous. When Drovetti opened it the extraordinary document had been reduced to mere scraps which have been arranged and rearranged during the past hundred years, but so much had disappeared in dust on that ride on donkey-back that only the barest outline of the original document remains today.[73]

Where was the papyrus found? Where was Drovetti riding? What is the source for the whole story? None is given, but a footnote refers to Farina. For those who can consult this rather rare work their surprise will be considerable: Farina asserts that the story of the papyrus' destruction after its finding is a totally unfounded legend. Note the vital word on which the whole account hinges: 'apparently'. This is excellent historical method! Sufficient to destroy the whole fabrication is the fact that the first Drovetti collection was already in Europe by 1820, so the papyrus could not possibly have been found in '1823 or 1824'.

Fact is, as usual, much more exciting than fiction. The Torino Canon was purchased by the museum in 1823 with the rest of the first collection and arrived in the museum by February 1824.[74] In June of that year Champollion arrived to study everything. It was not until October that he turned to the papyri, and naturally first studied the magnificent editions of the 'Book of the Dead' as it is known to moderns. He immediately understood that only the longest copies were anything like 'complete', and that the shorter versions were only extracts for those who could not afford more. There were less attractive papyri in packets, 'blackened and eroded by time'. Amongst other things Champollion recognised the plan of the tomb of Ramesses IV. The most remarkable discovery still, however, awaited him. He learned by chance that there were other fragments, but

31. The 'Royal Canon' of Torino Museum

in very bad condition. He insisted on seeing them. What was his emotion on confronting a table ten feet long covered to a depth of six inches with 'papyrus debris'. He attempted to calm his anguish by pretending that they were merely fragments of the usual funerary papyri, but the first piece he picked up showed that they were historical documents. He thereupon resolved to examine every piece on the table: 'a million leaves, the shapeless remains of books written more than thirty centuries ago.' Among them he identified forty-eight fragments of what he instantly recognised as a 'chronological table', a 'royal canon', providing the names of almost two hundred kings.[75] It is thus another imperishable contribution of Champollion to have sorted and saved the remains of this invaluable papyrus which might have been consigned to oblivion.

Two years later, in 1826, the unreliable Gustav Seyffarth, best remembered for his fantastic rejection of Champollion's decipherment, came to Torino, searched for further fragments, and attempted to put them in order. A total of three hundred fragments were reunited to form 164 and arranged in twelve columns. This first arrangement has been very variously evaluated, and was questioned by Champollion's colleague Ippolito Rosellini as early as 1832[76] but was used by many others, notably Lepsius, who published the Canon in his *Auswahl der wichtigsten Urkunden des ägyptischen Altertums*, 1842. It was Francesco Barucchi, assistant director of

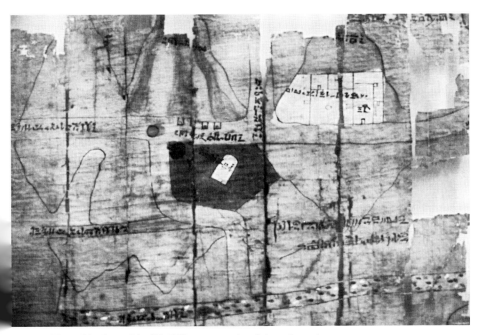

32. The gold mines of the Wadi Hammamat (south is at the top)

33. A signature of Rifaud on a statue of Ramasses II

the Torino Museum 1835-1860, who, referring to this publication by Lepsius, gave the simplest explanation of the papyrus' fragmentary state, namely that it had not been packed properly for the journey from Egypt to Italy.[77]

The eminent English scholar John Gardiner Wilkinson visited Torino in 1849 to make a further examination of the fragments and publish the second edition.[78] He paid special attention to the arrangement of the fibres, and also took notice of the writing on the verso, a vital clue to the arrangement. Wilkinson had the highest praise for the work of Seyffarth and Lepsius. On the history of the papyrus, he offered no information earlier than Champollion's discovery of the fragments in 1824.

Enormous steps were then taken with the discovery and publication of various other king-lists: from Karnak (1845), Sakkarah (1860), and Abydos (1864). This freed the investigation of ancient Egyptian chronology from reliance on the latest and most deformed of the lists, that of the third century BC Greek priest, Manetho, which was all Seyffarth had to help him. The superiority of the Torino Canon became clear – and its damaged state therefore all the more lamented. It alone had given a complete list of names, as well as the years reigned by each king and periodical totals.

268

34. The Acrobat (ostrakon from Deir el Medineh)

Emmanuel de Rougé, Curator of the Louvre collection 1849-1872, visited Torino to re-examine the fragments. He declared that Seyffarth's arrangement was 'tampering of lamentable skill'. De Rougé began to reconstruct the length of the columns of the papyrus based on his incomparable understanding of the earliest dynasties.[79] By the end of the century, however, Wallis Budge gave a melancholy verdict:

> ... beyond supplying the names of a number of kings, many of which do not appear elsewhere, the royal papyrus of Turin in its present state is of no use in our investigations, for it affords us no information as to the period of the beginning of Egyptian civilisation, and it does not give us the order of the succession of the kings whose names it records; we cannot even make use of the fragments of it which are inscribed with numbers and contain the lengths of the reigns of certain kings stated in months, years and days, for it is uncertain to which names they apply.[80]

More encouraging was the great Eduard Meyer in his *Ägyptische Chronologie*, 1904.[81] He stated that even in its present condition the Torino Canon was basic to the study of all the other king-lists; yet he lamented that it was disregarded by most Egyptologists. Meyer also went out of his way to compliment Seyffarth, accounting his work as generally brilliant.

Scholars were still relying on the work of Seyffarth, Lepsius and Wilkinson indeed until 1939, when a new edition of the papyrus was published under the editorship of Giulio Farina, Curator of the Torino Museum.[82] This was the result of six years' work, 1928-1934. The papyrological experts and restorers involved were Ermina Caudena and Hugo Ibscher. The latter was world famous as the restorer at the Berlin Museum from 1894 who worked all over Europe. By now the guiding criterion for new arrangement of the fragments was the fibre pattern.

Finally, in 1959, another edition was undertaken by the doyen of English Egyptologists, Alan Gardiner assisted by Rolf Ibscher (Hugo's son).[83] This twentieth century work has finally established the Torino Canon as the most invaluable of the king-lists. It provides, in particular, very important periodic totals: 55 years for the third dynasty (cf. 214 in Manetho), 181 years for dynasties 6-8 (cf. 349 in Manetho), and a grand total for the Old Kingdom of 955 years (cf. c.1400 in Manetho). For the tortured 'Second Intermediate Period' (dynasties 14-17), the Torino list of names, despite its tragic destruction, is the starting-point.[84] May one of the most outrageous of all libels against Drovetti, that he reduced the papyrus to its present state by his own carelessness, be finally laid to rest. It must be admitted, however, that the papyrus was probably intact when it left Egypt.

The Drovetti collection brought many other famous papyri to Torino: the map of the gold-mine (ill. 32),[85] the plan of the tomb of Ramesses IV,[86] the judicial papyrus containing accusations against officials of Ramesses III,[87] the journal of the Theban necropolis in the late XXth. dynasty, relating to the famous tomb robberies,[88] the famous satirical papyrus,[89] a collection of love poetry,[90] and a 'magical' papyrus.[91] What is most extraordinary to anyone who consults the various editions of these documents is that Drovetti's name is almost universally unmentioned and that there is no interest in the vital matter of provenance.

Where, then, were the great treasures of the collection found? Most of the statuary came from Thebes. Many of the largest and most valuable pieces are still inscribed with the name of Rifaud and the year 1818 and the fact that he was working at Thebes for Drovetti (ill. 33). Apart from that, the statues of the goddess Sekhmet came from the temple of Mut at Karnak, the colossus of Seti II from his chapel in the courtyard of Amun there, and the head of Tuthmosis I from his funerary temple.[92] Many items came from Deir el Medineh, but it has been suggested that they were not the result of direct excavation, but rather were acquired from native collectors.[93] One of the most striking examples is the famous ostrakon of the acrobat or dancing girl (ill. 34). Drovetti was working there with Rifaud from 1818, however, and paying squads of Arabs. This was mainly in the northern and north-western sectors. No cemetery has enriched the Torino Museum more than this.[94] From Abydos, on the other hand, came the stele of Meru of the 11th dynasty,[95] and from near Tell el Amarna the mummy case of Djedthoth.[96] From Memphis came both the wooden cubit of Amenemapet[97] and the bilingual cippus.[98]

The identity of the collector of this great assemblage of antiquities is appropriately kept alive by the bust of Drovetti at the entrance to the Torino Museum. The identity of the sculptor has been controversial, but a recent discussion suggests that it cannot be by Albertoni, the sculptor of the bust on Drovetti's tomb, but that it is rather Carlo Marocchetti, who also produced a medallion of the Consul. He was well known to Drovetti.[99] Yet Drovetti is hardly mentioned in the museum apart from this. His name is found on only a handful of cards attached to the exhibits.[100]

The second collection

On 16 October, 1822, Frédéric Cailliaud returned from Ishmael's expedition to the Sudan, and was instantly asked by Drovetti to stay at his house. He gives us valuable evidence on the continuing interest in antiquities by the Consul-General. One of the many things Cailliaud saw on the quay at Alexandria was a beautiful sarcophagus, found at Memphis. This site was not the chief object of Drovetti's explorations, or at least Arab activity on his behalf, and Cailliaud gave a long list of small objects being added to the collection: part of a mummy case encrusted in mosaic, gold bracelets, necklaces, sandals, a gold cup, rings, scarabs and amulets. Drovetti allowed his friend to make drawings and take wax impressions of those with hieroglyphs, and he was able, thanks to what he knew of Champollion's work, to make out the names of Amenophis I and Tuthmosis II; he therefore thought that Memphis must have been the site of these kings' tombs.[101]

The first mention of the second collection as such comes in May 1824, in a letter significantly from François Artaud, Director of the museum at Lyon. Knowing Drovetti's activity, he was sure that he was busy assembling a second collection 'for the sake of science'.[102] In August of the same year, Jomard informed Drovetti that the Minister for the Navy had given orders for the monolithic shrine which Drovetti had presented to the King to be carried to Paris. Jomard advised him to write about it formally to the Minister of the Maison Royale. This letter would help Jomard in negotiations about the sarcophagus. As for the measure, he suggested that it be sent separately.[103]

Further news was sent from Jomard to Drovetti via General Boyer in November 1825. He announced the King's decision, on the advice of the

Minister of Fine Arts, that there would not be a special Egyptian gallery in the Louvre. Jomard rightly called this decision 'strange', and said that he was glad at least to have acquired the sarcophagus, although Drovetti had been poorly paid and his loyalty abused: if he had spent 22,000 francs on it, he had made only 8,000 (the price therefore was 30,000 francs). There was therefore some talk of an increase in Drovetti's salary as Consul-General.[104]

The first public notice of the collection came in the same year, 1825, in the form of a letter by Jomard in the *Bulletin universelle*.[105] By this time, the collection was on offer, and sixty stone monuments had already arrived in 'our harbours' (meaning Europe), not to mention several thousand other objects. A granite sarcophagus, 8´8´´ long and weighing 25,000 kgs, had been brought to Paris on two carriages. It had been found in a tomb at Memphis and required three months' work to extract it. The cover was extraordinary, in that it was cone-shaped with a cylindrical head. It dated to the seventh century BC. Champollion-Figeac identified the owner as Ousirphthaor, priest of Amon and Anubis, in charge of the cult of Psammetichos, and so it dated to c.650 BC. It belonged, in fact, to the high-priest Djedhor (N344).

Drovetti had given King Charles X a monolithic shrine, Jomard announced. It also was of granite and weighed 25,000 kgs. The King had ordered a special room to be assigned to it in the Louvre. Jomard hoped that this would be the beginning of a collection which, if it could not rival those of London or Torino, would allow France to show herself worthy of her cultural position. Jomard's letter was thus a ringing call for the acquisition of the second Drovetti collection. Other articles were also devoted to the sanctuary.[106] It was of pink granite and had been discovered at Sais. It was 8´ high, 5´ wide and 4´ deep. The four sides were decorated with religious scenes. Champollion-Figeac declared that it was dedicated to Neith by Amasis of the 26th. dynasty. This is correct; it is now N381.

The two major objects which were the subject of the above publicity show very clearly Drovetti's methods in making his second collection indispensable to the French. Treasures were sent to Paris to demonstrate the quality of the antiquities and the King was won over by gifts. Influential individuals were the key. Jomard was obviously determined that France would not let slip a second chance, as had happened only a few years before. Apart from him, the main people who had to be won over were the duc de Doudeauville, Minister of the Maison Royale, and the vicomte de la Rochefoucauld, Minister of Fine Arts. The moving forces behind the scenes were the duc de Blacas, Premier Gentilhomme de la Chambre du Roi (chief chamberlain) and recipient of Champollion's letters from Italy, who examined the collection at Livorno, and none other than Champollion himself, who stressed its great historical and artistic importance.[107]

It was also Champollion who provided the most detailed catalogue of the collection at Livorno in April 1826.[108] He divided the list into the obvious categories:

1. 98 papyri, the longest 20´, both hieroglyphic and hieratic, and mostly funerary. There were also demotic texts (Ptolemaic) and fourteen Greek papyri.
2. more than 400 objects in bronze, including 200 of divinities or sacred animals of which he details about a dozen.
3. wooden objects, more than 200, including sixty of gods, kings or other human figures, toilet articles, furniture, painting and writing palettes.
4. 15 objects in ivory.
5. 36 objects made of palm-leaves.
6. 21 objects of leather.
7. 34 terracotta vases, 21 of porcelain, 26 in stone, 50 in alabaster.
8. 1,400 pieces of adornment, including figurines, rings, and necklaces of all kinds, and described in detail.
9. 900 amulettes and figurines.
10. glass and enamel ware, more than 200 pieces.
11. Greek or Roman engraved stones (11).
12. funerary monuments: 10 mummies, various masks, vases, 17 funerary caskets, mummified animals, 32 funerary statuettes, 260 funerary images (including a set of figurines of kings) of all materials, and 60 large funerary scarabs.
13. 40 terracotta figures.
14. 10 'adoration tables'.
15. 50 stelai (17 described in detail).
16. stone statues and statuettes of divinities, kings and others, of which he details about twenty.
17. large sculpture: Ramesses the Great adoring Amon (cippus); lower part of a colossus of Amenhotep III (pink granite); monolithic chapel of Ptolemy II from Philae; cippus in pink granite of Tuthmosis I; 17 blocks of the 'numerical wall' of Seti from Karnak; the sarcophagus of Ramesses III from his tomb in Thebes; a royal sphinx in pink granite.

The most important pieces in this collection came from the excavations of Rifaud at Thebes, then in the Fayum, and finally at Tanis.

The contract of sale was signed, in fact, on 11 October, 1827.[109] The price of 150,000 francs was to be paid in five instalments, the first of 50,000 immediately, the other four of 25,000 each by October 1830. The final clause stipulated that on the arrival of the whole collection in Paris, experts were to evaluate it afresh, and that the price might thus be diminished, but not increased![110] The collection thus acquired in 1827 had all reached the

Louvre by the next year. In the 1830 Revolution, however, when the mob invaded the Louvre, all valuable objects, notably gold, were stolen.[111]

Another item acquired for the Louvre by Drovetti deserves a special note; for the story is remarkable. In September 1828, Champollion wrote to Mechain, Consul at Larnaca, asking that his news be passed on to Drovetti.[112] Amongst other things, he had been taken by none other than the leading English collector Lord Prudhoe to see a trilingual inscription, of which part was visible, serving as a doorstep of a little mosque in Cairo. This was the first known copy of the Canopic decree of Ptolemy III (237 BC). Champollion urged Drovetti to obtain it; for it had been refused to Salt. He regarded it as possibly a consolation for the loss of the Rosetta Stone. Drovetti followed this up in May of the next year, writing to the Foreign Minister.[113] In an interview with Mehemet Ali, he had requested that it be added to the antiquities given to Charles X in 1827. The British Consul and English travellers were furious with him and Champollion, he reported. This was understandable, since back in the previous November, approval was given to Salt by his government to try to obtain the stone, following a letter of the traveller James Burton, an associate of Robert Hay, John Gardner Wilkinson, Edward William Lane and Joseph Bonomi, addressed to the Marquis of Lansdowne. Perhaps the reason for the English failure is that Salt was authorised to employ 'reasonable and moderate expense'.[114] This would have availed little against the zeal of Drovetti and Champollion, especially where the Rosetta Stone was mentioned. It was not, however, obtained without a struggle. The English in April 1829 recovered the stone and took it to their consulate. None other than the Viceroy then intervened, and it was taken off to a store in Boulaq. Attempts to have it sent on from there to Alexandria required a second intervention by Mehemet Ali, and Boghos also played a role, sending it on to Drovetti.[115] The greatest trouble had been taken for so little, and Champollion's talk of a second Rosetta Stone was mistaken: almost the whole of the three versions of the decree was effaced and there was not a single intact line.

The third and smallest collection made by Drovetti went to Berlin in 1830 for 30,000 francs, although he had sought twice that amount. The purchase was made on the advice of Richard Lepsius.[116]

There is a curious footnote which associates Drovetti's name with the other of the greatest European museums, albeit falsely. In the ninth edition of the *Encyclopaedia Britannica* (1875-1889), in the article on glass, it is noted that the earliest glass known was made by the Egyptians.

> A small lion's head of opaque blue glass of very fine colour, but changed externally to an olive green, was found at Thebes by signor Drovetti, and is now in the British Museum; on the underside are

hieroglyphs containing the name of Nuantef IV, whose date according to Lepsius's chronology was 2423-2380 BC.[117]

This piece is BM 59619. It was acquired in 1873, presented by the executor of Felix Slade. It bears the name Nubkheperre and is dated probably later than the eighteenth dynasty.[118] The note in the encyclopaedia is, therefore, a mistake, and we cannot, unfortunately, connect Drovetti with the British Museum.

Drovetti's finds went to many other European museums, thanks to his generosity: Lyon, Marseille, Geneva, Dresden, Munich, Vienna, and the Vatican.[119]

Drovetti and the pyramids

A most extraordinary story is recorded by Edouard Montulé, a French traveller in Egypt 1818-1819, who had much to do with Drovetti at Thebes. It was to him that the ex-consul, now devoting himself to travel and excavation, confided the following story.

During the first years of my residence in Egypt,' said he, 'I never thought or dreamed of anything but antiquities; one night in particular; I imagined that I had penetrated into a pyramid which had not yet been explored. I proceeded for some time along a corridor, dark and silent, when, on a sudden, I conceived myself to be in a vast chamber, from which a narrow passage led to a second, at the top of which, at about twenty feet from the soil, I saw an opening. As time and space count for nothing in a dream, I sent for ladders, and perceived, in the middle of another apartment, a carcase extended upon a bed, near which there burned a sepulchral lamp. This vision struck me so forcibly, that I resolved to visit the pyramids of Dassour, the interior of which was not yet known. I caused the rubbish from the first passage to be cleared away, and on viewing the first chamber my astonishment was excited, being precisely similar to that figured to me in my dream; out of this a passage presented itself, into which I crawled with pain, and found a second, when raising my regard, how was I stupefied on beholding at the summit, a square aperture, precisely similar to that my dream had depicted. I sent for a ladder, and got into the corridor, which conducted me to a third apartment, but as to the bed, the lamp, and the body, not a vestige of either (sic) appeared.'

On reciting this adventure, M. Drovetti still seemed astonished, and almost displayed symptoms of terror at the similarity of his dream with the actual contemplation of facts. The pyramid in question is precisely what he described it to be; the chambers are from thirty to thirty-five feet high, fifteen wide, and terminate at a point, by the successive projection of eleven layers of stone laying about six inches over each other, which would completely display a vaulting if the angles were taken away; the joints would, however, be horizontal, while they are in the direction of the radii of the vaults. At the higher extremity of the second chamber, about forty feet in length, is found the square opening above alluded to, but having no ladder I could not mount to explore it. This pyramid slopes more than all the others, and, in some places, still preserves its rampart, which simply consists of the stones of its surface chiselled slantingly, and well joined.[120]

This is, of course, the Bent Pyramid at Dahshur. The features referred to by both Drovetti and Montulé may best be appreciated from the plans in the classic study by I.E.S. Edwards, *The pyramids of Egypt*.[121] The pyramid is remarkable for having two entrance passages, on both the northern and western sides. The 'first passage' is, in fact, 241' long. There are three internal chambers, but the first is rather a vestibule. The difference between the floor levels of the vestibule and the first chamber is 20'. Access from the latter to the second chamber is gained via a rough passage from the roof of the first chamber. No trace of a sarcophagus has been found in either.

Montulé's technical information is very approximate. The vestibule measures 16' in length, 14´6´´ in height; the first chamber 20´6´´ by 16´6´´ and 57´ in height. The corbelled roof to which he refers is made, in fact, by stepping in the chamber's fifteen uppermost courses. The pyramid does slope more than others, but surely its most outstanding feature is the change in its angle. It is true that this pyramid still preserves more of its casing than any other major example.

Much more relevant to the story of the dream, however, is the fact that in Drovetti's time the Bent Pyramid was perfectly well known to travellers:

we know from the accounts of early European travellers that the interior of the Bent Pyramid was accessible to visitors as early as the Seventeenth century and that in the year 1660 it was entered by the English traveller Mr Melton, and that twenty years later, M. le Brun discovered in it one of the chambers. After 1660 and during the Eighteenth century, the cemetery of Dahshur was visited by many travellers, but their accounts are not of much value to us because the passages inside the pyramids were almost blocked by debris and large stones. It was only in 1839 that the site of Dahshur was visited by Perring, who was no doubt the first real investigator of those pyramids...[122]

The upper chamber had certainly been found before Perring, but of the two entrances, that on the west was discovered by him in 1839, although accessible in ancient times. When we turn to Vyse and Perring, however, we find mention of Melton and le Brun as entering the pyramid, but Nathaniel Davison in 1763 is said to have found the northern passageway blocked, and when Perring arrived it was accessible only to some 140´ and had to be cleared (September-October, 1839).[123] Drovetti's dream would seem to have to be taken with the customary grain of salt but the story published by Montulé as early as 1821 seems to constitute a hitherto unnoticed chapter in the exploration of the Bent Pyramid.

Twenty years later, Drovetti wrote to his friend Giuseppe Baruffi a letter which is for the most part devoted to a discussion of the purpose of the pyramids.[124] The main stimulus seems to have been the publication of Peter Wilhelm Forchhammer's *de pyramidibus* (Kiel, 1837), suggesting that they were really underground cisterns. This was far from a new idea, as Drovetti knew. The letter is a most lively, slightly disjointed refutation of such a 'bizarre' view. Drovetti asked where, in that case, were the tombs of the Memphite kings? Why did one find within the pyramids of Gizeh and Dahshur the usual equipment of tombs, admittedly violated and therefore much destroyed? The underground sections are full of mummies; the areas are quite unsuited to cisterns. The proximity of the bodies to water would, moreover, be quite unthinkable, given the usual Egyptian care to bury them in the driest places. If such underground cisterns existed, why had the canals from the Nile necessary to fill them not been found? The Egyptians always preferred fresh water from the river to that kept in reservoirs. If the pyramids were cisterns why are they not found near all major cities? Many, to the contrary, have artificial lakes. That the pyramid was the classical form of tomb is proved by many other examples, from Halikarnassos to America to Rome (the tomb of Cestius). The underground of the Great Pyramid, finally, had been thoroughly investigated, notably by Caviglia, and no trace of cisterns had been found. In conclusion, Drovetti expressed his aversion to such criticism of new ideas and conjectures, but was 'impelled by a strong desire' to share his views with Baruffi, despite their crowded and even 'tortured' form.

One could hardly ask for a more exhaustive or more cogent series of arguments against the 'cistern theory'. The letter is interesting on various counts. It reminds us of the arguments still flourishing at the time concerning the understanding of these great monuments. For the biographer of Drovetti, it is significant to observe how passionate Drovetti was about such matters, needing to pour forth his response to Baruffi. The letter suggests, in addition, that he had a serious interest in Egyptian antiquities beyond that of a mere collector. The letter, it must be remembered, was written a decade after his retirement from Egypt.

Drovetti as excavator

One of the earliest commentators on the value of Drovetti's work was his collaborator and admirer, Edme Jomard. In 1822 he wrote:

> in the course of his labours, which have been continued for more than ten years with the same perseverance and the same success, he unceasingly discovers new works of the ancient inhabitants of the Thebaid, useful in revealing the most interesting details of the arts, customs, sciences and practices of this industrious people.[125]

It is significant that the doyen of the members of the Napoleonic expedition stressed Drovetti's contribution to the knowledge of 'everyday life' of the ancient Egyptians, notably in the Thebaid where his collecting was concentrated. That his judgement was flattering is no surprise given their close relationship. With this we may compare the views of one of the earliest scientific excavators in the country, Henry Rhind:

> Of nearly all those researches there remain only the most imperfect records: of the great majority there are absolutely none. Prosecuted with ardour more than forty years ago, the mode of procedure was by no means of a satisfying nature. Mr Salt and Signor Drovetti entered at the same time actively on the pursuit, and their official influence, as Consuls-General for England and France, obtained for them the necessary permission and facilities from the native government. Various of ancient sites were fixed upon, and in particular the Necropolis of Thebes was, so to say, mapped out between the working parties employed by those two gentlemen. But nearly all their explorations were conducted under the supervision of agents whose instructions, while it is only just to believe that they had in some respects broad scientific ends in view, would seem, by some oversight, to have been to attend to the accumulation of relics, rather than to the circumstances under which they were found. At least we look in vain for sufficient accounts of the latter. As regards Drovetti's collection, now at Turin, there are, I believe, no means of ascertaining the individual history of its constituents; or rather, there are no

particulars preserved as to the previously undisturbed tombs, if any, which fell to the lot of those who formed it.[126]

Rhind's account is remarkably restrained, considering how much effort he was to devote to finding a few plundered and late tombs, when obviously just a few years before others had looted so much which was as yet untouched. Both Drovetti and Salt each made no fewer than three collections, and they were not the only assiduous collectors operating at the time. The removal of antiquities from their provenance without any record must have been on a gigantic scale. Rhind rightly reminds us also of the contemporary – but isolated – vandalism of even Champollion's expedition in the tomb of Seti and of Lepsius in the 1840s. Even 'scientific expeditions' often adopted 'the economics of a mining speculation rather than the scope of a scientific survey'.[127] Rhind himself was remarkable for his time.

The father of the Egyptian Antiquities Service, Auguste Mariette, recalled Drovetti in a memorable metaphor:

> after the great shipwreck of the Egyptian monuments, the explorers whom I have mentioned (Drovetti, Anastasy, Mimaut) were the first to collect the floating wrecks, leaving to their successors only the booty of the debris, which we must now search for at the bottom of the waves which have engulfed them.[128]

Drovetti and his contemporaries, therefore, were able to collect the 'flotsam' while Mariette and his generation had to scour the sea-floor for the remaining debris. It must be remembered, however, that Mariette was not a model excavator or publisher. He regretted – to change the metaphor – that he certainly found that the cream of the visible and more portable remains of ancient Egypt had been more than skimmed off in the preceding generation. He at least was to struggle to keep new finds in Egypt.

National prejudices are rarely far below the surface when attempts are made to assess such collecting. A rather prim verdict was delivered early this century by a Scottish divine who was a voluminous writer on ancient Egypt, even though he never visited the country: James Baikie.

> ... the early story of Egyptian exploration is not the story of pure research, conducted for the love of truth and of antiquity, but very often merely the story of how the representative of France strove with the representative of Britain or Italy (sic) for the possession of some ancient monument whose capture might bring glory to his nation or profit to his own purse ...

It must be almost a nightmare to the modern excavator, with his ingrained appreciation of the importance of even the smallest object which may add to the knowledge of ancient lands and peoples, to think of the priceless material which was destroyed by the undiscriminating zeal of men like Belzoni, Drovetti and their fellows, or if not destroyed, at least deprived of half its value by being torn from its historical place and connection.[129]

We may detect the influence of the work of men such as Petrie in the principles underlying these sentiments, and Baikie indeed knew him well. By this time the ways of archaeology had changed beyond recognition. The discerning reader will also note that although there is reference to diplomats of various nations, when the villains of the piece come to be named, they are Italians such as Belzoni and Drovetti. A famous English Consul of the same period is, however, missing.

At almost the same time, in the 1920s, the outstanding Italian archaeologist Evaristo Breccia issued an even severer judgement:

the modern scientist, who excavates while studying the stratification of the objects, collecting the smallest fragments, experiences horror thinking of the wealth of documents which must have been irremediably lost, not only by the actions of collectors and dealers (a tribe which has not disappeared but still fairly flourishes), but also through the work of laudable discoverers, most worthy of respect and gratitude.

For more than thirty years, in the first half of the nineteenth century, private individuals and consuls devoted themselves to a veritable ransacking. If the passion for the antique and the more or less indirect contribution which the collectors made to the progress of Egyptology, enriching museums and awakening an increasing interest in the new discipline, have led to a favourable evaluation of the activity of many of them, we must not allow ourselves to be drawn away by any apologetic temptation or by complaints in poor taste over claimed forgetfulness or ingratitude towards people whose merits are rather debatable.[130]

Here again is the theme of mere fragments left to the modern excavator in comparison with the treasures so recently to hand and so carelessly lost. Breccia's language is, however, stronger than that of most: the early nineteenth century excavations were a 'veritable ransacking', the benefits of which can easily be overestimated: they did add objects to museums and they did increase interest in Egyptology, but one must be on guard against mistaken claims to gratitude. The supposed benefits were declared roundly to be 'rather debatable'. He then went on to compliment Drovetti for his great 'taste and flair'![131]

The indefatigable Giovanni Marro devoted one of his innumerable articles on Drovetti to a study of him as an archaeologist. He summed up his contribution as follows:

> He was truly the first to collect on a vast scale every kind of object from Pharaonic civilisation, relying on a special organisation of men and means, and always generously favoured by Mehemet Ali the Viceroy, never being impeded, like the other Europeans, by the native population, by whom he was regarded as a great benefactor.[132]

Marro here returned to Jomard's notice of the scale of Drovetti's collection, comprising every kind of antiquity from monumental sculpture to the most common objects. He rightly stressed his unique relationship with the Viceroy, without which such collecting would not have been possible. His judgement on Drovetti's relations with the natives also seems correct. The only important rebuff he ever suffered was in his failure to induce them to assist him in clearing Abu Simbel.

Marro went on to give Drovetti credit for stimulating others to follow in his footsteps: some in geographical exploration, such as Gau, Cailliaud and Belzoni, others in the search for antiquities. Not to be forgotten, as Marro also recalled, was the tribute paid to Drovetti by Jomard and others in inviting him to contribute to the *Description de l'Egypte*.

Just one century after Drovetti's death, Evaristo Breccia again attempted an assessment of his contribution. It was to be very different from his remarks of a quarter of a century before.[133] He, like Marro, stressed his influence with the Viceroy and suggested that his use of it must have been 'very indiscreet'. He could capitalise on Mehemet Ali's indifference towards the relics of the past and his anxiety to gain political and commercial concessions by his generosity. The Viceroy may not have known the scientific value of the antiquities, but it surely would not have taken him long to understand their commercial value! It is the judgement of Drovetti which is, however, most interesting and so different from Breccia's summary in the 1920s. When Belzoni was using methods which now make an archaeologist horrified, how could one expect Drovetti to be prudent in excavation, and careful and precise in recording what he found? How could he be expected to see the monuments only as material for scientific study, keeping as much as possible of its original place? How could he not see them as sources of prestige and profit? For all this, he was not to be blamed, given the times: they were 'venial sins, redeemed by undeniable merits'! Breccia was now in his seventies, his long career as a museum curator over, but his very different attitude to Drovetti is probably to be ascribed simply to the occasion. Celebrations of centenaries often produce striking distortions and tendencies to eulogise.

Various commentators, notably Breccia, have referred to Drovetti's relations with Mehemet Ali. Apart from the apparent ease with which he granted firmans to his favourites and the terrible stories of destruction of classical monuments for the construction of sugar refineries and the like, the most illuminating story is told by Cailliaud.[134] The Viceroy came to visit Gurneh, and was appalled by the parts of mummies scattered everywhere by the pillaging Arabs; arms, heads, and half-broken bodies were the prey of scavenging animals. Mehemet Ali reproached the consuls and other Europeans taking part in the excavations. Were these corpses not previously men like them and him? He rebuked them for thinking only of brilliant collections and forgetting to treat flesh and bones with respect. Cailliaud noted the superior sensibility of the Albanian, who was commonly regarded by Europeans as a barbarian. The Arabs were ordered by him to bury the remains.

VIII   The measure of the man

The first quarter of Drovetti's life laid the foundation of all that followed.[1] He began life with the advantage of being born into a family of lawyers with high political connections and the local standing that naturally was accorded professionals and notables, but soon showed his own qualities. He followed the family tradition and graduated in law. That was momentarily put aside to take up a very different calling, arms, and in the service of France, where he soon distinguished himself, attaining the rank of cavalry major by the age of twenty-four, and attracting the favour of very high officers. His legal and military brilliance then combined to stand him in the best of stead when he entered politics as a member of the Provisional Government, 1798-1799, in its last hectic days, where his bravery and determination were well tested. On the restoration of French power in northern Italy, he returned to his original métier as judge in one of the most important courts.

Highly placed friends clearly seconded his interests, but his own merits in these very varied capacities ensured his further career in one of the most responsible posts in the French Empire. It is, then, as a diplomat for the next quarter of a century that Drovetti played a not inconsiderable part in the politics of the Levant with all their repercussions on the wider Mediterranean and European stages.

The young officer and lawyer who came to Egypt at the age of twenty-seven and was so soon to find himself the chief French representative immediately showed skills in diplomacy of the highest order. No sooner had he arrived than the crisis arose over the European consuls' safety; Drovetti played a leading role in organising the remarkable resistance and the successful outcome. His powers of prescience and prediction were remarkable. He very early decided against supporting the Mamelukes and trying to wean them away from the English. In this he marked a complete break with the views of his short-lived superior, Matthieu de Lesseps – which was fortunate for the French prestige during the long reign of Mehemet Ali. He saw clearly from 1804 that the Mamelukes were incurably divided. From as early as 1805 he correctly analysed Mehemet Ali's ambitions, even during the governorship of Kurchid, when he was only an Albanian commander, and sought instructions how to proceed. As early as 1806 Drovetti supported Mehemet Ali's requests for French military backing, and his position was considerably weakened when, as so often, the government disregarded his advice, and the English were ready to provide what was asked.

The high-point of his first tour of duty was the *annus mirabilis*, 1807. Drovetti was instrumental in Mehemet Ali's surviving the English invasion and then in negotiating for an English withdrawal rather than attempting a costly expulsion. Following these crucial events, Drovetti's influence paradoxically suffered a decline. Missett was succeeded by a much more astute agent, Petrucci, who seems to have been able to act without hindrance, and the English were supplying Mehemet Ali with arms and gaining control of the Egyptian economy. Drovetti's position in these years was especially difficult, well-nigh impossible; for the French government refused to give him instructions even in the event of a much feared second English invasion.

To be a leading diplomat in an Oriental despotism meant that one was constantly vulnerable to destruction by intrigue. This was a vital test of skill. Such a test occurred in 1810, when Drovetti was accused of dealing with the Mamelukes. When he rushed to the Citadel to explain himself, Mehemet Ali was just entering his harem. The young Consul explained and survived. This year saw his recovery of his old position, but he still had no support from his government, and he could not help Mehemet Ali's ambitions to become a naval power. In these years Drovetti fought constantly against English influence which was economically based: buying grain and selling arms.

A most telling testimony to Drovetti's diplomatic skills is revealed in the sequel to his temporary replacement in 1815, during the six years that he remained in Egypt, supposedly as a private citizen. His standing with the Viceroy could not have been higher, and his indispensability to Europeans was even greater. Even the French government instructed Roussel to cultivate Drovetti as France's most experienced representative in this vital country. The attention paid to him by the comte de Forbin, Director-General of Museums, on his visit 1817-1818 is another unmistakable indication of his standing in official eyes. At the same time began his friendship with Edme Jomard and the other members of the 1798 expedition, who were preparing the *Description de l'Egypte*. His status was so little obscured that other powers vied for his services: Piedmont offered him the position of Consul-General. The French for their part were to find what they had lost when Pillavoine arrived in 1819. The Viceroy's continued reliance on Drovetti is demonstrated by his participation in, and considerable contribution to, the expedition to Siwah, where he employed his diplomacy on behalf of the defeated Siwans.

It was precisely his political skills which gained and maintained the support of many highly placed people, and which resulted in his reappointment in 1821. Noteworthy among them were Beaujour, Inspector of Consuls in the Levant, and the comte de Marcellus, secretary to the Ambassador in Constantinople. Apart from his official diplomacy as French Consul, Drovetti was involved in many other delicate situations. One of the most insistent was the resort to him by the hierarchy of the Order of the Terra Santa. These Catholic priests were continually at war with the Greek Orthodox, mostly over control of the sanctuaries in the Holy Land. There was also wrangling within the Order between the various nationalities, notably the French and Italian. Intervention required the greatest skills, and Drovetti must have had them, given the frequency with which he was called upon, and the fact that he was awarded the Order of the Holy Sepulchre in 1824. A similar religious crisis was the appointment of a 'bishop' of Memphis in 1824; the man seems to have owed his life to Drovetti.

The Greek war began a period of great difficulty for Drovetti as French Consul. By 1825 he made clear that he found Greek atrocities intolerable, and this was at a time when the French government, like most of the rest of Europe, was making no secret of its support for the Greek cause. Drovetti was also outraged by the way the European officers who had tried to help them had been insulted by the Greeks. Apart from his own feelings, which he did not attempt to conceal, his political position was very uncomfortable, considering that he was accredited to precisely the country which was bearing the brunt of the fighting for the Ottoman Empire against the insurgents. Even the European programme for the education of Egyptians was imperilled. In all of this, it must be remembered that similar views were held by many leading French figures in the Levant, such as David at Smyrna and Admiral de Rigny.

The Europeanisation of Egypt was a process fraught with problems, despite Drovetti's wholehearted support. No crisis excited by imported Europeans equalled that of the army instructors in 1826. There had been constant antagonisms and jealousies at the highest level, and even assassination attempts. General Boyer departed, taking other officers with him, after he had fallen out with his erstwhile confidant, Gaudin. Drovetti's diplomatic skills had been constantly employed, both to obtain for them the best conditions of service, and to reconcile them one with another. Now he had to prevent the English taking over the whole training scheme for the army.

No test of the Consul's conciliatory skills equalled the situation for a European consul in October 1827. Drovetti was, of course, on leave in Europe. Striking testimony to his reputation was the government's immediate return of him to Egypt to represent the nation's interests and conciliate Mehemet Ali. It must be admitted that the task was not as difficult as at first it must have seemed: Mehemet Ali perceived his own untenable position, caught between the Sultan and the European powers. He was to be extricated from Greece, but at what cost! The Viceroy's total calm must in part, however, have been due to his having at his side his oldest confidant.

Drovetti's greatest achievement as a diplomat was the Convention of Alexandria. This was negotiated between him for Mehemet Ali and the English admiral Codrington. He was expressly commissioned by the Viceroy to arrange for the evacuation of Greece in the way least humiliating for Egypt. The prelude to the appearance of a new independent nation in Europe was thus negotiated by a man who was no friend of that people.

By this time, to judge from a very pointed remark which Drovetti made to Pierre Hamont, who came to take service as a veterinarian, he was somewhat exasperated with Europeans in Egypt; for he advised Hamont to avoid them, and to make friends with the Turks. His reputation was such, however, that with the Russo-Turkish war and the departure of the Russian Consul-General, Drovetti as before acted as a mediator between Mehemet Ali and the Russian admiral.

The Convention of Alexandria might have been eclipsed as Drovetti's claim to international diplomatic fame had his plan for Mehemet Ali and the Egyptians to subdue the Bey of Algier been acceptable to the French. It was a very bold plan – too bold, indeed, to be accepted – but it would have suited the Viceroy and saved the French much anguish. Not for the first time, Drovetti was outwitted by the English, as in his early years, but the extraordinary clumsiness of the French government was largely to blame.

One question of vital importance for a diplomat in the polyglot Levant was language. Drovetti was, as anyone who reads his correspondence can see, equally fluent in Italian and French. This was not, after all, so extraordinary for a Piedmontese, and inescapable for someone who had served in the French army and then as a French diplomatic representative for some thirty years. That Drovetti's post was in Egypt naturally raises the question whether he could speak any eastern languages. This also would seem almost inevitable, but there are few pieces of evidence in all the voluminous sources about Drovetti. One comes from the highest source, although the text is coloured: Mehemet Ali's attempt to defuse the Sultan's suspicions of his having engaged in a plot with the French over the Algerian affair. Drovetti was present at an interview between the Viceroy and some Arab envoys, and understood perfectly what they said.[2] The other reference is in a very antagonistic source. La Contemporaine abused him for not doing more for the poor Egyptian peasants, although he spoke Arabic and Turkish fluently. The author would hardly have invented this information, which in a way flattered him. In addition, the ease with which Drovetti moved around in Egypt, and more to the point, his dealings with the natives in his archaeological work made his competence in Arabic almost indispensable.

To this we may add a most tantalising possibility, that he also understood English. There are again two pieces of evidence. The letter he received from the American confidence-man George English was written in that language, with the assumption that he could read it. More decisive is the subscription taken out by Drovetti's agent Morpurgo for an English paper, so that he could keep abreast of European affairs.

It is in Egypt that Drovetti made his most lasting impression, as the chief adviser to Mehemet Ali in his programme of modernisation, which embraced so many different fields. Among the most successful were education and health. A very adventurous education programme was conceived as early as 1811, even if it did not come into operation until more than a decade later. It required the sending of dozens of young Egyptians to Europe to be given a western education. The concept of the plan must, it seems, be credited to Edme Jomard, but it would have come to nothing had Drovetti not adopted it and convinced Mehemet Ali to approve of it. Drovetti was then also crucial in the choice of France over Italy as the best place to send the students, and the appointment of Jomard as director. The programme was a most bold one for an illiterate and autocratic ruler; he may not, indeed, have made the best use of the new teachers and experts when they returned, but their influence was to be dominant in the new Egypt.

An even more far-reaching revolution was accomplished at a very different level by the health programme. This helped banish the diseases which were the scourge of the poor fellahin. The vaccination programme overcame enormous prejudice. The *Epistolario* contains letters from all the Italian and French doctors participating in the campaign, not only informing Drovetti of its progress, but also seeking his help in the many difficulties encountered. The doctors may well have been recruited in Europe on Drovetti's initiative. This seems not to have been true of the founder of the medical school, Antoine Clot, but he also turned frequently to Drovetti and made a point of sending him regular reports on the progress of the school. Drovetti was also responsible for the establishment of quarantine regulations in Egypt.

Other programmes in which Drovetti was intimately involved were successful or failed, according to different perspectives. The formation of a modern army and navy on European lines owed most to him. General Boyer, the chief instructor, described the Consul as 'the main instigator and adviser of the regular army'. The instructors were mostly Italian or French, and Drovetti's hand in their recruitment may be surmised: they corresponded constantly with him and resorted to him to solve any problems. It was precisely to Drovetti that Boyer looked in the midst of total disorder for 'coherence and method'. Despite the debacle of 1826, the European officers created a large and very efficient army which made Egypt the leading military power in the Levant, almost able to overthrow the Ottoman Empire. It must be admitted, however, that the burden on the economy was enormous, and horrible on the poor conscripted fellahin.

It is a similar story with the navy. A considerable fleet was built in Europe, thanks to the Italian and French connections of Drovetti. The Egyptians proved brilliant sailors. Again, however, the cost was utterly crippling to the economy, and the pride of the navy with its crews was sent to the bottom at Navarino.

The history of the Egyptian economy is a very different matter. The Viceroy's policies were an unmitigated disaster, and Drovetti was commonly blamed by contemporaries; his position at 'court' made him the first suspect as conceiver or instigator of the policies. For the monopolies imposed on agriculture and commerce and the attempt to establish European-style industries, Drovetti was not only not responsible, but also constantly argued against them. One of the most revealing accounts he gave, in 1816, confesses, however, that even he had to exercise circumspection in dealing with a man like Mehemet Ali when he had set his heart on anything. One does not have to know Drovetti very well to realise how dear to his heart was the proper management of agriculture. As early as 1812, he had described the policies being pursued in this area as defying the circulation of the blood. Ten years later, he roundly condemned the industrialisation as absurd and impractical, and described the collapse of Egyptian commerce.

Apart from Drovetti's very varied part in these major policies, there survive striking testimonies from various employees of the regime. None other than the all-powerful Boghos, secretary and minister, admitted that he owed his entire position to Drovetti. His successor, Abro, was exiled to Smyrna for some crime, but was then recalled thanks to Drovetti's intervention. Lascaris was employed as tutor to one of the Viceroy's sons on Drovetti's recommendation. The Italian doctors who served with Ibrahim in the Wahabite war, Gentili, Tedeschini and Scotti, and the French officer, Vaissière, all corresponded with Drovetti, indicating his part in their employment and his continuing protection. Giovanni Baffi, the chemist, called Drovetti his 'great patron'. The mineralogist Frédéric

Cailliaud states that it was Drovetti who said to him, 'I will make you the Pasha's mineralogist', and so it happened. He therefore owed to Drovetti, as he happily admitted, all the benefits which he had received in Egypt. As late as 1842, he spoke of his 'happy fate' which he owed to his friend, and much more significantly, he spoke of 'the good which you have done so many times before my eyes to people who have not always shown themselves worthy of it.' General Boyer stated that Drovetti was 'the soul and linch-pin' of his coming to Egypt. His colleague, General Livron, summed up more broadly in 1825: he could not too often praise Drovetti's services in Egypt. 'He enjoys the entire confidence of the Viceroy, and it is to him that France owes the influence which she enjoys in the country.'

There was yet another field in which Drovetti made a name for himself, better known than the above, but so often misrepresented and belittled because of jealousy. It was his release from consular duties in 1815 which allowed him to devote himself to antiquities and exploration. Drovetti was an explorer at a time when so many historically important journeys were being undertaken. He failed to gain a prominent place in the history of such exploration often by only a very small margin. He was not the first European in modern times to reach Abu Simbel. That was Burckhardt in 1813. He also failed to induce the natives to help him clear the entrance to the temple. That was managed by Belzoni with Irby and Mangles in the very next year after Drovetti had been there, and was a most dangerous and taxing feat. He was similarly not the first European to reach Dakhla oasis in 1819, being anticipated by a matter of days by the Scotsman Edmonstone; the oasis did not, however, contain very much of interest. Siwah had also been visited many times by Europeans before 1820, but its historical interest was of the highest order. Here Drovetti participated in the expedition sent by the government which forced the fiercely independent Siwans to grant access to the outside world for the first time. There was much to be observed in architecture, natural history, language and antiquities. Drovetti compiled a small lexicon of the dialect, but failed to identify correctly the site of the famous oracle.

From at least 1811 Drovetti had been fascinated by antiquities and busily collecting them. A list of sites at which he or his agents are known to have worked covers most of Egypt: Thebes, the Second Cataract and Abu Simbel, Shanhour, Abydos, Dendereh, Apollinopolis, Hawarah, Athribis, Sakkarah, Tanis, Girgeh and Manfalut. His agents included Jacques Rifaud, Antonio Lebolo, Youssef, Giuseppe Rosignani, Father Ladislaus, Piccinini and Antonini.

Excavators of more recent times, for example, Petrie and Woolley, have realised how important it is to treat the native workmen generously and fairly. The success of Drovetti's collecting indicates that he understood the same rule, and both the comte de Forbin and Carlo Vidua testify to his reputation with the Egyptians in this regard. There are few witnesses to contradict this, and they are otherwise hostile: Irby and Mangles were gleeful that the natives had refused to help him at Abu Simbel and claimed that Drovetti had a chief beaten for daring to work for the English at Thebes, and Athanasi told of Drovetti's rejection of (admittedly ordinary) funerary figurines.

The first collection was finally sold to Piedmont in 1823, after a long saga of negotiations. There had been offers from many sides, and France narrowly missed out. The reasons were not so much the price as the disrepute into which Egyptian antiquities had been plunged after the scandal and fraud of the Dendereh zodiac, and ecclesiastical opposition to sources which might imperil (as they surely did) trust in Biblical history and chronology. The irony is that the much more Catholic Piedmont dared to buy what the French did not. This was thanks to the large group of intellectuals, especially at court, well known to Drovetti, who saw the value of the collection, and who were shortly afterwards to give Champollion so generous a welcome.

In keeping with other collectors of the time, especially Salt, it may be frankly admitted that economic motives were uppermost in Drovetti's mind. He had served long in Egypt in an arduous and expensive post, he had reason to fear that his health had been seriously affected, and he had many family members who had a claim on his renowned generosity. The final terms were enough to ensure him an income the equivalent of half of his final consular salary, and a lump sum equal to a little more than three years, which was soon deeply eroded by family obligations, such as paying off the debts of his elder brother and reestablishing his spendthrift son Giorgio. The second collection cost France only 150,000 francs, and that sum was paid in full within three years.

There is little evidence that Drovetti was interested in Egypt for the sake of science. Salt, by contrast, gave the impression of being a scholar, and participated in the hieroglyphic debate between Champollion and Young. On the other hand, Salt was as avid a collector as Drovetti. The latter must be given the very great credit of having encouraged those who did come to Egypt for scientific purposes, and of having facilitated their travels; he always seems to have gained their respect as well. That hardly any of the Drovetti pieces in museums have a provenance strikes us now as appalling, but that was usual at the time. Museums wanted imposing pieces, and a general indication such as 'Thebes' was enough to satisfy curiosity or suggest an evocative context. It should also be recalled that antiquarians such as William Gell found Drovetti 'well-informed'. He was, most remarkably, invited by Jomard to contribute anything he would offer on the excavations in Egypt since 1798 with the promise that it would be published in the *Description de l'Egypte*.

In particular connection with the pyramids, however, there are two episodes for which he deserves credit. Some time before 1818 Drovetti had entered the Bent Pyramid at Dahshur and was able to give Edouard Montulé a detailed account of its unusual and complicated interior. Standard accounts imply that during the eighteenth century and during the nineteenth until 1839, the interior was inaccessible. Although the whole story as told to Montulé was couched in the form of a dream, the description cannot be discounted. Drovetti also should be given credit for his 'review' of Forchhammer's *de pyramidibus*, which was published in 1837. He relentlessly and with the soundest arguments demolished the old view, here being reworked, that the pyramids were cisterns.

Judgements on Drovetti's activity as a collector have varied greatly according to time. John Carne went so far as to accuse him of throwing down an obelisk at Karnak, but the charge seems to be a confusion, albeit malicious. James St John, visitor in the early 1830s, denounced the 'ravages' committed in Drovetti's name by Ladislaus as less forgivable than the activities of modern grave-robbers. Commentators in this century have complained bitterly at the lack of provenance and recording of the finds, and described the actions of Drovetti and his contemporaries as a 'sack' of Egypt, constituting an irreparable loss. Others have praised him for the breadth of his collecting and excused him as hardly likely to have been able to resist the fame and fortune to be gained by exploration in Egypt in the age of Belzoni. It is most melancholy to contemplate what has been destroyed by hunting for antiquities in the past, evidence which would have solved innumerable problems which still plague us. It has often been stated, however, and is obvious, but also inescapably true, that we cannot judge the past by the standards of the present. We cannot expect Drovetti to have been a Flinders Petrie or a Woolley ages before his time. What will archaeologists a century from now say of current work?

During the twenty-six years that Drovetti was in Egypt, most of the time as French diplomatic representative, there was a constant influx of travellers of all kinds and all nations. Sometimes they were aristocrats now able to extend the Grand Tour to take in the sights of the East and acquire a few antiquities for ancestral collections, but often they were scientists with more serious purposes.

It is not without interest to know something of travel conditions in Egypt at this time. One of the few travellers to leave some guidance for others was the English officer John Pringle, who made the journey in 1824.[3] First and foremost he advised avoidance of the season of the plague. This came to Alexandria at the end of February, reached Cairo a few weeks later, and lasted until mid June. At Alexandria a hotel kept by a Maltese was recommended for three or for days, while ten were required at Cairo, where a French hotel cost a dollar a day. Here one was advised to buy some wine, and to make sure that it could be carried by camel. Good powder was recommended for presents. The journey up river visiting the antiquities was estimated to take one month to Thebes, with another fortnight to visit Aswan. The usual mode of travel was by *kanja*, a boat about seventy feet in length with two large sails, and a crew of seven or eight. A cabin at the poop served two passengers, and the hire was twenty or thirty Spanish dollars per month.

Of general observations, Pringle counselled against wearing Turkish dress; European was much more respected. There was now no need to take a janissary, but pistols and hunting guns were necessary, and insurrections were a danger against which the traveller had to be prepared. This was presumably in the light of the revolt that very year (1824), when Europeans were reportedly massacred. All in all, travel in this part of the world was arduous and one might be called upon to defend one's life.

Of the French travellers who had to do with Drovetti one may mention Chateaubriand, Cailliaud, Firman Didot, the comte de Forbin, Linant de Bellefonds, Montulé, Huyot and Lachaise, the comte de Marcellus, Pacho, the two Labordes, Champollion, and baron Taylor. From Germany came Bramsen, Gau, the Minutolis, Scholz and Parthey, and from Switzerland Burckhardt. Italian visitors were fewer: Finati, Vidua, Belzoni, Ricci, Frediani, Brocchi and Rosellini. Among the English who met him were Hester Stanhope, Turner, Irby and Mangles, Richardson, Hyde, Edmonstone, perhaps Carne, Hay, and Madden.

Tributes were lavished on Drovetti from all sides by these visitors. The earliest came from Chateaubriand on his famous journey from Paris to Jerusalem, and he singled out Drovetti from all the other consuls in the Levant: to the others he was grateful, but with Drovetti he had found true friendship. He sketched his character as marked by both simplicity and warmth and recorded the emotion of their parting. William Turner nearly a decade later remembered Drovetti's protection of the English prisoners in 1807, and noted that even during the critical juncture of the Hundred Days, when Drovetti made clear his attachment to both Napoleon and Murat, the Consul came to pay his respects. The Prussian Bramsen described him as 'well informed, polite and attentive to travellers of all nations'. The comte de Forbin, a very high official of the Restoration government who had replaced the old Bonapartist Denon as Director of Museums, again forged the closest links with the Consul. He described his character as one of 'disinterested benevolence', not thinking of himself. Gau, the famous Nubian traveller, stated bluntly that his whole success was due to Drovetti's zeal and perseverance on his behalf; he had indeed found himself penniless in Egypt. Even more striking is the testimony in Drovetti's favour by John Hyde, who mixed so much with the English diplomatic and antiquities establishment: he paid high (probably too high) tribute to the Consul's intellectual accomplishments. Vidua noted that his influence while out of office was greater than that of all the other consuls, and that he had declined to make a fortune with the Viceroy. He still devoted himself to helping all the 'poor foreigners' who came to Egypt. Vidua was to repay this generosity by being the one who above all others secured the first collection for Piedmont. The Royalist Marcellus immediately formed a 'sincere reciprocal friendship' with Drovetti based on political insight and service in common and a shared fascination with antiquity. The party of the Minutolis and Hemprich, finally, paid Drovetti high compliments from their varied vantage-points: Drovetti gave every attention to the mission sponsored by the Prussian government and especially won the heart of the baroness by his courtesy and hospitality, but also facilitated her husband's travels. The naturalist Hemprich was able to visit Dongola thanks 'to Drovetti's arrangement of the firman'. We may allow Cailliaud to have the last word. His *Voyage à Méroé* was published in 1826:

> May I be allowed to express here the feeling of profound gratitude which I owe him for the services which he had not failed to render French travellers and those of all nations and for that untiring generosity which nothing has been able to discourage, not even black ingratitude, injustice and jealousy.[4]

Apart from this constant stream of visitors and travellers, there are several other special cases which deserve separate discussion. Drovetti's relations with them have often been depicted in a way used to discredit him, and not always with justice. The great adventurer and excavator Giambattista Belzoni is one of the most tantalising of his acquaintances in Egypt. The truth about their relations is of the highest importance, since it is Belzoni's own account which has been used as the prime source by English writers interested even momentarily in the French Consul. Belzoni was in Egypt from 1815 until 1819. On his arrival, Drovetti as a fellow Italian was obviously his first resort, as he tried to set himself up as an hydraulic engineer, and found himself baulked by the oligarchy entrenched around the Viceroy, notably Bokhty. Drovetti lent him money and intervened in his quarrels.

Relations changed when Belzoni became a rival in the antiquities trade. At first Drovetti was not worried about the removal of the 'Head of Memnon', thinking the task impossible, and he even gave Belzoni a sarcophagus lid from a Theban tomb. The Paduan was then obstructed at Thebes by Rifaud and Cailliaud, Rosignani and Lebolo. In the same year, 1817, however, Drovetti was shown over the newly discovered tomb of Seti by Belzoni. The monopoly of the area around Gourneh by Drovetti's agents forced Belzoni to turn to the Valley of the Kings. The two were again corresponding, albeit in some disagreement, in 1818 over rumours that Belzoni had not found the tomb by himself but bought the knowledge of its site. The source was again one of Drovetti's agents, Rosignani. Drovetti allowed Belzoni to excavate at Luxor, which must have been in his own concession, and joked that someone looking like Belzoni seemed to want to harm him, but at the same time Belzoni was part of the social circle of both Salt and Drovetti.

The Philai obelisk was another bone of contention. Drovetti conceded the object to Salt, but again his agents attempted to obstruct its removal. The success of this operation and its being tied up at Thebes was the act of provocation which led to the famous attack on Belzoni on Boxing Day 1818. Yet again agents, Rosignani and Lebolo, led the party and, being armed, it is difficult to say where it might have ended but for Drovetti's appearance. Belzoni certainly refused to stay any longer in Egypt.

It is hard to exonerate Drovetti completely of ruthlessness in all this, after Belzoni became not only a rival in the collection of antiquities but also a much more spectacular success. The prizes of the Head of Memnon and the obelisk were too considerable to be surrendered without a struggle. The *modus vivendi* that Drovetti had established with Salt between two gentlemen and equals was one thing; the ingenious and temperamental giant was too threatening to be so accommodated. Salt, who knew him better than most, found him erratic and untruthful.

That suggests the obvious comparison, Drovetti's relations with Salt. By 1817 the English Consul was also greatly interested in antiquities. He was there with Richardson and Drovetti in the tour of the tomb of Seti. The next year at Thebes Belzoni provides us with a picture of convivial evenings with Salt, Bankes, baron Sack and Drovetti. He also mentions Salt taking sorbets with Drovetti at his famous house on the ruins of Karnak. It was here that Drovetti ceded the Philai obelisk to Salt; whether it was he who then attempted to prevent its being removed is a matter for speculation. When Salt married in 1819, it is almost certain that Drovetti was present. Evidence for their relations in the 1820s is much rarer. When, for example, the two consuls were asked to accompany Mehemet Ali on a tour to review the army in the south in 1824, they are known to have travelled separately. Drovetti was absent from Egypt when Salt died in 1827, but would have deeply regretted the loss of a man he respected and with whom he had shared so much.

The other person with whom Drovetti's relations have often been considered blameworthy is Champollion. For the first time the present study assembles the full evidence, and again the picture is more complex than previously admitted. When the first proposals were made in 1826 for the decipherer's visit to Egypt, Drovetti was most encouraging, although he hinted at less than stable conditions, owing to the Greek war. Early the next year he was positively urgent that Champollion should come before too many monuments were destroyed.

All this was transformed by the battle of Navarino in October 1827. Champollion and Rosellini had both met Drovetti during his leave in Europe, but the Consul's return seemed to be enough to ensure the security of the scientific expedition. Serious problems existed, however, in the interior of the country. In May 1828 Drovetti notified Champollion that the Viceroy had not approved of his coming until conditions improved. Not to be overlooked is the fact that Egypt and France were at war. Drovetti himself doubtless was anxious that no danger befall such eminent visitors; as Consul, he would be held responsible in Europe.

The expedition arrived nonetheless in August 1828. Drovetti was compromised with Mehemet Ali, who thought that he had disregarded his orders. Every attention, however, was lavished on the travellers by Drovetti. And when a scene developed at the audience with the Viceroy over firmans for excavations, it was resolved, be it noted, by Drovetti's ceding some of his own rights. It was only now, indeed, that Champollion began to think that warnings about coming to Egypt had ulterior motives.

When the expedition set off up the Nile, the Consul was most generous in providing the best of provisions, and also arranged for the repatriation of the ill Bibent. There was, however, a problem with mail for the French members; certainly the Italians received theirs more regularly. Again Champollion had his suspicions. Apart from that, however, he frequently expressed his gratitude to Drovetti, and when the Consul was to leave his post, Champollion keenly regretted a zealous friend and protector.

On Drovetti's departure, Champollion considered himself much more 'affectionately' treated by the new Consul, Mimaut, and thereupon turned about and denounced Drovetti and Jomard (his old foe in Egyptology) as the two ruiners of Egypt, and claimed that Drovetti was cursed by all the French there. Aware that this constituted an almost total volte-face from his previous statements, he went so far as to admit that he had been totally hypocritical in maintaining good relations. On his release from quarantine in 1830, however, he again consulted closely with the ex-consul; for now he wished to obtain an obelisk for France, and Drovetti was one of the delegation sent by the government to consult with him.

In all of this, Drovetti may have been nervous about an expedition sponsored by two governments with large sums to spend on excavations, and may have indulged in the creation of small inconveniences such as retarding mail, but this is in total contrast to all his care for the expedition's comforts. Champollion's erratic and over-critical nature, often an accompaniment of genius, led him into hasty suspicions. That is all that can be asserted with certainty.

It is now opportune, after considering Drovetti in Egypt, to turn to a more general discussion of his political life. From his entry into the French army in 1796 until the collapse of the Napoleonic regime, there is no doubt where his loyalty and enthusiasm lay. His part in the Provisional Government in Torino and then in the Italian campaign of 1800 reveals a young man committed to revolutionary reform in his own country, with outside intervention. In looking to France at this time, he was characteristic of so many idealists and intellectuals. He does not, however, seem to have suffered any disillusionment during the Napoleonic empire, unlike so many others who found that French intervention meant domination. His post in Egypt at the other end of the Mediterranean undoubtedly protected him from the sharper realities.

He was so highly regarded in some influential military quarters that on their recommendation Napoleon nominated him as second in command in a country most central to his own plans, where he had himself led an expedition only five years before in an attempt to strike a deadly blow at the English Empire, and when Drovetti's superior retired, Napoleon did not for all the remainder of his régime either replace him or appoint a new Consul-General. Those conversant, however, with the Emperor's arrangements for Rome, theoretically the 'second city' of the empire, will see parallels there and not be sure how far Napoleon knew what he was doing. Drovetti's passions are, on the other hand, absolutely clear, as his reactions to the Hundred Days demonstrate.

The continuing adherence to radical reform on Drovetti's part can easily be documented by his promotion of all the programmes to modernize Egypt during the 1820s. If one were to select one example more telling than others, it would surely be the famous plan for the education of not only Egyptians but also Africans. Drovetti firmly rejected any idea that these people were intellectually inferior; they were simply isolated. He was sure that they were perfectly capable of benefiting from educational opportunities in Europe.

As for his native country, the *Epistolario* reveals close connections with the pro-French and more reformist side of the Piedmontese royal family, namely the Prince of Carignano. In all the disasters of the House of Savoy, proverbial with Italians, this was one of the saddest. When the prince came to the throne as Carlo Alberto he betrayed his ideals and the great trust placed in him on which so many hopes relied. His first great failure was as Regent in 1821, which led to a revolution which was put down by Austrian intervention and repression by Carlo Felice. We have the most fascinating insight into Drovetti's reaction to this regime, and the papal government, in the letter which he wrote in 1826 concerning the Egyptian education programme. When he was consulted about the best European country to which the young Egyptians should be sent, he replied with a very frank comparison of Italy and France. His unwavering preference went to France, and Paris in particular. His reasons were not simply educational, but highly political. Since the revolution of 1821, education in Italy was subject to police and governmental control, he stated, and toleration, both political and religious, was unknown. Education was impossible, in his view, without freedom of expression and of the press. One might object, Drovetti realised, that this implied that there were no men of principle in Italy. They existed, he admitted, but they were in great danger.

By the 1840s, two decades later, we have further evidence for Drovetti's political views. It seems that by now he was interested in the famous neo-Guelph proposal of Vincenzo Gioberti for a papal federation. Although Drovetti is known to have had an audience with Pius IX, almost certainly he was shocked by the events of 1848, and came to agree that the temporal power of the papacy was the main stumbling block to Italian independence. Drovetti would also have been horrified, given his outstanding military career, at the fiasco of Carlo Alberto in 1848, but also with the part played in that collapse by the strife among the political factions. This is demonstrated by his letter to his son Giorgio in 1851 bitterly criticising those members of his family who had 'under the names of liberty, equality and fraternity ... espoused subversive principles of every kind in society'. The radical principles of his youth were now seen by him in his old age to be 'subverted'; the results were failure and strife.

His views in old age are complicated, but perhaps more consonant with those of his youth than at first appears. He was still very much in favour of reform, and such a stance in Italy in these times, after 1848, had clear political implications. His charitable foundations for the poor and their children reveal a man who believed in the duty of those who were better off to assist others less fortunate than themselves. This grouped him with those of the centre, attacked by both the reactionaries, who regarded such actions as encouraging the aspirations of the lower classes, and the radicals, who thought such charity patronising and who wanted more far-reaching changes. On the other hand, such charity was in accordance with progressive policies which were inevitably to lead to improvements for the working-classes and their increased self-awareness.

The Bielle speech concerning agriculture is the best illustration of his last ideals. While giving full credit to those who provided work, as benefactors of society, he openly expressed his horror at the backwardness of Piedmontese agriculture. Opponents of progress were to blame. He denounced usury and the misery of the peasants. It is significant, of course, that he placed so much stress on the contribution of the priesthood. One might view this as reactionary, but at the same time, he specified that priests were to conduct workers' education classes on Sundays. Literacy would have been the most politically explosive gift to the peasantry. And among the priests were to be found men of the stamp of Ugo Bassi.

There are many portraits of Drovetti: the famous view of him and his team at Thebes in 1818 which was published by Forbin, the romantic bust of his tomb, that in the Torino Museum, but undoubtedly best of all is the fine engraving by Franz Gau (frontispiece). The face is distinctively handsome, and the gaze fascinatingly direct, expressive of the qualities for which he was renowned, and which privilege must have refined since childhood. He manifests an awareness, the mark of a man with the gift of understanding, one humbled and made generous by both a striving for excellence and a sense of the lack of it – not always deserved – in others. Here is a man who knew both the intensity of political aspirations and the dangers to which they gave rise. At the age of a little more than forty, Drovetti looks out calmly at the world, already well acquainted with the possibility of death, and aware of the complications of life. He had by now long exercised considerable power in a most volatile environment, where consuls of European nations were both a law unto themselves and yet servants of an Oriental despot. In his face may also be traced the sad detachment of an Italian obliged to live in foreign places, of one reared in a sub-Alpine landscape and trained in the discipline of law, who had turned to arms, and then been diverted to politics in the heat of the Levant. In sum, however, one can understand how such a man would have attracted the responsibilities which were thrust upon him.[5]

The events of his life allow us to broaden and deepen this character sketch. From the earliest notice we have of him, certain traits are prominent. It is not surprising that he graduated from Torino University at a young age. He came from a well established and comfortable family with diverse professional backgrounds. He must have been an adolescent of intelligence and application, however, to win the scholarship to the Collegio delle Provincie, despite what we know of the way in which they were often awarded.

His mature qualities were immediately evident when he joined the French army and gained rapid promotion. They were even more obviously manifested in his selection for the vital post which he held in the

Provisional Government and the frankness and self-confidence which he displayed in 1799, as well as his bravery, patriotism and dedication. His two very high positions in the army and the courts in 1801 were awarded for his professionalism, the breadth of his competence, his leadership and energy, his learning in law, his absolute incorruptibility, and above all, his humanity. In these posts he was esteemed by all and long remembered.

Even with this array of qualities it was an awesome responsibility for a young man of 27 to be despatched at this time to Egypt, a country which combined the most vital importance with the gravest dangers. It is Drovetti's bravery which is his dominant virtue, displayed notably in 1803, when Alexandria was threatened with civil war, and in the famous English invasion of 1807. His life would have been forfeit (so it was intended) but for his valour, decisiveness and clear-sightedness.

If there is one constant running through Drovetti's character as revealed by his life it is his generosity. No-one he ever met seems not to have been helped by him, especially throughout his official years in Egypt. It seems that anything which he could give and which anyone else needed or wished to have, he gave to them. Among many examples, Rignon received perfume and dates, Dubois Ayme a whole array of relics of ancient Egypt, including mummified animals, Gau money, Huyot the usual provisions for his journey (wine, spirits, vinegar, oil), Hyde classical coins, the comte de Marcellus antiquities, the Minutolis hospitality, Wilhelm of Wurtemburg and the Prince of Carignano horses, Lajard fossils and seals, Delile seeds, and probably much more for the various botanists and anatomists in France, to judge by their requests, the Lyons Museum stelai, Sekowski and Fischer in St. Petersberg papyri and plant samples, the museum at Geneva antiquities, the King and the Prince of Carignano this time antelopes and an oryx, Nota precious stones, the baron di Barbania coffee, the Dresden Museum a Greek manuscript, Clot money for his tour in Europe, Canina coffee and chocolates (and probably the requested gifts for the Papal Museum), Sclopis tobacco, and Carlo Botta a gift of 4,000 francs. As well, not by any means to be forgotten, although the animal was actually donated by the Viceroy, is Drovetti's part in transporting the famous giraffe to Paris in 1826.

One would only expect that a man who was so generous to friends and people whom he had recently met would also care for his own family. Drovetti's son Giorgio, subject to disabilities of mind and body, was a constant responsibility. His brother Luigi, a priest, was the recipient of much kindness at various stages of his career, but one might have thought that Drovetti's elder brother, the notary Giuseppe, could have stood on his feet. He was, to the contrary, apparently so irresponsible that on his death he left his numerous family in heavy debt, and they naturally turned to Drovetti.

There are few cases recorded of any meanness in his character. One striking example is his refusal to allow Thomas Young make copies of a bilingual inscription in 1821, which might have helped him in the race to decipher hieroglyphs. The doctor's interests were purely scientific. It may have been, as Young asserted, pure 'cupidity' on the collector's part, but Drovetti did not want the collection, on which he relied for his retirement, devalued. Champollion would for once have agreed with the English doctor, adding what he saw as Drovetti's attempt to prevent his excavating in Egypt.

Closely connected with Drovetti's generosity may be placed his humanitarianism. This was first illustrated by his actions as a judge in Torino before his appointment to Egypt, when he was well known for his concern for political prisoners and his visits to the gaols. The most famous illustration, however, is his care for the English prisoners taken during the invasion of 1807, and even his standing surety for their letters of credit. Again in the cause of the defeated, he intervened for the sake of the Siwans in 1820, after they had been battered into submission by the Viceroy's artillery. Drovetti ameliorated the terms which had been imposed on them. The most extensive example of this virtue in his character is his eager promotion of reforms in Egypt, mostly in health and education. As a child of the French Revolution, he favoured the export to continents like Africa of the advantages of European science and culture. The poor fellahin, now beginning to escape from the clutches of scourges such as smallpox, had reason to bless his name. There were other unfortunates among the Europeans: Drovetti urged Mehemet Ali to pay pensions to the officers who were invalided or to their families if they were killed. And finally, again in stark contrast to his own feelings, as in 1807, his innate humanity triumphed during the Greek war. As has been made abundantly clear, he was no friend of the Greeks for a variety of reasons. When it came to individuals, however, he spared no exertion and no expense to recover and repatriate Greeks enslaved and carried to Egypt, and his actions were officially recognised by the Greek government.

One aspect of his character has occasionally excited adverse comment. It was held against him by some when he was to be reappointed in 1821 that he was very emotional. His friend Roussel defended him against this by first of all admitting the charge, but then by saying that his emotional nature was being moderated by age, and that it was balanced by his 'natural obligingness' and ability to win favour. He was, besides, the most important adviser to Mehemet Ali and his son. This last could hardly be true of a man who either betrayed or was carried away too often by his emotions. His position in Egypt, as Drovetti himself stated, was much more demanding than that of an ordinary diplomat. Special delicacy had to be used with an Oriental autocrat.

There are only a few occasions in all the documentation of his life when we are told that Drovetti manifested anger. Salt reported that he was 'in a raging passion', when action was being taken over the attack on Belzoni. He was also obviously very angry with his subordinate Thédénat-Duvent over the handling of the Adda affair in 1822, but the man had acted most incompetently. There are, on the other hand, the testimonies of people such as the comte de Marcellus, who wrote of Drovetti's 'calm and reflective reason', and William Gell who was impressed with his amiability, not to mention Carlo Vidua who praised his most elegant manners and very great desire to please.

Among the most potent dangers for a European in the Levant was sickness. The matter of Drovetti's health looms large in his biography, with good reason. Many were the Europeans who succumbed to the rigours of the climate, and for Drovetti, coming from the north-west of Italy appropriately called Piedmont, the change must have been abrupt. His tour of duty and the intervening break comprised twenty-six years in all, and was very long by any standards.

The first hint of ill-health is in 1812, and the reactions of diplomatic colleagues suggest that his disease was mental rather than physical, although there were discomforts of the latter kind manifested in some skin complaint. Drovetti was so far indisposed as to request leave. We then hear nothing until 1824. His release from duties and the great physical activities into which he threw himself during the 'interregnum' seem to have stimulated his recuperation. His eyes now began to trouble him, an affliction not uncommon in the East, and he suffered from sciatica; this was apparently the same as the pains in the joints (dengue fever) which Champollion stated that he was suffering from in 1828. At the same time we have the formal report by three doctors who attended him: a 'herpetic humour', chronic gastro- enteritis, and sciatica going back seven years (so to 1821). Even Champollion thought that Drovetti would be dead within the year if he did not escape. The next year he returned to Europe and lived another twenty-three years.

There were more than personal illnesses to be dreaded in early nineteenth-century Egypt. The plague was a constant menace. In 1813, for example, sixty to eighty persons a day were dying in Alexandria, and even the Viceroy's physician was among the victims. There were also endless intrigues which could involve even a man of Drovetti's position and status. The most interesting was a danger partly of his own creation. He had indulged in satirical comments on Egyptian politics and when his intimate Lascaris had died, his papers were sequestered. Had these been examined, Drovetti's position would not have been enviable. The rivalry between the European powers could also endanger the life of a man like Drovetti. His friend Chayolle claimed that the English had induced the Arabs to assassinate French officers going to India during the American war. Other very highly placed employees of the régime, such as doctors, were poisoned, and shots were fired at some people. Drovetti himself had been fired upon at thirty paces shortly after his arrival. He summed up his life in Egypt better than anyone else could in 1816, although the words are those of his friend Rignon who had just received his letter: always menaced by the plague or by a massacre, or in danger of falling victim to the inclemency of the climate.

In connection with his health, there is one tantalising question raised by just one witness as early as 1806. Chateaubriand in his widely published *Itinéraire de Paris* à Jerusalem stated that Drovetti had a 'mutilated' hand. Tradition connected this with his participation in the battle of Marengo in 1800. It is incredible that only one of all those who knew him mentions this disability. The only explanation is that it must not have been very noticeable or incapacitating. It is a strange coincidence that Drovetti's counterpart, Ernest Missett, was severely handicapped in all his limbs, as every English visitor commented. In the famous engraving of Drovetti and his team in the album of Count Forbin (Pl.15), Drovetti in his right hand holds a measuring-cord against the head of the colossus, while his left hand hangs rather limply by his side. Keen eyes have detected the loss of some fingers.

We may finally attempt to select from the hundreds of people whom he knew well those who could be counted among his close friends. They form an interesting group, of very varied character, background and profession. Going back to Drovetti's early adult life and lasting until the other's death in 1837 was a friendship with Carlo Botta, a fellow Canavese but almost ten years older. They entered French service in the same year, were colleagues in the Provisional Government, and then shared exile in France, where Botta spent almost the entire period of his remaining life, mainly writing history. The link between the two men could not be more strongly demonstrated by Drovetti's gift of 4,000 francs in 1825, and his invitation to Botta to visit him in Egypt, and Botta's letter to Drovetti in 1835 full of family news addressed to 'mon cher et bien cher Drovetti'.

We could also include Colonel Vincent Boutin, four years older than Drovetti, but another Bonapartist who fought, amongst other campaigns, in Italy in 1800. A close intimacy between the Consul and the secret agent was established when they both travelled south in 1811, and then when Boutin left Egypt until the time of his assassination near Baalbek in 1815 he kept up a regular correspondence. He was solicitous of Drovetti's health, and discussed military events such as the Russian campaign and the volatile events of 1812 and the next years. Boutin looked forward to seeing

Drovetti in Paris on leave. Drovetti wrote to him frequently after Boutin left for Syria, and they commiserated over France's great defeat and the resultant political chaos.

Among diplomatic colleagues none was closer than David, Consul at Smyrna until 1826. He was a remarkable person, highly intelligent and educated, with a fine epistolary style and a great sense of humour. He shared so many convictions and attitudes with Drovetti, notably their hostile view of the Greeks. In the early 1820s there are preserved no fewer than seventeen letters from David to Drovetti as they sought comfort from each other in the endless eastern crises.

There were also most highly placed French officers in the Levant, namely the commanders of the French fleet. Henri Gauthier, the comte de Rigny, held this post from 1822 until 1830. He had fought in all the Napoleonic wars before being appointed at the age of forty to this command. He was remarkable for his courage and humanity, and he also shared with Drovetti his view of the Greek war, being particularly outraged at Greek piracy.

Other eminent Frenchmen came to Egypt during Drovetti's term there and became his close friends. Two leading examples are the mineralogist Frédéric Cailliaud, eleven years younger, and the administrator the comte de Forbin. Cailliaud's first visit was 1815-1819: as well as his investigation of mines, he accompanied Drovetti to the Second Cataract in 1816, and visited Kharga oasis in 1818, just six months before his friend. On his second tour (1819-1822), he visited Siwah in 1819, again only a few months before Drovetti. The two men shared a great interest in antiquities. Cailliaud was still recording his gratitude to Drovetti for his help twenty years later. Forbin came to Egypt in 1817, met Drovetti and became a life-long admirer. He was almost two years younger than the Consul, and had succeeded the famous colleague of Napoleon, Vivant Denon, as Director-General of Museums. Their brief meeting in Egypt made Forbin a committed supporter of Drovetti's reappointment as Consul in 1821. The latter had the task of seeing safely transported from Egypt to France the large antiquities which Forbin had acquired for the Louvre. Forbin also found Drovetti an invaluable source of information about so many personalities in Egypt, and was a fervent advocate of the acquisition of the first collection. He died in 1841.

Beyond all others, however, Edme Jomard is revealed by Drovetti's correspondence as his closest friend, although they did not meet until 1827. Jomard was almost two years younger than Drovetti. His first surviving letters date from July 1819, and from that time the two men cooperated indefatigably in the programme of Egyptian modernisation. Drovetti persuaded Mehemet Ali to appoint Jomard as director of studies in Paris, and they worked together without the slightest trace of disagreement for the rest of their lives, commiserating on the enormous difficulties they faced on all sides, both in Egypt and in France. The partnership is instructive, between Jomard, the leading figure in the intellectual establishment (member of the Académie des Inscriptions, Keeper of the Bibliothèque Nationale), and the lawyer, soldier and diplomat.

Not to be forgotten in the same connection is the enormous circle of intellectuals with whom Drovetti maintained the closest relations on his return to Europe. Apart from names already mentioned, such as Botta and Jomard, there was the antiquarian William Gell, Dr Etienne Pariset, Cesare Balbo, the scientist and traveller Giuseppe Baruffi, the philanthropist the marchese di Barolo, the poet and patriot Silvio Pellico, the linguist Pietro Giordano, the sculptor Carlo Marochetti, the painter Count Benevello, the lawyer Giuseppe Bertalazone, the antiquarian and architect Luigi Canina, the lawyer and politician Federigo Sclopis, and the Egyptologist Emmanuel de Rougé.

From all those who knew Drovetti we may conclude by recalling some of the many tributes paid to him. Visitors to Egypt whose scientific aims had been accomplished and whose travels had been facilitated and even whose lives had been preserved thanks to Drovetti's patronage and protection, not to mention the comforts provided by his personal generosity, paid him the highest compliments, as we have already seen. There were many others who had known him in other capacities.

Few higher compliments could have been paid the notorious Bonapartist than that by the restored Bourbon government, which in 1817 expressed its gratitude for his 'praiseworthy and disinterested conduct' as Consul. His successor, Joseph Roussel, doyen of the French consuls in the Levant, went out of his way in 1820 to write to a State Councillor in support of Drovetti's reappointment, rebutting point by point the various objections which had been raised. In 1817 he called Drovetti appropriately 'a walking dictionary' of Egypt. The man with whom Drovetti worked most closely in Europe was Edme Jomard. One of the best sixtieth birthday presents Drovetti received was undoubtedly his friend's tribute: 'without you, I could not have succeeded; without you, the Pasha would have dared nothing, would have dreamed nothing.' Dr Etienne Pariset visited Egypt only at the very end of Drovetti's term, yet they forged a close friendship, and had hoped to travel together in the East in 1837. Pariset's own avowals of affection for Drovetti are fulsome. More significant, however, is his statement that in his circle in Paris there was a veritable cult of Drovetti. Only a little later, Giuseppe Baruffi assured him of the longing of so many friends and acquaintances for his 'happy company'. Drovetti was plainly a man who inspired great affection on many sides, whose company was much in demand, and whose services, but even more, his cooperation in great undertakings, were highly valued.

His life spanned one of the most tumultuous generations in European history. He had shown great capacities in many professions: most importantly he had been France's indefatigable agent in representing her interests in one of the most vital areas of her foreign policy. He was a man of considerable passion, of fierce loyalty on the one hand, and a formidable rival on the other to those on whom he did not look kindly. His most lasting contributions are undoubtedly in the two very disparate fields of the laying of the foundations of modern Egypt and in the creation of the first museum of Egyptian antiquities.

Appendix 1

The Drovetti Family

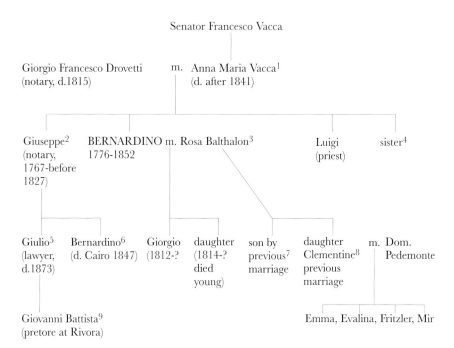

Senator Francesco Vacca

Giorgio Francesco Drovetti
(notary, d.1815)

m. Anna Maria Vacca[1]
(d. after 1841)

Giuseppe[2]
(notary,
1767-before
1827)

BERNARDINO m. Rosa Balthalon[3]
1776-1852

Luigi
(priest)

sister[4]

Giulio[5]
(lawyer,
d.1873)

Bernardino[6]
(d. Cairo 1847)

Giorgio
(1812-?)

daughter
(1814-?
died
young)

son by
previous[7]
marriage

daughter
Clementine[8]
previous
marriage

m. Dom.
Pedemonte

Giovanni Battista[9]
(pretore at Rivora)

Emma, Evalina, Fritzler, Mir

Notes

1. Mentioned 1841 (*Ep.* 692).
2. Dead by 1836 (*Ep.* 656). See also Bertolotti, 7.331.
3. The name is given variously as Barthalon or Balthalon. The latter seems the more reliably transmitted.
4. Her husband is given variously as Calos (*Ep.* 504) or Boggetti di Leone (Bertolotti, 7.325).
5. See Bertolotti, 7.331.
6. A nephew so named is mentioned by Champollion, *Lettres* 2.25. Don Buzzo kindly found his will.
7. Mentioned by Belzoni (see below, p.327), and Driault, *La formation de l'empire de Mohamed Aly*, 185.
8. Named in *Ep.* 695. The vital link that she was Drovetti's step-daughter is provided by La Contemporaine (see above, p.164).
9. See Bertolotti, 7.331.

Appendix 2

EUROPEAN OFFICERS IN THE EGYPTIAN ARMY, 1825
(CORR.5, 93)

French (all serving in Egypt, unless otherwise specified):

General Boyer
Captain Pujol Samville
Lieut. Ledieu
Colonel Gaudin
Major Adolphe de Tarle
Cav. Capt. Paulin de Tarle
Lieut. Planat (artillery)
Lieut. Barras (infantry)
Capt. Ristori
Capt. Cadeau (Sennar)
Capt. Doumerc (Mecca)
Artificer Dotte
Colonel Rey
Berthier (controller)

Spanish:
Colonel Costa (Morea)
Lieut.-Col. Lescure
Capt. Cormano
Lieut. Canals (artillery)

Neapolitans:
Capt. Ximenes
Capt. Acerbi
Eng. Chianti
Second Lieut. Fiorentini
Lieut. Attomar (Morea)

Piedmontese:
Col. Cresia
Capt. Brunetti
Capt. Serras
Capt. Riccini
Capt. Riba
Capt. Playo
Lieut. Ario
Capt. Grillotti
Capt. Vigna
Capt. Salusolia
Capt. Eng. Piantanida
Capt. Gobernatis (Mecca)
Col. Soultz (Morea)
Capt. Trona
Capt. Albertini
Serg. maj. Luchesi

Appendix 3

The Drovetti Collection in Torino: major items (S. Curto, *Museo egizio di Torino*, 1984)

The numbers on the left are catalogue numbers.

6281: prehistoric knife (pl.48)

1874: Turin canon (55)

3065: princess Redief (dyn. III) (61)

3147: head of a young man in painted limestone (FIP) (77)

1447: chancellor Mery's stele (FIP) (86)

1534: stele of Abekau (Middle Kingdom) (93)

1613: stele of scribe Horhernakht (94)

1547: stele of Warkha I from Abydos (100)

3082: little tabernacle in yellow Limestone with family group (Middle Kingdom) (104)

1381: king of dyn. XIII-XIV (105)

1374: Tuthmosis I (108)

1372: Amenophis I in painted limestone (111)

1387: head of Tuthmosis I (from Karnak ?) (113)

1376: Tuthmosis III in majesty (115)

1375: Amenophis II ofering vases of wine, red granite (117)

836: Amon as ram protecting Tuthmosis IV, red granite (118)

86: Ptah of Memphis in black granite, from Karnak (121)

1408: sphinx of Amenophis III (122)

566: Queen Tiy and hippopotamus (124)

1377: priest Anen, brother of Q. Tiye, black granite (125)

1378: head with cartouches of Amenophis IV (128)

768: Tutankhamon with Amon (131)

1379: Horemhab with Queen Mutnedmut (133)

1380: Ramesses II in majesty (145)

767: Ramesses II between Amon and Mut (151)

1383: colossus of Seti II (155)

1875: judicial papyrus (159)

1392: Ramesses III with prisoner of war (160)

1885: papyrus of tomb of Ramesses IV (164)

2031: the Satirical Papyrus (165)

1584:   stele of Ensef (late XVIII) (167)

1555:   stele of the scribe Pai (169)

1465:   stele of the scribe Mahu (171)

1464:   cornice of the shrine of Ramesses II (173)

The following items to 3048 all come from *Deir el Medineh*:

2082, 2083, 2073: journal of the Theban necropolis, Ramesses IX (183)

1554:   stele of the scribe Pai (187)

3038:   statuette of Sekai (187)

1603:   cusp of the pyramid of the scribe Ramese (188)

1579:   stele of the scribe Maia (189)

1517:   relief of four women and two children, from tomb 215 (190)

1549:   stele of Baki (Seti I, tomb 298) (192)

1454:   stele of the priest Nakht Atum (dyn. XIX) (192)

7357:   stele of the worker Ipi (193)

1636:   stele of the sculptor Kara (Ramesses II, tomb 330) (193)

1635:   stele of the sculptor Ken (dyn. XIX, tomb 4) (195)

3032:   worker Paensheenabu with Amon (tomb 322) (197)

3048:   statue of Paenbui (199)

1628:   stele of Kha and Merit (203)

1009, 986, 914: standards of Toth, Horus and a jackal in coloured wood (Ptolemaic) (221)

1460:   Tuthmosis III before Min (223)

251:    Sekhmet seated, from Karnak (224)

255:    Sekhmet standing (225)

3017:   statue of a worshipper offering to Ptah (227)

3035:   statuette of priest of Amon carrying Amon as ram (228)

7358:   stele of Anherka worshipping Amon, Maat and Amenophis I (dyn. XIX) (230)

3016:   statue of a worshipper of Anuket (Ramessid) (232)

3016:   statuette of Iner, from temple of Hathor, Deir el Medineh (235)

1601:   goddess on a lion (237)

2446:   tabernacle dedicated to the Elephantine triad (237)

1558:   stele of Paimesha (237)

1750:   foot of a basin dedicated by Seti II (238)

1751:   altar dedicated by Nektanebo II (239)

1570:   stele of Pashedu (240)

1546:   ear stele (241)

1593:   'stele of miracles' (242)

1993, 1995, 1996: magic papyrus (late Empire) (243)

2236:   sarcophagus of the scribe Butehamon (247)

1782:   book of Neskhensuisit (253)

1768:   Book of the Dead of Nebhepet (253)

1808:   Book of the Dead of Hor (253)

2805:   mummy and ba (257)

1769:   Book of the Dead of Mishisekeb (257)

1966:   papyrus of love poetry (259)

7052:   ostrakon of the dancer (opp. pl.260)

6278, 6259: oboe case in wood (262)

6347:   cubit of Amenope (263)

1879, 1899, 1969: gold mine map (270)

6850:   scarab (271)

518:       Isis protecting the king (272)

866:       statue of lion in limestone (272)

6402:   lion feet for furniture (275)

Third Intermediate period:

3063:   priest Merienptah (279)

1760:   offering table (280)

2201:   sarcophagus of vizier Gemenefherbak (283)

1673:   relief showing pressing of lily oil (286)

3138:   head of male statue in white limestone (dyn. XXX) (287)

1752:   offering table (288)

Ptolemaic:

1763:   stele

38:        statue of Bes (302)

433:       child Horus in Bronze (304)

1668:   Isis as Aphrodite Anadomene (304)

173:       Isis feeding Horus (304)

7148:   stele of Serapis and Isis (306)

7149:   relief of Serapis and Isis (309)

2230:   sarcophagus of Petamonofi (313)

6080:   papyrus (318)

3030:   statue of priest with stele of Horus (319)

Byzantine:

865:       Coptic lion (324)

7193:   bronze lamp (329)

There are here, in all, one hundred items, with illustrations and notes.

List of Abbreviations

Corr. 1: G. Douin (ed.), *L'Egypte de 1802 à 1804*, 1925.

Corr. 2: G. Douin (ed.), *Mohamed Aly, pacha du Caire 1805-1807*, 1926.

Corr. 3: E. Driault (ed.), *Mohamed Aly et Napoléon, 1807-1814*, 1925.

Corr. 4: E. Driault (ed.), *La formation de l'empire de Mohamed Aly de l'Arabie au Soudan, 1814-1823*, 1927.

Corr. 5: E. Driault (ed.), *L'expédition de Crète et de Morée 1823-1828*, 1930.

Corr. 6: G. Douin (ed.), *L'Egypte de 1828 à 1830*, 1935.

DBF: *Dictionnaire de biographie française*.

DBI: *Dizionario biografico degli italiani*.

Ep.: Drovetti, *Epistolario*, ed. S. Curto and L. Donatelli, 1985.

FO: records of the English Foreign Office, Public Record Office, London.

MFA: Minister of Foreign Affairs.

WWWE: *Who was who in Egyptology*, 3rd ed., 1995.

Notes

Introduction

1. I consign the following horrible examples to a footnote. The appalling maltreatment –
    if he is mentioned at all – in every kind of standard work surpasses belief. F.G. Bratton,
    History of Egyptian archaeology, 1967, mentions him only twice, as a 'naval (sic) explorer'
    (could this be 'rival explorer'?) and as someone who trotted around on expeditions with
    the English consul, Henry Salt (68). B. Fagan, *The rape of the Nile*, 1975, says he was
    born at Barbaria (sic), that he went to Egypt with Napoleon, that his successor as
    consul was Foussel (for Roussel!) and that he died in a lunatic asylum (86f, 236, 248).
    A recent book by C. Traunecker, *Karnak, resurrection d'un site*, 1984, manages five
    mistakes in one small paragraph (119). Given the fame of the authors, one cannot pass
    over another gem: Belzoni was a rival of Drovetti, 'who represented the French consul'
    (H. Carter and A. Mace, *The tomb of Tutankamen*, 1923, 1.68). Worst of all are the
    biographical dictionaries. The article in the *Dictionnaire de biographie française* (11.836) by
    d'Amat is a scandal.
    On the other hand, Drovetti's name does not even appear in the *Cambridge history of
    Africa* (vol. 5, c.1790-c.1870), 1976. On this matter, see below, chap. 6.

2. See S. Fumagalli, *Giovanni Marro, 1875-1952*, Pinerolo, no date (!), cited by Marta
    Petricioli, *Archeologia e mare nostrum*, 1990 (p.400); it is inaccessible to me.

Chapter One

1. A century ago, these were grain, rye, chestnuts and potatoes, but incredibly not
    enough for the inhabitants, so that food had to be imported. G. Casalis, *Dizionario
    geographico-storico-statistico-commerciale degli stati di S.M. il Re di Sardegna*, 2.1834, 129-134
    (Barbania).

2. The correct date is found in the parish registers (see illustration). It is also given in the
    records of the Order of SS Maurizio e Lazzaro: an extract from a baptismal certificate
    was required for admission. The error of 7 January was introduced authoritatively on
    Drovetti's tombstone by his executors, who also wrote the first biographical sketch with
    the same date; followed by G. Marro, 'La personalità de B. Drovetti studiato nel suo
    archivio inedito', *Mem.Accad.Torino* 2.71.1951, 39-151 at 5. The origin of this error is
    obvious: the register could easily if carelessly be misread as 7 January, since the name
    Druetto is written in the margin opposite the third line of a four-line entry, and the
    next is, in fact, of that date.
    Hilarious if they were not appalling would be French biographical dictionaries: Rabbe,
    Biographie des contemporains 5.1834, 170: born at Livorno in 177-; *Nouv. biog. gén.* 13.1855,
    806: born at Livorno in 1775, copied by *Grande dictionnaire universelle du XIX siècle*, 1865,
    6.1299; d'Amat, *DBF* 11.1967, 836: born at Barbania, near Livorno! Barbania in
    Piedmont and Livorno in Tuscany are separated by c. 300 kms.

3. G. Ferreri, *Brevi cenni su Barbania canavese*, 1904, 38f.

4. The Canavese is 'the subalpine district extending from the level moraine ridge of the
    Serra d'Ivrea up to the foot of the Gran Paradiso', Blue Guide *Northern Italy*, 1978 (7th
    ed.), 61.

5. The best history is AA.VV. *Storia del Piemonte* (2 vols), 1960. Torino lacks the grandiose
    multi-volume histories devoted to, for example, Milan or Naples. See F. Cognasso,

Storia di Torino, 1961; Ada Peyrot, *Torino nei secoli*, 1965. In general, H. Hearder, *Italy in the age of the Risorgimento 1790-1870*, 1980; S. Woolf, *A history of Italy 1700-1860*, 1979.

6. Giovanni Fabroni, quoted by Woolf, 150.

7. *ibid.*, 154.

8. I. Macario, *Cenni biografici del fu cav. Bernardino Drovetti*, 1885, 15.

9. On everything to do with the Collegio delle Provincie, see Marina Roggero, *Il sapere e la virtù*, 1987.

10. Archives of the University of Torino, Registro degli esami di baccalaureato, licenza, laurea 20 luglio 1791-28 giugno 1805 (73C), and Verbali degli esami 15 maggio 1789-4 aprile 1795 (77C). My most sincere thanks to the University for copies of these records, and to Father Geoffrey King, canon lawyer.

11. Ugo Bottone, Luigi Colla and Amedeo Avogadro, his later colleagues, all graduated in law at 18, and GB Balbis and Carlo Botta graduated as doctors aged 20.

12. Torino (S. Chiara) Governo Francese, mazzo 71 (tribunali).

13. Archives du Ministère des Affaires Etrangères, série Personnel, lère série, carton 105 (henceforth 'Drovetti dossier'). This is unknown to Drovetti's Italian biographers.
There is strangely no trace of a dossier of Drovetti in the very extensive records in the Torino archives of Piedmontese who served in the French armies (S. Chiara), Governo Francese.

14. Compare Carlo Botta, also from the Canovese, who enrolled as a doctor in the French army of the Alps in precisely the same month (*DBI* 13.365).
Bonaparte wanted to enrol Italians from 1796, but the Directory refused (R. Faino, *I soldati italiani di Napoleone*, 1914, 10f). The Lombard and Aemilian legions were formed, and then the Italian legion under Lechi in 1800. From then on, thousands of Italians were enrolled. The less fortunate were incorporated in French regiments, and so their exploits are largely unknown. Faino calculates (p.24) that by 1812, 100,000 Italians were in French regiments or the Italian army.
Following the defeat of Piedmont in 1796, the army had been thoroughly reformed and reduced in numbers. By the Treaty of Bologna (25 February, 1797), a defensive and offensive alliance was struck between France and Piedmont and 6,000 infantry (later raised to 9,000) and 1,000 cavalry were to serve under French command. The commander-in-chief was Fontanieux, with Colli as chief-of-staff (F. Pinelli, *Storia militare del Piemonte* 1854, 2.23f).

15. According to Colli's reference in 1801, in year 5 (1796/7) he 'entered the service of the Republic' as a soldier in the 15th Half Brigade in which he attained the rank of Sergeant. In A.B. *Histoire régimentaire et divisionnaire de l'armée d'Italie*, 1844, there is no mention of the 15th.

16. This was a family tradition: G. Drovetti, 'Il mio glorioso avo Bernardino Drovetti', *Torino rivista municipale* 1931, no 8, 57-61, and known to Macario (n.8) 16, but not to C. Cagnone and C. Mosca, *Notizie biografiche sul cav. B. Drovetti*, 1857.

17. One of the most interesting Italian generals on French service, the Milanese Giuseppe La Hoz (c.1766-1799). Having reached the grade of lieutenant in the Austrian army, he passed to the French in 1795 as adjutant of General La Harpe and fought at Lodi. Adjutant to Bonaparte, he organised and commanded the Lombardy legion and the Cisalpine troops. On the foundation of the Cisalpine Republic, he commanded at Milan and was a member of the Great Council, but in 1798 went to Paris to complain over the changed constitution. Becoming disenchanted with the French, he resigned his rank, but was reinstated. He tried to organise an independence movement, rejoined the Austrians and Russians, and fell at the siege of Ancona.

18. Luigi Colli, marchese di Felizzano (1757-1809), attained the rank of colonel in the Piedmontese army by 1795 after valorous action in the endlessly incompetent resistance by the Austrians and Piedmontese. As negotiator of the Peace of Leoben (1797), he came to Bonaparte's notice. On the fall of the Piedmontese monarchy (December 1798), Colli was made Brigade General in the Italian Army, and was

captured at Novi (May 1799), but freed the next year. He was appointed head of the General staff in Piedmont in March 1801 and promoted to General in September 1802 with command in Corsica 1803. He retired under a cloud in 1806 and died in Alessandria three years later.

19. A.B. (sic), *Histoire régimentaire et divisionnaire de l'armée d'Italie*, 1844, 29-39. The author is unfathomable to the British Library Catalogue, and does not appear in H. Barbier, *Dictionnaire des ouvrages anonymes*, 1872.

20. P. Duhesme, *Essai sur l'infanterie légère*, 1814.

21. Woolf (n.8), 177.

22. The story was already circulated in the authoritative *Nouvelle biographie générale* 13.806 (Beauvois): lieutenant-colonel (which he was not until 1829!) he saved the life of Murat, and had a hand mutilated; followed by Larousse, *Grande dictionnaire universelle du XIX siècle*, 6.1865, 1299, and *DBF* (d'Amat): Murat's aide-de-camp. The assertion was made even by the great biographer of Champollion, Hermine Hartleben, *Champollion, sein Leben und sein Werk*, 1906, 1.484, and in one of the early articles of G. Marro, 'B. Drovetti et Champollion le Jeune', *Atti Accad. Torino* 58.1922/3, 548-582 at p.548, and in the otherwise charming and instructive L. Greener, *The discovery of Egypt*, 1966, 119.

23. Hearder, *(N.8)*, 49.

24. The main source for the history of the Provisional Government is the *Raccolta delle leggi, provvidenze e manifesti emanati dai governi francesi e provissori* (2 vols), 1799. There is no trace of Drovetti in these documents.

25. Torino, Epoca francese, 2nd series, 1.

26. Torino, Epoca francese, 1st series, cart. 3, fasc. 8.

27. Torino, Epoca francese, 2nd series, 1: Decreti e letter per impieghi, p.61.

28. Torino, Epoca francese, 2nd series, 1, Processi Verbali, under that date. This is not mentioned by the early biographers (Cagnone and Mosca, Macario).

29. The index of these letters is preserved in Torino, Epoca francese, 135: letters and decrees.

30. F. Pinelli, *Storia militare del Piemonte*, 1854, 2.113f. Macario (p.30) gives him great credit for his tact and skill and care for a 'just and ordered liberty'; his prudence is said to have avoided many upsets, as for example when Favria revolted against the regime.

31. G. Drovetti (n.16), 59.

32. Marro, 'Personalità', 6. There is no trace of any such decrees in the *Raccolta* (n.24).

33. Torino, Epoca francese, 1st series, cart. 3, fasc. 8, pp.433-434.

34. Felice Bongioanni (1770-1838), lawyer, for a short time member of the Provisional Government, resigned over opposition to the annexation; professor of law, procurator at Ceva and Genova; unemployed 1814-1822, then assessor at Genova and fiscal advocate at Savoia.

35. F. Bongioanni, *Mémoires d'un jacobin*, 1958, 171.

36. Copies of three of his letters are preserved in Torino, Epoca francese, 1st series, cart. 2, fasc. 7.

37. C. Botta, *Lettere inedite*, ed. Pavesio, 1875, 147.

38. Bongioanni, *Mémoires*, 208.

39. *Ibid.*, 163. The Avogadro is apparently Amedeo, but the biography in *DBI* 4.689 knows nothing of him between 1795 and 1801!

40. The Drovetti dossier in Paris (n.13); Colli's reference (n.12), but without date; Cagnone and Mosca, 3; Macario 16 dates this after Marengo.

41. N. Brancaccio, *L'esercito del vecchio Piemonte*, 1922, 115; Pinelli, (n.30) 2.113, 122.

42. The Drovetti dossier; Colli's reference; Cagnone and Mosca, 3; Marro, 'Personalità' 7.

43. Not in Cagnone and Mosca; Macario 16 suggests that this was after the Provisional Government when Drovetti 'returned' to France, and that he was appointed by Murat as commander of the vanguard. This gives a date in 1800. Marro, 'Personalità', 6, simply notes him as Murat's aide-de-camp.

44. G. Drovetti (n.16), 59. (7

45. Drovetti, *Epistolario*, 1985 (henceforth Ep.), 13f, from Benzi, chaplain to Caroline Murat, 26 Jan. 1805, and Marro notes that two letters of the Marshal once in the correspondence have been lost. Not one letter, however, addressed to Drovetti survives in all the eight volumes of Murat's preserved correspondence (5169 letters only to 1810), *Lettres et documents pour servir à l'histoire de Joachim Murat*, ed. P. le Brethon, 1908-1914.

46. Count Cugnac, *Campagne de l'armée de réserve en 1800*, 1900-1901, 2.401f.

47. *Ibid.*, 2.574f.

48. See below, p.43; Marro, 'Il movimento civile...' *Atti del XXIII Congresso di Storia del Risorgimento italiano*, 1935, 1940, 257-280, at p.257.
    For those who like their history with a strong dash of romance, M. Disher in his ill-titled *Pharaoh's fool*, 1957 (a biography of Belzoni!), 92, states that Drovetti had 'lost a hand while saving the life of Murat'. The same page claims that he served as lieutenant-colonel under Napoleon (his highest active rank was major) and that in c.1817 'he was forming two magnificent collections, one for Paris, the other for Turin' (see below, chap. 7).

49. C. Botta, *History of Italy during the Consulate and Empire*, Eng. trans. (2 vols), 1828, 1.65.

50. Count Cugnac carried out a model of historical research on this campaign, publishing first the entire documentation in two fat volumes of 1,300 pages: *Campagne de l'armée de réserve en 1800*, 1900-1901, followed by a volume of historical narrative based upon them: *La campagne de Marengo*, 1904, in which myth after myth was demolished.

51. The vital Austrian despatches telling of this fell into the hands of Murat and Berthier, but they had no officer who could read German! Cugnac, *Marengo*, 160.

52. C. Botta (n.49), 1.108.

53. It is here that the numerous examples documented by Cugnac of Napoleon's rewriting of history reach their climax. It was even claimed that the retreat had been voluntary and that the army performed a 'pivot' manoeuvre which led the enemy against fresh reserves (Desaix) and blocked their retreat. The rewritten Marengo was, in fact, put into operation at Austerlitz. Napoleon went so far as to destroy the documents, but one copy survived: Cugnac, *Marengo*, 239f.

54. Drovetti dossier; Cagnone and Mosca, 3; Macario 16; Marro, 'Personalità' 7.

55. Drovetti dossier; Colli's reference; Cagnone and Mosca, 3; Marro, 'Personalità' 7.

56. N. Brancaccio, (n. 41), 259.

57. Drovetti dossier.

58. *Ibid.*

59. *Ep.* 4, from Colli, 12 March, 1801.

60. Cagnone and Mosca, 3; Maccario, 16, Marro, 'Personalità' 7.

61. *Raccolta di leggi, decreti, proclami, manifesti e circolari pubblicati dalle autorita' constituente*, vol.6 (ND), 109f. The standard statement that Drovetti was judge in a special *military* tribunal is thus completely misleading.

62. See above, p.7.

63. *Ep.* 301, from dal Pozzo, 12 April 1824.

64. As soon as this promotion became known, arrangements were made to have him replaced: Torino, Governo francese 71, fasc. 5.

65. *Ibid.*, 72 (correspondence), 19 December 1801; 72. fasc. 7.

66. *Ibid.* 72, fasc. 6.

67. Macario, 17.

68. C. Botta, *History* 1.214.

69. There is a copy of the decree in G. Wiet, 'Les consuls de France en Egypte sous le règne de Mohammed Ali', *Revue du Caire* Oct. 1943, 459-476, p.460.

70. *Ep.* 11f, from Colli, 13 August; cf. 12, 24 October.

71. Woolf (n. 5), 196.

72. D. Thomson, *Europe since Napoleon*, 1966[2], 122.

Chapter Two

1. See H. Bunbury, *Narratives of some passages in the Great War with France from 1799-1810*, 1927, 54f.
2. H. Dodwell, *The founder of modern Egypt*, 1931, 9.
3. G. Douin, *L'Egypte de 1802 à 1804*, 1925 (= *Corr. 1*), 6: Bonaparte to Sebastiani, 5 Sept., 1802.
   Horace Sebastiani (1772-1851), a Corsican and ardent Bonapartist. He distinguished himself in the Italian wars 1794-1800, including at Arcola, Verona and Marengo; special Ambassador to the East, 1802-1803; general at Austerlitz (wounded); ambassador to Constantinople 1806-1807, where he organised the defences against the English fleet; Minister of the Navy and Foreign Affairs, 1830-1834; Ambassador to London, 1835-1840.
4. Talleyrand was Minister of Foreign Affairs, Dec. 1797 – August 1807.
5. *Corr. 1*, 8: Sebastiani to Talleyrand, 20 Oct.
6. *Corr. 1*, 26: Khosrew to Talleyrand, 6 Nov.
7. *Corr. 1*, 30: Stuart to Ibrahim, 11 Dec.; Stuart to Khosrew, 16 Dec.
8. Corr.1, 11f: Sebastiani to Napoleon, Jan. 1803.
9. *Corr. 1*, 32: Brune to Talleyrand, 25 Jan. Guillaume Brune was Ambassador to Constantinople 1802-1804.
10. *Corr. 1*, 34: Stuart to Khosrew, 13 Feb.
11. S. Ghorbal, *The beginnings of the Egyptian question and the rise of Mehemet Ali*, 1928, 208. Ibrahim and Murad were virtually rulers in concert, 1775-1798.
12. *Corr. 1*, 39. Matthieu de Lesseps (1774-1832), so only two years older than Drovetti. He had had a remarkably precocious career, serving in his early 20s as Consul in Morocco, Tripoli and Spain before Egypt. Following the last, he served in Livorno (1806), the Ionian Islands (1808-1815), Philadelphia (1819), Syria (1821) and Tunis (1827). He was, of course, the father of the engineer of the Suez canal.
13. In a later letter, Napoleon made it perfectly clear that he meant that one must be circumspect in dealing with the Mamelukes, although they were to be told that he supported them, because the Turks might, with the Sultan's help, gain control: *ibid.* 76: Talleyrand to de Lesseps, 26 Sept., reporting the instructions of Napoleon.
14. *Corr. 1*, 47: Brune to Talleyrand, 9 Apr.
15. There is no article on Missett in the *DNB*.
16. Hester Stanhope, *Travels* (3 vols) 1846, 1.218; by 1811 he was crippled in both hands and feet: *Corr. 3*, 132: Saint-Marcel to MFA, 3 July, 1811.
17. FO 24.2.19, 69f.
18. Antonio Goddard to Sturmer, Austrian envoy at Constantinople: A Sammarco, *Il regno di Mohammed Ali nei documenti diplomatici italiani inediti*, 1.1930, 75.
19. E.W. Lane, *Notes and views in Egypt and Nubia made during the years 1825-1828* (BM Add. MS 34080) p.10f.
    I cannot forbear also recording the wicked remarks of Richard Burton later in the century:

    > Let others describe the once famous Capital of Egypt, this City of Misnomers, whose dry docks are ever wet, and whose marble fountain is eternally dry, whose 'Cleopatra's Needle' is neither a needle nor Cleopatra's; whose 'Pompey's Pillar' never had any earthly connection with Pompey; and whose Cleopatra's Baths are, according to veracious travellers, no baths at all.

    Pilgrimage to al-Madinah and Meccah (Memorial ed. 1893), 1.9-10.
20. *Corr. 1*, 50: de Lesseps to Brune, 9 June.
21. *Corr. 1*, 55: de Lesseps to Talleyrand, 9 July.
22. *Corr. 1*, 69: de Lesseps to Talleyrand, 20 Sept.
23. *Corr. 1*, 71: Brune to Talleyrand, 25 Sept.
24. *Corr. 1*, 79: Drovetti to Ali Pasha, 6 Oct.
25. *Corr. 1*, 89: de Lesseps to Talleyrand, 2 Nov.

26. *Corr. 1*, 81: Drovetti to de Lesseps, 23 Oct. On Vincenzo Taberna, the English intelligence agent, see FO 24/6/16.
27. *Corr. 1*, 82f: de Lesseps to Talleyrand, 24 Oct.
28. *Corr. 1*, 92: Drovetti to de Lesseps, 15 Nov.
29. *Corr. 1*, 97: Drovetti, Briggs, Goddard, Soler, Fantozzi, and Stavracchi, 20 Nov.
30. *Corr. 1*, 109: report of the consuls, 27 Nov.
31. *Corr. 1*, 107: Bonaparte to Talleyrand, 24 Nov.
32. *Corr. 1*, 120: Drovetti to Brune, 1 Dec.
33. *Corr. 1*, 122: Drovetti to Talleyrand, 2 Dec.
34. *Corr. 1*, 132: de Lesseps to Talleyrand, 17 Dec.
35. *Corr. 1*, 139: de Lesseps to Brune, 12 Jan. 1804.
36. *Corr. 1*, 141: de Lesseps to Drovetti, 21 Jan.
37. *Corr. 1*, 144f: de Lesseps to Talleyrand, 21 Jan.; January bulletin; de Lesseps to Drovetti, 27 Jan.
38. *Corr. 1*, 155: de Lesseps to Talleyrand, 7 Feb.
39. *Corr. 1*, 149: de Lesseps to Talleyrand, 25 Jan.
40. *Corr. 1*, 158: Drovetti to de Lesseps, 9 Feb.
41. It is another telling indication of how incompetent French communications were at this time that at the same time, the Ambassador in Constantinople, Brune, was still fussing over the Alexandrian crisis of Nov.-Dec. and the actions of Ali Pasha: *ibid.* 162: Brune to Talleyrand, 11 Feb. The last would not, in addition, receive the letter for weeks.
42. *Corr. 1*, 161: Drovetti to de Lesseps, 11 Feb.; 165: Drovetti to Brune, 18 Feb.
43. *Corr. 1*, 167: Drovetti to Brune, 20 Feb.
44. For misunderstandings concerning supposed English support for Elfi, see Ghorbal (n.11), 216f.
45. *Corr. 1*, 170: de Lesseps to Talleyrand, 23 Feb.
46. *Corr. 1*, 173: de Lesseps to Talleyrand, 23 Feb.
47. *Corr. 1*, 173: de Lesseps to Talleyrand, 25 Feb.
48. *Corr. 1*, 177: Drovetti to Talleyrand, 25 Feb.
49. *Corr. 1*, 183: Talleyrand to de Lesseps, 5 March.
50. *Corr. 1*, 184: Talleyrand to Drovetti, 9 March.
51. *Corr. 1*, 189: de Lesseps to Talleyrand, 16 March.
52. *Corr. 1*, 198: de Lesseps to Talleyrand, 9 Apr.; same, 10 Apr.
53. *Corr. 1*, 205: Brune to Napoleon, 18 Apr.
54. *Corr. 1*, 220: de Lesseps to Talleyrand, 23 May.
55. *Corr. 1*, 226: de Lesseps to Talleyrand, 29 June.
56. *Corr. 1*, 230: de Lesseps to Talleyrand, 14 July.
57. *Corr. 1*, 243: de Lesseps to Talleyrand, 12 Oct.
58. *Corr. 1*, 245: de Lesseps to Talleyrand, 10 Dec. Dodwell (n.2), 20 rightly compliments Drovetti's insight as an analyst in contrast to the 'tavern-keeping' Lesseps. This is a reference to de Lesseps' attempts to win over the Albanians by supplying them with liquor (WO 1.347: Missett to Hobart, 3 Sept. 1804).
    'Never was there a more ludicrous spectacle of ineffective busybodies than that presented by Major Missett and M. de Lesseps.' (Ghorbal [n.11], 207)
59. It will be convenient here to assemble the little known of Mme Drovetti (needless to say, the index of the *Epistolario* omits her completely).
    She and Drovetti were married obviously by 1807, and she remained in Alexandria during the English invasion. Drovetti knew that his own life could be saved only by desperate measures, but obviously trusted his wife's safety to English chivalry. Boutin expressed his regard for her in 1814 (*Ep.* 50), as did the comte de Forbin in 1819-1819 (108, 124).
    She was in France 1821-1822 (*Ep.* 179, 206) and again 1827-1830 (in Paris with Giorgio) (527, 565, 619), in Italy 1832 (632). Is she the Madame recorded by her son-

in-law as suffering from migraines in Egypt in 1833 (638)? She was back there with Giorgio in 1840 (681), and was interested in Giorgio's pension in 1841 (690). That same year she and he were in Malta, coming to Italy in summer (695). In December 1842 she was at Livorno (702).

The last notices of her are back in Egypt in 1846, where she was very busy in Alexandria with repairs and building and troubles with tenants; Pedemonte ascribed her health to her active life (716); she was probably in her 60s, a little older than Drovetti. She was still with her family in Alexandria in 1851, but suffering from leg trouble (728).

There seems, then, to have been in effect a separation between Drovetti and his wife, but no-one refers to any rancour, and everyone expects him to be interested in news of her. She seems to have devoted much of her time to her son Giorgio by him, but then returned to Egypt to her daughter's family and died there.

The indefatigable researches of Jean-Jacques Fiechter have discovered the separation notice of June 1804 in the archives (*La moisson des dieux*, 23) and her lack of sympathy with her husband's obsession with antiquities (153).

60. *Ep.* 13f: from Fr. Benzi, 26 Jan. 1805.
61. G. Douin (ed.), *Mohamed Aly, pacha du Caire 1805-1807*, 1926 (= *Corr. 2*) 7.
62. *Corr. 2*, 11: Drovetti to Talleyrand, 11 Apr.
63. *Corr. 2*, 14: Drovetti to Talleyrand, 23 Apr.; 16: Drovetti to Talleyrand, 28 Apr.
64. *Corr. 2*, 19: Drovetti to Talleyrand, 6 May.
65. *Corr. 2*, 23f: Drovetti to Parandier, 16 May.
66. *Corr. 2*, 29: Drovetti to Menghin, 23 May.
67. *Corr. 2*, 30: Drovetto to MFA, 23 May.
68. *Corr. 2*, 58: bulletin, 12 July.
69. *Corr. 2*, 62: Talleyrand to Drovetti, 22 July. Ghorbal (n.11) comments (p.229): 'Drovetti obeyed'. He had, to the contrary, been foreseeing the future since May, and soon acted accordingly.
70. *Corr. 2*, 67f: Drovetti to Talleyrand, 4 Aug.
71. *Corr. 2*, 71: 'Journal historique', 19 Aug.
72. *Corr. 2*, 75f: Drovetti to Talleyrand, 31 Aug.
73. *Corr. 2*, 82: Drovetti to Talleyrand, 16 Oct.
74. *Corr. 2*, 87: Drovetti to Talleyrand, 24 Dec.
75. At this time Missett analysed the Mamelukes as being in three parties: Mohammed Elfi, Osman Bardissi (two inveterate enemies) and Osman Hassan. The first was very pro-English, and consulted Missett continuously. Bardissi was very pro-French. Hassan was pro-English. Mehemet Ali was entirely under French influence, although Missett assured him that they were interested only in discord (FO 24.2.106: Misset to Mulgrave, Jan. 1806).
    It was here that Missett began his disastrous insinuations: if the British government 'judged it expedient to interfere by force of arms in the affairs of Egypt, a very small armament would be sufficient' (*ibid.*, 108).
76. *Corr. 2*, 91-105: February-June, 1806.
77. *Corr. 2*, 101: Talleyrand to Sebastiani, 21 June.
78. *Corr. 2*, 109: Drovetti to Talleyrand, 30 June. Dodwell's assertion (21) that Drovetti 'did not at this time desire the continuation of his (Mehemet Ali's) administration', is incomprehensible. Misset in Sept. noted Drovetti's open support for the Albanian, and the English disadvantage in being seen as the supporters of the Mamelukes (FO 24/2/129f). Missett actually negotiated with Mehemet Ali on behalf of Elfi (133f).
79. *Corr. 2*, 109f: Drovetti to Talleyrand, 1, 10, 15 July.
80. *Corr. 2*, 122: Talleyrand to Drovetti, 28 July.
81. *Corr. 2*, 129f: Drovetti to Talleyrand, 25 Aug.
82. D. Cameron, *Egypt in the nineteenth century*, 1898, 70, rightly credits Drovetti with playing a leading role in saving Mehemet Ali in this crisis.

83. Chateaubriand, *Itineraire de Paris à Jérusalem*, Paris, 1859, 2.122.
84. *Corr. 2*, 147: Dec. report.
85. *Corr. 2*, 151: Drovetti to Talleyrand, 2 Feb. 1807.
86. FO 24/2/108.
87. *Corr. 2*, 154f: Drovetti to Sebastiani, 25 March.
88. G. Douin and E. Fawtier-Jones, *L'Angleterre et L'Egypte*, 1928, using the War Office records.
89. *Ep*. 15: General Fraser to Drovetti, May 1807.
90. Fraser informed Windham, Minister of War, on 27 March that Drovetti had escaped from Alexandria and was urging Mehemet Ali to return from the south (Douin and Jones, 34f).
91. *Corr. 2*, 154f: the very important letter of Drovetti to Sebastiani, 25 March. See the letter recalling these events written two years later: *Ep*. 20, to Abbot Benzi, 16 Jan. 1809. To the Prussian traveller, Johannes Bramsen c. 1815, Drovetti gave assurance that 'owing to his intimacy with several of the beys up the Nile, he had been the cause of cutting off the supplies from the English army. He pretended that, had the army of that nation taken Rosetta before proceeding up the Nile, they would have obtained provisions, in spite of the beys.' (Bramsen, *Travels in Egypt, Syria and Cyprus*, 1820 (2nd ed.), 182).

    One of the most amazing documents is the letter of Ibrahim Bey to General Fraser, 2 April (Douin and Jones, 56), explaining that the beys could not leave their wives for fear that they would be violated by the Turks, and offering to meet the English in Cairo after they had captured Rosetta! On 14 July, Ibrahim wrote to Fraser saying that the beys were ready to attack Mehemet Ali, and were only awaiting the instructions of the English government, but that the Nile would rise in thirty days, and then their cavalry would be useless. Such were the straws on which Missett relied.
92. Douin and Jones, 26.
93. *Corr. 2*, 171: Drovetti to Sebastiani, 7 May.
94. As an example of the fundamental law of war that no-one knows what is happening, 24 days later Castlereagh, Minister of War, wrote to General Fox, stating that he had laid before the King the letters about the successful occupation of Alexandria, which had weakened the French operations in the Mediterranean and even Italy. 'The efforts of any hostile force that can be assembled by the Turks within the country cannot be very formidable to a British corps of 6,000 men, supported by a superior fleet.' (Douin and Jones, 105) This was weeks after the expedition had been reduced to a fiasco.
95. *The diary of Sir John Moore*, ed. Maurice (2 vols), 1904, 2.172-174.
96. J. Fortescue, *History of the British Army*, 6.24.
97. This is confirmed by an anonymous account of the whole expedition, first published in the *United Service Journal*, 1837-1838, reprinted by Douin and Jones 183f. The lives of four hundred prisoners were thus saved.
98. Douin and Jones, 74. Another English soldier who owed a debt to Drovetti was Lieut. Matheson of the 78th, whom he freed from slavery (*ibid*. 136).
99. *Ep*. 15, General Fraser to Drovetti. About eight years later, Drovetti showed this letter to the Prussian traveller Johannes Bramsen (*Travels*, 182).
100. Min. Affaires Etrangères, Personnel, 1.105.
101. Douin and Jones, 118: Hallowell to Thornbrough, 21 May.
102. Bramsen, *Travels*, 182.
103. *Corr. 2*, 180: Drovetti to Sebastiani, 27 May. And now in May the English discovered that, despite Missett's claims, there was 'no difficulty in securing abundant supplies of every kind' – so the whole rationale for the disastrous fragmentation of forces had been completely fraudulent (Douin and Jones, 118: Admiral Hallowell to Adm. Thornbrough, 21 May).
104. *Corr. 2*, 183: Drovetti to Sebastiani, 14 June.
105. Douin and Jones, 132, 147.

106. Petrucci, agent at Rosetta, had been badly treated by the Turks, thanks to Drovetti, and then imprisoned in Cairo (Douin and Jones, 136). He had no reason to like Drovetti. He won over Mehemet Ali by lending him 40,000 piastres during the troops' mutiny.

107. On 8 August, 1807, Champagny, duc de Cadore, replaced Talleyrand as Foreign Minister, a post he held until 16 April, 1811.

108. *Corr. 2*, 195f: Drovetti to Sebastiani, 19 August.

109. FO 24/3/10f. Petrucci served England brilliantly. It is not, then, very amusing to find him in April 1809, after seven years' service to England, begging for some reimbursement for his expenses and gratification for services: FO 24/3/72.
    For evidence of Drovetti's difficulties in obtaining information at this vital juncture, see *Ep.* 17f, from his agent Mengin, in September.

110. Cameron (n.82), 70.

111. *Corr. 2*, 205f: Drovetti to Sebastiani, 10, 20, 31 October.

112. *Mohamed Aly et Napoléon*, ed. Driault, 1925 (= *Corr. 3*), 9f: Drovetti to Talleyrand, 8 April 1808, although Talleyrand had been succeeded as Foreign Minister in August 1807!

113. *Corr. 3*, 17f: Saint-Marcel to Champagny, 10 July.

114. *Corr. 3*, 20: Drovetti to MFA, 10 August.

115. FO 24/3/59f.

116. *Corr. 3*, 31: Saint-Marcel to MFA, 15 March 1809.

117. *Corr. 3*, 35: Drovetti to MFA, 9 April (received 11 December, note).

118. *Corr. 3*, 37: Champagny to Drovetti, 17 April.

119. *Corr. 3*, 43f.

120. *Corr. 3*, 57f: Drovetti to Champagny, 12 March 1810.

121. FO 24/3/75f.

122. *Corr. 3*, 62: Champagny to Drovetti, 31 March.

123. *Corr. 3*, 65f: Drovetti to Champagny, 28 April.

124. *Corr. 3*, 69-83: Drovetti to Champagny, 19 May – 1 September.

125. *Corr. 3*, 85: Mehemet Ali to Drovetti.

126. *Corr. 3*, 93: Drovetti to Champagny, 28 November.

127. *Corr. 3*, 113: Drovetti to Champagny, 4 March, 1811. Dodwell, 36 suggests that Drovetti was at first not very upset over the massacre because the Mamelukes were friends of the English, but later realised that the English were delighted and then came to describe the punishment of the Mamelukes as inexcusable. Dodwell's reference to Driault (p.184) is, however, wrong.

128. Within a couple of months, Drovetti informed his minister that from what Mehemet Ali later said to him, the massacre had been instigated by the English, to punish the Mamelukes for not coming to their assistance during the invasion of 1807, and also to clear themselves of imputations that they were in league with the Mamelukes to overthrow the Pasha: *Corr. 3*, 122: Drovetti to MFA, 8 May.

129. *Corr. 3*, 116f: Drovetti to MFA, 27 March.

130. *Corr. 3*, 118f: Drovetti to MFA, 19 April. On 17 April, Champagny was replaced as Foreign Minister by Maret, duc de Bassano, who held office until November 1813.

131. Napoleon, *Correspondence*, 20.121. J. Goby published a further letter of Napoleon stressing that Boutin's journey was to be 'masked under every possible pretext'. ('Une lettre de Napoléon I relative au voyage en Orient du col. Boutin', *Cahiers d'hist. eg.* 2.1950, 329-332). See L. Berjaud, *Boutin, agent sécret de Napoléon*, 1950.

132. Auriant, 'Le voyage politique du colonel Boutin en Orient', *Revue bleue*, 6 Sept. 1924, 594-599, using Missett's papers (see FO 24/4/26f), Stanhope and Burckhardt, but very careless about dates. We may now add his many letters to Drovetti: *Ep.* 35f, August 1812, looking for communications between lakes Moeris and Mareotis and the sea; October 1812, and still in November, hopeful chatter about the Russian campaign; June 1813, the battle of Lutzen and the death of General Bessières, the reasons why Murat remained in Naples; July 1813, the battles of Bautzen and

Wurschem, the scandal of the Princess of Wales, the Austrian alliance, the Swedish position. All this time Boutin was in Cairo. *Ep.* 49f, January 1814, the Peninsular War; March, announcing his departure the next day, journeying overland, and concerned about plague in Syria. He was robbed by his servant and not well received by some consuls (*Ep.* 59). By July he was in Aleppo (*Ep.* 61), in the midst of rampant plague, commiserating with Drovetti on the fall of Napoleon; he planned to leave within a fortnight. This is the last letter in the *Epistolario*.

133. *Corr. 3*, 125: Drovetti to MFA, 5 June.

134. *Corr. 3*, 144: Saint-Marcel to Bassano, 1 Sept.

135. Leinon to Drovetti, 2 October 1811, published by Marro in *Boll. Ist. Zool. Torino* 2.1949/50, 560 (not in *Ep.*).

136. FO 24/4/3-25, 107.

137. *Corr. 3*, 153.

138. *Corr. 3*, 164: January bulletin, 1812. See below, chap. 6.
The episode of this frigate, the *Africa*, was of the greatest importance for Anglo-Egyptian relations. The ship was coppered and equipped as a British war sloop at government expense! This generosity of the English government 'entirely allayed the irritable feelings produced by the unsuccessful expedition against Egypt in 1807', and hence induced Mehemet Ali to supply both grain and horses for the English armies in the Napoleonic wars, and even to offer them Cleopatra's Needle! (FO 78/112/91f).

139. *Travels of Lady Hester Stanhope* (3 vols), 1.160.

140. *Corr. 3*, 176f: Drovetti to MFA, March-May.

141. *Corr. 3*, 178: April Bulletin.

142. *Corr. 3*, 184: May Bulletin. See also the letter of Burckhardt FO 24/4/63 on the Mamelukes.

143. *Corr. 3*, 190: July Bulletin.

144. *Corr. 3*, 195: Drovetti to Bassano, 18 August.

145. *Corr. 3*, 196f: September-October Bulletins.

146. *Corr. 3*, 203: Drovetti to MFA, 28 November; 208: Saint-Marcel to Bassano, 30 December.

147. Asselin de Cherville (1772-1822), Orientalist and Second Dragoman at the Cairo Consulate from 1806, then Vice-Consul and First Dragoman from 1816 until his death. His linguistic researches were financially supported by Drovetti in 1812 (Boutin and some Englishman also offered him assistance, which he declined, *Ep.* 33). He acquired one of the largest private libraries of Arabic, Persian and Turkish works, most of which went to the Bibliothèque Nationale. See *DBF* 3.1292.
In 1814 he wrote to the Minister of Foreign Affairs about his plans to analyse the origins of nations by studying comparative languages (*Ep.* 55), which Drovetti fully supported. He also was an ardent Bonapartist (*Ep.* 59f), and a very close confidant of Drovetti (*Ep.* 87, 172). It is obviously in connection with this linguistic study and acquisition of MSS that Didot in 1816 noted Asselin as a good Orientalist, and recorded that he and Drovetti were pestering the Patriarch of Alexandria to be allowed to see some MSS in his library (*Notes d'un voyage fait dans le Levant en 1816 et 1817*, ND, 187, 196).

148. *Ep.* 30, 32, 34, 36, 38.

149. The story of this only son is one of tragedy. It can be traced through the *Epistolario*, and may be summarised here. He was apparently in Paris in 1827, (studying?) where he was seen by Jomard and Rosetti (*Ep.* 517, 527), and in 1829 by Carlo Botta (612: Drovetti was anxious about his son's health). In 1832 he was in Florence, Siena and Livorno with Etienne Abro, when Drovetti was very angry with him; Abro assured the father that Giorgio would be worthy of him with more time and care: this at the age of 20 (632). He was in Alexandria 1833 (637), 1834 (644: known to Clot Bey), 1836: employed by his brother-in-law the Sardinian consul, Pedemonte, and when the latter lost his post, his father tried to find Giorgio another career (656). By 1841 he had returned to Egypt via Malta (690, 695), but there was talk of his being in Paris (697),

where he was certainly seen by Jomard in 1843 (709). Drovetti was paying him an allowance (683, 690). By this time, when Giorgio was about thirty, Drovetti became more concerned about him. The father's agent, Morpurgo in Livorno, shared his view 'about the state of health of this unfortunate young man', who now talked of going to Barcelona or Cadiz, purpose and means unknown (702). In 1851 he was travelling around in Upper Egypt (728). The full story of these last years while his father was still alive is told in one of the last letters his father wrote (see below, p.198)

His death at a young age, but after his father's demise, is mentioned in family tradition: he died of heart failure at the Torino Hotel, looked after by a faithful negro servant, the only witness of his death. Not even the family knew why had returned to Torino (Drovetti, *Rivista municipale* 1931, 57).

150. Drovetti's colleague, Saint-Marcel at Cairo, was also ready to retire, being more than sixty years of age and having given 35 years of service (*Corr. 3*, 228). There is a very noticeable decline in the amount of correspondence from 1813 in the published archives.

151. *Corr. 3*, 211: Drovetti to MFA, 18 January 1813.

152. *Corr. 3*, 212f: January, February Bulletins; Saint-Marcel to MFA, 20 March; March and May Bulletins.

153. *Corr. 3*, 212: February Bulletin.

154. *Corr. 3*, 219: Drovetti to MFA, 4 June.

155. See below, chap. 6. In September 1813 there arrived in Alexandria the English traveller James Silk Buckingham (1786-1855), who visited Thebes and also crossed the Red Sea. His *Autobiography*, 1855 makes much of his extensive diary and he boasted of being a confidant of Mehemet Ali. His care for accuracy is somewhat undermined by his only reference to Drovetti as the Piedmontese Consul (2.159): he thought that Asselin was the French Consul-General! On leaving Egypt in October 1814, he went east as far as India, where he was expelled by the East India Company, although later they had to pay him compensation.

156. *Corr. 3*, 233: Boutin to de Caux, 14 December.

157. *Ep.* 62, from Boutin, July, 1814.

158. Talleyrand succeeded Caulaincourt April 1814-1815, save for the Hundred Days, when Caulaincourt returned. The marquis de Caulaincourt was Foreign Minister November 1813 – April 1814.

159. *Corr. 3*, 249: MFA to Roussel, 25 September.

160. *Corr. 3*, 251f: Drovetti to Talleyrand, 14 January, 1815. This is almost the last letter from Drovetti's first period in office.

In September 1815 Talleyrand was succeeded as Foreign Minister by du Plessis, duc de Richelieu, who held office until December 1818.

161. *Ep.* 69, from Gandolfi, 16 Feb.

162. Turner, *Journal of a tour in the Levant*, 1820, 2.330, 517. William Turner (1792-1867) was on the staff of the British embassy at Constantinople, 1811-1816, then travelled in the East, before being envoy to Columbia, 1829-1830.

That considerable trouble occurred over the flag we know from Asselin de Cherville (*Ep.* 79, from him, 29 August). As Vice-Consul in Cairo, he had to request official permission from the Pasha to 'salute' the white flag. The Pasha, advised by Boghos, replied that that flag could not be recognised again without implying that the government had recognised another. The situation was an impasse which Asselin was unable to solve, and he left the handling of it to Drovetti.

163. Turner, *Journal* 2.312.

164. see below, chap. seven.

165. Turner, *Journal* 2.338f.

166. See the splendid biography by S. Mayes, *The great Belzoni*, 1959.

167. *Ep.* 76, from Belzoni, 2 August; 77: 14 August; 78: 25 August.

168. Giovanni Baffi (also known as Osmar Bey) was an Italian chemist who established a nitrate factory near Cairo and a very close friend of Drovetti. No article in *DBI*.

169. Belzoni, *Narrative of the operations and recent discoveries within the pyramids, temples, tombs and excavations in Egypt and Nubia* (3rd ed.), 1822, 1.13f. See also Missett's account, FO 24/6/33.

170. Thédénat-Duvent (1756-18??) made two collections of antiquities and wrote *L'Egypte sous Méhémed Ali*, 1822.

171. To the duc de Richelieu, 23 October 1819, in the Drovetti dossier.

Chapter III

1. *La formation de l'empire de Mohamed Aly de l'Arabie au Soudan 1814-1823*, ed. E. Driault, 1927 (= *Corr. 4*), 4: Thédénat-Duvent to Talleyrand, 30 Nov., 1815.

2. *Ep.* 89: from Rignon, 1 July, 1816.

3. see below, p. 250f.

4. *Corr. 4*, 18: Thédénat-Duvent to Richelieu, 14 April, 1816; Halls, *Life and correspondence of Henry Salt*, 1834, 1.451.

5. It carried off the Austrian Vice-Consul and his wife, *Corr. 4*, 27: Thédénat-Duvent to Richelieu, 28 June.

6. There are sixteen letters from Boghos to Drovetti in the *Epistolario*, 1814-1823, and two from Drovetti, 1825-1826.

7. *Ep.* 85: from Rignon, 19 November.

8. on whom, see below, p. 252f.

9. Frédéric Cailliaud (1787-1869), otherwise called Murad Effendi, mineralogist, who first visited Egypt in 1815-1819. He accompanied Drovetti to the Second Cataract, investigated the mines in the eastern desert, and went to Khargha Oasis. His second visit, 1819-1822, included a visit to Siwah just before Drovetti in 1819, then he accompanied Ishmael in the Sudanese war 1820-1822. He retired to his birth-place, Nimes, where he was curator of the Museum of Natural History.

10. *Ep.* 88: from Boghos, 13 May, 1816.

11. Marro, *Personalità*, 44; *Aegyptus* 32.1952, 126. This claim was probably taken from Carlo Vidua, *Lettere* (3 vols), 1834, 2.190, who seems to have had it from Drovetti himself. Vidua was followed by G. Farina, *Bernardino Drovetti archeologo*, 1921, 20.

12. Irby and Mangles, *Travels in Egypt, Nubia, Syria and Asia Minor in 1817 and 1818*, 1844, 5; L. Christophe, *Abu Simbel*, 1970, 15f.

13. Irby and Mangles, 10; also Belzoni, *Narrative of the operations* (3rd ed.), 1822, 1.132.

14. Cailliaud, *Voyage à Méroe en Nubie* (4 vols), 1823-1827, 1.316f (with notes). The entry on Cailliaud, *DBF* 7.863 by Prevost has him now going only to the First Cataract, not the Second, and then duplicates his visit to Abu Simbel under 1818 and refers to his unsuccessful attempts to open the temple – when it was with Drovetti. This article is almost as careless as that on Drovetti.

15. Christine Desroches-Noblecourt and C. Kuentz, *Le petit temple d'Abou Simbel*, 1968, 2.pls 59 and 91; Christophe, *Abu Simbel*, 278.

16. M. Dewachter, 'Graffiti des voyageurs du XIX s. relevés dans le temple d'Amada en Basse-Nubie', *BIFAO* 69.1971, 131-169, at 141f, with pl.23.

17. *ibid.*

18. A. Blackman, *The temple of Dendur*, 1911, p.52b.

19. H. Gauthier, *Le temple de Kalabchah*, 1911-1927, 2.pl.28A.

20. This is the first mention of Drovetti in Belzoni's *Narrative*: 1. 46.

21. *ibid.*, 1.67.

22. *ibid.*, 1.85.

23. *ibid.*, 1.173, 196.

24. *Corr. 4*, 31: Roussel to Richelieu, 1 September; 38: 7 December.

25. *Corr. 4*, xxiv; Belzoni, *Narrative* 1.201.

26. See his *Voyage à l'oasis de Thèbes et dans les déserts*, 1821. In the letter which he wrote to Drovetti when he left Egypt at the end of 1818, Cailliaud stated that he owed Drovetti

all the benefits which he had received in the country, *Ep.* 119: from Cailliaud, 3 January, 1819.

27. *Ep.* 94f, from Cailliaud, 22 January, 1817.
28. Nagel, *Egypte*, 1969, 647.
29. *Corr. 4*, 49: Roussel to Richelieu, 24 February. Belzoni, *Narrative* 1.213f.
30. *Corr. 4*, 51: Roussel to Richelieu, 1 March.
31. see below pp. 233.
32. *Ep.* 93, from Boghos, 9 December, 1816, and from Luzzi, 18 January, 1817.
33. *Ep.* 96, from Vaissière, 10 February.
34. Belzoni, *Narrative* 1.223f.
35. *ibid.* 1.229f.
36. *ibid.* 1.239f, 308.
37. An obituary of him by Burckhardt was published in England.
38. *Corr. 4*, 22: Roussel to Richelieu, 22 July.
39. Cailliaud, *Voyage à l'oasis de Thèbes*, 68.
40. Irby and Mangles, *Travels in Egypt*, 44.
41. Belzoni, *Narrative* 1.320f, 357f.
42. Nagel, *Egypte*, 515f.
43. *Corr. 4*, 85: Roussel to Richelieu, 13 October.
44. R. Richardson, *Travels along the Mediterranean 1816-1818* (2 vols), 1822, 1.307f; cf. Belzoni, *Narrative* 1.357f. Robert Richardson (1779-1847), a Scottish doctor, who in this capacity travelled with the Earl of Belmore and Viscount Mountjoy in Egypt and the Holy Land.
45. J. Halls, *Life and correspondence of Henry Salt*, 1834, 2.308.
46. see below, p. 81.
47. Belzoni, *Narrative* 1.343.
48. Giovanni d'Athanasi, *A brief account of the researches and discoveries in Upper Egypt*, 1836, 58. d'Athanasi, born 1799, servant of Salt, for whom he excavated at Thebes, was known to all travellers in Egypt from c.1817 to c.1835.
49. P. Coste, *Mémoires d'un artiste*, 1878, 1.35.
50. *Ep.* 98-100, from Forbin, 27 December, 1817, 6 and 11 January, 1818; 102: 22 January; 123: 1 March; 129: 25 May.
51. Comte de Forbin, *Travels in Egypt in 1817 and 1818*, 1819, 23f.
52. see above. His account is preserved in *Corr. 4*, 129f.
53. *Ep.* 104, 109f, from A. Gentili, 10 July, 24 September.
54. *Ep.* 118, from Scotti, 1818.
55. *Ep.* 107, from Corancez, 30 July.
56. *Ep.* 122, from Dubois Ayme, 15 February, 1819.
57. *Ep.* 138, from Dubois Ayme, 15 October; 143, 15 April, 1820.
58. Cailliaud, *Voyage à l'oasis de Thèbes*, 1821, 82.
59. Forbin, *Travels*, 46.
60. Cailliaud, *Voyage à l'oasis de Thèbes*, 56. Many French also remained and joined the Mamelukes in Cairo and then served Mehemet Ali. By Cailliaud's time, 1816, they numbered only forty out of an original 400, under Selim of Avignon!
61. J.J. Fiechter, *La moisson des dieux*, 40f.
62. Champollion, *Lettres* 2.466.
63. Cailliaud, *Voyage à l'oasis de Thèbes*, 83. Richardson also records that 'an active young Frenchman, Mr Riphaud (sic), was then engaged in making excavations, so as to form plans of the temples for Mr Drovetti, the ci-devant French consul at Cairo, and his labours have been crowned by many interesting discoveries.' (*Travels* 2.92) Fiechter has put the flesh on these bones (94f): Rifaud discovered the temple of Mut, four great statues of Sekhmet, the granite relief of Rameses II between Amon and Mut, the canopic statue of the scribe Bakenkonsu, the two statues of Seti II from his temple at Karnak, finds mostly now in Torino.
64. Vidua, *Lettere* 2.176, not noticed by *WWWE* 3rd ed. 241. Belzoni's description of him

and Rosignani is most valuable (*Narrative* 1.343). Lebolo 'had left Piedmont after the fall of the late government', i.e. 1815.

Rosignani was 'the renegade who had deserted from the French army when in Egypt and entered the service of the Bashaw'.

65. Firman Didot, *Notes d'un voyage fait dans le Levant en 1816 et 1817*, ND. 187. Didot (1790-1876), the publisher, visited the Delta in 1816.

66. Irby and Mangles, *Travels in Egypt*, 44.

67. Belzoni, *Narrative*, 2.11-12.

68. G. Parthey, *Wanderungen durch Sicilien und die Levant* 1833-1840, 2.542. On Parthey (1798-1872), see below p. 119.

The division of Thebes between Drovetti and Salt is noted by one of the most rakish adventurers in Egypt at this time, Giovanni Finati. Born in Ferrara, he was conscripted by the French, deserted in the Tyrol, crossed to Dalmatia, deserted again, fled to Albania, converted to Islam, fled to Egypt in 1809, where he killed a fellow soldier, and took part in the Wahabite war: *Narrative of the life and adventures of G. Finati*, ed. W. Bankes, 1830. In 1815, he accompanied Wm. Bankes to Upper Egypt and the Second Cataract (2.72f), was with Belzoni, Irby and Mangles at Abu Simbel in 1817 (2.191f); accompanied Bennet and Fuller to Nubia; and in 1818 helped Belzoni, Bankes, Ricci and Linant remove the Philae obelisk (2.201f). In 1819 he returned to Abu Simbel with Henniker (2.348f) and two years later accompanied Linant and Ricci to Meroe (2.354f). It is strange, then, that in all this detail he mentions Drovetti only twice: the situation at Thebes (2.212-213) and the question of the obelisk (304).

69. *Ep.* 210, from Rifaud, 14 June, 1822.

70. *Ep.* 112-115, from Belzoni, 29, 30, 31 October, 2 November, 1818.

71. Belzoni, *Narrative* 2.100.

72. *ibid.* 2.102.

73. *ibid.* 2.106, 110-126. By a strange error, at first sight very damaging to Belzoni's case, the particular way of writing the month in French, 9bre, has been misunderstood and written out as September instead of November! This implies that Lebolo had been at Philae months before the conversation with Drovetti. S. Mayes, *The great Belzoni*, 1959, 228, has nothing to add on Drovetti's behaviour beyond Belzoni's insinuations.

It was the inscription of Cleopatra on this obelisk which was to give Champollion his vital clue in the decipherment of hieroglyphs, by comparing the transliteration of Ptolemy on the Rosetta Stone. Bankes kindly sent copies of it around Europe.

74. E. Montulé, *Travels in Egypt during 1818 and 1819*, 1821, 26. Montulé defeats J. Carré, *Voyageurs et écrivains français en Égypte* (2 vols), 1932, who knows nothing of him.

75. F. Gau, *Antiquités de la Nubie*, 1822, 5.

76. *Ep.* 115, from Gau, November-December, 1818; 144f: 10 May, 1820, further expressions of gratitude, notably the intention to put Drovetti's portrait at the front of the work 149: 19 August. Note also the enormous problems in getting the work published, settled in 1820: 166, 10 December.

77. Belzoni, *Narrative* 2.126-135.

78. E. Montulé, *Travels* 100f.

79. Halls, *Life and correspondence of Henry Salt*, 2.115.

80. *ibid.* 2.21; Belzoni, *Narrative* 2.235f.

81. J.J. Fiechter, *La moisson des dieux*, 148f.

82. *Ep.* 120, Drovetti to Huyot (?), 11 January, 1819.

83. This journal is preserved in the British Library: Add.MSS 42, 102. Very little is known of Hyde's life. After reaching the Second Cataract he went across Asia to India, where he died in 1825.

84. Hyde, 39, 55, 56.

85. *ibid.* 63 (Rifaud was born 1786, so he was in his early 30s), 216, 229, 234.

86. *Corr.* 4, 149: Thédénat-Duvent to Dessolle, 22 February. On 28 December, 1818, marquis de Dessolle replaced duc de Richelieu as Minister of Foreign Affairs, and remained in office until 17 November, 1819.

87. *WWWE* 3rd ed. 79 corrects the errors of the second edition.
88. Jomard (ed.), *Voyage à l'oasis de Thèbes*, 53; Marro, *Personalità* 45 makes no such claims, being more interested in the MS copy of Drovetti's journal, preserved among his papers.
89. A. Edmonstone, *Journey to two of the oases of Upper Egypt*, 1822, 59, 148. Sir Archibald Edmonstone (1795-1871), of whom nothing more is known.
90. H. Winlock, *El Dakhleh oasis*, 1936, 4, declared that Drovetti's journal was a very good guide to Dakhla, except for some confusion in the points of the compass, 'which, I suspect, is due to Jomard's transcription of Drovetti's manuscript.'
91. *Corr. 4*, 137: Roussel to Dessolle, 15 February, 1819.
92. Winlock, 4.
93. Winlock considered Drovetti's deception over the date as deliberate, 'which surely was the impression of some who knew him' (*ibid.*). The end of 1818 was still given by Farina, *Bernardino Drovetti, archeologo*, 1921, 20, who did not make any statement about this being the first visit, but who also praised, inexplicably, the notes on the places and inhabitants and their customs – unless he mistook Cailliaud's account for Drovetti's (the footnote, however, refers correctly to chap. 3 of the book). Edmonstone was fiercely upheld by J.G. Wilkinson, *Modern Egypt and Thebes*, 1843, 2.362.
    Travellers in the nineteenth century after Edmonstone and Drovetti included John Hyde (unpublished) in December 1819, Cailliaud in February 1820 (*Voyage à Méroe*, 1826), Wilkinson, 1824 (*Modern Egypt and Thebes*, 1843), Gerhard Rohlfs, 1874 (*Drei Monate in der libyschen Wüste*, 1875), Henry Lyons 1893/4 (*Quarterly Journal of Geological Soc. of London* 50.1894, 531-549) and Hugh Beadnell, 1898 (*An Egyptian oasis*, 1909).
94. E. Montulé, *Travels*, 55.
95. *Ep.* 125, from Spagnoli, March.
96. *Ep.* 139, from Dubois Ayme, 15 October.
97. *Corr. 4*, 155: Thédénat-Duvent to Dessolle, 30 May.
98. *Ep.* 126, Drovetti to the barone di Barbania, 23 April.
99. On his previous travels, see above, n.9.
100. *Ep.* 134-135, from Jomard, 29 July; 140, from Cailliaud, 10 November.
101. *Ep.* 139, from Dubois Ayme, 15 October. Vidua, *Lettere* 2.209 reports that Mehemet Ali was very impressed. Marro, *Personalità*, 65 for some reason dates the award to 1820.
102. *Corr. 4*, 159f: Pillavoine to Dessolle, 19 July.
103. *Corr. 4*, 165f: Pillavoine to Dessolle, 14 August.
104. *Corr. 4*, 170f: Pillavoine to MFA, 7 September. Louis' anniversary cannot be his birthday (17 November), and his accession seems inappropriate (8 July, 1795).
105. *Corr. 4*, 178f: Pillavoine to Dessolle, 23 October.
106. Count Marcellus, *Souvenirs de l'Orient*, 1839, 2.176f. The wicked Fiechter announces that this whole story was an invention of Pillavoine. Mrs Salt came from the Livornese family of the Santoni, and her brother, a banker, was already known to Salt (*La moisson des dieux*, 160).
107. Halls, *Life and correspondence of Henry Salt*, 2.225f.
108. *Corr. 4*, 185: Pillavoine to MFA, 17 January 1820. The duc de Pasquier succeeded the marquis de Dessolle in November 1819 and held office until December 1821.
    It is interesting that Belzoni in a letter to Peter Lee, English Consul at Alexandria, in December 1820 (Hay, BM Add.MS 25,658, f.1f) also mentions a son-in-law of Drovetti, called Balctolon (sic), who claimed to have thrown someone into the Nile at Girgeh. The solution to the reference is that 'beau-fils' in French means both son- in-law and stepson.
109. W.E. Browne, *Travels in Africa, Egypt and Syria*, 1799; F. Hornemann, *Journal of Frederick Hornemann's travels from Cairo to Mourzouk*, 1802.
110. His journey, along with that of Drovetti, from their respective notes, was published by Jomard, *Voyage à l'oasis de Syouah*, 1823. *DBF* 11.837 ascribes the publication to Drovetti himself. The publication of Drovetti's account, in which he wished to use the illustrations by Linant, caused some disquiet to Cailliaud ('this work is absolutely the

duplicate of what I have obtained'), although he admitted that Drovetti's route was quite different from his own and that therefore everyone would be interested, and supported the idea that Drovetti's notes and drawings should be published, together with Cailliaud's own notes by Jomard, rather than by a bookseller who knew nothing about Egypt (*Ep.* 158f, from Cailliaud, 9 October). Drovetti wrote an account to, amongst others, Gau (*Ep.* 165, from Gau, 10 December).

111. Belzoni, *Narrative*, 2.168f.

112. Louis Linant de Bellefonds (1799-1883): after beginning a career in the navy, he accompanied Forbin to the East in 1818-1819, went with Drovetti to Siwah, then with Bankes to Dongola, the first of many journeys south. He became Minister of Public Works in 1869.

Allessandro Ricci (d. 1832), an Italian doctor from Siena, employed by Bankes and Belzoni as a draftsman, member of the Salt-Bankes expedition to Abu Simbel, 1818-1819; with Drovetti to Siwah, 1820; with Linant to Sinai, 1820; with Minutoli to Upper Egypt, 1820-1821; with Ibrahim to the Sudan, 1821; with Champollion and Rosellini, 1828-1829.

Enegildo Frediani (1783-1823), a pharmacist with the Neapolitan army c. 1806- 1814, attaining the rank of captain; in Rome, where he met Canova, before coming to Egypt 1817. He accompanied Belmore and Richardson to the Second Cataract, was with Belzoni at the opening of the Second Pyramid (March, 1818), and after a year in Asia, joined the Siwah expedition. His account of this so pleased Mehemet Ali that he was sent with Ishmael to the Sudan, 1820, where he went insane. He was brought back to Cairo by Ricci, where he died. G. Waddington, *Journal of a visit to some parts of Ethiopia*, 1822, 89, claimed that Drovetti had Frediani appointed tutor to Ishmael.

Frediani stated that Linant and Ricci joined the expedition on the insistence of Henry Salt. Carlo Vidua *(Lettere* 2.194f) avowed that had he not been in Nubia, he also would have joined.

113. Nagel, *Egypte*, 701-702. That mystique lasted well into the twentieth century. The first visit by a member of the Antiquities Service was by James Quibell in 1917 ('A visit to Siwa', *Ann.Serv.* 18.1919, 78-112).

114. Published by A. Wolynski, 'Il viaggiatore E. Frediani', *Boll. soc. geog. ital.* 1891, 90-125, 295-324, 397-406.

115. Cailliaud, *Voyage à Méroé* 1.246f, 251, 289. Cailliaud says that Drovetti returned to Cairo on 2 April. This must be a mistake. They left the Nile on 2 March, arriving at Siwah a fortnight later, but did not enter the town until the 29th. Extensive exploration and then two weeks' return journey will not fit into four days! Drovetti was able, however, to present Cailliaud to Mehemet Ali before the latter set out again on 22 April.

116. 'Un cimelio del viaggio di B. Drovetti all'oasi di Giove Ammone', *Bull. Soc. roy. de Geog. Cairo* 191.1934, 1-20.

117. Cailliaud, *Voyage à Méroé* 1.409-418; and compare that with the running texts provided by Quibell (n.113), 97f.

118. See L. Greener, *The discovery of Egypt*, 1966, 82f.

119. *Corr. 4*, 195: Pillavoine to Pasquier, 6 May.

120. see above, p. 91.

121. *Corr. 4*, 201: Pillavoine to MFA, 29 July.

122. Thédénat-Duvent had his revenge. Among other things in his *L'Egypte sous Méhémed Ali*, 1822, 99, he claimed that, whereas in 1816 90 out of 100 ships at Alexandria were French, now only ten were, and he blamed Pillavoine for this collapse of French trade.

123. Vidua, *Lettere* 2.162, to his father Count Pio Vidua, 20 January, 1820. Carlo Vidua (1785-1830) travelled as far as the Second Cataract, December 1819-August 1820. He was later to be instrumental in acquiring Drovetti's first collection for Piedmont (see chap. 7).

124. See also M. Dewachter, 'Le voyage nubien du comte Carlo Vidua', *BIFAO* 69.1970, 171-187.

125. Vidua, *Lettere* 2.194f.
126. *ibid.* 2.211, 200.
127. *ibid.* 2.333, to the Countess Incisa di S. Stefano.
128. Marcellus, *Souvenirs de l'Orient*, 1839, 2.167f, 192f.
129. *ibid.* 2.167.
130. Baron Heinrich Minutoli (1772-1846) and his wife Baroness Wolfradine (dates not given, naturally!). The baroness published her *Souvenirs d'Egypte*, 1826, which were translated into English the following year. See pp. 3, 14.
131. Yet another name butchered in the *Epistolario*: Bacciuti (174), Brucciarti (204).
132. Baron Minutoli, *Reise zum Tempel des Jupiter Ammon*, 1824, 7f.
133. *ibid.* 244; 248: no part of the temple complex of Hathor at Dendereh seems to accord with this detail; 280 (Apollinopolis); 300 (Athribis); 268 (papyri).
    The baroness also mentions Father Ladislaus superintending excavations at Abydos (113) and Drovetti's discovery of the avenue of sphinxes at Edfu but she notes that this was after the Minutolis' visit (153).
134. St John, *Egypt and Mohammed Ali*, 1834, 1.297.
135. Minutoli, 295f. Cf. J.-P. Lauer, *Saqqara*, 1976, 11. Firth, Quibell and Lauer, *The Step Pyramid*, 1935, 1.4, mention Minutoli's visit, but nothing more. R. Vyse and Perring, *Operations carried out at the pyramids of Gizeh* (3 vols), 1840-1842, 3.41f cite Minutoli's opening and his finding of a sarcophagus.
136. Minutoli, 299, 307. This is presumably the journey to Syria mentioned by Luigi Gandolfi in August 1821 (*Ep.* 173).
137. *Ep.* 156f, from Wilhelm of Wurtemburg, 30 September, 1820; 170 from his Foreign Minister, 11 April, 1821; 159, from Baron de Barbania, 6 November, 1820.
138. *Ep.* 160, from Prospero Balbo, 6 November.
139. L. Cibrario, *Descrizione storica degli ordini cavallereschi*, 1846, 1.17f.
140. Documents in the archives of the Order in Torino.
141. G. Douin, 'Le conquète du Soudan', *Revue du Caire* Sept. 1944, 413-442.
142. Cailliaud, *Voyage à Méroé*, 3.51. Dodwell, *The founder of modern Egypt*, 1931, 52, notes that Mehemet Ali tried to moderate his son's cruelty, while at the same time demanding more slaves: 'It is difficult simultaneously to conciliate and to enslave a population...'
143. *Ep.* 150, from Drs Rossignoli, G. Gentili, and Brunetti, 6 September, 1820.
144. A Greek Armenian, grandson or nephew of Giovanni Bozari, the doctor of Mehemet Ali. After poisoning his rivals, he had all the medicines thrown in the Nile when he was unable to do anything for the troops in the rainy season, and then tried to get rid of Ricci when he was curing Ishmail of dysentery. At the end of the expedition, he was impaled for his cruelties.
145. Cailliaud, *Voyage à Méroé*, chap. 24. G. Marro, 'Un drammatico episodio della spedizione al Sennar', *Atti Accad. Torino* 67.1931-2, 263-287, is devoted to an analysis of these letters in their historical context. He carefully distinguishes the chemist G.A. Gentili from the surgeon Andrea Gentili, who accompanied Ibrahim to Arabia and lost a foot. The index to the *Epistolario* obliterates the distinction.
146. V. Denon included a large plate of it in his *Travels* (pl. 59); also *Description de l'Egypte*, 4 pl.21.
147. L. Greener, *The discovery of Egypt*, 130, claims that Drovetti had just been reappointed. His account of the plundering of the temple reads more like an act of heroism than vandalism.
148. Coste, *Memoires* 1878, 35.
149. P. Saulnier, *Notice sur le voyage de M. Lelorrain en Egypte*, 1822, Eng. trans. 78- 79.
150. *Ep.* 304, from Artaud, May 1824.
151. Reprinted in Champollion, *Lettres* 2.154f.
152. *Ep.* 190, from Jomard, 2 January, 1822.
153. Drovetti dossier, Ministry of Foreign Affairs, Paris. It would be appropriate here to list the expenses of the consulate, information not found in the French records as published but vouchsafed by Salt, who must have got it from Drovetti (FO

78/135/155). It relates to 1825, when Drovetti's salary had been slightly increased:

consul's salary	24,000 francs
extraordinary expenses	3,000
chancellor	5,000
chief interpretor	4,800
second "	2,500
assistant "	1,300
hospital contribution	210
four janissaries	1,920
flags	500
correspondence and visits	800
	44,030 francs

Salt estimated a properly run and financed English equivalent would cost about £20,000 (about the same sum).

154. *Ep.* 172, from Gandolfi, 25 August, 1821; 176, from Halgan, 7 September; 181, from Auban, 3 December; 182, from Allery, 1821; 185, from David, 3 January, 1822.
155. *Ep.* 172, from Asselin de Cherville, 31 July, 1821. Asselin was to die by early 1823 (*Ep.* 244).
156. *Ep.* 129, From Forbin, 25 May, 1819.
157. *Ep.* 134, from Jomard, 29 July.
158. Drovetti dossier, Ministry of Foreign Affairs, Paris: declaration of Allary, 16 August, 1819.
159. *ibid.*: Roussel to the comte d'Hauterive, 24 November, 1820.
160. Thédénat-Duvent, *L'Egypte sous Méhémed Ali*, 1822, 99.
161. Drovetti dossier, Ministry of Foreign Affairs, Paris: from Cailliaud to Minister of the Interior, 'analysé 4 March'.
162. See above, p. 111.
163. See pp. 107, 207.
164. This adds particular poignancy to Italian claims such as by Donadoni that Drovetti 'nonostante avesse sempre conservato la nazionalità piedmontese' (*Il museo egizio di Torino*, 17).

Chapter Four

1. G. Guémard, *Les réformes en Egypte*, 1936, 108, justly describes Pillavoine as 'sottement jaloux' of Drovetti, making 'ridiculous accusations', and receiving the deserved response – the order to hand the consulate back to Drovetti.
2. *Corr.4*, 223: Drovetti to Pasquier, 17 August, 1821.
3. J. Halls, *Life and correspondence of Henry Salt*, 1834, 2.194. Further notes are provided about the same time by Giovanni Battista Brocchi, *Giornale* 1.91-92. The consuls were judges of all maritime, civil and criminal matters of individuals subject to the sovereigns they represented. In civil judgements, appeal in the case of the French could be made to the tribunal at Aix, against both the Consul and Vice-Consul. The two diplomats could employ 'assessors' from the most respected merchants in more serious cases. In criminal cases, they could impose fines up to 100 francs or prison of up to one month; otherwise the case went to France. In sum, Europeans had much greater freedom in Egypt than in Europe.
4. *Dictionary of national biography* 9.135.
5. Nagel, *Égypte*, 1969, 497.
6. J. Carne, *Letters from the East*, 1826, 130f. The letters were first published in the *New monthly magazine*, 1824.
7. R. Pococke, *Description of the East*, 1743, 1.95; *Description de l'Egypte*, vol.3, pl.18. There is no help in any of the following on the history of the obelisks: Bertha Porter and Rosalind Moss, *Topographical bibliography*, 1927-1952, 2.27-29; W. Budge, *Cleopatra's Needle and other Egyptian obelisks*, 1926, 98f; Baedeker, *Egypt*, 1929, 288; Nagel, *Égypte*,

1969, 489, 495; *Lexikon der Aegyptologie*, 1975-1985, 4.542-547 (Spycher); Virginia Seton-Williams, *Egypt*, 1983, 516; W. Murnane, *Penguin guide to ancient Egypt*, 1983, 230.

8. *Ep.* 176, from Halgan, 6 September.

9. Salt supported the idea that the English should supply the frigates, seeing that the French otherwise would get the contract, 'Drovetti knowing well how to make the most of such a business': Halls (n.3), 2.189, from FO 78/103/236. The English government replied to Salt in January 1822 that it would not supply the frigates, because it would be a breach of neutrality (78/112/13).

10. *Corr.4*, 225f: August and September bulletins.

11. *Ep.* 184, from Hemprich, without date; 191f, 20 February 1822; 203f, 20 May. Fr. Wm. Hemprich (1796-1825), doctor and geologist. He accompanied Minutoli to Egypt, along with his friend Christian Ehrenberg. The two then made their own tour of Egypt, Nubia, Sinai, Lebanon and the Red Sea coasts. Hemprich died of malaria at Massaua, after making enormous collections of minerals, plants and animals (34,000 of the last alone!). W. Hemprich and C. Ehrenberg, *Reisen in Aegypten, Libyen, Nubien und Dongola*, 1828.
    In the absence of the Prussian Consul, Hemprich and Ehrenberg were also recommended to Henry Salt (FO 78/103/213).

12. G. Marro, 'Louis Alexis Jumel et Bernadino Drovetti', BIE 31.1949, 279-295: another letter not in the *Epistolario*!

13. R. Cattaui, *Le règne de Mohamed Aly d'après les archives russes en Egypte*, 1931, x. See also *Ep.* 282, from Daschwoff, January 1824.

14. Pasquier was replaced as Foreign Minister in December 1821 by the duc de Montmorency, who remained until Chateaubriand's second term in 1823.

15. *Corr.4*, 234-247.

16. *Corr.4*, 248: Drovetti to Montmorency, 6 June.

17. *Ep.* 214, from David, 9 July.

18. They were freed in August by Commodore Hamilton, *Ep.* 227.

19. *Ep.* 216f, from David, 23 July.

20. *Ep.* 227, from David, 9 September.

21. Marro, *Personalità*, 64. Felix Lajard (1783-1858), famous for his theories on the eastern connections of Greek culture, and for his writings on Mithraism.

22. Marro, 38: the letters do not appear in the *Epistolario*.

23. *Ep.* 219f, from Lajard, 25 July.

24. *Ep.* 245f, from Delile (14 February 1823). Alire Raffencau-Delile (1778-1850), botanist, member of the Egyptian expedition, professor of botany at Montpellier 1818-1850. He compiled the flora of Egypt in the *Description*.
    Georges Cuvier (1769-1832), professor of natural history at the Central Schools, 1795; Permanent Secretary of the Academy of Physical Sciences, 1803; professor at the Collège de France, 1800; Chancellor of the University, 1821-1827; member of the Académie Française, 1818; the founder of comparative anatomy and a leading palaeontologist. He had declined to go to Egypt in 1798.

25. *Ep.* 225f, from Cailliaud, 15 August.

26. See the report FO 78/119/55.

27. Cailliaud, *Voyage à Méroe*, 3.225-226.

28. *Ep.* 228, from Bastiani, 10 September.

29. *Ep.* 246, from Lajard, February 1823. There is no evidence that Drovetti ever learned any hieroglyphs.

30. Gustav Parthey (1798-1872), *Wanderungen durch Sicilien und die Levant*, 1833-1840, 2.47f.

31. One of the most interesting visitors to Egypt at this time was James Burton, otherwise known as Haliburton (1788-1862). He visited Egypt twice: 1822-1828, and 1830-1835, and travelled over the whole country, being noted especially as a surveyor of the eastern deserts. He was known to John Gardiner Wilkinson, travelled with Edward Lane, made drawings for Robert Hay, and was a friend of Joseph Bonomi. His copious manuscripts are preserved in the British Library (Add MS 25,613-25,675) and are a

treasure-house of information on antiquities, geography, modern customs etc, as well as containing innumerable drawings. He mentions most of the earlier travellers, being very critical of St. John, 'who differs in his conclusions from other travellers (to make a book)' and knew Anastasi's agent, Piccini, but paradoxically does not seem to have mentioned Drovetti.

32. *Ep.* 242, from English, 10 January, 1823. See the *Dictionary of American biography*, 3.165.

33. John Moyle Sherer, *Scenes and impressions in Egypt and Italy*, 1824, 111. On Rifaud, see 88f.

34. *Ep.* 188, from de Rigny, January 1823, misdated by the editors to 1822. Henri Gauthier de Rigny (1782-1835) had his first command in 1803, then took part in many of Napoleon's land campaigns; commander of the Levant navy 1822-1830, rear-admiral 1825; commander of the French fleet at Navarino; Minister of the Navy, 1831, of Foreign Affairs, 1834-1835.

35. *Ep.* 249, from David, 20 March.

36. *Ep.* 252f, from Ladislao, 15 June.

37. *Corr.4*, 287: Drovetti to Chateaubriand, 20 July.

38. *Ep.* 260, from Brocchi, 7 August.

39. *Ep.* 262f, from Pacho, 16 August. Jean Pacho (1794-1829), artist and botanist, visited Egypt 1818, 1822-1825, when he explored Lower Egypt and Cyrenaica. Drovetti and Salt gave him letters of recommendation. He committed suicide in a fit of melancholy. See his *Relation d'un voyage dans la Marmarique*, with 'Notice sur la vie et les oeuvrages de M. Pacho.'

40. *Moniteur universel* 29 August, 1823; *Ep.* 264, from Jomard, 23 August; 266, from Forbin, 30 August.

41. *Ep.* 451, from Jomard (January 1826). For the complete story of the editing and publication, see C. Gillespie and M. Dewachter, *The monuments of Egypt*, 1987, 23ff.

42. *Ep.* 270, from Osman, 29 October.

43. H. Westcar, *Diary* (copy in British Library, Manuscripts), 46.

44. See below, chap.6.

45. *Ep.* 273, from Bastiani, 21 December.

46. *Corr.4*, 299: Drovetti to Chateaubriand, 9 February, 1824.

47. See below, chap.7.

48. *Il primo secolo delle R. Accademie delle Scienze di Torino*, 1783-1883, 1883, 225.

49. *Ep.* 283, from Rifaud, 28 January, 1824.

50. *Ep.* 331, from Rifaud, 7 October.

51. W. Murnane, *The Penguin guide to ancient Egypt*, 1983, 183.

52. Petrie, *Seventy years in archaeology*, 1932, 91f, 97f.

53. E. Driault (ed), *L'expédition de Crète et de Morée 1823-1828*, 1930 (= Corr.5) 11: Drovetti to Chateaubriand, 30 March = *Ep.* 296; see also Salt's account, FO 78/126/238.

54. *Corr.5*, 12: Drovetti to Chateaubriand, 10 April. A first-hand account of the perils of Europeans caught up in this revolt is given by Henry Westcar (*Diary* 150f). Helen Rivlin, *The agricultural policy of Muhammad Ali*, 1961, 202, claims that many soldiers joined the rebels and that the revolt was finally crushed only by Turkish and Bedouin troops, but gives no sources.

55. *Ep.* 306f, from David, 25 May. See L. Marchand, *Byron, a portrait*, 1971, 452f.

56. *Ep.* 307.

57. *Ep.* 314, from Bastiani, 20 July; Register of the Order (thanks to the Latin Patriarch in Jerusalem). Marro, *Personalità* 65 strangely misdates the award to 20 April. It is amusing that both Champollion and Rosellini were offered the decoration in 1829 at a cost of a mere 100 louis. Champollion indulged in irony on the price of three inches of ribbon, and declined, saying that he would have to be *thought* worthy of it (*Lettres* 2.388). Cf. the cost given as 100 Venetian sequins (*Ep.* 388).

58. *Ep.* 316, from Bastiani, 20 July.

59. *Ep.* 309, from Guilleminot, 14 June.

60. *Ep.* 311, from Guilleminot, 15 June.

61. *Corr.5*, 18: Chateaubriand to Drovetti, 1 June.
62. *Corr.5*, 20: Villele to Drovetti, 11 June. Baron Damas was Foreign Minister from August 1824 until January 1828.
63. *Ep.* 319, from Rambaud, 31 July.
64. *Ep.* 329f, from David, 5 October.
65. *Corr.5*, 32: Drovetti to Damas, 1 September.
66. *Ep.* 325, from David, 20 September; 329, from Guilleminot, 4 October.
67. *Corr.5*, 39f; cf. *Ep.* 340f.
68. The fulminations of the French officers present are enlightening: 'I never expected to find so many different kinds of death to combat: sickness, fire, drowning, projectiles, and what is more annoying, the pride, arrogance, cowardice and jealousy of the haughty Turks' (*Ep.* 341, from Guerand on Ibrahim's flagship, 8 November); Ibrahim commanded 'a rabble not worth the cord to hang it' (344, from La Solimuelle (?), 20 November).
69. *Corr.5*, 36f: Drovetti to Damas, 20 October; FO 78/126/259f (Salt's account).
70. *Ep.* 325, from David, 20 September.
71. *Ep.* 329f, from David, 5 October; 334, 22 October.
72. *Ep.* 348, Drovetti to Damas, 2 December (not in *Corr.5*); 358, Drovetti to Damas, 28 December (also lacking). See also Salt on their arrival (FO 78/135/93): Boyer adopted Turkish dress!
73. G. Douin, *Une mission militaire française auprès de Mohammed Ali*, 1923, 14; 40: Boyer to Jomard, May 1825.
74. *Ep.* 352, from Dr. Cani, 24 December.
75. *Ep.* 349, from Cozza de'Luzzi, 5 December; 354, from same, 26 December.
76. *Ep.* 368, from David, 22 January, 1825.
77. *Ep.* 371, from Guilleminot, 25 January.
78. *Corr.5*, 53: Damas to Malivoire, 11 February.
79. *Ep.* 377, from Balbis, 12 February. Giovanni Battista Balbis (1765-1831), member of the Jacobin club, fled to France in 1794. Deputy chief physician to the Italian army 1797, member of the Provisional Government (1798-1799), along with Drovetti. Director of the Torino Botanical Garden 1801, professor of botany 1806-1814, professor at Lyons 1819-1830, where he gave refuge to Piedmontese refugees.
80. *Ep.* 388, Drovetti to Drouault (?), 30 April.
81. *Ep.* 400, from Guilleminot, June.
82. Boyer claimed that Ibrahim had had no map of the Morea for almost a year. On the capture of Navarino, 1,800 members of the garrison were conducted out to safety. Boyer thought at this time that Drovetti wanted him to go to Greece as adviser to Ibrahim (Boyer to Belliard, June = Douin, *Mission*, 43).
83. *Corr.5*, 66: Drovetti to Damas, 12 July.
84. *Corr.5*, 67: Drovetti to Damas, 13 July.
85. Douin, *Mission*, 49f; 55, Boyer to Belliard, August; 62; 68f.
86. 'Had he met the Greeks, he would almost certainly have perished', Dodwell, *The founder of modern Egypt*, 1931, 75. Some might think that the Egyptian navy should not be dismissed so easily.
    Salt provides interesting further details (FO 78/135/187): it was widely thought that Mehemet Ali had fled from the Captain Pasha, his pursuit of the Greeks was so incredible. Salt and Drovetti played a leading part in entertaining the Turkish admiral in the Viceroy's absence.
87. *Corr.5*, 76f: Drovetti to Damas, 6 September.
88. *Ep.* 415, from Romanzoff, September.
89. Marro, *Boll.Ist.Zool.Torino*, 2.1949/50, 561.
90. *ibid.*, Fischer to Drovetti, 15 November (also not in *Epistolario*).
91. *Corr.5*, 82: Malivoire to Damas, 28 September; 87: Drovetti to Damas, 7 October.
92. *Corr.5*, 92: Livron to MFA, October.
93. *Corr.5*, 95: Drovetti to Damas, 30 October.

94. *Ep.* 433, from Brunetti, 24 November.
95. *Ep.* 455, from Boyer, 22 January, 1826; 459, from Boyer, 8 February.
96. *Corr.5*, 96f: Malivoire to Damas, 2 November; Drovetti to MFA, 8 and 9 November.
97. *Ep.* 437f, from Guilleminot, 30 November.
98. Richard Madden, *Travels in Turkey, Egypt, Nubia and Palestine in 1824-1827*, (2 vols), 1829, 1.214. Madden (1798-1886) was a friend of Byron, visited Egypt (1825-1827), and was Colonial Secretary in Western Australia 1847-1850.
99. *ibid.* 239.
100. *Ep.* 395, from Rifaud, quoting Drovetti, 20 June.
101. *Ep.* 394f, from Rifaud, June; 405, from Rifaud, August; 408f, from Rifaud. For invaluable analysis and identification of Rifaud's finds at Tanis, see J.J. Fiechter, *La moisson des dieux*, 233f.
102. Boyer to Belliard, June = Douin, *Mission*, 47.
103. The most celebrated Arabist of his day, Edward Lane (1801-1876), compiler of the great Arabic lexicon and translator of the Thousand and one nights, made his first visit to Egypt 1825- 1828. The resulting Notes and views, with more than 100 drawings, was never published (the Ms is in the British Library, Add MS 34,080-34,082). There is no reason why this appalling waste should not now be remedied! Although he made several journeys up the Nile, in 1826 and 1827, and stayed more than four months in all at Thebes, and mentions people such as Yanni and an Italian working for Bokhty, the Swedish Consul, as well as many of the exploits of Belzoni, there is not a word of Drovetti.
104. Confirmed to me by the Director of the Library; the Society was unfortunately unable to tell me anything more. Marro, *Personalità* 64 gives the date as 1 March. The letter from Count de Laveau, Secretary of the Society, informing Drovetti of his election, is dated 22 June: Marro, *Boll.Ist.Zool.Torino* 2.1949/50, 565f – again not in *Epistolario*.
105. *Ep.* 391, from Boissier, 1 June.
106. The Drovetti dossier, Ministry of Foreign Affairs, Paris.
107. *Ep.* 407, from Daschwoff, August; also Drovetti dossier.
108. *Corr.5*, 113f: Drovetti to Damas, 8 January, 12 February, 1826. It was in April that Salt complained that Drovetti 'is admitted openly into the counsels of His Highness and follows him from Alexandria to Cairo whenever he moves.' He was trying to convince Mehemet Ali, Salt claimed, to dismiss all Turks who would not enter the New Army, and from the civil service, and to replace them with Arabs. Salt was increasingly the victim of the 'intrigues and machinations of the French party': he referred to his isolation in Alexandria (1824-1826) (see above, p. 128). According to his rival, Drovetti's position was, then, still dominant, because England was held responsible for Egypt's failure quickly to subdue the Greeks. Relations with the Viceroy were much improved for Salt by September (see below, n.132).
109. Boyer to Belliard, January 1826 = Douin, *Mission*, 94f.
110. Boyer to Belliard, February = Douin, *Mission*, 104f.
111. *Corr.5*, 136: Drovetti to Damas, 10 March.
112. *Corr.5*, 141f: Drovetti to Damas, 25 March.
113. *Ep.* 468, from Forbin, 29 March. Laborde published many important works, including *Voyage de l'Arabie Petrée*, 1830, *Voyage en Orient*, 1837, and works on the history of printing, of libraries, on Renaissance art.
114. See above, p. ...
115. *Corr.5*, 148f: Malivoire to Damas, 4 April.
116. *Ep.* 462, from the Prefect of the Propaganda, 5 March.
117. *Ep.* 464, from Mont'Asola, 14 March.
118. *Ep.* 469, from Noureddin, 1 April.
119. *Ep.* 470, from Mont'Asola, 8 April.
120. *Corr.5*, 171f: Saint Sauveur to Damas, 31 May.
121. *Corr.5*, 159f: Malivoire to Damas, 12 May.
122. *Corr.5*, 174: Boghos Youssef to Drovetti, 8 June.

123. *Ep.* 473, Drovetti to Malivoire, 2 May; 485, 10 June; 486, 16 June; 489, 26 June.
124. *Ep.* 223, from de Rigny, 2 August – misdated by the editors to 1822!
125. Drovetti dossier, Ministry of Foreign Affairs, Paris; *Corr.5*, 228: Chayolle to MFA, 11 January; Marro, *Personalità*, 65.
126. Aime Champollion-Figeac, *Les deux Champollions*, 1887, 195. Vaucelles was author of *Chronologie des monuments antiques de la Nubie*, 1829. There is a short article in *WWWE*, 3rd ed., 425, but he is unknown to Carre, *Voyageurs et écrivains français en Egypte*.
127. Champollion, *Lettres* 1.70, 303.
128. *Ep.* 502, from Champollion-Figeac, 22 November.
129. Champollion, *Lettres* 1.424.
130. See below, chap.6.
131. Thomas, tenth Earl of Dundonald, *Autobiography of a seaman* (2 vols), 1869.
132. *Corr.5*, 207f: Drovetti to Damas, 29 September. FO 78/147/103 (Salt's interview).
133. *Ep.* 500, from the duc de Vandermiet, 8 November; 500, from baron de Barbania, 12 November.
134. *Ep.* 501, from Damas, 21 November.
135. G. Dardaud, 'L'extraordinaire aventure de la girafe du Pacha d'Egypte', *Revue des conférences françaises en Orient*, 13.1951, 1-72. I thank Prof. Leclant most sincerely for sending me a copy of this precious and first-rate article.
    Further light is thrown on the story by the *Epistolario*. The first mention of the scheme was 1825 (425, from Jomard, 31 October). The Museum of Natural History sent a portrait of the animal to Mehemet Ali, to be carried back by Drovetti (523, from Saint-Hilaire, 22 October, 1827: an old member of the 1798 expedition, who expressed also a wish for Egyptian independence!). Salt was at great pains to declare the English animal the more handsome, but was instructed to use the greatest economy in getting it to England. In return George IV sent bucks and does and a pair of kangaroos! FO 78/147/92, 127; 78/160/45.
136. *Ep.* 475, from Rifaud, May.
137. *Ep.* 479, from Rifaud, May.
138. There is a short and very poor article on him in the *Dictionary of national biography*, 25.275; see *WWWE* 3rd ed., 194. His diary is preserved in the British Library (Add. MS 31,054), 470 pages of faint pencil, inaccurately bound (the opening pages have Hay at Abu Simbel and the pencilled date 1824, which should be 1825).
139. Hay, *Diary* 117f, 115, 126f. Salt complained to him about Belzoni, for the Consul had paid for all the Italian's operations, including 200 pounds to clear Abu Simbel, but admitted that the account by Mangles and Irby was 'strictly correct' (50).
140. *ibid.*, 90, 98.
141. *Corr.5*, 226f: Chayolle to Damas, 11 January, 1827. Chayolle is unknown to the *Dictionnaire de biographie française, Nouvelle biographie générale, Index biobibliographicus hominum notorum*. He lived in the rue Fosse Mont Martre in 1808 (*Ep.* 18), acted for Drovetti frequently 1822 (190), 1824 (351, 376), 1827 (516), and was known to Jomard (611).
142. *Corr.5*, 231: Drovetti to Chayolle, 15 November, 1826.
143. *Corr.5*, 234f: Drovetti to Damas, 22 January. See also FO 78/160/91.
144. *Corr.5*, 238-248.
145. *Corr.5*, 248f: Malivoire to Damas, 25 April.
146. *Corr.5*, 251: Drovetti to Damas, 1 May.
147. Clairambault's report to Damas is preserved in the Drovetti dossier, Ministry of Foreign Affairs, Paris.
148. *Ep.* 515, from Jomard, 1 July.
149. *Corr.5*, 266: Malivoire to Damas, 10 August.
150. *Corr.5*, 268: Malivoire to Damas, 26 August. FO 78/160/195f.
151. *Ep.* 518, from Halgan, 22 August.
152. For events in September, see especially G. Douin, *Les premiers frigates de Mohamed Aly*, 1926.
153. *Corr.5*, 277f: Malivoire to Damas, 20 and 26 October.

154. Marro, *Personalità*, 65. This was the first of the orders of merit, established by Louis XIV in 1695, and the first open to the bourgeoisie and officers from the ranks. Its conferring required at least ten years' distinguished service and that the recipient be a Catholic! The cross bore the legend 'Bellicae virtutis praemium' (the prize for courage in war). The order was abolished in 1792, restored in 1814, and again abolished in 1830.

155. See chap.7 for the second collection, and chap.6 for his educational ideas.

156. *Corr.5*, 282: Damas to Malivoire, 27 October.

157. *Corr.5*, 283: Damas to Drovetti, 27 October. The King authorised the new arrangements on 30 December. Damas informed Drovetti that he had wanted to raise his salary to 36,000 francs, but that a cut in the consular budget for the present prevented this (letter of 3 January, 1828, in the Drovetti dossier, Ministry of Foreign Affairs, Paris).

158. FO 78/146/346. Malivoire mentions it in one of his letters to Damas, 20 November (*Corr.5*, 295). He reported that everyone was grieving for this widely esteemed man, famous for his conciliatory spirit. A kind of epitaph was composed by Salt for himself: 'It is well to play a respectable part in life, but whether that part extend to a third, fourth or fifth act, it matters little' (Halls 2.210).

159. *Corr.5*, 302: telegram from Prefect at Toulon to Minister of the Navy.

160. One of the earliest accounts of the battle was transmitted to Drovetti just as he was about to return to Egypt at the end of the year, from his old friend, the Commandant de la Bretonnière, who was badly wounded in the battle. He had commanded the *Breslau*, and asked Drovetti to assure Mehemet Ali when he saw him that he regarded it as an honour to fight against the Egyptian frigates, which had covered themselves with glory. Not one of them hauled down its flag, even when on fire or about to sink. De la Bretonnière asked himself why the Egyptians and French were not still friends, and was overcome with regret (*Ep.* 528).

Two English comments are too important to omit: the Foreign Secretary, Dudley, expressed his regret to Salt, but stated that the Allies had to intervene, otherwise the result would have been 'the extermination of the weaker party' (i.e. the Greeks) (FO 78/160/58, 7 December). And Salt himself had insisted, as long ago as August 1826, that the Viceroy 'never had the remotest idea' of any advantage for himself from the Greek war (78/147/99).

161. *Corr.5*, 286: Livron to Damas, 5 November; confirmed by FO 78/146/352.

162. *Corr.5*, 291: Malivoire to Damas, 20 November.

163. *Corr.5*, 295: Damas to Drovetti, 21 November. Durand-Veil, *Les campagnes navales de Mohammed Aly et d'Ibrahim*, 1935, 415, makes the astonishing claim that when Drovetti returned to Egypt he represented English interests as well as those of France.

164. G. Douin (ed), *L'Egypte de 1828 à 1830*, 1935 (= Corr.6), 9: Drovetti to Damas, 28 December.

165. *Corr.6*, 10: d'Oysonville to Chabrol, 9 January, 1828. Baron Damas was replaced as Foreign Minister on 4 January by the comte de la Ferronays, who remained in office until May 1829.

166. *Corr.6*, 13f: Drovetti to MFA, 15 January; 19: Drovetti to la Ferronays, 20 January.

167. *Ep.* 538, from Rosellini, 11 February. This is the sole substance in Marro, 'Ippolito Rosellini e Bernardino Drovetti', *Scritti in memoria di I.R.*, 1949, 1.89-94. Marro was rebuked for his uncritical attitudes by his fellow-countryman, Evaristo Breccia (see below).

168. *Ep.* 540, from Champollion, 18 February.

169. *Ep.* 545, from Mont'Asola, 10 March.

170. *Corr.6*, 24: Drovetti to la Ferronays, 20 March.

171. *Corr.6*, 29: la Ferronays to Drovetti, 20 April.

172. *Corr.6*, 34: Drovetti to la Ferronays, 6 May.

173. *Ep.* 540, from Champollion, 18 February; 551, from Drovetti to Champollion, 3 May.

174. Champollion, *Lettres* 2.41, 43. Marro goes far beyond this evidence when he claims that as soon as Champollion arrived Drovetti offered him 'most lively and cordial congratulations that the letter sent to him in May advising against his departure had not reached him'(!): 'Bernardino Drovetti e Champollion le Jeune', *Atti Accad.Torino* 58.1922, 548-582 at p.564.

175. P. Coste, *Mémoires d'un artiste*, 1878, 1.45.

176. Champollion, *Lettres* 2.23.

177. *Corr.6*, 83: Drovetti to MFA, 22 October.

178. *Ep.* 550, from Lajard, 21 April.

179. Baron I. Taylor, *L'Egypte*, 1857, 2, 387-388. Isidore Taylor (1789-1879), man of letters and artist, travelled in Flanders, Germany and Italy, 1811-1813, served in the army, 1814-1815, visited Holland, England and Spain, 1816-1819, then served as aide-de-camp to General d'Orsay in Spain, 1823. He was appointed to manage the Théatre Française, 1825. In Spain again in 1835, he succeeded in assembling a vast collection of Spanish art for the French King, and was appointed Inspector-General of Fine Arts, 1838. See C. François, *Le baron Taylor*, 1879.

180. *Corr.6*, 41f: Drovetti to la Ferronays, 20 June. The same account to Guilleminot, the same day (*Ep.* 561f). The very day that Drovetti sent off these two letters, A. Drenier of the Ministry of Foreign Affairs asked Drovetti to send him a quintal of Arab beans (*Ep.* 565)!

181. *Corr.6*, 45: la Ferronays to Drovetti, 22 July.

182. *Corr.6*, 48: Drovetti to la Ferronays, 29 July.

183. *Ep.* 567, from d'Oysonville, 8 August.

184. *Corr.6*, 57: Drovetti to la Ferronays, 10 August. The text of the convention is given 60f, with clause 1 on the restoration of slaves, 2 on the evacuation of Greece, and 6 on the small garrison to be left (1,500 men).

On 24 November, Drovetti wrote complaining to la Ferronays (*Corr.6*, 88) that the English papers were attributing the agreement to Codrington and the Viceroy. Drovetti could not believe that the English admiral was behind this; for he knew that when he arrived everything had been arranged, so that the agreement could be signed immediately. Drovetti asserted that he was not given to boasting of his services, but that he had played such a positive part that the Viceroy had given him one of the two original copies.

Champollion mentions the 'laborious preparations' of Drovetti (*Lettres* 2.31), but then proceeds to claim that the whole thing was arranged by de Rigny and Drovetti. This is supported by D. Dakin, *The Greek struggle for independence 1821-1833*, 1973, 253, who states that these two stressed the possibility of an allied invasion of the Morea, which was crucial in convincing Mehemet Ali. Drovetti acted 'approximately according to instructions from La Ferronays'. Then de Rigny heard that the English had recalled Codrington, which he considered unjustified, so he sailed to Corfu and told Codrington of the agreement, so that he could end his career spectacularly and have his revenge on an ungrateful government.

Cameron, *Egypt in the nineteenth century*, 1898, 144, names the English consul Barker as responsible for the convention!

185. A letter recommending Champollion to Drovetti was written from Paris by the comte de Forbin, dated 16 July (*Ep.* 566).

186. Champollion, *Lettres* 2.24, 29, 34, 35.

187. There was another hurdle, apart from firmans, namely funds. Champollion asked for money to excavate for the Louvre when he proposed the expedition. This was struck out (*Lettres* 2.456: Hartleben's footnote on p.88 states that Drovetti had asked Forbin, Jomard and others to prevent the money being granted!). Champollion never ceased urging his brother to obtain the money, and he was finally granted 10,000 francs just as he was leaving Thebes in May 1829, thanks to the intervention of de la Rochefoucauld, Director-General of Fine Arts (407ff). This did not prevent the French

side of the expedition alone bringing back more than 100 pieces in some 20 cases (418).

188. Champollion, *Lettres* 2.44-45, 10 September. And so Rosellini. Breccia published extracts from his letters. On 1 September he wrote to his wife Zenobia that the dangerous conditions were all an invention of Drovetti in order not to have his excavations disturbed and that Mehemet Ali had said not a word about danger and knew nothing of the expedition! ('Ippolito Rosellini e Bernardino Drovetti, *Aegyptus* 32.1952, 138-142, at p.139). These claims are contradicted by all the above evidence.

189. *Corr.6*, 66f: Gros to la Ferronays, 29 August.

190. Drovetti dossier, Ministry of Foreign Affairs, Paris.

191. Champollion, *Lettres* 2.42: 29 August.

192. See below, on the trilingual stone. *Ep.* 568, from Champollion, 29 September. The vexed question of Champollion's letters may be summarised here. It seems that he thought that Drovetti was holding them up. The expedition arrived in Egypt in August 1828. The first mention of any correspondence received is 9 November, for Rosellini (*Lettres* 2.140). Champollion finally received some early in December, sent by his wife in mid August and his brother in late August and early September (172). More letters came for the Italians early in January 1829, but nothing again for Champollion (198), until 9 February, when he received a batch written from September to November. More from late December arrived in March. Early in July he replied to letters dated 30 January, 22 March and 10 April, admittedly late, but he had been very busy (385). Letters were thus taking about three months to come from France to the expedition in Upper Egypt, but even 'couriers' sent from Thebes to Cairo took months (406). There is certainly no statement in his letters as published by Hartleben that Drovetti deliberately retarded his mail. The missing source is his letter to Drovetti of 14 January, 1829 (*Ep.* 581), thanking him for the only two letters he had received since leaving Alexandria. Champollion stated bluntly that he was afraid that Drovetti's staff in Alexandria were not zealously sending on packets from Europe which had to be forwarded to Cairo. This reminds us that Drovetti himself would not have been engaged in mail sorting! Most importantly, this conflict is quite out of character with everything else one knows of their relationship, as the sequel shows.

193. *Ep.* 570, from Champollion, 9 October.

194. *Corr.6*, 76: Drovetti to la Ferronays, 14 October.

195. *Corr.6*, 78f: Gros to la Ferronays, 16 October.

196. *Ep.* 574, from Jane Porter, 28 October. The wish was granted by Champollion (see below).

197. *Ep.* 578, 579, 580, from the Greek state.

198. *Corr.6*, 89: la Ferronays to Mimaut, 28 November.

199. *Ep.* 580, from Artaud, 20 December.

200. The three letters are referred to by Marro, *Boll.Ist.Zool.Torino* 2.1949/50, 565; they are not in the *Epistolario*.

201. P. Hamont, *L'Egypte sous Mehemet Ali*, 1843, 2.115f.

202. *Corr.6*, 94f: Drovetti to la Ferronays, 15 January, 1829.

203. *Corr.6*, 96f: Gros to la Ferronays, 20 January.

204. Durand-Veil, *Les campagnes navales de Mohammed Aly et d'Ibrahim*, 1935, 1.474.

205. *Ep.* 581, from Champollion, 14 January.

206. *Ep.* 586, from Champollion, 13 February.

207. *Corr.6*, 108: Drovetti to la Ferronays, 14 March.

208. *Ep.* 589, from Champollion, 12 March.

209. *Ep.* 597, from Mont'Asalo, 24 March.

210. *Ep.* 600, from Count Stirda, April; 605, from de Valmy, May; 606, from Macardle, May.

211. On 14 May, 1829 the comte de Portalis succeeded de la Ferronays as Foreign Minister, but held the post only until August.

212. See J. d'Ivray, 'Une aventurière sous l'Empire', *Les oeuvres libres* 18.1936, 175-206, who sums up, 'la vie entière de cette femme ne fut que folies et mensonges.'

213. *La contemporaine en Egypte*, 1.262f. Mimaut is mentioned favourably, *passim*.

214. *ibid.* 1.254f. See below.

215. *ibid.* 2.53, 3.9, 4.237.

216. *ibid.* 4.272. Louis Sebastien Fauvel (1753-1838), an artist who worked for the comte de Choiseul-Gouffier in the East, lived in Athens 1792-1799, sold 24 cases of antiquities to the Directory. Appointed by Talleyrand as Deputy-Commissioner at Athens 1801-1838. His notes and casts were lost in the uprising of 1829. See R. Stoneman, *Land of the lost gods*, 1987, 165f.

217. Not that Drovetti was her only bête noir. Equal was Dr Pariset, 'médecin de la peste' and a pretentious schemer (2.1f, 41, 79f; 3.59f, 181). She admired Clot Bey (1.355f), and was impressed with Mehemet Ali (2.42f): 'digne de régner' (3.27). Her most charming note on him is that French editors believed he could read French, because of his subscriptions to journals such as *Le Constitutionel*, until it was revealed that they were for Boghos (2.21).

218. 'le premier moteur de mon voyage', she informs us as late as vol.3, p.279.

219. *ibid.* 1.285, 2.166, 3.196, 4.265.

220. Especially the hanging of the Archbishop of Constantinople (2.55f), Ibrahim's mercy (3.324), Greek massacres of Turkish prisoners (3.29f), le Tellier and Navarino (3.42f), and the human shields (3.50f).

221. d'Amat *DBF* 11.837 dates Drovetti's 'renunciation' of the title of Consul-General to 1826. He knows that he did not leave Egypt until 1829 (kept back only to make things difficult for Champollion), when he went to take up 'his post in Torino'. This is piling absurdity on absurdity. Mme Drovetti stayed behind in Alexandria, although she later visited Europe (see above, 318). It was not until July 1831 that Drovetti was accorded a pension, a mere 5,430 francs (Drovetti dossier, Ministry of Foreign Affairs, Paris), but that was almost double the 3,000 frs for a Vice-Consul.

Chapter Five

1. See below, p. 172.

2. S. Woolf, *History of Italy 1700-1860*, 1979, 234.

3. H. Hearder, *Europe in the nineteenth century, 1830-1880* (2nd ed.) 1988, 22.

4. *ibid.*, 31.

5. H. Hearder, *Italy in the age of the Risorgimento 1790-1870*, 1980, 53.

6. Woolf, 250-251. In fact, with the adoption of the Spanish constitution in Naples in 1820, there was a split in the Piedmontese liberals, with Balbo and others opposing this constitution, and Santarosa and the majority claiming that it was the only way to unite the Italians, and using Piedmontese military intervention to drive out the Austrians and form a large kingdom in northern Italy (*Storia del Piemonte*, 1.329, Romeo).

   Count Santore (1783-1825), sub-prefect under Napoleon, captain in the Piedmontese army in 1815, organised the conspiracy of 1821, was condemned to death, fled, fought for the Greeks and died at Sphakteria. His *De la Révolution piemontaise* 1821 was instantly translated into English.

   On Balbo, the conservative, who worked for an independent Italy through the Piedmontese monarchy, so that she would take her place in Christian Europe, see *Storia del Piemonte*, 1.354f. (Romeo)

7. *ibid.* 2.333, 339.

8. For all the relevant documents, see G. Douin, *Mohammed Ali et l'expédition d'Alger 1829-1830*, 1930.

9. *ibid.*, 35f, cf. 121.

10. *ibid.*, 97f.

11. *ibid.*, 80.

12. *ibid.*, 149.

13. *ibid.*, 136f.
14. *ibid.*, 195f.
15. FO 78/192 quoted by Douin, lxxxviif.
16. Champollion, *Lettres* 2.413, 450, 465, 469f.
17. *ibid.*, 2.473. It is precisely this evidence which is missing from G. Marro, 'Bernardino Drovetti e Champollion le Jeune', *Atti Accad. Torino* 58.1922/3, 548-582, which quotes only the letters of Drovetti's *Epistolario*, and therefore tells only half the story! Marro went to extraordinary lengths to give the version he preferred, which backfired to Drovetti's discredit.
18. *Ep.* 611, from Jomard, 7 August, 1829.
19. *Ep.* 612, from Doncour, 2 January, 1830.
20. *Ep.* 613, from d'Armandy, 25 March; 625, June.
21. *Ep.* 617, from Nota, 3 April.
22. *Ep.* 618, from Bianco di Barbania, 4 April.
23. *Ep.* 619, from Huder, 26 April.
24. *Ep.* 621, from Sartorio, 23 June; 635.
25. *Ep.* 622, from Monte d'Asola, 5 July.
26. Marro, *Personalità* 64 quotes the Society's letter to Drovetti of 15 August, not in the *Epistolario*. My own enquiries revealed that his name could not be found in the archives, but that nothing was usually recorded of corresponding members. I thank the Society.
27. *Ep.* 626, from Trompeo, 22 November.
28. Correspondence with J. Rathenez, writing from Cairo at this time is most strange. In November 1831, he spoke of buying Drovetti a horse. Perhaps the one belonging to the military instructor Brunetti would suit. He was at Alexandria, so Drovetti could see the horse and talk to him about it (*Ep.* 627). In January, 1832, he talks of Drovetti's return to Cairo, and the pleasure of seeing him again in a few weeks (*Ep.* 630). In June of the same year, he asks how Drovetti is acclimatizing himself in Egypt, at Alexandria (*Ep.* 633).
    Drovetti was definitely in Torino in June 1832 (*Ep.* 632) and Jomard was sending him news of events in Alexandria in summer of the same year (*Ep.* 635). The dating of letters in the *Epistolario* is utterly unreliable.
29. D. Thompson, *Europe since Napoleon*, (2nd ed.), 1966, 165.
30. Woolf (n.2), 317.
31. *Ep.* 631, from Dr Bosio, 2 February, 1832.
32. *Ep.* 632, from Abro, 5 June.
33. *Ep.* 628f., from Jomard, 15 January; 635, 20 September. See chapter 6.
34. *Ep.* 637, from Pedemonte, 20 February, 1833.
35. Clot, *Mémoires*, 1949, 260.
36. *Sir William Gell in Italy*, ed. Edith Clay and M. Frederiksen, 1976, 108 from Naples, 13 April, 1833.
37. C. Botta, *Lettere* 1841, 62.
    It is most infuriating that yet another of the letters in the *Epistolario* is misdated which, for want of a solution, must be mentioned here. It is no.469 (p.612), and is addressed to Carlo Botta from Drovetti in Alexandria, and dated 10 November, 1829. Everyone knows that Drovetti left Egypt on 20 June.
    The letter refers to his colleague Tourneau (mis-transcribed Tomneau!) and to the younger Botta's plans to come to Egypt, which he did for the first time in 1831. A moment's consultation of the original would suffice to solve the problem, but this is the last thing which will be allowed. Allowing the month (abbreviated 9bre) to be reliable (at least one of the last four of the year), I suggest 1828.
38. *Ep.* 638, from Morpurgo, 10 December.
39. *Ep.* 639, from Tumigni, 19 December.
40. *Storia del Piemonte*, 1.343f. (Romeo)
41. *Ep.* 642, from Clot, 13 March, 1834.

42. *Ep.* 644, from Gillio, 19 August.
43. *Ep.* 645, from dal Pozzo, 8 October. Like Drovetti, dal Pozzo (1768-1843) was a lawyer who had served in the Provisional Government 1798-1799, then been a member of the French government in Rome, 1809-1814. He made his peace with Vittorio Emmanuele, and was Minister of the Interior during the Regency 1821. He then went into exile in Switzerland, London (1823-1831) and Paris (1831-1837), before being allowed to return to Piedmont. His restless policies seem to have alienated all parties; for he finally came to defending Austria.
44. *Ep.* 646, from Falkenstein, 14 November.
45. *Ep.* 647, from Balbo, 1834?
46. *Ep.* 650, from Jomard, 20 May, 1835.
47. *Ep.* 652, from Botta, 27 October.
48. See chap.7.
49. *Ep.* 655, from Jomard, 7 June, 1836.
50. *Ep.* 679, from Clot, 12 January (1840).
51. *Ep.* 656, Drovetti to the Sardinian Consul (unnamed), 19 January, 1837.
52. *Ep.* 657, from Jomard, 18 February.
53. C. Botta, *Lettere*, 1841, 153.
54. *Ep.* 659, from Pariset, 8 October.
    Etienne Pariset (1770-1847), son of poor peasants, served in the army 1792-1794, then studied medicine. He was a member of the Académie de Médicine, and permanent secretary of it from 1842.
55. *Ep.* 531, from Drovetti to Baruffi, egregiously misdated by the editors of the *Epistolario* a decade too early.
    Giuseppe Baruffi (1801-1875), educated at his birthplace Mondovì, then like Drovetti at the Collegio delle Provincie in Torino; ordained a priest in 1824, professor of mathematics at Torino University 1833-1862. He was a prolific author of popularising works, especially in science, and of *Una peregrinazione da Torino a Londra, 1835, Pellegrinazioni autumnali*, 1840-1841, *Viaggio in Oriente*, 1847 (Greece and Turkey), *Viaggio da Torino alle Piramidi*, 1848.
56. *Ep.* 661, from Pellico, 15 January, 1838.
57. *Ep.* 661, from Giordani, 26 February.
58. *Ep.* 662, from Jomard, 31 August.
59. *Ep.* 667, from del Signore, 23 February 1839.
60. *Ep.* 666, from Marochetti, no month or day.
61. *Ep.* 669, Drovetti to Jomard, 25 February.
62. There was talk of the Viceroy himself leaving for Syria at this time (*Ep.* 683, from Morpurgo, July 1840). On the refusal of the proposals, *Ep.* 685, from Morpurgo, August 1840. On the Napier treaty and the expected arrival of Ibrahim by ship, *Ep.* 690, from Morpurgo, February 1841. On the incompetence of French diplomacy, *Ep.* 691, from Jomard, February 1841.
63. Dodwell, *The founder of modern Egypt*, 1931, 191.
64. *Ep.* 671, from Baruffi, 23 March.
65. *Ep.* 672, from de la Rue, 3 May.
66. *Ep.* 676, from Benevello, 24 December. The conte di Benevello (1788-1853) first studied law, then turned to art and literature, which took him to Paris. Under Carlo Alberto, he was noted for his interests in charity, education and agriculture. As a painter he specialised in landscapes and historical scenes. He was made a senator in 1849.
67. *Ep.* 678, from Clot, 12 January 1840.
68. Clot, *Mémoires*, 341.
69. *Ep.* 681, from Abro, 31 January.
70. *Ep.* 683, from Morpurgo, 24 July.
71. *Ep.* 684, from Clot, 4 August.
72. *Ep.* 686, from Bertalazone, 1 August. The writer was a lawyer, and member of the

Regia Società Agraria di Torino; there is no article in *DBI*.

This letter was the subject of a special study by Marro, 'Relazione inedita sulla riunione degli scienziati a Torino nel 1840', *Rassegna storica del Risorgimento* 1949, 43-50, but he adds little to the contents of the original.

73. A. Philips in the *Cambridge Modern History* vol.10, 1907, 128; see also *Enciclopedia italiana* vol.11, 146f.

    Giovanni Rosini (1776-1855) was professor of eloquence at the University of Pisa, and author of *La monaca di Monza*, 1829.

74. *Ep.* 687, from Canina, 16 October.

75. *Ep.* 691, from Jomard, 1 February, 1841.

76. *Ep.* 692, from Dantas, 25 March; 694, 16 April; 697, from Pedemonte, 6 November.

77. *Ep.* 698, from Cailliaud, 17 March, 1842.

78. *Ep.* 700, from Benevello, 1 June.

79. *Ep.* 702, from Morpurgo, 30 December.

80. *Ep.* 702, from Anselmi. The editors of the *Epistolario* date this letter referring to Gioberti's book published in 1843 '1842-1843 ?'.

81. Drovetti probably quoted Gioberti in his speech to the Società biellese in 1845 on the position of the priesthood, where he refers to a famous modern 'author, philosopher, philanthropist and catholic' (see below, 191). The *Primato* is called by Hearder 'this inflated, chauvinist and extraordinary book' (*Italy in the age of the Risorgimento*, 197) which made the cause of Italian unity and independence respectable. Second only to Gioberti's influence was Cesare Balbo's *Speranze d'Italia*, 1844, agreeing with a Papal federation, but anxious also for the expulsion of Austria. Woolf (n.2) 338f. is much more critical: Gioberti said nothing original; there was nothing about Austrian rule, nothing about reform in the Papal States; the unity of Italy was rejected as unhistorical; power was to be retained by princes. The Italic federation under the Pope was to be based on the support of the Piedmontese army. Gioberti attacked the Jesuits to win over the central Italian moderates.

82. *Ep.* 705, from Jomard, 2 August 1843.

83. *Ep.* 706, from Baruffi, 15 August.

84. *Ep.* 707, from Canina, 22 and 24 August.

85. A letter from a friend in February 1844 shows that Drovetti had been in Barbania all winter, Zavati, 'Lettere inedite di Bernardino Drovetti', *Oriente moderno* 1965, 878-888, no.7.

86. *Ep.* 709, from Jomard, 7 September.

87. Ferreri, *Brevi cenni su Barbania canavese*, 1904, 27f.

88. *Ep.* 710, from Jomard, 1 June, 1844.

89. *Ep.* 712, from Jomard, 15 January, 1845.

90. *Atti della Società biellese* 8.1845, 4-16. It seems to be this speech to which a friend refers in April 1846; Drovetti had sent him a copy, causing the friend to remark that he never stopped doing good, and that when he might enjoy a retirement earned by so many services, he used it to profit his fellow creatures (*Ep.* 713, from A. Menier, 26 April, 1846).

91. Woolf (n.2), 275f, 281, 321f.

92. *Storia del Piemonte*, 1.366 (Romeo).

93. *ibid.* 1.314, quoting Saluzzo, *Memorie*.

94. Bertolotti, *Passeggiate nel canavese* 7.329f.

95. *Storia del Piemonte*, 1.363f (Romeo).

96. *Ep.* 714, from Pedemonte, 19 November.

97. *Ep.* 717f, from Bonfort, 14 October, 30 October, 12 November; from Nubar, 31 December 1847. There is not a hint of explanation of Drovetti's behaviour in Marro, 'Ibrahim Pacha dans les archives privées du consul Drovetti', *Cahiers d'histoire égyptienne* 1.1949, 66-77.

    This episode is not to be confused with the tour to France and England made by Ibrahim, August 1845 – August 1846. He was given a royal reception in Paris, but the highlight of the tour was apparently England, where he was received by Albert, dined with Victoria, visited factories and mines in England and Ireland, and attended the Commons for the resignation of Peel in June, and a military review with Wellington. See G. Wiet, 'Le voyage d'Ibrahim Pacha en France et en Angleterre', *Cahiers d'histoire égyptienne* 1.1949, 78f.

98. Macario, *Cenni biografici del fu cavaliere Bernardino Drovetti*, 1885, 31f. The rest of the section in Macario seems to be his own, rather than Drovetti's observations, in particular defending Pius from a charge of having abandoned Rome.

The last major honour conferred on the ageing Drovetti was the rank of commendatore in the Papal Order of S. Silvestro on 24 April (Marro, *Personalità*, 65.)

99. Fiechter, *La moisson des dieux*, 252.

100. Hearder, *Europe in the nineteenth century, 1830-1880*, 208.

101. *Storia del Piemonte* 1.376f, 386f (Romeo).

102. *Ep.* 721, from de 'Negri, 11 March 1848.

103. *Ep.* 723, from de 'Negri, 24 May. Giovanni Corboli Bussi (1813-1850) was perhaps the leading councillor of Pius IX in his first liberal phase. As Secretary of the Congregation of Ecclesiastical Affairs, he was warmly in favour of Italian revolt against the Austrians, but the Pope's renunciation of war denied his policy and he retired for a time (see *DBI* 28.775-778). Mazzini returned from England to Milan in April, following the great uprising against the Austrians. His proclamations were his constant propaganda for Italian unity rather than federalism. Giovanni Durando (1809-1869) was sent by the Papal government to assist the revolt of the Veneto against Austria, but he was defeated at Vicenza. He was division commander at Novara in 1849 and at Solferino 1859. Andrea Ferrari (1770-1859) served in Egypt, then under Murat. He fled to France in the 1820s, and fought in the Algerian war in 1831. He was commander of the Papal army in the Veneto alongside Durando, but they quarrelled. Ferrari took his last stand for the defence of Rome in 1849.

104. Italy is indeed fortunate in having one of England's greatest historians, George Trevelyn, devote himself to Garibaldi's exploits in his immortal trilogy, *Garibaldi's defence of the Roman Republic*, 1907, *Garibaldi and the Thousand*, 1909, *Garibaldi and the making of Italy*, 1911.

105. For a sympathetic assessment of Ibrahim – notably for his bravery and defending him against charges of cruelty – see R. Curzon, *Visits to monasteries in the Levant*, 1849, 245f. Curzon met Ibrahim in Egypt in 1833 and again in London in 1846.

106. *Ep.* 725, from Reyneri, 16 March.

107. Having been President of the Council of Ministers 16 December 1848 – 20 February 1849, after the battle of Novara Gioberti was sent to Paris as minister, but soon retired and died there in October 1852.

108. *Ep.* 727, from de Rougé, 1849.

109. *Ep.* 728, from Mir Pedemonte, 6 January. I thank most sincerely the Consul for the Netherlands in Melbourne, Mr W.M. van Gennip for his great kindness in obtaining these biographical details for me.

110. *Ep.* 729, Drovetti to Giorgio, 8 March 1851.

111. *Ep.* 731, from C. Sperino, 2 April.

112. *Ep.* 732, Drovetti to the President of the Academy, 23 December.

113. Macario (n.98), 35.

114. Cagnone e Mosca, *Notizie biografiche sul cavaliere Bernardino Drovetti*, 1857, say nothing of the cause of death; Macario (n.98), 35 says that in his last year Drovetti was subject to insomnia, and that the autopsy showed ossification of the cerebral arteries which had produced noises in his head, which he attributed to evil influences. This must be the origin of other statements that 'his sense altered a little' (Bertolotti, *Passeggiate nel canavese* 7.330), which becomes elsewhere, 'vers la fin de sa vie, il était tombé en démence' (*Novelle biographie générale* 13.807), or worse in English: 'his mind gave way and he died in an asylum' ($WWWE^2$ 90). It should be noted that there is absolutely no sign of mental disturbance in his last letters, and that S. Salvario was not a mental hospital.

115. The will is in Archivio di Stato, Torino: Sezione Riunite, Insinuazione di Torino 1852, libro 3, vol.3, cc.1777r-1782v. I cannot thank too warmly the Archivist of Vercelli, Dr. Maurizio Cassetti, for having found this for me.

116. A descendant talks of his 'austere and modest' resting-place at Barbania: G. Drovetti, 'Il mio glorioso avo Bernardino Drovetti', *Torino Rivista municipale* 1951, 57-61, 58. It is claimed that a funeral service was held at Barbania on 4 April at which the oration was delivered by the notary Giovanni Ferreri: Ferreri, *Brevi cenni su Barbania canavese*, 1904, 58.
There is an element of mystery about Drovetti's burial. In my first enquiries at the Cemetery of Torino, it was revealed that there was no sign of a record of burial under the appropriate date. This induced me to suggest (*DBI* 41.715) that knowing his wish to be buried with his parents, he was first inhumed at Barbania, and only later transferred to Torino. In 1990, I visited the cemetery again, and officials in the office found an entry concerning him out of place, but I foolishly failed to obtain a photocopy of it. I determined that the story of his burial must be solved once and for all. In 1994 I again went to the cemetery, and for the first time confirmed that Drovetti's body indeed lies in the vaults at ground level just under his monument (between arcades 160 and 161). A very kind official, Dr Mario Capitolo, began a search for me, which finally produced the documents sighted four years earlier and confirmed the date of the burial. It was 11 March 1852, just two days after Drovetti's death. The tomb cost the large sum of 800 lire and was designed for six people. It was, however, to be used only for Drovetti and his parents, whose remains were to be transferred from Barbania. That was never done, so Drovetti, despite his last wishes and the sums expended, remains alone. The record can be found, out of place, under Prima Ampliazione arcata no.274, instead of 160. The cemetery can give no explanation for this.

117. see above p. 1.

118. Baruffi, *Passeggiate nei dintorni di Torino*, 9.60; Curto, 'All'ombra dei cipressi', *Boll. SPABA* 23/24.1969/70, 5-9; Debiaggi, 'Un appunto sul busto di Bernardino Drovetti nel museo egizio di Torino', *Boll. SPABA* 27-29.1973-1975, 82-83.

Chapter Six

1. R. Madden, *Egypt and Mohammed Ali*, 1841, 11f, 21f, 27, 29.

2. P. Thédénat-Duvent, L'*Egypte sous Méhémed Ali*, 1822, 187f.

3. P. Hamont, *Egypte sous Méhémet Ali* (3 vols), 1843, book 2, chap.6. Hamont was director of the Veterinary School at Cairo, and died in 1848. There is no article in *Dictionnaire de biographie française*.

4. Clot, *Aperçu général sur l'Egypte* (2 vols), 1840, 1.44f.

5. J. St John, *Egypt and Mohammed Ali*, 1834, 2.368, 430. On St John (1801-1875), see *Dictionary of national biography* (*DNB*) 17.634.

6. D. Cameron, *Egypt in the nineteenth century*, 1898, 122. There is no article on Cameron (1856-1936) in the *DNB*. See *Who was who* 1929-1940.

7. H. Dodwell, *The founder of modern Egypt*, 1931, 37-38. There is no article on Dodwell (1879-1946) in the *DNB*. See *Who was who* 1941-1950. He comments in characteristic style that English observers 'commiserated with the fellahin because they did not live in brick cottages and eat beef' (p.192).

8. Helen Rivlin, *The agricultural policy of Muhammad Ali*, 1961, 105f.

9. A. Abdel-Malek, *La formation de l'idéologie dans la renaissance nationale de l'Egypte*, 1969, 123.

10. *Ep.* 168, from Saluzzo, 12 February, 1821.

11. *Ep.* 525, from Jomard, 18 November (1827).

12. Joseph Agoub (1795-1832), a Cairene, who came to France with the French army, and was appointed professor of Arabic at the Collège Louis le Grand in Paris, 1820-1831.

13. *Ep.* 425, from Jomard, 31 October, 1825.

14. For all this, see 'Note sur l'établissement d'une école égyptienne à Paris', *Bull.Soc.Geog.* 5.1826, 673f; A. Silvera, 'The first Egyptian student mission to France under Muhammed Ali', in E. Kedourie and Sylvia Haim (eds), *Modern Egypt, studies in politics and society, 1980*, 1-22, p.7; Abdel-Malek (n.9), 119f. For the military schools, see below.

15. *Ep.* 446, Drovetti to Boghos, 7 January 1826.

16. The most complete list of students is that given by Jomard, J. *Asiatique* 2.1828, 109-112, for 1828. He listed 44 students in all, of whom 37 were then undertaking special studies in Paris; two others had gone to Toulon (obviously for naval training), and three had returned to Egypt. Were these students the ones who had arrived in 1826? Another two are listed as 'recently arrived'. For lists of the 44 (sic) students who arrived in 1826 see also Heyworth-Dunne, *Introduction to the history of education in modern Egypt*, 1939, 159-163.

    Silvera (n.14), 8, distinguished between the 'four gifted Armenian Catholics', all protegés of Boghos, and the rest, belonging to the ruling families, chosen 'out of favouritism rather than (sic) ability'. Their ages on arrival ranged from 15 to 37. Silvera made excellent use of many contemporary sources, but did not unfortunately have Jomard's letters in the *Epistolario*. There is a brief allusion also in the official correspondence, *Corr.5*, 149f: Malivoire to Damas, 4 April, 1826.

17. *Ep.* 483, Drovetti to Agoub, May-June.

18. Hamont (n.3), 2.84f.

19. *Ep.* 487, from Jomard, 25 June.

20. The French general Boyer claimed that Drovetti convinced the Viceroy against great opposition from people such as Boghos, Osman and naturally the English (G. Douin, *Une mission militaire française auprès de Mohammed Ali*, 1923, 104f.)

21. *Ep.* 494, from Agoub, 24 July.

22. J. Tagher, 'Les locaux qui abritèrent la mission scolaire égyptienne à Paris existent encore', *Cahiers d'Hist. égyptienne* 2.1950, 333-336.

23. Silvera, (n.14), 13; (Sheik Refaa), 'Relation d'un voyage en France', *J. Asiatique* 11.1833, 222-251.

24. *Ep.* 517, from Jomard, 4 August, 1827.

25. *Ep.* 525, from Jomard, 18 November.

26. 'Note sur l'établissement d'une école égyptienne à Paris', *Bull. Soc. Geog.* 5.1826, 673-674.

27. 'Essai sur la civilisation de l'intérieur de l'Afrique d'après un projet de M. Drovetti', 8.1827, 137-142. On Pacho see 332.

28. The British abolished slavery in their empire in 1833, followed by the French in 1848, the United States in 1862, and South America by the 1880s.

29. Jomard communicated with Drovetti about the plan in October, while Drovetti was still on leave (*Ep.* 521), expressing the great interest of the Société, which had already extended such educational opportunities to natives from Senegal and Madagascar, and established schools in Senegambia. Jomard also revealed rewards for the benefactors: French educated natives could guide French travellers on government missions!

30. Jomard, 'L'école égyptienne de Paris', *J. Asiatique* 2.1828, 96-116.

31. *Ep.* 543, from Jomard, 8 March, 1828.

32. *Ep.* 595, from Jomard, 20 March, 1829.

33. *Ep.* 602, from Jomard, 25 April.

34. *Ep.* 607, from Jomard, 22 May.

35. *Ep.* 611, from Jomard, 7 August.

36. *Ep.* 621, from Jomard, 1 July, 1830.

37. *Ep.* 628, from Jomard, 15 January, 1832.

38. *Ep.* 635, from Jomard, 20 September.

39. *Ep.* 650, from Jomard, 20 May, 1835.

40. *Ep.* 654, from Jomard, 7 June.

41. *Ep.* 711, from Jomard, 1 June, 1844. Artin is called Artur by the editors of the *Epistolario*.

42. For a brief summary, see Marro, *Personalità* 28f, or 'La civilizzazione dell'Africa nel progetto di B. Drovetti', *Italiani nel mondo* 10 Aug. 1951, 17-20: the two versions correspond *verbatim* most of the time. He does not single out Jomard as he should, and gives as much credit to the short-lived Italian programme as to the ten years' French one (of course). cf. *Atti Accad. Torino* 69.1933/4, 58, where Marro claims that all the merit for this initiative in sending young Africans (sic) to Europe belonged to Drovetti. The first mention of Drovetti's plan for European education of Africans going back as far as 1811 is in the article of 1827. In 1814 the English traveller James Silk Buckingham, who was visiting Egypt, had an audience with Mehemet Ali. His own account of this interview tells how he explained that the main deficiency of Egypt was knowledge. Buckingham therefore proposed that one hundred or more youths should be sent to be educated in Europe or America. They might then return to Egypt to teach others. He stated that the Viceroy was convinced by his arguments and acted upon his advice. All this was published for the first time in 1855 in Buckingham's *Autobiography* (2.266f). One wonders what he meant by 'Europe': certainly not Italy or France!

43. On Jomard's part in the formulation of the whole design, see Silvera (n.14), 5: in 1839 in a memorandum to Mehemet Ali through the Consul Cochelet, Jomard referred to his urging the Viceroy to send students to France. This was 'some dozen years after the French conquest' (i.e. 1811). Mehemet Ali refused him, saying that his subjects could not benefit from Europe, but Noureddin went to Paris, and when he returned in 1817, Jomard tried again, also without success. See also A. Silvera, 'Edmé François Jomard and Egyptian reforms in 1839', *Middle Eastern Studies* 7.1971, 301-316.

   In a letter of Jomard himself to Artin Bey, dated October 1844 (G. Wiet, 'Une lettre de Jomard au sujet de l'école militaire égyptienne en 1844', *Revue du Caire* Oct. 1944, 562-577), he claimed that in 1826 the Viceroy wanted to have some Egyptians educated in Europe, and entrusted their studies to Jomard, with the 'material administration' looked after by three Effendis. 'Ainsi était réalisé le plan que j'avais formé douze ans après mon retour d'*Egypte*, à l'époque de la paix générale, plan soumis à Son Altesse par le Consul-Général de France, et six ans après par Osman Bey Noureddin' (p.565). The idea was thus Jomard's in 1811; the unnamed Consul was, of course, Drovetti. The two branches of arts and sciences were united under Jomard in 1836 and a military school added in 1845.

   At the annual dinner for the Egyptian expedition in 1861, Jomard again referred to his plan for civilising Egypt through education, a plan submitted through Drovetti in 1811 (*Banquet de l'Expédition d'Egypte, 31 mars, 1861*, 1862, 7). Silvera notes that he can find no trace of this document in Cairo or in Jomard's papers.

44. Hamont (n.3), 2.84f, 194.

45. Abdel-Malek, (n.9), 119f. Dodwell (n.7), 203, claimed that the Arabs were not very successful replacements for the Turks.

46. Silvera (n.14), 18f; Guémard, *Les réformes en Egypte*, 1936, 138f.

47. Clot, *Mémoires*, 156f.

48. *Ep.* 202, from Abro, 19 May, 1822.

49. *Ep.* 204, from Boissier, 24 May.

50. *Ep.* 324, from Massari, 18 September; 333, 21 October; 350, 19 December, 1824.

51. *Ep.* 335, from Daumas, 23 October; 337, 31 October.

52. *Ep.* 339, from Arthaud, 4 November.

53. *Ep.* 347, from Dr Cani, 1 December.

54. *Ep.* 352, From Cani, 24 December.

55. *Ep.* 359, from Daumas, 1 January, 1825; 364, from Cani, 7 January; 373, from Dr Massari, 7 February; 403, from Cani, 13 July.

56. *Ep.* 423, from Cani, 19 October; 434, from Massari, 26 November; 444, from Cani, 6 January, 1826; 452, 18 January.

57. *Ep.* 467, from Cani, 22 March; 506, from Cani, 1826.

58. Clot in his *Mémoires*, 156f, states that he presented a plan to Mehemet Ali to deal with

the scourge of smallpox. He gives no dates, and does not mention Drovetti. Since he arrived in Egypt only in 1825, his own part was obviously very limited.

59. *Ep.* 549, from Clot, 10 April 1828: the report is unfortunately not included in the *Epistolario*; 591, 12 March, 1829.

60. *Ep.* 642, from Clot, 13 March, 1834.

61. Clot, *Aperçu générale sur l'Egypte* 2.304, mentions only in general terms Drovetti's help in establishing Mehemet Ali in power, and the English invasion (1.50).
Heyworth-Dunne (n.16), 122-123, characterises the *Aperçu* as 'purely apologetic and propagandistic in nature', designed 'to give the impression that the Pasha was an enlightened monarch who had the interests and welfare of the Egyptians at heart, and that he had done everything in his power to introduce and encourage learning and science in his country.' See the very unfavourable French review in *Revue des deux mondes* 4.23.1840, 905-920, and the much more favourable English one in *For. Quart. Rev.* 27.1841, 362-393.

62. Clot states that for an army of 150,000, there were only fifty doctors, medics and chemists (*Mémoires* 58f).

63. This is much more extensive than the list in his *Mémoires* 58f, save that Cherubini replaced Gaetani.

64. Clot, *Mémoires* 35.

65. *ibid.*, 84f, 90f.

66. *ibid.*, 109.

67. *ibid.*, 158f.

68. *ibid.*, 169.

69. Hamont (n.3), 2.84f.

70. Heyworth-Dunne (n.16), 152.

71. *Ep.* 48, from Boghos, 27 January, 1814; 52, 4 April. Drovetti is recognised as instrumental in the establishment of quarantine at Alexandria by Guémard (n.46), 239. He refers to the bulletin of May 1813, which mentions the plague, but nothing more.

72. Thédénat-Duvent (n.2), 84.

73. *Corr.4*, 41: Roussel to Richelieu, 7 January, 1817.

74. Bramsen, *Travels in Egypt, Syria and Cyprus*, 1820, 184. A European hospital was established, which is mentioned by Brocchi in the early 1820s: it was begun in 1817, but contained only 12 beds. Its funds came from contributions by merchants and consuls, but the latter constantly bickered, Brocchi says, over its control: *Giornale* 1.110.

75. *Ep.* 272, from Boghos, 20 December 1823; *Corr.4*, 296: Drovetti to Chateaubriand, 29 Dec.; *Corr.5*, 18: Chateaubriand to Drovetti, 1 June 1824.

76. St John (n.5), 2.535.

77. It is strange that Marro, *Personalità*, does not devote any space to this aspect of Drovetti's great contributions to Egypt. There is a brief listing of headings in Cagnone and Mosca, *Notizie biografiche sul cav. B. Drovetti*, 1857.

78. Rivlin (n.8), 21.

79. *ibid.*, 42f.

80. *ibid.*, 124, 53.

81. *Corr.3*, 157f: Mengin to MFA, 20 January, 1812; 176f: Drovetti to MFA, March.

82. Rivlin, 61; *Corr.3*, 231: September bulletin 1813.

83. *Corr.4*, 266f: Drovetti's report, July 1822.

84. Belzoni, *Narrative* 2.172.

85. St John (n.5), 2.376, 452f, 462.

86. Madden (n.1), 29f.

87. Hamont (n.3), book 1, chap.4, chap.7; book 4, chap.10 (agricultural school). chap.4 (veterinary school). Clot, *Aperçu* (n.4), 2.337f. Clot was one of the few to defend Mehemet Ali's 'land reform' in the abolition of the religious estates (*ibid.* 2.446f).

88. These figures are from Rivlin, 124f.

89. *ibid.*, 112.

90. Guémard (n.46), 355, citing Roussel to MFA, 22 July 1817. The letter says no such thing.
91. *Corr.3*, 198f: October bulletin, 1812.
92. *Ep.* 649, from Jomard, 20 May 1835; also 654.
93. *Ep.* 669, Drovetti to Jomard, 25 February 1839.
94. *Ep.* 441, from Benso di Cavour, 6 December 1825. Not the least interest of this letter is the light it throws on the writer's personality.
95. From the Torino archives, noted by Marro, *Personalità*, 26.
96. Hamont (n.3), book 4, chap.9.
97. *Corr. 3*, 176: Drovetti to MFA, 21 March 1812.
98. *Ep.* 91, from Boghos, 3 December 1816.
99. *Corr. 4*, 57f: Roussel to Richelieu, 31 May 1817. Drovetti was by now, of course, relieved of office.
100. *Corr. 4*, 63f: Roussel to Richelieu, 22 July; 88: 19 December; 91f: report of Basil Farsali; 151: Thédénat to MFA, 9 March, 1819; *Ep.* 136, from Baffi, 14 August.
101. *Corr. 4*, 266f at 274: Drovetti's report, July 1822.
102. F. Menghin, *Histoire de l'Egypte sous le gouvernement de Mohammed Aly*, 1823, 2.375f; Brocchi, *Giornale* 1.163, 172, 204, 254, 276.
103. *Corr. 5*, 26f: Drovetti's report, July 1824. This and the further report made by Drovetti on 9 June 1825 were first published by Auriant in *Bulletin de la Société d'encouragement pour l'industrie nationale*, 1923, 420-432, but with virtually no annotation, save some notes on Jumel.
104. Rivlin (n.8), 143.
105. *Ep.* 426, from Jomard, 31 October, 1825.
106. *Corr. 5*, 100: Malivoire to Damas, 10 November.
107. *Ep.* 429, from Cadeldevans, November.
108. Corr. 5, 125f, Malivoire to Damas, 21 February, 1826; Douin, *Une mission militaire* (n.20), 89f: Boyer to Belliard, 1 January.
109. Corr. 5, 139: Drovetti to Damas, 20 March; 191: 14 August.
110. St John (n.5), 2.409; P. Mouriez, *Histoire de Méhémet Ali* (5 vols), 1855-1888, 3.67f.
111. Rivlin (n.8), 194f.
112. *Corr. 3*, 103f: Saint-Marcel to Champagny, 7 January, 1811.
113. *Corr. 3*, 120f: Saint-Marcel to MFA, 6 May; 133: 14 July; 144: Saint-Marcel to Bassano, 1 September.
114. Dodwell (n.7), 30.
115. *Corr. 3*, 149f: Drovetti's October and November bulletins; 168: February 1812 bulletin; 170: Saint-Marcel to Bassano, 3 February.
116. *Corr. 3*, 179: Saint-Marcel to Bassano, 2 May; 182: 20 May.
117. *Corr. 3*, 187: Drovetti's June bulletin; 189: Saint-Marcel to MFA, 20 July.
118. *Corr. 3*, 197: September bulletin; 202: Drovetti to MFA, 28 November; 206f: December bulletin.
119. *Corr. 3*, 212: February bulletin, 1813; 219: May bulletin; 241f: March 1814 bulletin.
120. *Corr. 4*, 44: Roussel to Richelieu, 10 January, 1817.
121. *Corr. 4*, 46: Roussel to Richelieu, 24 February; 57f: 31 May.
122. *ibid.*; see below, chap.6.
123. *Corr. 4*, 71f: Thédénat-Duvent to Richelieu, 27 September.
124. *Corr. 4*, 81f: Roussel to Richelieu, 30 September; 91f: report of Basil Farsali, 7 January 1818; 104f: Roussel to Richelieu, 9 June; 123f: 6 November; 170f: Pillavoine to MFA, 7 September, 1819.
125. *Corr. 4*, 266f: Drovetti's report, July 1822.
126. Douin (n.20), 40f; *Corr. 5*, 63: Livron to Belliard, 10 July, 1825.
127. *Ep.* 389, Drovetti to Boghos, May 1825.
128. *Corr. 5*, 216: Drovetti to MFA, 10 November.
129. *Corr. 5*, 217: Malivoire to MFA, 1 December; 221: 23 December.
130. Guémard (n.46), 333f.

131. E. Jomard, *Coup d'oeil impartial sur l'état présent de l'Egypte*, 1836, 14f.
132. Rivlin (n.8), 174.
133. The copy is headed with the date 7 September, from Cairo; the year, added in another hand (1821?) has been scratched out. See 'Four unpublished letters by or relating to Bernardino Drovetti', *CdE* 69.1994, 206f.
134. Also in the dossier, Archives of the Ministry of Foreign Affairs, Paris.
135. *Corr. 4*, 51: Roussel to Richelieu, 1 March 1817. So Salt in April (FO 78/89/42f).
136. *Ep.* 92, from Boghos, 9 December, 1816.
137. *ibid.*
138. *Corr. 4*, 64: Roussel to Richelieu, 22 July, 1817.
139. *Corr. 4*, 152: Roussel to Dessoles, 20 March, 1819. F. Coste, *Mémoires d'un artiste*, 1878, 25f.
140. *Corr. 4*, 178: Pillavoine to MFA, 7 September.
    Jean Huyot (1780-1840) was brought to Egypt by the comte de Forbin. He took Drovetti's advice and went to Upper Egypt as far as the Second Cataract, drawing all the monuments, before being called in to solve the problem of the levels and the filtration from the lakes into the canal. He then undertook a prolonged tour of Asia Minor, Greece and Rome, compiling an enormous collection of drawings. He was later professor of architectural history at the Ecole des Beaux-Arts. See *Nouvelle biographie générale* 25.681-683.
141. *Corr. 4*, 188: Pillavoine to MFA; 197: 6 May. Coste, *Mémoires*, 25f, gives the opening date as February 1821.
142. Comte de Marcellus, *Souvenirs de l'Orient*, 1839, 179f, but he was in Egypt in 1820; Thédénat-Duvent (n.2), 17f, but the work is dedicated to the Viceroy! Rivlin (n.8), 218f, accepts Thédénat-Duvent's figure in 1817, with wages of 30 paras a day; workers increased in 1819 to 300,000 and paid 1 piastre.
143. Rivlin, 216.
144. The main sources for the army reforms are Drovetti's official correspondence, his *Epistolario* (far more revealing), and G. Douin, *Une mission militaire auprès de Mohamed Aly*, 1923 (the Boyer-Belliard correspondence: henceforth Douin, *Mission*). And see Guémard (n.46), 114f.
145. *Ep.* 419, from Boyer, 3 October, 1825. Dodwell (n.7) gives Drovetti credit for suggesting the use of fellahin, and notes its success, contrary to expectations. Guémard (n.46) 121 goes only so far as to say that the native army was perhaps Drovetti's idea, perhaps deriving from Napoleon – but which army of his used such soldiers?
146. As a child Sève (1788-1860) was totally uncontrollable, and so was sent to sea at the age of eleven. He was wounded at Trafalgar. For striking an officer he was to be executed, but was reprieved by another whose life he had saved. He enlisted in the 26th Hussars in Italy in 1807, and was captured by the Austrians and held prisoner for two years. He took part in the Russian campaign, and never forgave Napoleon for deserting the army. Wounded at Posen in 1813, he was promoted to lieutenant in the 14th Hussars in 1814, but refused a decoration by the Emperor. At the end of the wars, he left the army and became a dealer in carriages and horses, but in Italy he was recommended to Mehemet Ali by his protector, the comte de Segur.
    He arrived in Egypt in July 1819, and was known henceforth as 'Colonel' Sève. He was first employed as an engineer to find coal at Aswan, and explored the eastern desert. As army instructor he was the object of the usual assassination attempts, and recalled that in training bullets were often whistling around his head. When he saved Mehemet Ali by bringing six regiments to Cairo and forced the Albanians to leave or join the new army, he was given the title Bey and appointed colonel of the 6th. In 1824, when the Wahabite Maugrabian led 20,000 rebels on Cairo, Sève again saved the Viceroy and showed what the new army could do. In the Greek war he captured Sphakteria and guarded Tripolitza. He fell out with Ibrahim as the siege of Missalonghi made the Egyptian more savage.
    Heyworth-Dunne (n.16), 111, states that Drovetti introduced Sève to the Viceroy –

which is quite possible. A. Vingtrinier, *Soliman Pacha*, 1886, does not mention Drovetti once. Salt's report (p. 235) implies the closest cooperation between Drovetti and Sève.

147. *Ep.* 278, from d'Andre, 1 January, 1824.
148. FO 78/126/219-231, 8 February, 1824.
149. *Ep.* 274, from Besson, 28 December 1823. *Ep.* 281, from Besson, 8 January 1824.
150. *Ep.* 277, from Cacherano de Bricherasio(!), 30 December, 1823.
151. Pierre Paul Boyer (1787-1864) served in all the Napoleonic campaigns, including Russian, attaining the rank of chef d'escadron (major, the same as Drovetti). His entry in the *Dictionnaire de biographie française* (7.108) jumps from 1816 to 1830! He was then aide-de-camp to Louis Philippe and the duc de Nemours; at Constantine (1837), in Algeria (1841); he attained the rank of lieutenant-general.
     Pierre Livron (1770-1831) was an emigré in 1792, but served in Egypt and Italy (1798-1800). He entered Neapolitan service in 1806, was colonel and aide-de-camp to Murat, and was in Russia; he left Naples for Trieste, and was captured by the Austrians (1815). Allowed to serve Mehemet Ali in 1824, he returned to France in 1826 (*DBF* 2.127-128).
152. Douin, *Mission*, 5, 19.
153. *Corr. 5*, 45: Boyer to Minister of War, 1 December.
154. Douin, *Mission* 25f; *Ep.* 351, from Boyer, 16 December.
155. *Ep.* 359, from Boyer, 1824 (?); 361, 4 January, 1825; Douin, *Mission*, 20f.
156. *Ep.* 365, from Boyer, 15 January.
157. *Ep.* 381, from Boyer, 22 February; 383, 8 April; 385, 25 April; Douin, *Mission*, 68f.
158. Douin, *Mission*, 68f.
159. *Ep.* 413, from Noureddin, 8 September; 418, from Boyer, 3 October.
160. *Corr. 5*, 82: Malivoire to Damas, 28 September; Douin, *Mission*, 88f.
161. *Corr. 5*, 93.
162. *Ep.* 430, from Boyer, 17 November. It transpires that it took Mariani six months before he was accepted, and that his salary was a miserable 250 piastres with keep and uniform.
163. *Ep.* 449, from Boyer, 8 January, 1826.
164. E. Jomard, 'Ecole égyptienne de Paris', *J. Asiatique* 2.1828, 113f.
165. *Ep.* 454, from Boyer, 22 January; 458, 8 February; Douin, *Mission*, 89 (Frangini), 104f (Boyer to Belliard, 26 February).
166. Douin, *Mission*, 120.
167. *Corr. 5*, 128f: Malivoire to Damas, 25 February; 135f, Drovetti to Damas, 10 March.
168. *Ep.* 457, from Boyer, 4 February.
169 *Corr. 5*, 188; Drovetti to Damas, 7 August.
170. *Corr. 5*, 202: Malivoire to Damas, 16 September.
171. Guémard (n.46), 157.
172. Corr. 5, 229f: Drovetti to Chayolle, 15 November. The departure of the French meant that the officers remaining were Piedmontese, Neapolitan and Spanish, as Salt noted (FO 78/160/102).
173. *Ep.* 454, from Boyer, 22 January.
174. Cameron (n.6), 131.
175. Guémard (n.46), 134f; see also Hamont (n.3), book 4, chap.5.
176. Mouriez (n.110), 3.88.
177. Rivlin (n.8), 201f. Hamont (n.3), book 4, chap.1.
178. Dodwell (n.7), 223f; Guémard (n.46), 206f; on Cerisy, see *ibid.*, 218f; on Besson, *DBF* 6.334f; Heyworth-Dunne (n.16), 139, on the naval school; Jomard (n.131), 33f.
179. The basic collection of sources with narrative is G. Douin, *Les premiers frigates de Mohamed Aly*, 1926.
180. *ibid.*, 22f.
181. *ibid.*, 28f.
182. *ibid.*, 43.
183. *ibid.*, 45f.

184. *ibid.* 58f.

185. *ibid.*, 65f.

Chapter Seven

1. For some of the revolting details, see K. Dannenfield, 'Egypt in the Renaissance', *Studies in the Renaissance* 6.1959, 7-27.

2. R. Pococke, *Description of the East*, 1743, 1.94.

3. W. Kalnein and M. Levey, *Art and architecture in 18th century France*, 1972, 331.

4. V. Denon, *Voyage dans la Basse et la Haute Egypte*, Eng. trans. 2.65f, cf. 283.

5. C. Vidua, *Lettere*, 1820, 2.239f; Minutoli, *Recollections of Egypt*, 1827, 3; G. Bertolotti, *Passeggiate nel canavese* 7.328.

6. E. Jomard, *Voyage à l'oasis de Thèbes*, 1821, 56.

7. E. Montulé, *Voyage en Amérique, en Italie, en Sicile, et en Egypte pendant les années 1816-1819*, 1821, Eng. trans. 45. G. Botti, 'La collezione Drovetti', *RAL* 5.30.1921, 128-135, 143-149 at p.129 suggested that the main campaigns were carried out at Thebes between 1818 (or a little earlier) and 1820. The most important statues are engraved 'found at Thebes by Rifaud, sculptor in the service of M. Drovetti, 1818'. G. Marro, 'Il R. Museo di Antichità di Torino e Champollion le Jeune', *Boll. SPABA* 7.1923, 7-26, p.14, dates the collecting to the first fifteen years of Drovetti's stay in Egypt (i.e. 1803/4-1818/19); so 'Documenti inediti sulla cessione al Piemonte della collezione egiziana Drovetti', *Atti Accad. Torino* 69.1933/4, 44-78, p.44, and 'Bernardino Drovetti, archeologo', *Aegyptus* 32.1952, 120-130, p.124. S. Curto, *Storia del museo egizio di Torino*, 1976, 46, dates Drovetti's 'researches' unadventurously 1811-1827.

8. *Corr.3*, 153: Saint-Marcel to Bassano, 15 December 1821; 165: 30 January.

9. W. Turner, *Journal of a tour in the Levant*, 1820, 2.321. Cf. *Description de l'Egypte* vol.2, Pls 49-50.

10. J. Burckhardt, *Travels in Nubia*, 1819, lxxix. At about the same time, Hester Stanhope's doctor saw the collection in the company of Burckhardt. He mentioned Drovetti's hope of selling it in Europe (a footnote states that it was, in fact, sold to Munich!) and that its value was estimated at 3,000 guineas, which the doctor regarded as generous (*Travels of Lady Hester Stanhope*, 1846, 3.218). The collection at Alexandria is mentioned, without details, in 1816 also by Ambrose Firmin Didot, *Notes d'un voyage fait dans le Levant en 1816 et 1817*, (ND), 187.

11. J. Halls, *Life and correspondence of Henry Salt*, 1834, 1.472. Irby and Mangles claimed in 1817 that Drovetti had offered his collection to Salt, of all people, on his arrival in 1816, for 7,000 pounds, and that rivalry between the two had forced up the price of papyri from 8-10 piastres to 30-50: *Travels in Egypt and Nubia*, 1844, 44.

12. Forbin, *Travels in Egypt in 1817-1818*, 1819, 23f; 72f.

13. The same claim is made by Forbin's contemporary in Egypt, Edouard Montulé (n.7), 46: 'The Arabians, by whom he is adored, uniformly convey to him the results of their labours.'

14. Vidua, *Lettere* 2.162f, 239f.

15. J. Scholz, *Travels in the countries between Alexandria and Paratonium*, 38.

16. *Ep.* 90, from Rignon, July 1816.

17. *Ep.* 102, from Forbin, 22 May 1818.

18. *Ep.* 108, from Forbin, 30 July.

19. *Ep.* 124, from Forbin, 1 March, 1819.

20. *Ep.* 128, from Forbin, 25 May.

21. *Ep.* 131, from Rignon, 22 July.

22. *Ep.* 133, from Jomard, 29 July.

23. See above, p. 92.

24. *Ep.* 142, from Saluzzo, 30 March 1820.

25. *Ep.* 145, from Gau, 10 May.

26. *Ep.* 147, from Gau, 20 June.

27. Vidua, *Lettere* 2.197f.
28. G. Botti, *art.cit.* (n.7), 131, and G. Marro, 'Bernardino Drovetti, archeologo' (n.7), 124, add that the Grand Duke of Tuscany also was interested. He acquired part of the Nizzoli collection in 1824. Marro, 'Il R. Museo' (n.7), 14, claims that Drovetti refused very tempting offers from England, Germany (Prussia and Bavaria) and Rome.
29. In the Drovetti dossier, Ministry of Foreign Affairs, Paris.
30. Vidua, Lettere, 2.211.
31. Marro, 'Documenti inediti' (n.7), 51.
32. *Ep.* 160, from Prospero Balbo, 6 November 1820.
33. *Ep.* 168, from Saluzzo, 12 February 1821, refers to Drovetti's letter of 6 December, which Marro, 'Documenti inediti', 58, 62, misdates to January.
34. *Ep.* 196, from Incisa de St. Etienne, 15 April, 1822.
35. *Ep.* 179, from Vidua, 28 September 1821.
36. See above, p.152f, 154, 157f.
37. *Ep.* 290, from Cordero di San Quintino, 20 February 1824. T. Young, *An account of some recent discoveries in hieroglyphical literature and Eg. antiquities*, 1823, 34f.
38. The episode is unknown to A. Wood and F. Oldham, *Thomas Young*, 1954.
39. *Ep.* 194, from Vidua, 12 March 1822.
40. *Ep.* 234, from Vidua, 19 October.
41. The original is in the Torino archives, Patenti Controllo Finanze vol.33, p.213, and a copy in *Ep.* 737f. Nothing at all is added to this story by G. Marro, 'Elementi ignorati sulla fondazione del museo egiziano di Torino', *Atti XXVI Cong. stor. subalpino*, 1933, or by C. Bianchi, 'Bernardino Drovetti e il museo egizio di Torino', *Edilizia* 22.1976, 13-15, or by M. Bernardini, 'Come Torino procurò il tesoro egizio', *Bolaffi arte* 5.1974, 42-49, who dates the Siwan expedition to 1829, says that Drovetti was Consul-*general* from 1803, and that Belzoni worked for the English Consul Dalt. There is a very short account in S. Curto, *Storia del museo egizio di Torino*, 1976, 43f: only one of the Drovetti pieces is identified in the illustrations of this book, the statue of Ramesses. Among innumerable gross errors in the entry on Drovetti in the *DBF* (11.836-837) is the claim that the contract included the clause that Drovetti was to be keeper of the collection and that the price was 100,000 lire plus 10,000 a year.
42. Nothing is added on the small part played by San Quintino by G. Giorgi, *Un archeologo piemontese dei primi dell'Ottocento*, 1982, who neglects his letters on Drovetti. The two letters of Artaud and the two of San Quintino were published by G. Marro, 'Sull'arrivo della collezione egittologica Drovetti in Piemonte', *Boll. SPABA* 8.1924, 49-61.
43. San Quintino, 'Notizie intorno alla collezione di antichità egiziane del cav. Drovetti', *Giornale arcadico* 19.1823, 180-208.
44. S. Curto, *Storia* (n.41), 48.
45. *Ep.* 285f, from San Quintino, 3 February 1824.
46. *Ep.* 289f, from San Quintino, 20 February.
47. *Ep.* 290.
48. *Ep.* 291.
49. P. Barocelli, 'Il viaggio del dott. Vitaliano Donati in Oriente in relazione colle prime origini del museo egiziano di Torino', *Atti Accad. Torino* 47.1912, 411-425. See also S. Curto, *Storia* (n.41), 43f.
50. G. Marro, 'Il R. Museo' (n.7), 15, takes it seriously.
51. S. Curto, *Storia* (n.41), 43f, fig.55.
52. Champollion, *Lettres* 1.1ff.
53. *Ep.* 304f, from Artaud, 16 May, 1824.
54. *Ep.* 375, from Artaud, 12 February 1825.
55. *Ep.* 497, from Artaud, 23 October, 1826.
56. G. Marro, 'Il R. Museo' (n.7), 14.
57. S. Curto, *Storia* (n.41), 47.
58. G. Marro, 'Il R. Museo' (n.7) is very diffuse.
59. G. Botti, 'La collezione Drovetti' (n.7), 129.

60. C. Vidua, *Lettere* 2.201.
61. J. Halls, *Life and correspondence* (n.11), 1.467.
62. *ibid.* 1.498.
63. *ibid.* 2.295f. E. Miller, *That noble cabinet, a history of the British Museum*, 1974, 198f, states that Salt suffered from the 'misapprehension' that 'anything he collected would be accepted without question by the Trustees', but admits that Belzoni also found their offers unreliable, and that Banks simply decided that 'it would be unwise for the Museum to accept any more Egyptian antiquities' because they could not equal classical art. In sum, Salt was embittered, 'with good reason'. Miller makes the extraordinary assertion that the sarcophagus of Seti was discovered in the Second Pyramid!
    Drovetti is reputed to have offered 2,000 pounds ($10,000) for the sarcophagus, as did Minutoli (Halls, *Life and correspondence*, 2.308; Belzoni, *Narrative* 2.100, without giving prices).
64. Halls, *Life and correspondence* 2.245, 251, 253.
65. *ibid.* 2.39f (Thebes), 65f (Caviglia), 121f (second journey), 183f (third journey).
66. Catalogue no.1383.
67. Champollion, *Lettres* 1.111f; see also Hermine Hartleben, *Champollion, sein Leben und sein Werk*, 1906, 1.543f.
68. S. Curto, 'Il torinese colosso di Osimandia', *Boll. SPABA* 18.1964, 5-26.
69. J. Bramsen, *Travels in Egypt, Syria and Cyprus*, 1820, 181f.
70. See Pauly-Wissowa, *Realencyclopädie* 23.1763; W. Peremans and E. van't Dack, *Prosopographia ptolemaica* 1950-1963, 2.4315. The inscription is now Dittenberger, OGIS 99, where the editor says that its origin is unknown, and makes no mention of Drovetti.
71. Standard reference works on Egyptian art commonly illustrate a few of these: Amenhotep II (K. Michalowski, *Great sculpture of ancient Egypt*, 1978, 134); Tutankamon and Amon (W. Stevenson-Smith, *Art and architecture of ancient Egypt*, 1958, 138-139); Seti II (Stevenson-Smith, 159; Michalowski, 156; Irmgard Woldering, *The arts of Egypt*, 1968, 87).
72. Stevenson-Smith, 22; Michalowski, 85.
73. H. Winlock, *The rise and fall of the Middle Kingdom*, 1947, 4.
74. See above p. 257f.
75. Letters from Torino, 30 October, 6 November 1824, published in *Bull. Universelle* 1.1824, 297-303. See also Champollion, *Lettres* 1.84f.
76. I Rosellini, *Monumenti storici* 1.1832, 147.
77. F. Barucchi, *Discorsi critici sopra la cronologia egizia*, 1844, 29.
78. J.G. Wilkinson, *The fragments of the hieratic papyrus at Turin*, 1851.
79. E. de Rougé, 'Recherches sur les monuments des six premiers dynasties', *Mem. Acad. Insc.* 25.1866, 225f.
80. E.A. Budge, *History of Egypt*, 1.1902, 118.
81. E. Meyer, *Ägyptische Chronologie*, 1904, 105f.
82. G. Farina, *Il papiro dei re restaurato*, 1939.
83. A.H. Gardiner, *The royal canon of Turin*, 1959.
84. For the most accessible edition of the Torino Canon, especially comparing it with the other lists, see A.H. Gardiner, *Egypt of the pharaohs*, 1961, 429f.
85. F. Chabas, *Les inscriptions des mines d'or*, 1862, 30f; F. Lauth, 'Die älteste Landkarte nubischer Goldminen', *SB Akad. Munich*, 1870, 337-372 (neither is interested in provenance or mention of Drovetti).
86. R. Lepsius, 'Grundplan des Grabes König Ramses IV in einem Turiner Papyrus', *Abh. Akad. Berlin*, 1867, 1-21 (no provenance).
87. T. Deveria, 'Le papyrus judiciaire de Turin', *J. Asiatique* 6.1865, 227-261, 331-377, 8.1866, 154-195, 10.1867, 402-476 (no provenance, no Drovetti). For a translation of this text, see Breasted, *Records of ancient Egypt* 4.416f.

88. G. Botti and T. Peet, *Il gironale della necropoli di Tebe*, 1928. The editors mention p.5 Drovetti and the lack of information on the papyrus' provenance, and suggest, p.7, that it comes from Deir el Medineh, unless Cerny is right that it was found at Medinet Habu, the archives of the temple of Ramesses III: they are only about one kilometre apart.

89. J. Omlin, *Der Papyrus 55001 und seine satirisch-erotischen Zeichnungen und Inschriften*, 1973. The editor mentions Drovetti, gives the provenance of the papyrus as Deir el Medineh, and dates it not later than Ramesses III (p.17f).

90. See *Love poems of the New Kingdom*, 1974, translated by J. Foster.

91. For a translation, see J. Pritchard, *Ancient near eastern texts*, 12f.

92. *The Egyptian Museum in Turin*, Eng. ed. by J. Shiffman, 1988, 30, 34.

93. M. Bierbrier, *The tomb builders of the pharaohs*, 1982, 130.

94. M. Tosi and A. Roccati, *Stele e altri epigrafi de Deir el Medineh*, 1972.

95. F. Rossi, *Atti Accad. Torino* 13.1877/8, 905-924: 'Illustrazione di una stele funeraria dell' XI dinastia'.

96. E. Lefebure, *Ann. Serv.* 20.1920, 207-213.

97. R. Lepsius, 'Die altägyptische Elle', *Abh. Akad. Berlin*, 1865, 1-64, p.14.

98. T. Young, *An account of some recent discoveries* (n.37), 34f, cf. Lebolo ap. *Ep.* 290.

99. C. Debiaggi, 'Un appunto sul busto di Bernardino Drovetti nel museo egizio di Torino', *Boll. SPABA* 27-29, 1973-5 (1977!), 82-83.

100. The labelling in the museum in general is of the poorest standard, many items without one, and no attempt is made to educate the visitor with 'essay-style' placards on major periods or themes, as are frequently found in museums in England or Germany.
The newest guide to the collection is an elegant edition in four languages, 1988. The English translation, by J. Shiffman, is excellent (n.92). The book is thoughtful, with a mythological and artistic glossary, as well as good illustrations. Drovetti is, however, hardly mentioned, apart from the historical introduction. In the chapter on the statuary gallery, Schiaparelli's finds are frequently identified, but Drovetti's name never appears!

101. F. Cailliaud, *Voyage à Méroé*, 1826, 3.327-331.

102. *Ep.* 306, from Artaud, 16 May 1824.

103. *Ep.* 321, from Jomard, 14 August.

104. *Ep.* 436, from Jomard via Boyer, 29 November 1825.

105. Jomard, *Bull. universelle* 3.1825, 225-227.

106. *Moniteur universelle* 22 March 1826, p.368. The same note is repeated almost verbatim in *Bull. universelle* 5.1826, 282-283. For Drovetti's letter announcing its embarkation, see *Ep.* 288, along with 8 horses and an elephant given by Mehemet Ali to the King and the Dauphin, as well as presents for all the chief ministers.

107. *Bull. universelle* 5.1826, 283-285, probably by Jomard.

108. *Bull. universelle* 5.1826, 373-382, 445-454.

109. Reprinted in *Ep.* 741f.

110. By a happy coincidence, Mme Kanawaty recently discovered the complete list of the collection in the papers of the Ministry of the Royal Household, which has allowed the identification of dozens of the more important items: 'Identification des pièces de la collection Drovetti au Musée du Louvre', *Revue d'Egyptologie* 37.1986, 167-171. There is a total lack of interest in the Drovetti collection by Christiane Aulanier, *Le musée Charles X et le département des antiquités égyptiennes*, 1961: pp.36, 80 make only incidental mention of him.

111. The horrible story is told by J.J. Fiechter, *La moisson des dieux*, 209f.

112. *Ep.* 569, Champollion to Mechain, 29 September 1828. A second copy of the decree in legible condition was found at Tanis in 1865 by a French engineer and published by Lepsius, *Das bilingue Dekret von Canopus*, 1866. A third and even better copy was found by Maspero at Kom el- Hisn in 1881, published by him in the *Journal des Savants*, 1883, 214-229. A. Bouche-Leclercq, *Histoire des Lagides*, 1903, 266, the standard work on the dynasty, makes no mention of Drovetti, of course. For a translation of the text, see G.

Mahaffy, *History of Egypt under the Ptolemaic dynasty*, 1899, 111f.

113. *Corr.6*, 115: Drovetti to Ferronays, 4 May, 1829.
114. FO 78/160/55, to Salt, 27 November 1827.
115. *Ep.* 604, from Mecique (?), 1 May 1828.
116. G. Ebers, *Richard Lepsius*, trans. Underhill, 1887, 97. There is no mention of Drovetti in the latest lavish catalogue, *Das Ägyptische Museum, Berlin*, 1991, but much about the Passalacqua, Minutoli and Lepsius collections. I have been promised further information by the Berlin Museum on various occasions.
117. *Encyclopaedia Britannica*, 9th ed. 1875-1889, 10.647 – but not in the classic 11th edition.
118. J. Cooney, *Catalogue of egyptian antiquities in the British Museum*, vol.4, *Glass*, no.362.
119. For identification of these, see J.J. Fiechter, *La moisson des dieux*, 248f, exemplary detective work.
120. E. Montulé, *Travels in Egypt*, 67.
121. I.E.S. Edwards, *The pyramids of Egypt*, 1991, 79, 81.
122. A. Fakhry, *The Bent Pyramid*, 1959, 4; see also 13, 49.
123. R. Vyse and J. Perring, *Operations carried on at the pyramids of Gizeh*, 1840-1842, 3.67.
124. *Ep.* 531f, Drovetti to Baruffi. The letter is undated but must be about 1837. By an egregious error the editors date it c.1827, because of references to work on the pyramids.
125. E. Jomard, *Description d'un étalon métrique*, 1822, 4.
126. A.H. Rhind, *Thebes, its tombs and their tenants*, 1862, 67-68.
127. *ibid.*, 261, 266. Rhind (1833-1863) was a lawyer who excavated at Thebes in the 1850s; his finds went to the Royal Scottish Museum and the British Museum. He also endowed a lectureship at Edinburgh. On Champollion, see 'Champollion in the tomb of Seti I: an unpublished letter', *CdE* 66.1991, 23-30.
128. A. Mariette, *Rev. Arch.* NS 2.1860, 24. This is the only reference to my knowledge in all Mariette's considerable writings. For an assessment of Mariette within his time and constraints, see 'Auguste Mariette, one hundred years after', *Abr-Nahrain* 22.1984, 118-158.
129. J. Baikie, *A century of excavation in the land of the pharaohs*, 1924, 8-9.
130. R. Almagia (ed.), *L'opera degli italiani per la conoscenza dell'Egitto*, 1926, 2. Breccia (1876-1967) was director of the Graeco-Roman museum at Alexandria 1904-1931, and then professor of history at Pisa.
131. 'molto gusto e finissimo fiuto', *ibid.* 6.
132. G. Marro, 'Bernardino Drovetti, archeologo', *Aegptus* 32.1952, 121-130, p.123.
133. E. Breccia, 'Ippolito Rosellini e Bernardino Drovetti', *Aegyptus* 32.1952, 138-142, p.141.
134. F. Cailliaud, *Voyage à Méroé*, 1.294.

Chapter Eight

1. The matters in this chapter, being a resume of earlier chapters, are not referenced except where they have not been cited before. Otherwise they can easily be traced through the index or by the year of the narrative.
2. Abdine archives, quoted and translated by G. Douin (ed.), *Mohamed Aly et l'expédition d'Alger 1829-1830*, intro. lxxxv.
3. J. Pringle, 'Route de l'Inde, par l'Egypte et la Mer Rouge', *Bull. Soc. Geog.* 5.1826, 651-660.
4. F. Cailliaud, *Voyage à Méroé*, 1.6.
5. I thank most sincerely my wife for providing me with her reflections on Drovetti's portrait, from which the above is drawn.

Bibliography

Archival sources
London: Public Record Office.
Paris: Ministère des Affaires Etrangères.
Torino: Archivio di Stato
      Università.

Books, articles and manuscripts
A.B., *Histoire régimentaire et divisionnaire de l'armée d'Italie*, Paris 1844.
Abdel Malek, A., *La formation de l'idéologie dans la renaissance nationale de l'Egypte*, Paris 1969.
Abu Lughod, A., *The Arab rediscovery of Europe*, Princeton 1963.
L'antico Egitto nel museo di Torino, Torino 1984.
Artin, Y., *L'instruction publique en Egypte*, Paris 1890.
Athanasi, G. d', *A brief account of the researches and discoveries in Upper Egypt made under the direction of Henry Salt*, London 1836.
Auriant, 'Un centenaire oublié: le coton Jumel. Deux mémoires du consul de France en Egypte Drovetti', *Bull. de la Société d'encouragement pour l'industrie nationale* 1923, 420-432.
--   'En marge des découvertes de la Vallée des Rois', *Le correspondent* 10 March 1924, 808-835.
--   'Le voyage politique de colonel Boutin 1811-1812', *Revue bleue* 6 Sept. 1924, 594-599.
Baedecker, *Egypt*, Leipzig 1929.
Baikie, J., *A century of excavation in the land of the pharaohs*, London 1923.
Balboni, L., *Gli italiani nella civiltà egiziana del XIX secolo* (3 vols), Alexandria 1906.
Barocelli, P., 'Il viaggio del dott. Vitaliano Donato in Oriente (1759-1762) in relazione colle prime origini del museo egiziano di Torino', *Atti Accad. Torino* 47.1912, 411-425.
Barucchi, F., *Discorsi critici sopra la cronologia egiziana*, Torino 1844.
Baruffi, G., *Passeggiate nei dintorni di Torino*, Torino 1858.
--   *Viaggio da Torino alle piramidi fatto nell'autunno 1843*, Torino 1848.
Belzoni, G.B., *Narrative of the operations and recent discoveries within the pyramids, temples, tombs and excavations in Egypt and Nubia* (2 vols), 3rd ed., London 1822.
Bernardi, M., 'Come Torino si procurì il tesoro egizio', *Bolaffi arte* no.44, 5.1974, 42-49.
Bertolotti, A., *Passeggiate nel canavese*, Ivea 1874.
Bianchi, C., 'Bernardino Drovetti e il museo egizio di Torino', *Edilizia* 22.1976, 13-15.
Boccardo, G., *Nuova enciclopedia italiana*, 6th ed. Torino 1875-1888.
Bongioanni, A. and Grazzi, R., *Torino, l'Egitto e l'Oriente fra storia e leggenda*, Torino 1994.
Bongioanni, F., *Memoires d'un jacobin*, ed. G. Vaccarino, Torino 1958.
Bosi, P., *Dizionario storico, biografico, topografico, militare d'Italia*, Torino 1869.
Botta, C., *History of Italy during the consulate and empire of Napoleon Bonaparte*, trans. Frances Moore (2 vols), London 1828.
--   *Lettere*, ed. P. Viani, Torino 1841.
--   *Lettere inédite*, ed. P. Pavesio, Faenza 1875.
Botti, G., 'La collezione Drovetti', *RAL* 5.30.1921, 128-135, 143-149.
Bussière, Renouard de, *Lettres sur l'Orient écrites pendant les années 1827 et 1828* (2 vols), Paris 1829.
Bramsen, J., *Travels in Egypt, Syria and Cyprus* (2 vols), London 1820.

Brancaccio, N., *L'esercito del vecchio Piemonte*, Rome 1922.

Breccia, E., 'L'esplorazione archaeologica', in R. Almagia (ed.), *L'opera degli italiani per la conoscenza dell'Egitto*, Rome 1926.

-- 'Ippolito Rosellini e Bernardino Drovetti', *Aegyptus* 32.1952, 138-142.

Brocchi, G.B., *Giornale delle osservazioni fatte nei viaggi in Egitto nella Siria e nella Nubia* (6 vols), Bassano 1841-1843.

Buckingham, J.S., *Autobiography of James Silk Buckingham* (2 vols), London 1855.

Budge, E.A.W., *Cleopatra's Needle and other Egyptian obelisks*, London 1926.

-- *History of Egypt* (8 vols), London 1902.

Bulletin universelle, 5.1826, 282f, 373f, 445f (unsigned articles).

Bunbury, H., *Narratives of some passages in the Great War with France from 1799 to 1810*, London 1927.

Burckhardt, J., *Travels in Nubia*, London 1819.

Burton (Haliburton), J., Diary (BM Add MS 25,613-25, 675).

Bus, C. du, 'Edmé François Jomard et les origines du Cabinet des Cartes (1777-1862)', *Comité des Travaux historiques et scientifiques: Bulletin de la section de géographie* 46.1931, 1-128.

Cagnone, C. and Mosca, C., *Notizie biografiche sul cav. Bernardino Drovetti desunte dai documenti scritti da esso*, Torino 1857.

Cailliaud, F., *Voyage à l'oasis de Thèbes et dans les déserts situés à l'Orient et à l'Occident de la Thébaide fait pendant les années 1815, 1816, 1817 et 1818* (ed. Jomard), Paris 1821.

-- *Voyage à Méroé* (6 vols), Paris 1823-1827.

Cameron, D., *Egypt in the nineteenth century*, London 1898.

Carne, J., *Letters from the east*, London 1826.

-- *Recollections of travel in the east*, London 1830.

Carré, J., *Voyageurs et écrivains français en Egypte* (2 vols), Paris 1956.

Casalis, G., *Dizionario geografico storico-statistico-commerciale degli stati di S.M. il Re di Sardegna* (28 vols), Torino 1833-1856.

Cattaui, R., *Mohamed Aly et l'Europe*, Paris 1950.

-- *Le règne de Mohamed Aly d'après les archives russes en Egypte*, Cairo 1931-1936.

Champollion, J.F., 'Antiquités égyptiennes. Collection Drovetti', *Revue encyclopédique* 22.1824, 767.

-- *Lettres à M. le duc de Blacas* (2 vols), Paris 1824-1826.

-- *Lettres écrites d'Egypte et de Nubie en 1828 et 1829*, Paris 1833.

-- *Lettres et journaux*, ed. H. Hartleben (2 vols), Paris 1909.

-- 'Papyrus égyptiens. Extrait des lettres de M. Champollion', *Bull. univ.* 1.1824, 297-303.

Champollion-Figeac, A., *Les deux Champollions*, Grenoble 1887.

Champollion-Figeac, J.J., *L'obelisque de Louqsor*, Paris 1833.

Charles-Roux, F., *L'Angleterre et l'expédition française en Egypte* (2 vols), Cairo 1925.

-- *Bonaparte, gouverneur d'Egypte*, Paris 1936.

Chateaubriand, F., *Itinéraire de Paris à Jérusalem*, Paris 1811 (many later editions).

Christophe, L., *Abu Simbel*, Torino 1970.

Cibrario, L., *Descrizione storica degli ordini cavallereschi*, Torino 1846.

Clot, A., *Aperçu général sur l'Egypte* (2 vols), Paris 1840.

-- *Compte-rendu des travaux de l'école de médecine d'Abou-Zabel, Egypte*, Paris 1833.

-- *Mémoires*, ed. J. Taylor, Cairo 1949.

Cognasso, F., *Storia di Torino*, Milano 1961.

'Collection de monuments égyptiens acquise par le roi de France', *Bull. univ.* 5.1826, 283-285.

Cooper, E., *Views in Egypt and Nubia*, London 1824-1827.

Coste, P., *Mémoires d'un artiste*, Marseille 1878.

Cugnac, comte, *Campagne de l'armée de reserve en 1800* (2 vols), Paris 1900-1901.

-- *La campagne de Marengo*, Paris 1904.

Curto, S., 'All'ombra dei cipressi', *Boll. SPABA* 23/24.1969/70, 5-9.

--   *Storia del museo egizio di Torino*, Torino 1976.

--   'Il torinese colosso di Osimandia', *Boll. SPABA* 18.1964, 5-25.

Dakin, D., *The Greek struggle for independence 1821-1833*, London 1973.

Dardaud, G., 'L'extraordinaire aventure de la girafe du Pacha d'Egypte', *Revue des conférences françaises en Orient*, 13.1951, 1-72.

Debiaggi, C., 'Un appunto sul busto di Bernardino Drovetti nel museo egizio di Torino', *Boll. SPABA* 27-29, 1973-1975, 82-83.

Denon, V., *Travels in Upper and Lower Egypt* (3 vols), London 1803.

Dewachter, M., 'Graffiti des voyageurs du XIX siècle relevés dans le temple d'Amada en Basse Nubie', *BIFAO* 69.1971, 131-169.

--   'Le voyage nubien du comte Carlo Vidua', *BIFAO* 69.1971, 171-189.

Dictionnaire de biographie française, Paris 1933-

Documenti inediti per servire alla storia dei musei d'Italia (4 vols), Rome 1876-80.

Dodwell, H., *The founder of modern Egypt*, Cambridge 1931.

Donadoni, Anna Maria et al., *Museo egizio di Torino*, Novara 1988.

Douin, G. (ed.), *L'Egypte de 1802 à 1804*, Cairo 1925.

--   *L'Egypte de 1828 à 1830*, Rome 1935.

--   *Mohamed Aly, pacha du Caire 1805-1807*, Cairo 1926.

--   *Mohammed Ali et l'expédition d'Alger 1829-1830*, Cairo 1923.

--   *Une mission militaire française auprès de Mohammed Ali*, Cairo 1923.

--   *Navarin (6 juillet-20 octobre 1827)*, Cairo 1927.

--   *La première guerre de la Syrie*, Cairo 1925.

--   *Les premiers frigates de Mohamed Aly 1824-1827*, Cairo 1926.

--   'La conquête du Soudan', *Revue du Caire* Sept. 1944, 413-444.

Douin, G. and Mme E. Fawtier-Jones, *L'Angleterre et l'Egypte: la campagne de 1807*, Cairo 1928.

Driault, E. (ed.), *Expédition de Crète et de Morée 1823-1828*, Cairo 1930.

--   *La formation de l'empire de Mohamed Aly de l'Arabie au Soudan 1814-1823*, Cairo, 1927.

--   *Mohamed Aly et Napoléon, 1807-1814*, Cairo 1925.

Drovetti, B., *Il corpo epistolare di Bernardino Drovetti*, ed. G. Marro, vol.1 only, Rome 1940.

--   'Discorso inaugurale detto dall'Ill.mo Sig. Bernardino Drovetti', *Società Biellese per l'avanzamento delle arti, dei mestieri e dell'agricoltura, Atti*, 1845, 4-16.

--   *Epistolario*, ed. S. Curto and L. Donatelli, Milano 1985 (rev. JEA 77.1991, 237-241).

--   'Idioma di Siwah' in G. Marro, 'Un cimelio del viaggio di B. Drovetti all'oasi di Giove Ammone', *Bull. Soc. roy. de Geog. Cairo*, 19.1934, 1-19.

--   *Journal d'un voyage à la vallée de Dakel, in Voyage à l'oasis de Thèbes...* (ed. Jomard), Paris 1821, 99-105.

--   *Voyage à l'oasis de Syouah, redigé et publié par M. Jomard ... d'après les matériaux recueillis par M. le chevalier Drovetti...* Paris 1823. See also Zavati.

Drovetti, G., 'Il mio glorioso avo Bernardino Drovetti', *Rivista municipale*, Torino 1931 (no.8), 57-61.

Duhesme, P., *Essai sur l'infantérie légère*, Paris 1814.

Durand-Viel, G., *Les campagnes navales de Mohammed Aly et d'Ibrahim* (2 vols), Paris 1952.

Ebers, G., *Richard Lepsius*, trans. Underhill, London 1887.

Edmonstone, A., *Journey to two of the oases of Upper Egypt*, London 1822.

Edwards, I.E.S., *The pyramids of Egypt*, Harmondsworth 1991.

The Egyptian Museum Turin, trans. J. Shiffman, Torino 1988.

Enciclopedia italiana, Rome 1929-

Encyclopaedia Britannica, 9th ed. Cambridge 1878.

Fabretti, A., Rossi, F., and Lanzone, R., *Regio museo di Torino ordinato e descritto, Antichità egizie*, Torino 1882.

Faino, R., *I soldati italiani di Napoleone*, Milan 1914.

Fakhry, A., *The Bent Pyramid*, Cairo 1959.

Farina, G., *Bernardino Drovetti, archeologo*, Torino 1921.

--   *Il papiro dei re restaurato*, Torino 1939.

Fermi, S., 'Dieci lettere inedite di P. Giordani a B. Drovetti', *Boll. stor. piacentino* 6.1911, 60-71.

Ferreri, G., *Brevi cenni su Barbania canavese*, Torino 1904.

Fiechter, J.J., *La moisson des dieux. La constitution des grandes collections égyptiennes 1815-1830*, Paris 1994.

Finati, G., *Narrative of the life and adventures of Giovanni Finati*, ed. W. Bankes (2 vols), London 1830.

Firman Didot, A., *Notes d'un voyage fait dans le Levant en 1816 et 1817*, Paris (1822 ?).

Forbin, comte de, *Le portfeuille du comte de Forbin*, Paris 1843.

-- *Voyage dans le Levant en 1817 et 1818*, Paris 1819: Eng. trans. *Travels in Egypt in 1817 and 1818*, London 1819.

Fortescue, J., *History of the British army* (13 vols), London 1899-1930.

Frediani, E., see Wolynski.

Fugier, A., *Napoleone e l'Italia* (2 vols), Rome 1970.

Gardiner, A.H., *Egypt of the pharaohs*, Oxford 1964.

-- *The royal canon of Turin*, Torino 1959.

Gau, F., *Antiquités de la Nubie*, Paris 1822.

Gazzera, G., 'Applicazione delle dottrine del Sig. Champollion Minore ad alcuni monumenti geroglifici', *Mem. Accad. Torino* 29.1825, 83-142.

Gell, W., *Sir William Gell in Italy*, ed. Edith Clay, London 1976.

Ghorbal, S., *The beginnings of the Egyptian question and the rise of Mehemet Aly*, London 1928.

Giddy, Lisa, *The Egyptian oases*, Warminster 1987.

Giffard, P., *Les français en Egypte*, 2nd ed., Paris 1883.

Gillespie, C. and Dewachter, M., *The monuments of Egypt. The Napoleonic expedition*, Princeton 1987.

Giorgi, G., *Un archeologo piemontese dei primi dell'Ottocento*, Torino 1982.

Gouin, E., *L'Egypte au XIX siècle*, Paris 1847.

Greener, L., *The discovery of Egypt*, London 1966.

Guémard, G., *Les réformes en Egypte 1760-1848*, Cairo 1936.

Halls, J., *The life and correspondence of Henry Salt* (2 vols), London 1834.

Hamont, P., *L'Egypte sous Méhémet Ali* (2 vols), Paris 1843.

Hartleben, Hermine, *Champollion. Sein Leben und sein Werk* (2 vols), Berlin 1906.

Hay, R., Diary (BM Add MS 31,054).

Hearder, H., *Europe in the nineteenth century 1830-1880*, 2nd ed., London 1988.

-- *Italy in the age of the Risorgimento 1790-1870*, London 1980.

Helck, W. and Otto, E., *Lexikon der Aegyptologie* (6 vols), Wiesbaden 1975-1985.

Henniker, F., *Notes during a visit to Egypt*, London 1823.

Heyworth-Dunne, J., *Introduction to the history of education in modern Egypt*, London 1939.

Hyde, J., *Journal London to Cairo and up the Nile* (BM Add. MS 42,102-42, 103).

Irby, C. and Mangles, J., *Travels in Egypt and Nubia*, 2nd ed., London 1844.

Jomard, E., 'Antiquités égyptiennes', *Bull. univ.* 3.1825, 225-227.

-- *Coup d'oeil impartial sur l'état présent de l'Egypte*, Paris 1836.

-- *Description d'un étalon metrique orné d'hieroglyphes découvert dans les ruines de Memphis par les soins de M. le chev. Drovetti*, Paris 1822.

-- 'L'école égyptienne de Paris', *J. Asiatique* 2.1828, 96-116.

-- *Lettre à M. Remusat sur une nouvelle mesure de coudée trouvée à Memphis par M. Drovetti*, Paris 1827.

Jomard (ed.), *Description de l'Egypte* (9 vols. text, 10 vols ills, 2 atlases), Paris 1809-1828.

-- *Voyage à l'oasis de Syouah ... d'après les matériaux recueillis par M. le chevalier Drovetti et par M. Frédéric Cailliaud pendant leurs voyages dans cette oasis en 1819 et 1820*, Paris 1823.

-- *Voyage à l'oasis de Thèbes et dans les deserts situés à l'orient et à l'occident de la Thébaide fait pendant les années 1815-1818*, Paris 1821.

Jonghe, Elzelina van Alyde (alias Ida Saint-Elme), *La contemporaine en Egypte* (6 vols), Paris 1831.

Kanawaty, Monique, 'Les acquisitions du Musée Charles X', *BSFE* 104.1985, 31-54.

-- 'Identification de pièces de la collection Drovetti au Musée du Louvre', *RdE* 37.1986, 161-171.

Laborde, L., 'Journal d'une voyage dans le Fayoum', *Rev. française* 7.1829, 47-83.

Lane, E., *Notes and views in Egypt and Nubia made during the years 1825-1828* (3 vols text, 6 of ills) (BM Add MS 34,080-34,088).

Larousse, *Grande dictionnaire universelle du XIX siècle*, Paris 1864-1890.

Lebas, J., *L'obélisque de Luxor*, Paris 1839.

Leclant, J., 'Voyage de N. Huyot en Egypte', *BSFE* 32.1961, 35-42.

Legh, T., *Narrative of a journey in Egypt*, London 1816.

Light, H., *Travels in Egypt, Nubia, the Holy Land, Mt. Lebanon and Cyprus in the year 1814*, London 1818.

Linant de Bellefonds, L., *Journal d'un voyage à Méroé dans les années 1821 et 1822*, (ed. Margaret Shinnie), Khartoum 1958.

Lumbroso, G., 'Descrittori italiani dell'Egitto', *Mem. Accad. Lincei*, 3.3.1879, 429-565.

Macario, I., *Cenni biografici del fu cavaliere Bernardino Drovetti*, Torino 1885.

Madden, R., Egypt and Mohammed Ali, London 1841.

-- *Travels in Turkey, Egypt, Nubia and Palestine in 1824-1827* (2 vols), London 1829.

Marcellus, comte de, *Souvenirs de l'Orient* (2 vols), Paris 1839.

Mariette, A., 'Lettre à M. le Vicomte de Rougé', *Rev. arch.* 2.1860, 17-35.

Marro, G., 'Di alcune letter inedite del grande naturalista G.B. Brocchi', *Commentari dell'Ateneo di Brescia* 1935, 369-390.

-- 'Sull arrivo della collezione egittologica Drovetti in Piemonte', *Boll. SPABA* 8.1924, 49-61.

-- 'Bernardino Drovetti, agricoltore', *Ann. Accad. di Agricoltura di Torino*, 93.1950/1951, 49-69.

-- 'Bernardino Drovetti, archeologo', *Aegyptus* 32.1952, 120-130.

-- 'Bernardino Drovetti e Champollion le Jeune', *Atti Accad. Torino* 58.1922/3, 548-582.

-- 'Il canale Mahmudieh e B. Drovetti', *Atti del XV Cong. geog. ital.* (Torino, 1950), 1952, 2.832-838.

-- 'Il casalese conte Carlo Vidua e le sue relazioni con Bernardino Drovetti', *Alexandria* 3.1935, 320-322.

-- 'Un cimelio del viaggio di Bernardino Drovetti all'oasi di Giove Ammone', *Bull. Soc. roy. de Geog. Cairo* 19.1934, 1-20.

-- 'La civilizzazione dell'Africa nel progetto di B. Drovetti', *Italiani nel mondo* 10 Aug. 1951, 17-20.

-- 'Documenti inediti sulla cessione al Piemonte della collezione egiziana Drovetti', *Atti Accad. Torino* 69.1933/4, 44-78.

-- 'Un drammatico episodio della spedizione al Senna d'Ishmael Pacha', *Atti Accad. Torino* 67.1931/2, 263-287.

-- 'L'Egitto e l'esploratore Bernardino Drovetti', *Italiani nel mondo* 10 Feb. 1951, 18-20.

-- 'Elementi ignorati sulla fondazione del museo egiziano di Torino', *Atti XXVI Cong. stor. subalpino*, 1933.

-- 'La fauna e la flora africana inviata in Europa da Bernardino Drovetti dal 1805 al 1829', *Boll. Ist. e Museo di Zoologia, Univ. Torino*, 2.1949/50, 559-572.

-- 'Una fonte dell'affermazione nostra in Egitto nel secolo passato', *Riv. delle colonie* 16.1942, 810-818.

-- 'Ibraham Pasha dans les archives privées du consul Drovetti', *Cahiers d'histoire égyptienne* 1.1949, 66-77.

-- 'Introduzione allo studio complessivo del corpo epistolare di Bernardino Drovetti', *Atti Accad. Torino* 70.1935, 595-617.

-- 'Ippolito Rosellini e Bernardino Drovetti', *Studi in memoria di Ippolito Rosellini*, 1949, 1.89-94.

-- 'Louis Alexandre Jumel e Bernardino Drovetti', *BIE* 31.1948/9, 279-295.

-- 'Il movimento civile e scientifico degli italiani nella prima metà dell'800 dall'archivio inedito di Bernardino Drovetti', *Atti del XXIII Cong. di storia del Risorgimento* (Bologna 1935), Rome 1940, 257-280.

-- 'La personalità di Bernardino Drovetti studiato nel suo archivio inedito', *Mem. Accad. Torino* 2.71.1951, 39-151.

-- 'Il R. Museo di Antichità di Torino e Champollion le Jeune', *Boll. SPABA* 7.1923, 7-26.

-- 'Relazione inedita sulla riunione degli scienziati a Torino nel 1840', *Rassegna storica del Risorgimento italiano* 36.1949, 43-50.

-- 'La vita e l'opera di Bernardino Drovetti', *Atti XXVII cong. stor. subalpino* (Torino 1934).

Mayes, S., *The great Belzoni*, London 1959.

Mengin, F., *Histoire de l'Egypte sous le gouvernement de Mohammed-Aly* (2 vols), Paris 1823.

Michalowsky, K., *Great sculpture of ancient Egypt*, New York 1978.

Michaud, J., *Correspondence d'Orient* (7 vols), Paris 1833-1835.

Miller, E., *That noble cabinet. A History of the British Museum*, London 1974.

Minutoli, Baroness, *Mes souvenirs d'Egypte*, Paris 1826; Eng. trans. *Recollections of Egypt*, London 1827.

Minutoli, Baron Menu von, *Reise zum Tempel des Jupiter Ammon*, Berlin 1824; Nachträge, 1827.

Le Moniteur universel, 1819, 1049; 1823, 1029; 1824, 367, 1135; 1826, 368; 1828, 246, 356 (unsigned articles).

Montulé, E., *Voyage en Amérique, en Italie, en Sicile, et en Egypte pendant les années 1816-1819*, Paris 1821. Eng. trans. *Travels in Egypt during 1818 and 1819*, London 1821.

Moore, Sir John, *Diary of Sir John Moore* (ed. Maurice), London 1904.

Mouriez, P., *Histoire de Mehemet Ali* (5 vols), Paris 1855-1858.

Murnane, W., *The Penguin guide to ancient Egypt*, Harmondsworth 1983.

Museo egizio di Torino, *Atti del centocinquantenerio 1824-1974*, Torino 1974 (39 pp).

Nagel, *Egypte*, Geneva 1969.

'Note sur l'establissement d'une école égyptienne à Paris', *Bull. Soc. Geog.* 5.1826, 763f (by Jomard ?).

Nouvelle biographie générale (46 vols), Paris 1855-1866.

Nuova enciclopedia popolare italiana, 4th ed., Torino 1856.

Pacho, J., 'Essai sur la civilisation de l'intérieur de l'Afrique d'après un projet de M. Drovetti', *Bull. Soc. Geog.* 8.1827, 137-142.

-- *Relation d'un voyage dans la Marmarique*, Paris 1827.

-- 'Sur un projet de M. Drovetti', *Revue encyclopédique* 37.1828, 344-348.

Parthey, G., *Wanderungen durch Sicilien und die Levante* (2 vols), Berlin 1833-1840.

Petrie, W.M.F., *Seventy years in archaeology*, London 1932.

Peyron, A., 'Saggio di studi sopra papiri, codici copti ed uno stele trilingue del Regio Museo Egiziano', *Mem. Accad. Torino* 29.1825, 70-82.

Pinelli, F., *Storia militare del Piemonte* (3 vols), Torino 1854.

Planat, J., *Histoire de la régénération de l'Egypte*, Paris 1830.

Pleyte, W. and Rossi, F., *Papyrus de Turin*, Leiden 1869-1876.

Pococke, R., *Description of the East* (3 vols), London 1743.

Porter, Bertha and Ross, Rosalind, *Topographical bibliography* (7 vols), Oxford 1927-1952.

Il primo secolo delle Accademie delle Scienze di Torino, 1783-1883, Torino 1883.

Pringle, J., 'Route de l'Inde, par l'Egypte et la Mer Rouge', *Bull. Soc. Geog.* 5.1826, 651-660.

PÅckler-Muskau, H., *Egypt under Mehemet Ali* (2 vols), London 1845.

Rabbe, A., *Biographie universelle et portative des contemporains* (5 vols), Paris 1834.

Raccolta delle leggi, provvidenze e manifesti emanati dai governi francesi e provvisori (2 vols), Torino 1799.

Raccolta di leggi, decreti, proclami, manifesti e circolari pubblicati dalle autorità costituente (6 vols), Torino ND.

Refaa, Sheik, 'Relation d'un voyage en France', *J. Asiatique* 11.1833, 222-251.

Rhind, A., *Thebes, its tombs and their tenants*, London 1862.

Richardson, Robert, *Travels along the Mediterranean*, London 1822.

Ridley, R.T., 'Auguste Mariette, one hundred years after', *Abr-Nahrain* 22.1983/4, 118-158.

-- 'Champollion in the tomb of Seti I: an unpublished letter', *CdE* 66.1991, 23-30.

-- 'Four unpublished letters by or relating to Bernardino Drovetti', *CdE* 69.1994, 203-214.

Rifaud, J., *Voyage en Egypte ... 1805-1827*, Paris 1830.

Rivlin, Helen, *The agricultural policy of Muhammad Ali in Egypt*, Cambridge 1961.

Roggero, Marina, *Il sapere e la virtó*, Torino 1987.

Rosellini, N.F.I.B., *Giornale della spedizione letteraria toscana in Egitto negli anni 1828-1829* (ed. G. Gabrieli), Florence 1925.

-- *I monumenti dell'Egitto e della Nubia* (8 vols), Pisa 1832-1844.

Rougé, E. de, 'Recherches sur les monuments qu'on peut attribuer aux six premiers dynasties', *Mem. Acad. Inscr.* 25.1866, 225-375.

St. John, J., *Egypt and Mohammed Ali* (2 vols), London 1834.

Salt, see Halls.

Saluces, A. de, *Histoire militaire du Piémont* (5 vols), 2nd ed., Torino 1859.

Sammarco, A., *Gli italiani in Egitto*, Alexandria 1937.

-- *Il regno di Mohammed Ali nei documenti diplomatici italiani inediti*, Cairo 1930.

'Sanctuaire monolithe égyptien arrivé à Paris', *Bull. Univ.* 5.1826, 282-283.

San Quintino, G. Cordero di, 'Interpretazioni e confronto di una bilingue iscrizione che sta sopra una mummia egiziana', *Mem. Accad. Torino* 29.1825, 255-325.

-- *Lezioni*, Torino 1824.

-- 'Notizie intorno alla collezione di antichità egiziane del cav. Drovetti', *Giornale arcadico* 19.1823, 180-208.

-- 'Osservazioni intorno all'età ed alla persona rappresentata dal maggiore colosso', *Mem. Accad. Torinio* 29.1825, 230-254.

Saulnier, S., *Notice sur le voyage de M. Lelorrain en Egypte*, Paris 1822.

Scamuzzi, E., *Egyptian art in the Egyptian Museum of Turin*, New York, 1965.

Schiaparelli, E., 'I papiri egiziani del R. Museo di Antichità di Torino', *Actes XII Cong. intern. des Orientalistes* (Rome 1899), 17-18.

Scholz, J., *Reise in die Gegend zwischen Alexandrien und Paratonium*, Leipzig 1822. Eng. trans., *Travels in the countries between Alexandria and Paratonium*, London, 1822.

Scott, C. Rochfort, *Rambles in Egypt and Candia* (2 vols), London 1837.

Senkowski, J., 'Länder und Völkerkunde. Bruchstück aus dem Reisetagebuch des Herrn J. von Senkowski', *Petersburger Zeitung*, 1822.

Seton-Williams, Virginia, *Egypt* (Blue Guide), London 1983.

Shaw, S.J., *History of the Ottoman Empire and modern Turkey: 2. Reform, revolution and Republic, 1808-1975*, Cambridge 1977.

Sherer, J., *Scenes and impressions in Egypt*, London 1824.

Silvera, A., 'Edmé François Jomard and Egyptian reforms in 1839', *Middle Eastern Studies* 7.1971, 301-316.

-- 'The first Egyptian student mission to France under Muhammed Ali', E. Kedourie and Sylvia Haim (eds), *Modern Egypt, studies in politics and society*, London 1980, 1-22.

Stanhope, Lady Hester, *Travels of Lady Hester Stanhope* (3 vols), London 1846.

Stevenson-Smith, W., *Art and architecture of ancient Egypt*, Harmondsworth 1958.

Storia del Piemonte (2 vols), Torino 1960.

Tagher, J., 'Les locaux qui abritèrent la mission scolaire égyptienne à Paris existent encore', *Cahiers d'Hist. égyptienne* 2.1950, 333-336.

Taverna, Donatella, 'Nella vecchia casa di Drovetti', *Piemonte vivo* 6.1974, 3-7.

Taylor, Baron I., *La Syrie, l'Egypte, la Palestine et la Judée* (2 vols), Paris, 1839.

-- *L'Egypte*, Paris 1857.

Thédénat-Duvent, P., *L'Egypte sous Méhémed Ali*, Paris 1822.

Thomson, D., *Europe since Napoleon*, Harmondsworth 2nd ed., 1966.

Turner, William, *Journal of a tour in the Levant* (3 vols), London 1820.

Vidua, C., *Lettere*, ed. C. Balbo (3 vols), Torino 1834.

Vingtrinier, A., *Soliman Pasha*, Paris 1886.

Vyse, R. and Perring, J., *Operations carried on at the pyramids of Gizeh* (3 vols), London 1840-1842.

Waddington, G., *Journal of a visit to some parts of Ethiopia*, London 1822.

Westcar, H., Diary (BM Add MS 52,283).

Who was who in Egyptology (2nd ed.), ed. W. Dawson and E. Uphill, London 1972; (3rd ed.) ed. M. Bierbrier, London 1995.

Wiet, G., 'Les consuls de France en Egypte sous le règne de Mohammed Ali', *Revue du Caire* Oct. 1943, 459-476; Nov., 41-53; Dec., 147-162.

-- 'Une lettre de Jomard au sujet de l'école militaire égyptienne en 1844', *Revue du Caire* Oct. 1944, 562-577.

-- 'Le voyage de Ibrahim Pacha en France et en Angleterre', *Cahiers d'hist. égyptienne* 1.1948, 78-126.

Wilkinson, J., *The fragments of the hieratic papyrus at Turin*, London 1851.

-- *Manners and customs of the ancient Egyptians* (3 vols), London 1837-1841.

Wilson, John, *Signs and wonders upon pharaoh*, Chicago 1964.

Wilson, R., *History of the British expedition to Egypt*, London 1803.

Wilson, W.R., *Travels in Egypt and the Holy Land*, London 1823.

Winlock, H., El Dakhleh oasis, New York 1936.

-- *The rise and fall of the Middle Kingdom in Thebes*, New York, 1947.

Woldering, Irmgard, *The arts of Egypt*, London 1968.

Wolynski, A., 'Gli itinerari Frediani, Belzoni e Drovetti', *Mem. Soc. geog. ital.* 5.1895, 435.

-- 'Il viaggatore Enegildo Frediani', *Bull Soc. Geog. ital.* 3.4.1891, 90-125, 295-324, 397-406.

Wood, A. and Oldham, F., *Thomas Young*, Cambridge 1954.

Woolf, S., *A history of Italy 1700-1860*, London 1979.

Young, T., *An account of some recent discoveries in hieroglyphical literature and Egyptian antiquities*, London 1823.

Zavati, S., 'Lettere inedite di Bernardino Drovetti', *Oriente moderno 1965*, 878-888.

Index

Cordero di San Quintino, Giulio (Egyptologist), 7, 257f, 263
Cossato, G.B. (Dr's executor), 200
Coste, Xavier Pascal (engineer), 76, 109, 155, 234
Cresia, Col., 240
Cuvier, Jean (palaeontologist), 118, 331

Dahshur, 276, 291
Dakhla Oasis, 88f, 289
Damanhur, 41f, 44, 49
Damas, baron (MFA 1824-1828), 128f, 144, 150ff, 241
d'Andre, Dr., 235
d'Armandry (Fr. agent), 173
Daumas, Dr., 214f
David (Fr. consul at Smyrna), 110, 117, 121, 125, 127ff, 285, 303
Deir el Medineh, 270
Delile, Alire Raffeneau (botanist), 118, 299, 331
del Signore, Dr., 235
Dendereh, 105, 250; Zodiac, 108, 259, 290
Denon, Vivant, 250
Derossi, Abbé, 252
Dessolle, marquis de (MFA 1818-1819), 87, 91, 110
Didot, Ambrose Firman (publisher), 81
Djedhor (priest), 272
Dodwell, Henry (historian), 204
Donati, Vitaliani (collector), 258
Doudeauville, duc de, 272
Douin, Georges (historian), x, 243
Dresden Museum, 299
Driault, Edouard (historian), x
Droualt, Capt., 129
Drovetti (Dr's nephew), 128
DROVETTI, Bernardino, birth, 1; education, 5f; military service, 7; Provisional Govt, 13f; captain, 16; at Marengo, 17; damaged hand, 17, 43, 302; major, 18; Chief of Staff, 19; judge, 19; to Egypt, 21, 26f; 1804, 33f; 1805, 37f; and Mehemet Ali, 38f, 283; 1806, 41f;

1807, 44f; English invasion, 45f, 62; move to Cairo, 45; eclipse, 49f; 1808, 50f; 1809, 51f; health, 52; 1810, 52f; 1811, 54f; English trade, 54f, 58f; Col. Boutin, 55, 57; antiquities, 57; return to Alexandria, 58; health, 59; 1813, 59f; 1814, 60; 1815, 61; and Belzoni, 63f, 293f; 1816, 69f; Second Cataract, 69; 1817, 72f; influence, 72, 284; at Thebes, 73-76; 1818, 77f; Jomard, 78; Thebes, 79f; Belzoni, 83f; 1819, 86f; Shanhour and Abydos, 87; Dakhla Oasis, 88f; Abydos, 91; Sardinian consulate, 91f; Legion d'Honneur, 92, 254; Pillavoine, 93f; 1820, 95f; business dealings, 95; Siwah Oasis, 96f; Dendereh, Athribis, Abydos, 105; eastern tour, 106; Order of SS Maurizio e Lazzaro, 106, 256; 1821, 109f; reappointment, 109f; naturalisation, 112; Thebes, 114f; warships, 115; Russian consul, 116; 1822, 116f; Greek war, 117, 130ff, 136, 139, 155, 157, 159f, 162, 285; Marseille Academy, 117; 1823, 119f; journey south, 122; 1824, 123f; Torino Academy, 123; Hawara, 123f; health, 125, 126f, 129; Order of Holy Sepulchre, 125; Sakkarah, 128; 1825, 129f; Livron, 132, cf. Madden, 134; Tanis, 135; Moscow Society of Naturalists, Museum in Geneva, Order of St Anne of Russia, 136; 1826, 138f; lieut. col., 142; military scandal, 143; and Champollion, 142f; Girgeh and Manfalut, 146; 1827, 146f; services to France, 146; leave, 148f; Order of St. Louis, 150; reorganisation of consular service, 150; 1828, 152f; return to Egypt; with Viceroy in south, 153; relations with Champollion, 154f, 157f, 161f, 295; house, 256; Convention of Alexandria, 156, 337; health, 157f, 162; Lyons

Linant de Bellefonds (artist), 84, 97, 118, 328

Livron, Gen. Pierre, 128, 132, 151, 236-242, 244f, 289, 350

London, Treaty of (1827), 148

Louis XVIII, 166, 199

Louvre Museum, 271f

Love, Lt. John, 47

Lyons Museum, 299

Macdonald, Gen., 174

Madden, Dr. Richard (traveller), 133, 202, 221, 334

Magnetto (Sardinian consul), 132, 140f

Mahmudieh Canal, 233f

Malivoire (Fr. consul), 130, 138, 140f, 147-151, 240ff

Mamelukes, 23-58; Cairene Vespers, 54, 220f, 228

Manfalut, 38, 53, 70, 121, 123, 146, 235, 243

Mangles, Capt. James, 74, 81

Marcellus comte de, 103f, 234, 285, 293, 299, 301

Marengo, battle of (1800), 17f, 316; 'Marengo affair', 140f

Maria Louisa, Archduchess of Parma, 184

Mariani, Dominique (musician), 240

Mariette, Auguste (Egyptologist), 198, 250, 279

Marochetti, Charles (sculptor), 182, 271, 304

Marro, Giovanni, xf, 281, 336f, 340, 345f, 347

Marseille, 117

Massari, Dr. Francesco, 214-216

Mazzini, Giuseppe, 196

Mehemet Ali, 33f; Pasha of Cairo, 38; pro-French, 41; Eng-lish invasion, 45-49; Viceroy, 51; treaty with England, 52; Cairene Vespers, 54f; Wahabite War, 56f, 73, 77f, 88; navy, 57; conquest of Siwah, 96f; conquest of Sudan, 107f, 118f; Greek War, 115f, 126, 131, 133, 136, 138, 141, 143, 147-150; new army, 121, 124f, 133; ambitions, 130, 136f; French military scandal, 143; and Navarino, 151f; evacuation of Greece, 156f; Russo-Turkish war, 161; Algerian crises, 169-171, Syrian war, 176f, 183; in Italy, 194; death, 197; appearance and assessment, 202f; agriculture, 220f; industry, 224f; commerce, 227f; army, 235f; and Drovetti as excavator, 281f

Melas, Gen., 16, 18

Memnon, head of, 72, 293f

Memphis, 271f

Mengin, Felix (Fr. consul), 124, 139

Menou, Gen. Joachim, 19, 23, 228

Meroe, 118

Metternich, Prince Klemens, 194f

Meyer, Eduard (historian), 269

Mimaut Jean François (Fr. consul), 160, 163ff, 169, 172, 179, 279, 295

Minutoli, baron Heinrich v. (traveller), 101, 104, 293, 299

Miollis, Gen., 52

Mirbel, Charles (Royal gardener), 160

Missalonghi, 132, 137, 139f

Missett, Ernest (Eng. consul), 26, 40, 45f, 49, 55f, 62

Montmorency, duc de (MFA 1821-1823), 116

Montule, Edouard (traveller), 84f, 91, 250, 275, 291

Moreau, Gen. Jean, 13, 15f

Morel (cloth manufacturer), 225

Morpurgo (Dr's agent), 185, 287

Mosca, Carlo (Dr's executor), 200

Mouriez, Pierre (historian), 227, 242

Mukhtar Effendi, Mustafa, 208f, 211, 213

Murad Bey, 223; Mme., 42

Murtar Bey, 212

Murat, Gen. Joachim, 17f, 21, 37, 52, 60, 65; Caroline, 37, 56, 178

Napier, Sir Charles, 183

Naples, kingdom of, 16, 44, 52, 168, 177, 195